Movies, Moves and Music

Genre, Music and Sound

Edited by Mark Evans, University of Technology Sydney

Over the last decade screen soundtrack studies has emerged as a lively area of research and analysis mediating between the fields of cinema studies, musicology and cultural studies. It has deployed a variety of cross-disciplinary approaches to illuminate an area of film's audio-visual operation that was neglected for much of the mid- to late 1900s. Equinox's *Genre, Music and Sound* series extends the emergent field by addressing a series of popular international film genres as they have developed in the post-war era (1945–present), analysing the variety and shared patterns of music and sound use that characterize each genre.

Published

Terror Tracks: Music, Sound and Horror Cinema
Edited by Philip Hayward

Drawn to Sound: Animation Film Music and Sonicity
Edited by Rebecca Coyle

Earogenous Zones: Sound, Sexuality and Cinema
Edited by Bruce Johnson

The Music of Fantasy Cinema
Edited by Janet K. Halfyard

Sounding Funny: Sound and Comedy Cinema
Edited by Mark Evans and Philip Hayward

Forthcoming

The Singing Voice in Contemporary Cinema
Edited by Diane Hughes and Mark Evans

Ludomusicology: Approaches to Video Game Music
Edited by Michiel Kamp, Tim Summers and Mark Sweeney

Movies, Moves and Music
The Sonic World of Dance Films

Edited by
Mark Evans and Mary Fogarty

SHEFFIELD UK   BRISTOL CT

Published by Equinox Publishing Ltd.

UK: Office 415, The Workstation, 15 Paternoster Row, Sheffield, South Yorkshire S1 2BX
USA: ISD, 70 Enterprise Drive, Bristol, CT 06010

www.equinoxpub.com

First published 2016

© Mark Evans, Mary Fogarty and contributors 2016

All rights reserved. No part of this publication may be reproduced or transmitted in any form or by any means, electronic or mechanical, including photocopying, recording or any information storage or retrieval system, without prior permission in writing from the publishers.

British Library Cataloguing-in-Publication Data
A catalogue record for this book is available from the British Library.

ISBN-13 978 1 78179 444 9 (hardback)
       978 1 84553 958 0 (paperback)

Library of Congress Cataloging-in-Publication Data
Evans, Mark, 1973- editor. | Fogarty, Mary, 1978- editor.
Movies, moves and music: the sonic world of dance films / edited by
   Mark Evans and Mary Fogarty.
Sheffield, Yorkshire; Bristol, CT: Equinox Publishing, 2016. |
   Genre, music and sound | Includes bibliographical references and index.
LCCN 2015030848| ISBN 9781781794449 (hb) | ISBN 9781845539580 (pb)
LCSH: Dance in motion pictures, television, etc. | Choreography.
LCC GV1779 .M68 2016 | DDC 793.3—dc23
LC record available at http://lccn.loc.gov/2015030848

Typeset by S.J.I. Services, New Delhi
Printed and bound by Lightning Source Inc. (La Vergne, TN), Lightning Source UK Ltd. (Milton Keynes), Lightning Source AU Pty. (Scoresby, Victoria)

Contents

Acknowledgements	vii
1. The Sonic World of Dance Films Mark Evans and Mary Fogarty	1
2. From Choreocinema to Experimental Screendance: A Personal Archaeology Greg Faller	14
3. From *Beat Street* to *Step Up 3D*: The Sound of Street Dance Films Mary Fogarty	43
4. Space, Authenticity and Utopia in the Hip Hop Teen Dance Film Faye Woods	61
5. The School and 'The Streets': Race, Class, Sound and Space in *Step Up* and *Step Up 2* Brian Su-Jen Chung and Afia Ofori-Mensa	78
6. The Essence and Momentum of *Honey*: An Interplay of Sound and Movement Diane Hughes	108
7. Gone in a *Flash(dance)*: The Estrangement of Diegetic Performance in the 1980s Teen Dance Film Kelly Kessler	129
8. 'Anything but Ballet': Individuality, Genre-Bending and Sexual Expression in *Center Stage* Gillian Turnbull	150

9. Zoot Suit Mayhem: Swing Dance and the Skewed History in Steven Spielberg's *1941* 167
Philip Hayward and Jon Fitzgerald

10. *Across the Universe* and Nostalgia: Re-presenting the Beatles through Moving Images and Dancing Bodies 184
Colleen Dunagan and Roxane Fenton

11. Looking for the Past in Pastiche: Intertextuality in Bollywood Song-and-Dance Sequences 207
Usha Iyer

12. The Call to *Rize* 227
Megan Anne Todd

13. Resounding Neurological Ecologies: Choreographing the Body's Lost Interactions with the World 247
Sarah-Mace Dennis

Index 265

Acknowledgements

This anthology has been a long time in rehearsal and many people have passed through the company in that time. Equinox would like to thank Pauline Manley for her early work and contributions to the volume. Natalie Lewandowski has provided invaluable editorial assistance over a long period. And, of course, thanks to the authors who have stayed committed for so long.

The editors would also like to thank New York University's Steinhardt School and Hip hop Education Center who granted us invaluable research fellowships that ensured completion of the volume. As usual, much thanks to the team at Equinox, especially Janet Joyce and Valerie Hall, for their belief and willingness to trust in this production.

A special thanks to our home institutions who have supported the completed of this volume. To colleagues at the University of Technology Sydney, and especially Professor Mary Spongberg, many thanks. And to those at York University's Dance Department, alongside Professor Simon Frith and Dr Kyle Devine.

Finally to those who have heard the phrase 'dance book' too many times, Lauren and Peter, we made it!

Mary Fogarty and Mark Evans

The Sonic World of Dance Films

Mark Evans[1] and Mary Fogarty[2]

The study of dance in cinema, and of its construction as a filmic practice, is still in its infancy. In one of the most notable contributions to the field to date, Erin Brannigan identifies a "modality that appears across various types of films" that she characterizes as "a *filmic performance* dominated by choreographic strategies or effect" (2011: vii; original emphasis). The modality she refers to encompasses a variety of ways that choreography is employed in cinema, from formalized genre practices, such as Hollywood and Bollywood musicals, through to more idiosyncratic ones. Rather than focus on the former areas, the dance films analysed in this volume weave spectacularized or normalized dance routines into their narratives in a variety of ways. Often the films discussed are about dance in some form, be it an audition, a competition, community event and so on. Importantly, the films discussed in this volume showcase the art of dance, or the expression of characters through the act of dancing, and how meaning is developed through these acts.

The scholarship around dance films has intersected with, among other things, the study of youth cultures (McRobbie, 1984; Frith and McRobbie, 1978), dance genres (Dodds, 2001), film genres (Feuer, 1980), and artistic oeuvres (Jeong, 2009), as well as providing detailed analyses of gender, race and sexuality (see Blanco Borelli 2014). What has been less noticeable is the intersection with music. As Theresa Buckland (1983) points out, the relationship between recorded music and popular dance is a tight-knit one; however, much scholarship neglects the significant role of music and sound in dance films. This disconnect is related to the continuing neglect of music in dance analysis. Some dance scholars have taken music seriously from a variety of diverse perspectives (e.g. Jordan, 1996; Johnson, 2012; Dodds and Cook, 2013), yet, in critical dance studies more broadly, there has been a lack of focus on popular culture dance films. As light entertainment marketed by Hollywood to mainstream audiences, most dance films still tend to be perceived as trivial and unworthy of analysis. Other related popular forms have also been similarly neglected. The form of music video for instance, in which various types of choreographed movement are often central, has only received sporadic attention from scholars (see Gorham and Nakache, 1993; and Perillo, 2008 for two very different approaches to the topic). Outside the field of popular culture, even relatively higher status forms of avant-garde dance film, such as those of Maya Deren and Yvonne Rainer, have not received sufficient scholarly attention in relation to dance practices outside of dance studies, especially given their critical acclaim (see Jeong, 2009).

In this volume, music and sound are considered to be central to the significance of dance in both popular dance films and the avant-garde traditions of screen dance. As such our anthology project is necessarily interdisciplinary (see Vize, 2003). Dancers and choreographers are crucial to the output of Hollywood and Bollywood as well as to the music industries. The authors in this volume thus consider how the experiences of such creative workers can inform an understanding of a film's significance. Likewise, the circulation and reception of dance films in various contexts are attended to in the attempt to account for the multiple perspectives through which viewers come to appreciate dance on screen.

In an early address to the form of music video, Goodwin and Grossberg (1993) argued that music television requires models of analysis that consider not only the televised show or music video as a "text", but also the music industries that work to inform and shape the reception of the music itself. Yet what this account lacks is a detailed understanding of how dance might fit into this relationship between music and images. Likewise, dance scholars have argued that to understand the embodied meanings of dance choreographies requires an account of how such movements might be read as gendered, racialized and sexualized. For Melissa Blanco Borelli (2014), critical dance studies provide the tools to "facilitate literacy in how bodies signify", that then can be acquired and applied to moving bodies on screen. For example, this can involve a detailed analysis of "micro-choreographies" such as the filmic close-up (Brannigan, 2009). However, the production of said films can also benefit from an understanding of how film, media and dance are linked to the music industry. For example, the 1970s and 1980s entries in the dance film cycle such as *Saturday Night Fever* (John Badham, 1977) and *Flashdance* (Adrian Lyne, 1983) operated as trans-media properties, selling soundtracks and dance styles alongside musical-cinematic experiences. In many ways, the aesthetics and reception of dance films with prominent musical soundtracks (soundtracks that were foregrounded both in the cinema and the record store) can be linked to the rise of music videos.

In 2001, the film critic and philosopher Noël Carroll called for a broad definition of moving-picture dance that would account for new trends in the field such as animation and kung fu cinema alongside more traditional musicals. His list includes "cine-dance, film dance, video dance, camera dance, and even screen dance" (Carroll, 2001: 47). In the contemporary context this list could be expanded to include documentaries about dance, filming yourself dancing in your bedroom and uploading it to YouTube, Vine video dancing and stunts, promotional videos for commercial dancers, and other intersections with new technologies and industries, all of which might find a place within Carroll's broad category of moving-picture dance.

Carroll's broad definition allows our concerns about the crucial role of music in dance films to expand to include other forms in this category of moving-picture dance. The first dance scholar to publish a full-length monograph on dance films, Sherril Dodds (2001), considered not only Hollywood productions but also experimental art (screen dance). This speaks to the uncertain emergence of dance as a discipline and the resulting need to locate the various dance practices within a framework of development. Historically, neither dance nor film has enjoyed the same status as music in terms of scholarly analysis. Relatively new to the academy, dance scholarship has developed only in the last forty years. The traces of dance left on film have been treated as valuable archives of historic performance, as well as performance works. As Musser (2004) notes, many of the earliest appearances of dancers in Edison films were designed to arouse the sexual desire of audiences assumed to be male. However, Loïe Fuller's appearance in the Lumière Brothers' film was deemed a classier act that could be appreciated by both sexes. As Brannigan (2011) argues, "dancefilm" truly begins with these early historic films that consider the body as a radical site of meaning-making for modernity.

Similarly, the oft-cited experimental work of amateur dancer and avant-garde filmmaking pioneer Maya Deren has been seen as inventing new ways of presenting movement in films such as *A Study in Choreography* (Maya Deren, 1945) and *Ritual in Transfigured Time* (Deren, 1945-56), where dancers leap into new settings through the power of editing. Time is slowed down and sped up, changing the qualities of the movements of dancers. Later, Yvonne Rainer's famous "Trio A" (1978) captured on film the essence of postmodern dance's commitment to pedestrian movements and the space between beginnings and endings of movements.

Although dance studies has prioritized ballet and modern dance as the "dance" to be studied seriously, this has not prevented a more nuanced consideration of the relationship between dance and all forms of movement from entering the discipline. Thus, the work of such scholars as Dodds and Blanco Borelli treats popular dance on film as being of equal interest to screen dance.

One area where dance *has* been adequately considered in relationship to music and film is in studies of the genre of the musical film. From Jane Feuer's (1980) reading of the dance in film musicals as folk dance, to Peter Wollen's (1992) detailed reading of *Singin' in the Rain* (Stanley Donen and Gene

Kelly, 1952), that incorporates analysis of both the movement and the musical meanings, dancing is represented as a spontaneous expression of happiness and celebration. This tradition of dance as an expression of human emotions contrasts with the innovative representations of dance in films that came earlier. For example, in 1933 Busby Berkeley choreographed *42nd Street* (Lloyd Bacon, 1933), a musical where "young and healthy" dancers are captured from unique camera angles that feature the *Ballet Méchanique*-style choreography of bodies moving through space on shifting platforms (Fernand Léger and Dudley Murphy, 1923–24). This backstage musical can provide a frame for understanding what is to come in the relationship between moves and music on film, as the representation of dance expands to encompass the capacities of a camera that can capture angles not possible on a proscenium stage. This feature was taken up again in *The Red Shoes* (Michael Powell and Emeric Pressburger, 1948) where a stage performance expands beyond the proscenium to include non-traditional settings requiring a suspension of disbelief on the part of the spectator. In this film, the relationship between the composer and the dancer becomes central to the narrative.

The manner in which the choreography of Bob Fosse in *Sweet Charity* (1969) and *The Mexican Breakfast* (1969) has been taken up in the music videos of Beyoncé illustrates how the past can be re-enacted in the present to make new meaning out of movements acquired by commercial dancers and musical artists, in different musical contexts. Likewise dance styles such as waacking, a West Coast 1970s black and Latino gay dance style, were inspired by musical sequences. Marilyn Monroe's 'Diamonds are a Girl's Best Friend' scene in *Gentlemen Prefer Blondes* (Howard Hawks, 1953) proved to be an inspiration for *Soul Train* dancer Tyrone Procter (Walker, 2012). In other words, the relationship between music and dance can move beyond cinema as "text" to be read to think through industry and production, aesthetics and social contexts, and finally how the past is recycled in the present.

Dance scholar Clare Parfitt-Brown's (2010) insight into what she calls the post-popular may be usefully applied to dance films which relate to both musicals and the early works of modern dancers and filmmakers. Parfitt-Brown suggests that consumption today of the "popular past" positions participants in a relationship with "modernist and colonialist politics" that must be negotiated. This notion of the "post" suggests not only the postmodern aesthetics of nostalgia and parody but also the meanings implicit in dance practices that explicitly reconstruct the past of popular dance as part of their contemporary appeal. Here she is referring to burlesque, the cancan and tango as key examples. The relationship between musicals, dance films and popular dance practices reveals a similar relationship of recycling that could indeed be thought of as "post-popular". For example, the current cycle of street dance films relate to the b-movies and cult classics that defined the emergence of hip hop as a cultural practice in the 1980s, yet stray quite significantly from the original content and meanings ascribed to the movies.

Since music underpins narrative film meaning (Gorbman, 1987), then sound is also worthy of consideration. The emergence of sound studies has been fruitful for film and music studies although the connections have been slower to develop within dance studies. Sound studies offer key insights into how listening practices were transformed throughout modernity and frame our experience of performance, such as dancing to music (Thompson, 2004). Listening to music through the body – especially through dancing – is an undervalued practice and way of listening. The relationship between sound and the body is another area of future development in the analysis of dance films. Central to these considerations will be precisely the act of listening to music while watching dancing, and the development of various sound systems is crucial to this discussion. The introduction of sound studies to considerations of the sonicity of dance films raises new questions about distinctions between noise and music, loudness and fidelity. These could then greatly impact the development of dance film as an area of academic research that is truly interdisciplinary encompassing considerations of both music and sound.

Overview of the Anthology

The chapters in this volume divide into two thematically related halves. After Greg Faller's rich archaeological mining of the terminology surrounding dance film in the opening chapter, the first sequence of chapters considers dance films, more specifically teen dance films, from the 1980s onwards. Within that there is a clutch of chapters concerned with hip hop and street dance films, and while they sometimes consider the same films, there is a difference of approach and reading that quickly becomes apparent. Reynolds (2010) makes the rather provocative assertion that dance audiences familiar with dance languages and tropes often seek out live, experimental performances, "whereas spectators without specialist knowledge can be attracted to dance in its more popular forms – notably on screen – because it is presented in contexts which are more familiar to them, such as well-known narratives or music" (20). Ignoring the potential elitism of this observation, the recourse to narrative is important, as Reynolds continues:

> In *Dirty Dancing* and *Billy Elliot*, as in other films such as *Saturday Night Fever* (1977), *Flashdance* (1983) and *Strictly Ballroom* (1992), narrative plays a crucial role in facilitating identification between spectator and dancer. These narratives foreground what McRobbie calls the "mysterious

transformative power" of dance, and "its ability to create a fantasy of change, escape or achievement". (Ibid.)

But where did this narrative begin and what is its relationship to sound and music? The answer to this question often begins with *Saturday Night Fever*, as Coyle and Fitzgerald note:

> *Saturday Night Fever* (John Badman, 1977) represented a turning point in the general history of the US movie musical. The film soundtrack generated five US No.1 hits on *Billboards*' singles charts, and clearly demonstrated that pop songs could be a primary force within the musical format. Songwriter and popular music producer Giorgio Moroder recalls: Saturday Night Fever *was an enormous hit and made everybody think "Wait. Let's try and do something similar", and that's when we started to have songs which were really driving the movie.* The success of subsequent movies such as *Flashdance* (Adrian Lyne, 1983), *Footloose* (Herbert Ross, 1984) and *Dirty Dancing* (Emile Ardolino, 1987) proved beyond doubt that movie musicals were highly effective vehicles for the creation of popular hits, especially when supported by intensive cross-media promotion. (2010: 226; emphasis original)

While Coyle and Fitzgerald refer to these films as "movie musicals", they could more readily be associated with their own "dance film" genre delineation (Vize, 2003). Labels aside, there is no doubt that *Saturday Night Fever* changed the way music operated in contemporary film, and the way the films themselves were conceived, as Jeff Smith observed from an industrial analysis:

> In the 1970s, the success of soundtrack albums such as ... *Saturday Night Fever* (1977), encouraged a new cycle of film and music cross-promotions. As a 1979 *Billboard* article noted, such cross-promotions depended on several components, among them: "Commercially viable music. Timing. Film cooperation on advance planning and tie-ins. Music that's integral to the movie. A hit single. A big-name recording star. A big-name composer." Certainly, some ingredients were more important than others, but promoters believed that the absence of one or two spelled the difference between a campaign's overall success or failure. (Smith, 2001: 411)

So music's place, and in particular pre-recorded popular music, became integral to film and especially to dance film (Grossberg, 1993: 191). This was a change from earlier musical or dance cinema where singers and musicians were most often visible in the diegetic world of the film (Creekmur, 2001: 394). Now the music drove the dance, which in turn drove the audience to the cinema. And the success of the films that followed this formula through the 1980s, irrespective of the subtle narrative differences between films, ensured it became entrenched. Indeed, it could be argued that a similar pattern remains today in relation to some music videos. In 2012 South Korean pop artist Psy released 'Gangnam Style' which became a huge hit worldwide, and that birthed a 'Gangnam' dance craze based on Psy's moves from the music video. The mimicry of Psy's moves is not far from the imitation of Travolta's signature moves in *Saturday Night Fever* – that can still be found on many Western wedding reception dance floors around the world today.

> Dance film communicates to us on many different levels creating a synergy of the aural, the visual and the cerebral to which the audience can relate and through which it can escape. Dance film reinforces its effect (and affect) doubly – through the music and the spectacle of the dance ... I believe we should analyse dance film *as* dance film, rather than as film which happens to feature music and dance. And in that analysis, we must acknowledge equally three elements of multimedia; music, film and dance. They interact with each other to create a new, different, "novelised" form in which music and dance propel the plot. (Vize, 2003: 25)

This anthology adheres to Vize's call above, for it does announce dance film unapologetically as dance film. Moreover, it concurs with the notion that there are multiple levels at which dance film operates, and multiple modes by which it can be examined. Extending Vize's tripartite breakdown though, this is a volume about the sonic in the world of dance film. As numerous chapters in the volume show, this extends further than music alone, and certainly further than the often voiced use of popular pre-recorded music in contemporary dance films.

As mentioned above, the first group of chapters (3–8) consider popular dance films from the 1980s onwards. The first of these, a consideration of street dance films by Mary Fogarty, highlights the extent to which sound, in all its manifestations, needs to be considered in dance film analysis. As she notes: "From considerations of musical taste to the use of multi-channel sound to facilitate different icons and the tagging of screen dance history, sound has long contributed to embodied portrayals of street dancers' lives." Fogarty explains that the immersive experience of hearing a street dance film is only made possible by the realization and even dramatization of external sounds.[3] These include the impact sounds of street dancing, the communal choruses of boos, whistles, yelps and shouts of affirmation that traditionally accompany battles. Indeed, as she shows, these external sounds often drive performance, building attitude and drive in the performer. The challenge is to represent these sounds adequately in the film and immerse the audioviewer enough to believe they are experiencing the dance along with the street crowd. Yet this is not easy: "The relationship in street dance films between cinematic sound (including music, effects and dialogue) and dance moves reveals a tension between production and reception, representation and labour." The tension comes through the proliferation of external sounds produced in the reception of the film, those noises, conversations, interruptions that come from the viewing audience. What Fogarty's analysis shows is the sheer number of sonicities that feed into the world of dance films.

Faye Woods (Chapter 4) identifies hip hop teen dance films as a cycle. She argues that this cycle, "illustrates that music and dance, with long held connections to minorities of the post-industrial city and their resistance to conservative forces, actually meet these conservative forces in the formulaic narratives and utopian pleasures of the classical Hollywood musical". In discussing the cyclical nature of these films, which she argues extends from *Grease* (1978) through to the latest *Step Up* film, Woods brings numerous films to the discussion. However she focuses on *Save the Last Dance* (Thomas Carter, 2001), *Honey* (Billy Woodruff, 2002) and *Step Up* (Anne Fletcher, 2006) whose "narratives celebrated hip hop performance, and depicted dance as a bridge between cultural boundaries, bringing together couples, communities and cultures. These films used hip hop to construct filmic spaces and identities while fragmenting hip hop soundscapes, limiting its expressive potential." Woods points to the tensions created through the partial integration of hip hop soundscapes, which once again suffer at the hands of narrative, and particularly "utopian fantasies". Despite this she demonstrates how the relationship between the body and sound works to resolve some of these tensions through dance.

Chung and Ofori-Mensa (Chapter 5) spin the hip hop dance film from another direction. Taking *Step Up* and *Step Up 2: The Streets* as their case studies, they carefully deconstruct the visual, verbal and aural components of the films. For them, the "'verbal' refers to the content of what characters say in monologues and dialogue, while 'aural' refers to the sounds of characters' voices, music, ambient noises, and silence". Once again we see how wide the sonic net is cast in fully registering how dance films are operating. Their purpose in mapping these elements is to reveal how the "films instruct audiences about race and social mobility through the discourses of colourblind meritocracy. Colourblind meritocracy refers to the evaluation of individuals on the basis of the quality of their performance and decidedly not on the basis of their race."

Rounding out the sub-section of hip hop related dance films is Diane Hughes's (Chapter 6) examination of *Honey*. Through her chapter Hughes asserts the need to consider the industrial apparatus behind a film, to fully understand the music production, choreography, and other music elements. She argues that the use of contemporary industry professionals, with pre-existing video and music production credentials, adds to the credibility of the film, and integrity of the relationship between sound and movement. For instance, she notes that it is through the "creative platforms and professional experiences of [choreographers] Woodruff, Jerkins and Gibson that *Honey* finds its strength and focus. From the film's outset, the crafting of macro visual to micro action, together with the manipulation of volume levels and film speed, typifies the interplay of sound and movement."

Kelly Kessler (Chapter 7) and Gillian Turnbull (Chapter 8) leave the world of the hip hop film and return to the teen film more generally. Both use their analysis to question the generic boundaries of dance film. Kessler interrogates the use of visual and aural aspects of so-called "classic song and dance" musicals, "spontaneous performance of integrated song and dance and a visual projection of full bodies in motion or multiple bodies in union", with techniques used in teen dance films, "largely underscored music, a lack of diegetically performed song, and camerawork that fractures the dancing bodies rather than showing the visual union or choreographed whole". What she shows is that the modern teen dance film is a hybrid, a sub-genre, that straddles the "ideological, aesthetic, narrative and aural qualities of the emergent music video and the more traditional Hollywood musical".

Turnbull (Chapter 8) turns her attention to the genres of dance morphed, altered and necessarily scrutinized via dance films. In relation to her study of *Center Stage*, she focuses particularly on the treatment of ballet. She argues that music, specifically popular music heard and responded to throughout the film, "functions to break the impenetrability of ballet, securing its place within a more commercial (or lowbrow) mainstream, while elevating popular music to the role of reconstructing ideas about classical dance". In terms of gender politics, Turnbull further shows how the use of rock and pop music enables the characters to use "alternative gestures in order to disentangle the standard gender roles that still dominate ballet". Similar debunking of traditional gender roles can be found throughout dance film history. Recalling *Saturday Night Fever* once again, we note that Stephanie there chooses an independent lifestyle rather than subservience to Tony (see Jordan, 1996), breaking with accepted societal norms.

History, Pastiche and Philosophy

The second half of the volume brings us away from the mainstream (teen) dance films of recent decades. The chapters in this section are broadly concerned with history, whether historical representations of dance, historical moments or historical contexts that have informed the sonic world of dance films. Related to this are notions of pastiche and parody that surround dance films, and, of course, the embodied philosophy that brings them into existence.

In discussing Stephen Spielberg's film *1941* (1979), Hayward and Fitzgerald (Chapter 9) analyse the "zoot suit" phenomenon of early 1940s' US society. In order to provide appropriate historical context to the music used in the film, Hayward and Fitzgerald detail the origins of Lindy hop/swing dancing styles in the 1930s; the nature of the Mexican-American *pachuco* culture that was central to zoot suiter oppression in California (and other areas of the US) in the early 1940s; and aspects of the cultural climate of late 1970s' North America relevant to the film's production. In line with Nattiez's (1990) semiological framework that calls for consideration of the poietic level of discourse, they provide a detailed reading of the producers' discourse on the film and its reception, as contained in the feature-length "Making Of" documentary by Laurent Bouzereau (1995).

Dunagan and Fenton (Chapter 10) bring us forward in time both musically and cinematically, to the Beatles inspired *Across the Universe*. Through a close reading of several songs in the film, their visual representation and integration, and the dance that accompanies them, they argue that the "merging of sound and image in *Across the Universe* activates nostalgia (both for the US in the 1960s and for the mythology of the Beatles) in order to create a visual and aural tribute to the philosophical outlook conveyed in the Beatles catalogue". More philosophically, they argue that the Beatles' catalogue of music as represented in the film offers moral and ethical lessons relevant to North American history. As Faller reminds us in the opening chapter of the volume, definitional divisions between dance films are fluid and slippery. *Across the Universe* highlights this well, combining song and dance but not in straightforward ways. It exists at the intersection of "film musicals, music videos, screendance and narrative dance films, making it a truly hybrid film and in places calling to mind the innovations of experimental and avant-garde cinema".

While the music of the Beatles may provide relevant commentary on moments in USA history, Usha Iyer (Chapter 11) clearly shows how Bollywood cinema has a lot to say about itself. She notes that: "Pastiche, tribute and parody are familiar structuring principles, the very profusion of these intertextual devices pointing to a certain kind of 'memorialization' in this self-reflexive cinema." But what is the nature of the narrative produced and why are filmmakers interested in perpetuating it? Through analysis of three key song and dance sequences from contemporary Bollywood cinema, 'Woh Ladki Hai Kahan' from *Dil Chahta Hai* (Farhan Akhtar, 2001), 'Dhoom Tana' from *Om Shanti Om* (Farah Khan, 2007) and 'Phir Milenge Chalte Chalte' from *Rab Ne Bana Di Jodi* (Aditya Chopra, 2008), Iyer demonstrates that song and dance intertextuality is "used as a lens to focus on the presences and *presentations* of the past in the present" (original emphasis).

In remembering that dance is political, music is political, and any cultural artefact can be used to provoke a society, Megan Todd (Chapter 12) provides an impassioned discussion of David LaChappelle's (2005) film *Rize*: "The dancing in this movie is political. It is charged in the call to *RIZE*." In detailing the krumping and clowning dance styles featured in the movie, Todd surmises that the "film brings to centre stage Africanist aesthetics in these featured dance genres, which break the continuous kinesthetic line, the mono-rhythmic orientation, detached performance personae, and the pseudo-apolitical assumptions many embodied Eurocentric art forms promote".

Sarah-Mace Dennis rounds out the anthology (Chapter 13) with her ficto-critical, philosophical musings about her own formation and production of a dance film. Drawing from embodiment theory, from an autoethnographic position, Dennis explains that after a severe car accident left her with brain trauma, she was forced to interact with the environments that surrounded her in various states of consciousness. "*Mondo Ghillies* (Dennis, 2010) – the short dance film that followed this – is a practical and experiential unfolding of the subjective and perceptual atmospheres that I came to see and hear as I moved through the world with a severely altered neurological architecture."

Conclusion

In following Vize (2003) the chapters outlined above suggest that dance film has much to say about contemporary popular culture and issues of "sexuality, gender, ethnicity, power and pleasure" that populate it (38). Music and sound are fundamental to our understanding of these issues and the feelings we embody towards them. But there is more at stake than even these sizable issues. There is also the spatial recognition we bring to the sonic world of dance films; our position as an audioviewer; and our willingness to immerse ourselves. There are obviously the political and industrial apparatuses at work, trying to incite or placate as the case may be. And there is the historical dimension of the sound, calling into question our beliefs, memories and readings of past events.

Our objective, in considering dance films across the range of production contexts including screen dance and Hollywood's street dance cycles, Bollywood, independent and avant-garde film, is to broaden considerations of movies, moves and music in academic scholarship. As Faller asks in Chapter 2, "what role does music and sonicity play in our reception and interpretation of screendance? Each screendance answers these questions in its own way, some more fully and/or successfully than others." It is the music and moves within the movies that should enable more voices to rise up, and to articulate the peculiar nuances of certain dance films, or sub-genres of them, that are attempting to speak into contemporary culture.

Notes

1. Mark Evans is Head of the School of Communication at the University of Technology Sydney. He is series editor for Genre, Music and Sound (Equinox Publishing) and executive editor of the (forthcoming) *Encyclopedia of Film Music and Sound*.
2. Mary Fogarty is an Assistant Professor of Dance at York University, Canada. Her work about hip hop dance, film and video appears in the following anthologies: *The Routledge Reader on the Sociology of Music* (2015), *The Oxford Handbook of Dance and the Popular Screen* (2014) and *Ageing and Youth Cultures* (2012). She is the lead facilitator/lecturer for the Toronto B-Girl Movement, a community programme that mentors girls and women in hip hop culture (www.keeprockinyou.com).
3. Diane Hughes (Chapter 6) agrees, noting that in *Honey* "crowd noise, or even the sound of a basketball hitting the ground, are used to focus attention on movement in its various contexts".

References

Blanco Borelli, M. (2014), *The Oxford Handbook of Dance and the Popular Screen*, New York: Oxford University Press.

Brannigan, E. (2009), 'Micro-choreographies: The Close-up in Dance Film', *International Journal of Performing Arts and Digital Media*, 5(2-3), 121–39.

Brannigan, E. (2011), *Dancefilm: Choreography and the Moving Image*. New York: Oxford University Press.

Buckland, T. (1983), 'Definitions of Folk Dance: Some Explorations', *Folk Music Journal*, 4(4), 315–52.

Carroll, N. (2001), 'Toward a Definition of Moving-Picture Dance', *Dance Research Journal*, 33(1), 46–61.

Coyle, R., and Fitzgerald, J. (2010), 'Disney Does Broadway', in R. Coyle (ed.), *Drawn to Sound: Animation Film Music and Sonicity*, London: Equinox, pp. 223–48.

Creekmur, C. (2001), 'Picturizing American Cinema', in P. Wojcik and A. Knight (eds), *Soundtrack Available: Essays on Film and Popular Music*, Durham and London: Duke University Press, pp. 375–406.

Dodds, S. (2001), *Dance on Screen: Genres and Media from Hollywood to Experimental Art*. Houndmills and New York: Palgrave.

Dodds, S., and Cook, S. (eds.) (2013), *Bodies of Sound: Studies across Popular Music and Dance*. Farnham: Ashgate.

Feuer, J. (1980), 'Hollywood Musicals: Mass Art as Folk Art', *JumpCut*, 23 (October), 23–25.

Frith, S., and McRobbie, A. (1978), 'Rock and Sexuality', *Screen Education*, 29, 3–19.

Goehr, L. (1992), *The Imaginary Museum of Musical Works: An Essay in the Philosophy of Music*. Oxford: Oxford University Press.

Goodwin, A., and Grossberg, L. (1993), 'Introduction', in S. Frith, A. Goodwin and L. Grossberg (eds), *Sound and Vision: The Music Video Reader*, London: Routledge.

Gorbman, C. (1987), *Unheard Melodies: Narrative Film Music*. Bloomington: Indiana University Press.

Gorham, R., and Nakache, A. (1993) 'Star Moves: Choreography in Australian Music Video', *Perfect Beat - The Journal of Research into Contemporary Music and Popular Culture*, 1(3), 23–37.

Grossberg, L. (1993), 'The Media Economy of Rock Culture: Cinema, Post-Modernity and Authenticity', in S. Frith, A. Goodwin and L. Grossberg (eds), *Sound and Vision: The Music Video Reader*, London: Routledge, pp. 185–209.

Jeong, Ok Hee (2009), 'Reflections on Maya Deren's Forgotten Film, *The Very Eye of Night*', *Dance Chronicle*, 32, 412–41.

Johnson, I. (2012), 'Music Meant to Make You Move: Considering the Aural Kinesthetic', *Sounding Out!* (18 June), http://soundstudiesblog.com/author/imanikaijohnson/ (accessed May 2013).

Jordan, C. (1996), 'Gender and Class Mobility in *Saturday Night Fever* and *Flashdance*', *Journal of Popular Film and Television*, 24(3), 116–22.

McRobbie, A. (1984), 'Dance and Social Fantasy', in A. McRobbie and M. Nava (eds), *Gender and Generation*, London: Macmillan, pp. 130–61.

Musser, C. (2004), 'At the Beginning: Motion Picture Production, Representation and Ideology at the Edison and Lumière Companies', in L. Grieveson and P. Kramer (eds), *The Silent Cinema Reader*, New York: Routledge, pp. 1–30.

Nattiez, J. (1990), *Music and Discourse: Toward a Semiology of Music*. Princeton: Princeton University Press.

Parfitt-Brown, C. (2010), 'Popular Past, Popular Present, Post-Popular?' in *Conversations Across the Field of Dance Studies*, Special Issue on Dancing the Popular guest-edited by Danielle Robinson, vol. XXXI, pp. 18–20.

Perillo, L. (2008), '"Smooth Criminals": Mimicry, Choreography, and the Discipline of Cebuano Dancing Inmates', *Congress on Research in Dance Conference Proceedings* 40 (supplement 1), pp. 197–202.

Reynolds, D. (2010), 'Glitz and Glamour or Atomic Rearrangement: What do Dance Audiences Want?', *Dance Research*, 28(1) (May), 19–35.

Smith, J. (2001), 'Popular Songs and Comic Allusion', in P. Wojcik and A. Knight (eds), *Soundtrack Available: Essays on Film and Popular Music*, Durham and London: Duke University Press, pp. 407–432.

Thompson, E. (2004), *The Soundscape of Modernity: Architectural Acoustics and the Culture of Listening in America, 1900–1933*. Boston: Massachusetts Institute of Technology Press.

Vize, L. (2003), 'Music and the Body in Dance Film', in I. Inglis (ed.), *Popular Music and Film*, London and New York: Wallflower, pp. 22–38.

Walker, K. (2012) 'Hip Hop Dance in New Zealand: Philosophies, Practices and Issues', unpublished MA thesis, online at https://researchspace.auckland.ac.nz/bitstream/handle/2292/19275/whole.pdf?sequence=2 (accessed 18 May 2015).

Wollen, P. (1992), *Singin' in the Rain*. London: British Film Institute.

From Choreocinema to Experimental Screendance
A Personal Archaeology[1]

Greg Faller[2]

Near the beginning of Maya Deren's *A Study in Choreography for the Camera* (1945), Talley Beatty steps from a forest into a room and helps Deren launch a new hybrid art form – screendance. Building on the cinematic 'discoveries' and editorial 'inventions' she made in her first two films (*Meshes of the Afternoon*, 1943 and *At Land*, 1944), Deren inaugurated an experimental approach to the film(ed) dance that offered an alternative to the Hollywood musical and documented proscenium performances. She explored the collaborative intersection between film and choreography in a way that, according to P. Adams Sitney, created a "simple and unified action ... through irrationally connected spaces within a more or less rational time" (1963–1964: 188). In other words, she fully exploited the temporal and spatial potential of the filmic medium. This was dance that used the camera and editing to recorporealize[3] the human body within a purely cinematic space. Since Deren's 'study', screendance has evolved and expanded into new realms that embrace digital technology and the internet. But whether labelled dance for the camera, video dance or hyperchoreography, the basic tenet of *A Study in Choreography for the Camera* remains relatively unchanged: how to (re)locate human movement within unlimited and fluid time and space.

This outline is a historical convenience. It provides a relatively clean aesthetic and theoretical genesis from which a multidisciplinary art form can be (chronologically) traced. It locates the first collaboration between an established (Black) dancer and a (woman) filmmaker in (alternative) cinema. It parallels the traditional history of American avant-garde film as a post-World War II phenomenon. But history, especially the birth of a new model of production, is messy and this anecdote does not reveal the contentious and even contradictory development of (international) screendance. Deren's work remains seminal, but it did not emerge in a vacuum. What else had happened and was happening? We should also ask: What is a screendance? Why this label?

How is it different from: (1) mainstream films (specifically musicals), which also use the camera and editing to create purely cinematic spaces, and (2) visual records and documentaries of dance performance? And finally, what is experimental screendance?

Figure 1: Annabelle Whitford Moore's Serpentine Dance (c. 1895)

The history of film dance arguably began with the history of film. Annabelle Whitford Moore appeared in a number of short films for the Edison Manufacturing Company and the American Mutoscope & Biograph Company between 1894 and 1897 (see Figure 1). These panoramic frontal tableaux[4] merely documented proscenium performances; we watch her 'Butterfly' and 'Serpentine' dances as if we are eighth row centre. Neither time nor space undergoes any manipulation; her flowing gestures remain firmly grounded in a pro-filmic reality. This approach to recording dance suggests little connection to Deren's work and the experimental screendance, but it demonstrates the basis of the Hollywood model: verisimilitude and the preservation of performance. Fred Astaire, Gene Kelly, Eleanor Powell, The Nicholas Brothers, Anne Miller, Judy Garland (all contemporaries of Deren) were shown full body with minimal editing. Editing, when used, employed 'match position' or 'match action' techniques so that even though time and space were interrupted at each cut, an illusion of contiguous space and continuous time dominated. An appearance of truth or reality preserved the integrity of the seemingly live stage performance as film(ed) choreography.

This panoramic frontal tableau approach to recording dance is also obviously the basis for the archival documentation of dance and dance documentaries. For historical, critical and pedagogical purposes, an uninterrupted, wide-shot visual record of choreography and performance seems to be preferred. Like many documentaries, the tenuous link between pro-filmic reality and filmic reality is hidden; real time and space become film time and space. Like the mainstream musical, verisimilitude and the preservation of performance dominate; but even more so. There is no illusion of reality, only the authenticity (or authenticating) of reality.

These branches of film dance are not screendance. Even though they offer dances shown on screens, and even though traces of these approaches are evident in some screendances, their drive for verisimilitude and their subjugation of the cinematic apparatus in favour of choreography and performance keep them from exploring the new potentials most overtly championed by Deren. To put it (perhaps too) simply, Annabelle Moore's filmed dances evolved into mainstream musicals and dance documentaries. My focus here lies in a different direction.

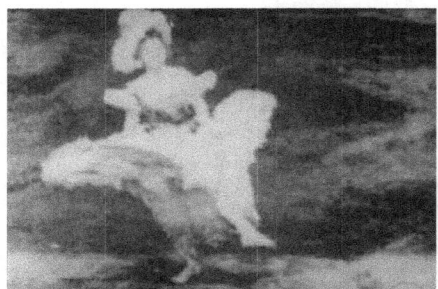 

Figures 2a and 2b: A Nymph of the Waves and Neptune's Daughters (c. 1900)

The seven-disc set, *Unseen Cinema* (Anthology Film Archives, 2005), devotes Disc 7 – 'Viva la Dance' – to an examination of early 'ciné-dance'. Showcasing 42 films made between 1894 and 1946, the collection provides many fascinating works of performance (including the Annabelle Moore dances), visual rhythm and abstract movement. Among them are three early superimpositions from 1900: *Davy Jones Locker*, *Neptune's Daughters* and *A Nymph of the Waves* (see Figures 2a and 2b). These three, 20-second panoramic frontal tableaux add a simple special effect: a double exposure. In *Davy Jones Locker*, an animated skeleton (or a marionette) dances 'on' a ship ploughing through the water. In *Neptune's Daughters*, four women dance 'on' waves crashing on a beach. In *A Nymph of the Waves*, a woman dances 'on' ocean swells. Time hasn't been manipulated, but a new, purely cinematic space has been created into which human movement has been relocated. As Bruce Posner states on the DVD, "The transformation of a stage dance into a unique ciné-dance could only be possible in cinema and never be presented as a live performance" (2005: ch. 10). These films exhibit the first tenuous steps towards modern screendance. Sidney Peterson, in an interview with Kathy Geritz, said that something as simple as a double exposure or a superimposition "did something to the space in which the movement occurred, which you miss when you just shoot a picture of dance stuff happening on the stage" (Geritz, 2010: 51). The importance of superimpositions to screendance can be readily noted in a number of significant works: Sidney Peterson, Hy Hirsch and Marian van Tuyl's *Clinic of Stumble* (1947) and *Horror Dream* (1947), Ed Emshwiller's *Dance Chromatic* (1959) and *Totem* (1963, with Alwin Nikolais), and Ed Seeman's *Frekoba* (1970).

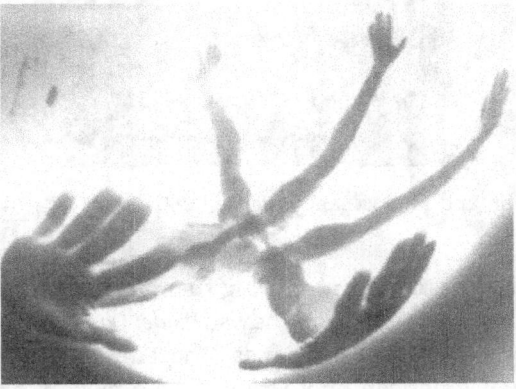

Figure 3: Sara K. Arledge's *Introspection* (1941–1946)

Superimpositions form the spine of Sara K. Arledge's *Introspection* (1941–1946), a film that questions *A Study in Choreography for the Camera*'s status as screendance's ur-text. David James calls it "the first abstract dance film", yet notes that it fails to integrate dance, structure and editing in any meaningful way (2005: 250). Superimposed low-angle medium shots of John Baxter's head turning inside an oval matte yield to superimposed and disembodied arms, legs and torsos moving through darkened voids. Superimposed arms and hands reflected off the concave surface of a Chrysler hubcap create a carousel effect (see Figure 3). The convex side of the hubcap provides fish-eye lens distortions of dancers' bodies. Combinations of these images and other variations in superimpositions and distortions complete the film. Like Deren's work, *Introspection* is a study in the potential of cine-dance, but doesn't connect the numerous spatial abstractions into a temporal whole. As the opening credits inform the viewer, *Introspection* is a "series of experiments" featuring "fragments of dancer imagery". The human body has been relocated in a unique filmic space (*Introspection* could not be performed on a stage), but we see disparate gestures, not choreography; isolated shots, not editing. Even though Terry

Cannon claims that *"Introspection* was one of the first films to utilize dance as a formal element of construction and is considered one of the pioneering examples of 'cine-dance', or dance made uniquely for and by the medium of film" (2001: 75), it remains a precursor to Deren's more accomplished film.

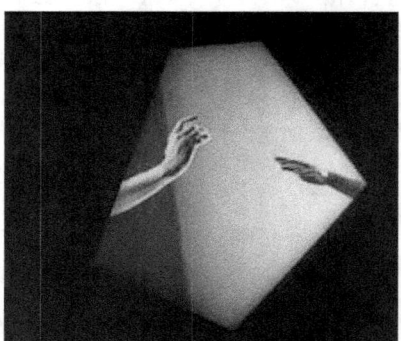

Figure 4: Stella Simon and Miklós Bándy, *Hände* (1927–1928)

Also playing with gestures, but moving them towards a sustained choreography is Stella Simon and Miklós Bándy's *Hände: Das Leben und die Liebe eines Zärtlichen Geschlechts* (1927–1928) [Hands: The Life and Loves of the Gentler Sex]. Simon was an American photographer who moved to Berlin in 1926 to study filmmaking at the Technische Hochschule. As the title indicates, the film uses close-ups of hands (and arms) to tell a story: a proto-feminist exploration of female subjectivity and romantic longing. As an early sound film, Marc Blitzstein provided an original musical score. Set against Constructivist and Expressionist sets (see Figure 4), hands dance a metaphoric narrative that can be followed by the inter-titles:

I. Prelude
   First Meeting
II. The Lonely (Female) Individual
    He Comes
    The Coquette Plays
    Everyone Goes to the Festival
    She and He Come to the Festival
    The Coquette Comes Too
    And Finally the Good One Comes
    Futile Games
    The Good One is Completely Lost
    Alone and Scared
III. Agreement

Jan-Christopher Horak says that "*Hands* can only be classified as a dance film in the widest sense" (1995: 44), but how wide is wide? *Hände* recorporealizes the human body within a purely cinematic space. It manipulates time and space through editing. It exploits camera techniques (framing particularly) in collaboration with set design, choreography and performance. *Hände* (especially the 'drowning' sequence) could not be performed on stage. And that a film dance could be shot exclusively in close-ups is certainly part of contemporary screendance – see, for example, Yvonne Rainer's *Hand Movie* (1966), Jonathan Burrows and Adam Roberts's *Hands* (1995), Cristina Capriola's *I Ti: Fingerdansen* (2002), Michael Slobodian's *Multiplicity* (2006) and Andy Wood and Zoe Solomon's *Gaze* (2006).

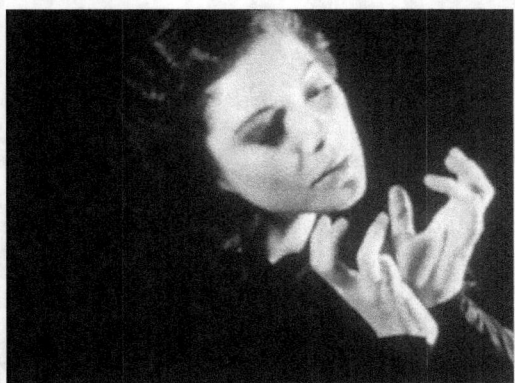

Figure 5: Norman Bel Geddes, *Tilly Losch in Her Dance of the Hands* (1930–1933)

Another film spotlighting hands, but integrating them into a more fully realized dance performance is Norman Bel Geddes's *Tilly Losch in Her Dance of the Hands* (1930–1933). Produced by Nutshell Pictures Corporation (Bel Geddes's crudely humorous name and credit sequence for his personal projects), the film features Tilly Losch dancing in a black studio space (see Figure 5), fully clothed in black except for her hands and head, lit so that her face and hands almost glow in the dark void, and accompanied by a piano score. If any one film prior to *A Study in Choreography for the Camera* truly challenges Deren's film as the first screendance, *Dance of the Hands* wins that position. Working with close-ups, medium close-ups and medium shots; employing a wide variety of camera angles and camera-subject distances; utilizing a moving, hand-held camera; playing with the edge of the frame; eschewing any locomotor movement but choreographing from the waist up; and using match-action and match-position cutting, Bel Geddes questions screen direction and gravity. Losch seems to float through an undefined 360-degree space with little sense of a floor. We see her in intimate detail, her emotionally charged movements fluid across numerous cuts. Like Deren, Bel Geddes explored the collaborative intersection between film and choreography in a way that exploited the temporal and spatial potential of the filmic medium. He used the camera and editing to recorporealize the human body within a purely cinematic environment. Perhaps the only significant difference between Bel Geddes's and Deren's films is space: Bel Geddes stayed in the studio; Deren jumped between exterior and interior locations. But this seems a matter of degree, creating end points on a spectrum. Deren underscored (almost reflexively) the large 'distances' travelled between match cuts while Bel Geddes used the same editing techniques to stress intimacy, bringing us closer to the heart of the dancer and dance. The final section of *Dance of the Hands*, with Losch's flowing dress seemingly anchored to the floor, suggests an influence on the final section of Liz Aggiss, Billy Cowie and David Anderson's *Motion Control* (2002) – a work that also explores the interiority of the performer. In 2008, Bel Geddes's film was extrapolated into a live performance by Diana Sherwood (with the film running on a monitor on the stage) and accompanied by the same score.[5]

These are some of the films that contributed to the artistic environment in which Deren created her *A Study in Choreography for the Camera*. Exactly where (and when) we locate the birth of screendance may not be particularly important or beneficial. What seems more important is to define screendance in greater detail and to continue to differentiate it from other forms of media which present recorded dance. This task will prove a bit awkward since the screendance canon, as it developed, presented many and often inconsistent definitions, descriptions, labels and explanations to separate mainstream musical/dance films, dance documentaries and archival records of proscenium performances from this other 'screendance' category.

Two of the earliest labels applied to the screendance include 'choreocinema'[6] and 'cine-dance'.[7] As video production superseded film production, the number of labels exploded: Dance for Camera, Dance for the Camera, Dance on Camera, Dance with Camera, Choreography for the Camera, Dance on Screen, Video Dance, Dance Film, Film Dance, Dance 4 Film, Moving-Picture Dance, and Screendance. An excursion into some of the terminology will shine a curious spotlight on this convoluted semantic and theoretical arena.

From a linked-in, global network perspective, Wikipedia offers a reasonable, popular culture commentary about the current dilemma in screendance. The posting for 'dance film' reads:

> Dance film is also known as the *cinematic* interpretation of existing dance works, originally created for live performance. When existing *dance* works are modified for the purposes of filming this can involve a wide

variety of *film techniques*. Depending on the amount of choreographic and/or presentational adjustment an original work is subjected to, the filmed version may be considered as Dance for Camera.[8]

In short, a dance for the camera is a dance film, but a dance film is not necessarily a dance for the camera. Then, with wonderful understatement, it concludes by saying, "These definitions are not agreed upon by those working with dance and film or video."[9] Say what you will about Wikipedia in academic research, but this entry is spot on.

The entry also says: "It has been suggested that this article be *merged* with *Videodance*."[10] When you access Videodance – which is also accessed through "dance for camera" – you see the following:

> Videodance is a genre of dance made for the camera. In videodance, movement is the primary expressive element in the work rather than dialogue (as in conventional narrative movies) or music (as in music videos). Other names for this form are screendance, dance film, cinedance, and dance for camera. Videodance is distinguished from other film genres by its emphasis on the craft and composition of movement in the work. A related genre that is often confused with videodance is the dance documentary film. This is the documentation of dance as it is practiced in real life such as a live performance or a journalistic profile of a dance company, figure, or community. Videodance is not a documentation of a dance that could be done in real time in a live setting. It exists only as a fictional or fictionalized dance for screen.[11]

Again, for a social website, this collaborative and anonymous explanation offers a primer on the field. It distinguishes between dance film and dance documentary on one side and videodance, dance for (the) camera, cinedance (or filmdance) and screendance on the other. All of these labels express (or are meant to express) the sensibility of Bel Geddes's and Deren's initial explorations: the collaborative intersection between film and choreography; the exploitation of the fluid temporal and spatial potential of the filmic medium; the recorporealization of the human body; no insistence of verisimilitude; and no drive to re-present, document and preserve live stage performance.

Noël Carroll, in his 'Toward a Definition of Moving-Picture Dance' (2001), offers a "philosophical characterization" that describes three types of moving-picture dance: the document, the reconstruction (essentially an adaptation of existing choreography) and the construction. He defines a construction as "a new work brought into being and shaped by ... editing, camera movement, camera placement, special effects, digital processing, motion capture, computer animation, and so on" (121–22). Jenelle Porter, in *Dance with Camera* (2009), offers a poetic explanation. A dance with camera is a "pas de deux between dancer and camera. Choreography is designed for the lens, with movements prescribed by the camera's frame" (11). Sherril Dodds, in *Dance on Screen* (2001), extends this description by adding that it is "not only the body that creates the dance, but also the camera and the cut" (xiv). Katrina McPherson, in her *Making Video Dance* (2006), states that:

> the term "video dance" does not exclude work that has been shot, or even edited, using a film format. It is rather a catch-all term to describe this relatively new art form that fuses avant-garde approaches to dance-making with innovation in video art, film, and television-making practice. The challenge ... is to invent a new language for the screen ... to find and communicate ideas that can only be expressed through this art form that combines the media of dance and video, using a style and a syntax that is unique to video dance. (p. 30)

These four descriptions, unlike the Wikipedia entries, emphasize synthesis – a blending of innovative camera/lens/editing and avant-garde choreography/dancer/movement in the drive to create a new and unique language for the screen. As Arlene Croce said, "Most successful screen dances lie somewhere between total cinematic illusion and passive recording ... A cleanly photographed dance can be pretentious and boring; a complex cinematic extravaganza can be utterly devoid of kinetic charms" (1978: 146).

At this point, a fairly prescribed model seems possible. The hierarchy starts with 'Dance Film' and offer four branches of potential production: (1) the archival record; (2) the dance documentary and journalistic profile; (3) cinematic adaptations or interpretations or reconstructions of stage/live performances; and (4) videodance (and its alternative names: dance for the camera, screendance, cinedance, film dance, dance with camera, dance on screen, moving-picture dance construction). When we look at some professional websites, these divisions begin to get messy. 'Dance film' seems to operate simultaneously as a specific category (screendance) and as the topmost stratum, excluding only the archival record. Videodance.org.uk prefers to use the label (not surprisingly) videodance, aligning it with screendance, yet also incorporating cinematic adaptations of stage performances.[12]

Physical TV Company offers a Venn diagram originally generated at Screendance: The State of the Art Conference (held at the American Dance Festival, Duke University, Durham, North Carolina, USA, 2006) with three intersections:

(1) dance on screen is essentially documented dance performance and shares only some elements of cinema and visual art (it resides almost exclusively in the Dance sphere); (2) dancefilm resides in the overlap between Dance and Cinema; and (3) videodance lies between Dance and Visual Art.

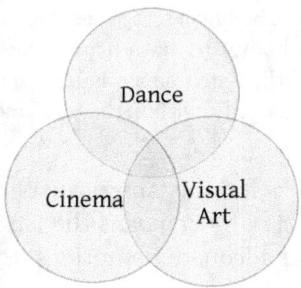

On their website, Karen Pearlman, co-founder and co-artistic director of the Physical TV Company, explains the areas of overlap:

> Unlike the typical result of these models, it was determined that the 'ideal' screendance production was not necessarily a mix of all three. Rather, each approach and each overlap provided a way of comprehending a given work: a *dance on screen* which prioritises dance as its central discipline will foreground the composition and exhibition of the danced movement; it has its origins in dance and is shaped by the impulse to capture and exhibit the dance and dancing; a dancefilm that is working in the overlapping areas of cinema and dance will prioritise the directorial vision and emphasise the collaborative coordination of all of the elements of cinematic production from script to mise-en-scéne to sound mix; it is created within the techniques, histories, and possibilities of cinema; a *video dance* that is based in the thinking of a video art maker, a performance art maker or a visual artist will have its effect through techniques, schools, theories and premises of those disciplines. (www.PhysicalTV.com.au, accessed 23 September 2013)

This model also foregrounds the hybridity and collaborative nature of screendance and allows for a continuum of production and reception but it fails to precisely define or explain screendance. You can see why Wikipedia said what it said. The discipline's terms and definitions are neither consistent nor shared.

Douglas Rosenberg is most sensitive to this problem and has provided a sustained argument for more theoretical rigour. In 'Video Space: A Site for Choreography' (2000), he developed a synthetic explanation that sees the camera/lens/video/film apparatus as the site for the creation of video dance. These are works *made for* video, not *recorded by* video; works with performances that occur *within* video, not *on* video. As a collaborative and hybrid form, neither the choreographer nor the camera can dominate. The videographer is not an archivist for the choreographer; the choreographer is not a content provider for the videographer. He calls for a

> recorporealization of the body via screen techniques; at times a construction of an impossible body, one not encumbered by gravity, temporal restraints, or even death. Video dance is in practice a construction of choreography that lives only within the site and architectural space of the camera. (280)

In the 2006 catalogue essay for the American Dance Festival's 11th annual Dancing for the Camera series, he bemoans the lack of theoretical grounding, consistent terminology and adequate definitions. He says,

> We have yet to define the terms of screendance to the degree that I had hoped for ... We are still lacking a critical framework for the genre, as well as a lexicon of theory and language that differentiates it from other moving image work and other body-centered media based work. In other words, practice is leading theory in its development and dissemination within the culture of screendance. (2006a: 1)

Note that Rosenberg has now adopted the term screendance. In this essay, he includes the '(Hu)Manifesto: Possibilities for Screendance' that was generated at the Opensource {Videodance} symposium held in Findhorn, Scotland, earlier that year.[13] The manifesto does not try to define screendance and stresses a continuum of ways to create a screendance (similar to Screendance's Venn diagram).

In his 'Proposing a Theory of Screendance' (2006b), Rosenberg begins to argue for well-articulated discourse, a master category of screendance and the creation of genres. As he explains:

> In our world, there is no delineation between comedic dance films and site specific dance films, or narrative and non-narrative work, or solo expressionistic dance films and intergenerational work. In other words, we have not made the effort to begin to parse screendance into frames of reference as other art forms have done in order to create a context for discourse. (12)

In 'Excavating Genres' (2010), Rosenberg continues this push. He offers a linguistic deconstruction of the most commonly used terms such as "dance for camera", describing it as "a kind of colonial space for which dance is simply another subjugated citizen" (64), and "video dance", as a term that "ultimately does little to illuminate the nature of the work in question" (67). He says that other, alternative labels in common use "are equally misleading or misrepresent the actual materiality of the hybrid of dance and its mediated image" (ibid.). Rosenberg re-emphasizes that screendance can provide the necessary master category from which numerous genres and subgenres can flow.

> Screendance, being a hybrid practice, contains at least two disciplines: dance and screen-based, technologically mediated methods of rendering.

> In this capacity, it is an overarching master category: screendance implies that the endpoint of the endeavor is a mediated image of dance on a screen, any dance on any screen. Indeed, by design and intent, screendance does not imply the materiality of rendering, nor does it describe a particular genre of dance practice. It could be shot in film or video, or manifest in a cameraless digital environment. The choreographic language of the work could be modern, post-modern, jazz, ballet or any other kind of dance. In order to particularize a discussion about a work of screendance, then, it is necessary to further articulate both form and content – both the method of rendering as well as the choreographic language. In this way it becomes possible to extrapolate meaning from the common and/or accepted shorthand that is used to describe a range of screendance practices. (2010: 67)

Over the course of 65 years (counting from Deren's work), the discipline has moved from calling its works choreocinema to screendance. For me, this label excludes archival records, dance documentaries and journalistic profiles because, even though consumed on a screen, they are only minimally mediated via technology (the camera has been subjugated by the dance), only minimally hybrid forms (maintaining instead the drive towards verisimilitude and preserving performance), and rarely collaborative. They are dances on screen rather than screendances. Screendances can be cinematic adaptations or interpretations of stage/live performances or – and most importantly here – works that are specifically "of the screen" (2010: 69). They require a collaborative intersection between film/video/digital media and choreography; the exploitation of the fluid temporal and spatial potential of the screenic[14] medium; the recorporealization of the human body; no insistence of verisimilitude; and no drive to simply re-present, document and preserve live stage performance. As Deirdre Towers stated, a screendance is an art form with the "potential to capture and express what neither live dance nor traditional film can" (2002: 189–92).

With this understanding I would like to propose a genre of screendance for analysis and debate: the experimental screendance. This category flows more from experimental media than from modern or postmodern choreography. As Amy Greenfield suggests, screendance can explore "the possibilities for the creative transformation of dance into avant-garde film" (2002: 21). An experimental screendance includes the attributes listed above, as well as the following:

> Non-narrative
> Short
> Visually abstract or non-objective/non-representational
> Reflexive
> Challenge taboos/conventions

Play with depth-of-field/focus and the flattening of space
Composition/Framing (to avoid the re-creation of a proscenium space)
Close-ups (for proximity and intimacy)
Lens movement (zoom)
Camera movement (pan, tilt, dolly, hand-held)
Camera angles, focal lengths and camera subject distance
Lighting
Exposure
Colour (costumes, set design, props, media)
Locations (exterior or interior but not studio space or stage)
Gravity free (no floor)
Multiple windows/screens
Abstract, extract, isolate and/or intensify movement

An experimental screendance does not need to use and exhibit all of these traits, but will typically integrate a significant number of them. Obviously all film/video/media can use and manifest these techniques, but the experimental screendance employs them in unconventional, innovative and oppositional ways. Sherril Dodds explains that screendance constructs dances and dancing bodies

> that could not be replicated on the stage: fragmented bodies, magnified bodies, and minuscule bodies; bodies seen from unconventional perspectives; unpredictable bodies that undermine spatial and temporal expectations; and bodies moving in ways that are physically impossible outside the film and television context. (2001: 79)

Even though ten years later Doug Rosenberg argues we should move away from this stage/live versus screen/mediated dialectic,[15] Dodds' list of screenic body images neatly summarizes much of the innovative nature associated with the experimental screendance. It embodies the unconventional not only to test new artistic forms but also to provide new ways of seeing and thinking. 'Experimental' suggests aesthetic and cultural innovation; it provides new aesthetic forms that lead to new ways of seeing and thinking which then generate opposition and challenges to the status quo. The ideal experimental screendance would accomplish all of this, but most focus on more specific (and limited) goals. 'Experimental' is not static or ahistorical; it changes over time and as culture changes. As André Breton said, the avant-garde will survive only by ceasing to exist; the cutting edge will be absorbed by the mainstream thus generating a new avant-garde. What was once innovative and challenging no longer appears as such and new technologies, techniques, styles, approaches, aesthetics and values assume that function.

The experimental screendance can be traced back to Simon, Bel Geddes, Arledge, and of course Deren. Their films established the groundwork for the recent expansion of the discipline. In the last two decades or so, there has been a profusion of work due to the internet and the growth of the screendance academically and professionally. Vimeo's 'screendance' group lists over 200 members and almost 500 videos; its 'dance on camera' group lists over 350 members and 900 videos. YouTube lists thousands of video clips under the various labels for screendance previously discussed (including 'videodanza'). Given the democratic nature of these sites, many postings (perhaps most) don't really qualify as screendances, but the numbers attest to an awareness (and an appreciation?) in popular culture. The Dance Films Association's Dance on Camera Festival is spotlighted on Hulu and TenduTV. Most associations maintain a website, including South East Dance, Dance Camera West, Dance Films Association, Dance UK, Contemporary Dance Australia, American Dance Festival, and Dance for the Camera.[16] Professional companies that create screendances have a web presence: Rosas, Ultimavez, DV8, LaLaLaHumanSteps, Mitchell Rose, and The Physical TV Company.[17] There are sites for festivals and networking, including ScreenDance Network, ChoreoVideo, Dance Media, Dance & Media Network, Dance-Tech/MoveStream, Move the Frame, The International Dance for the Camera Festival, and UMove Online Videodance Festival.[18] DVD anthologies are available, such as *Take 7*, *Dance for Camera*, *Evidentia*, *Dance for Camera 2* and *Dance Defying Gravity*. Two journals devoted to screendance are in publication: *The International Journal of Screendance* and the *Dance on Camera Journal*.[19] University programmes are emerging that focus on screendance.[20]

In this exponentially growing field, I can only discuss an extremely small percentage of the experimental screendances produced. I will focus on works that are short, non-narrative, collaborative, created originally for the screen, recorporealize the human body with some of the techniques listed above, exploit screenic time and space, and are (or were) innovative and oppositional. I realize this is an artificial category, one that ignores many important works because they are narratively structured and/or based on stage performances and/or are simply 'not short' (I feel particularly guilty for excluding exceptional films by Lloyd Newson/DV8 and Wim Vandekeybus/Ultima Vez),[21] but the gestation of a genre often begins with questionable restrictions and distinctions. I will also skip the early development of the screendance; much has already been written on Maya Deren,[22] Sidney Peterson,[23] Shirley Clarke,[24] Charles Atlas, Elliot Caplan and Merce Cunningham,[25] Norman McLaren[26] and Ed Emshwiller.[27] However, I will make exceptions in order to briefly discuss three seminal screendances: *Nine Variations on a Dance Theme* (1966) by Hilary Harris, *Breakaway* (1966) by Bruce Conner, and *Transport* (1971) by Amy Greenfield. Each of these films demonstrates "a merging of the principles of dance and film, not just the shift of dance onto film" (Siebens, 2002: 223).

Harris, probably best known for his documentary films such as *Seawards the Great Ships* (1961), winner of the 1962 Academy Award for Best Documentary

Short, and *Organism* (1975), a film about New York City that pioneered the use of time-lapse photography, builds on Bel Geddes and Deren and turns their initial steps into a compendium on how to "transform modern dance into cinema through specific techniques that reveal the structural essence of modern dance in a way possible only on the screen ... to use dance to reveal principles of cinematic motion" (Greenfield, 2002: 21). *Nine Variations on a Dance Theme* repeats a 55-second dance phrase performed by Bettie de Jong nine times (as the title tells us). It starts as a *filmic record* of her dance performance and ends as a *filmic dance performance* made possible only by the temporal and spatial manipulations of film. Harris's documentary eye yields to an editor's and choreographer's eye.

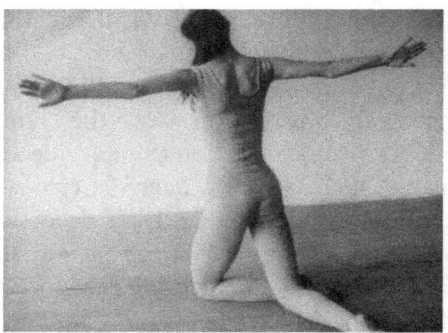

Figure 6: Hilary Harris, *Nine Variations on a Dance Theme* (1966)

The first two variations are single, long duration takes. In each one, the camera moves around de Jong in an intimate documentary fashion, recording real time and space though different angles and camera-subject distances (see Figure 6). Even though we share the space with de Jong (unlike an archival record), these variations strive towards verisimilitude and the preservation of the live performance; we see an uninterrupted and integral choreographic phrase. Variation 3 introduces match cutting and some medium close-ups, yet maintains the illusion of continuous time and contiguous space; it still runs at 55 seconds. The film has moved from dance documentary to the Hollywood model. Variation 4 begins the transition of the film into an experimental screendance. Extreme close-ups travel along de Jong's body and abstract it. This visual abstraction is intensified by cutting that jumps in time and space; some movements repeat, others are reduced or eliminated. Reconstructing the phrase in a non-linear fashion extends its running time; de Jong's actual performance is augmented by film techniques that recorporealize the body in a purely cinematic space.

Variations 5–9 continue this exploration by adding more and more film techniques, pushing the performance further away from the original documentation and increasing its running time. Variation 5 adds the use of overlapping shots, 360-degree screen direction, and focus on specific parts of the body (we see sections of the phrase only in close-ups). Variation 6 introduces fragmentation editing, shorter shots, and (consequently) a more rapid tempo. Variation 7 eliminates sections of the performance via larger editing jumps in time and space – and returns to the original running time of 55 seconds. Variation 8 reinstates rapid fragmentation editing, increases the visual abstraction through extreme close-ups and camera movements, and pulls de Jong out of time and space. Variation 9 runs at 3 minutes and 25 seconds. It reinstates a sense of space because it incorporates wide shots, yet its radical, non-linear construct wonderfully manifests the various types of screenic body images listed by Dodds: de Jong is fragmented, magnified, reduced, seen from unconventional perspectives, abstracted, unpredictable, undermines space and time, and moves in physically impossible ways. *Nine Variations on a Dance Theme* builds to a position of aesthetic and cultural innovation. It produces a completely new dance phrase from the combination of choreography and film techniques. It provides new ways of seeing and thinking about dance and film. It answers the question, how can a (screen)dance be created out of film?

Figure 7: Bruce Conner, *Breakaway* (1966).

Another important film from this period that also answers this question is Bruce Conner's *Breakaway* (1966). Often considered the father of assemblage/found filmmaking (through such works as *A Movie* [1958] and *Cosmic Ray* [1961]), and progenitor of the music video (through such works as *Mongoloid* [1978] and *America is Waiting* [1982]), Conner created this short experimental screendance mostly through editing (see Figure 7). As if following Soviet montage theory, Conner devises a dance pieced together from almost disparate shots. Perhaps the dance never existed as choreography; it emerged only when these images were combined. Similar to a flipbook or a movie on a hand-cranked projector, the film 'flickers' through a series of still poses, rapid zooms, slow, fast and reverse motion shots, and snippets of gestures to generate a frenetic and stroboscopic performance. At times producing a 'vibrating' effect similar to Ed Emshwiller's abstracted dancer in *Thanatopsis* (1962), *Breakaway* fully demonstrates the recorporealized screenic body.

Amy Greenfield may be occasionally underplayed in the screendance canon because her films seem based more on performance/body art than choreography. Nevertheless, her first four films – *Transport* (1971), *Dervish 2* (1972), *Element* (1973) and *Dialogue for a Cameraman & Dancer* (1974) – introduced a number of now standard aspects of screendance: pedestrian movement, untrained dancers, exterior locations, the interaction between performer and natural elements, and the use of video. These works established what she described as "filmdance".

> A filmdance ... is a film in which the filmmaker/choreographer transforms the ground rules of dance time and space through the kinetic use of camera lens, camera angles, camera motion, light, optical techniques, and ... editing. Through such filmic transformations of the human body in motion, the collaboration between film and dance creates a third experience, a new kind of dance often totally unrelated to live dance. (quoted in Porter, 2009: 87)

This "third experience" can be easily noted in *Transport*. Like Deren, Greenfield stepped out of the studio and into the real world. On a large dirt hill in a desolate urban area, two bodies (Greenfield and Lee Vogt) are repeatedly lifted and carried by three untrained performers; there is no stylized movement, only pedestrian actions. A hand-held camera moves roughly around, over and under them becoming another participant in a strange ritual. Jump cuts alternate with sequences of parallel editing, intensifying the rhythmic pattern until, like the diving sequence in Leni Riefenstahl's *Olympia* (1938), the carried bodies seem only to be flying. According to Greenfield, she was influenced by images of the dead of the Vietnam War and the nascent American space programme.[28] Whatever the inspiration, the choreography arises from the camera movement and editing. *Transport* manifests all the attributes of the experimental screendance; it challenges us to reconsider how we recognize, define and experience dance on the screen. Greenfield's influence could be traced to recent works such as Miriam King and Anthony Atanasio's *Dust* (1998), Jeannette Ginslov's *CoNCrEte* (2004), Carol Dilley's *We Sit* (2005) and Ben Dolphin's *Arising* (2009).

Life-long dance advocate, international teacher, founding chair of Dance UK and BBC producer for dance on television, Bob Lockyer nurtured initial screendance explorations into a fully cohesive – and respected – area of creativity. His *Tights, Camera, Action!* and *Dance for the Camera* series on BBC television in the 1990s produced about 50 screendances, many now considered seminal works. In his comparison between stage and screen, linear and non-linear time, and choreography and editing, he explained, "When selecting a project to go forward to production in the Dance for the Camera series, I'm looking, in very simple terms, for something that will work on the screen – a dance work that uses the film/video vocabulary, not one that could be seen on stage" (2002: 159). Screendances produced under his mentorship also aspired towards generating "third experiences".

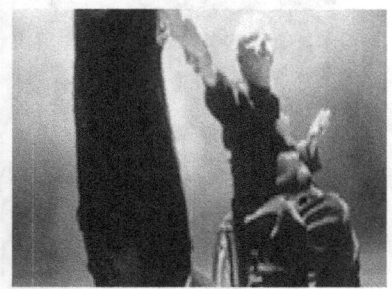 

Figure 8a: Victoria Marks and Margaret Williams, *Outside In* (1993)

Figure 8b: Victoria Marks and Margaret Williams, *Mothers & Daughters* (1994)

Two of the films that emerged from this very fertile period were by the well-known choreographer-director team of Victoria Marks and Margaret Williams (see Figures 8a and 8b). Their *Outside In* (1993) and *Mothers & Daughters* (1994) remain landmark examples of the fully realized screendance – which they define as "a piece that would exist only through the camera's lens and through the editing process" (Marks, 2002: 209). *Outside In* features the mixed-ability troupe CandoCo Dance Company in a series of thematically linked vignettes. Mixing dance, pedestrian movement, surreal images and special effects, six dancers interact in a smart, sexy and comedic tango that emphasizes power – the dancers', the choreography's and the film's – to challenge the dominant cultural notion of disability. *Mothers & Daughters* showcases eight mother–daughter pairs (of which only three daughters had some dance training) in an examination of the tension and sensuality of maternal (in)dependency. Again playing with dance, pedestrian movement, surreal images and humour, the film uses individual relationships to express some universal truths.

Two works, Philippe Decouflé's *Le P'tit bal* (1993) and Adam Roberts and Jonathan Burrow's *Hands* (1995), use the filmic frame to create a proscenium stage. In *Le P'tit bal*, Decouflé and Pascale Houbin sit behind a table set incongruously in a field of grass (see Figure 9). They perform a series of intricate hand gestures (sign language) to a whimsical song ('C'etait Bien' ['Although It Was']) while small objects randomly fall from the sky. Although editing, close-ups and variations in film speed are employed, the film depends on a wide two-shot that suggests a stage. What happens just outside the frame (what we can't see) contributes to the humorous absurdity of the film. Decouflé would again play with framing and compositional trickery in *Abracadabra* (1998).

 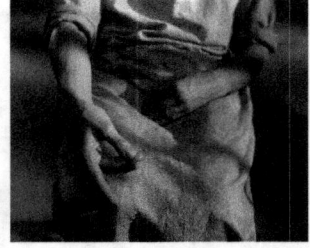

Figure 9: Philippe Decouflé, *Le P'tit bal* (1993)

Figure 10: Adam Roberts and Jonathan Burrow, *Hands* (1995)

Hands is nearly identical to the Edison films of Annabelle Moore; it is a single, long duration take. However, instead of employing a sustained wide shot, the film uses a sustained medium shot that frames a man's lap (a 'stage') on which his hands dance (see Figure 10). By also introducing the performer through a small tracking shot, *Hands* offers a postmodern twist on the panoramic frontal tableau.

Two other works, Wendy Houstoun and David Hinton's *Touched* (1994) and Mike Stubbs's *Man Act* (1996), use stylized pedestrian movement to explore the cultural meaning of social gestures. Both films use black and white stock, repetition, intercutting, and only medium shots and close-ups. *Touched* examines the almost ritualistic quality of public interactions (the film is set in a bar) and dating (the film focuses on the intimacy of friends and couples). *Man Act* aggressively depicts masculinity as problematic: violent, homophobic, competitive, potentially destructive (if not suicidal), and perhaps most disturbingly, as an attitude uncritically inherited by each new generation.

Figure 11: Rosemary Lee and Peter Anderson, *boy* (1995)

Perhaps the most famous film from this period is Rosemary Lee and Peter Anderson's *boy* (1995). Shot entirely on the coast of Norfolk, England, Tom Evans performs a series of animal-like jumps, leaps, runs, falls, poses and gestures that evoke the exuberant world of an eight-year-old boy (see Figure 11). He spies on, signals to and fights with an imaginary twin. Using traditional editing techniques (point of view, match action, eye-line gaze, shot/reverse shot) the film plays with subjective and objective perspectives, much like Maya Deren did in *Ritual in Transfigured Time* (1946). In Lockyer's parameters, *boy* is a dance work that uses film vocabulary and could not be seen on stage. In Greenfield's language, *boy* offers that unique, hybridized "third experience". In Dodds' words, *boy* exhibits an unpredictable body that undermines space and time. In Rosenberg's video space model, *boy* depicts choreography that can only exist within the camera. *boy* challenges us to reconsider how we understand dance, how we experience dance on the screen, and what larger truths might be revealed from individual expression. As Catherine Hale commented:

> Lee's art achieves a transcendence that has little to do with commonly held aesthetic values in dance. It is about engaging with a life force that is expressed, not through words but through the innocence of a body with no preconceptions of itself. In a sense Lee is making dances in uncharted territories ... that [are] very visceral and emotive. (2001)

Many other millennial works influenced my understanding and pedagogy of screendance, but I find myself returning to certain pieces again and again. They include: Philippe Baylaucq's *Lodela* (1996), Suzanna Hood and Michael Downing's *Cornered* (1997), William Forsythe and Thomas Balogh's *Solo* (1997), Bill T. Jones, Paul Kaiser and Shelley Eshkar's *Ghostcatching* (1999), Claudia Alessi's *Threads* (1999), Mitchell Rose's *Modern Daydreams* (2001), Danya and Gaelen Hanson's *Measure* (2001), Liz Aggiss, Billy Cowie and David Anderson's *Motion Control* (2002), Liz Aggiss and Billy Cowie's *Anarchic Variations* (2002), Reynir Lyngdal and Katrin Hall's *Burst* (2003) and Simona da Pozzo's *Walkabout of Alices* (2003). More recent works include: Kelly Hargraves's *Cargo* (2007), Peter Delaney's *Choreosplice* (2007), Carolina Alejos and Aitor Echeverria's *Aprop* (2007), Kitty Smith's *Corporate Line* (2007), Erika Janunger's *Weightless* (2007), Ally Voye's *Red* (2007) and Corrie Befort's *Slip Cadence* (2009). I would like to comment on all of them, but when combined with the hundreds of works I still need to see, this becomes a nearly infinite task – and one that I certainly cannot do here. Instead, I will conclude with two brief tangents from my initial archaeology into the experimental screendance.

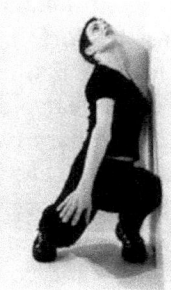 

Figure 12a: Suzanna Hood and Michael Downing, *Cornered* (1997)

Figure 12b: Liz Aggiss and Billy Cowie, *Anarchic Variations* (2002)

The first hopes to acknowledge intertextuality; the influence and cross-fertilization that screendance and screendance-makers have on one another. For example, *Cornered* features a woman trapped in a white room's corner (see Figure 12a). Her performance plays off the three intersecting surfaces (wall/wall/floor) but without any stability. The rotating camera eliminates gravity as all three surfaces change orientation and also become the ceiling. Changes in exposure, a score that combines percussion and ethereal vocals, a scratchy black and white film stock, and an editing strategy that is part match action and part jump cut, create an edgy, disquieting sense of entrapment and frustration. *Anarchic Variations* employs the same basic construct (a woman trapped in a white room) and explores the same basic theme (see Figure 12b). As Liz Aggiss explains on her website:

> *Anarchic Variations* ... confounds and disorientates the spectators' view of space, scale and sound based on the idea of theme and variations. The underlying physical concept centers on dislocation ... *Anarchic Variations* uses a neutral white box space as an antagonistic partner to the dancer.[29]

Made five years later than *Cornered*, *Anarchic Variations* employs new digital technology (for both image and sound) to generate a very different experience.

Figure 13a: Ami Ipapo and Matt Tarr, *Little Ease (outside the box)* (2008)

Figure 13b: Troika Ranch, *BKLYN* (2007)

Another interesting example is Ami Ipapo and Matt Tarr's *Little Ease (outside the box)* (2008), a reimagining of Elizabeth Streb's solo stage piece *Little Ease* (1985). By employing match action and match position editing, the performer is radically relocated mid-gesture from one location to another (see Figure 13a). The use of a literal box to confine the performer also echoes the second section of *Motion Control*. *Little Ease (outside the box)* was shot in Brooklyn, New York and offers a convenient segue to Troika Ranch's *BKLYN* (2007). Taking the basis of match action and match position editing to the extreme, matching a gesture on each *frame* instead of each shot, Mark Coniglio's algorithmic editing produces what Harmony Bench (2010) calls "anti-gravitational choreography". The intensely stroboscopic experience of watching the dancer violently and instantaneously transported around Brooklyn creates a tension between the choreography and the filmmaking that never seems resolved or synthesized (see Figure 13b). As Bench comments, the film "tests viewers' capacity to track a phrase of movement across rapid cuts, multiple environments, and fragmented gestures" (2010: 58). Mitchell Rose explores the same technique in *Advance* (2009), a two-minute film for two dancers that travels across 50 locations (see Figure 14). These pieces not only play off one another but also evoke the ghost of Maya Deren. Their extensive and extended reworking of *A Study in Choreography for the Camera*'s basic tenet cannot be overlooked.

Figure 14: Mitchell Rose, *Advance* (2009)

The second tangent enters the realm of future gazing. As I suggested earlier, the experimental screendance must continually advance aesthetic, cultural and technological innovation. So where does the screendance go next? How does it maintain its avant-garde nature? Can other screens and approaches be tapped? One avenue developing now (along with screendance installations and machinima-based virtual dance) is hyperchoreography (also known as web dance, cyberdance or hyperdance). As defined by hyperchoreography.org,

> hyperchoreography is a non-linear dance performance 'space', existing in an interactive, networked medium and using digital hypermedia. The elements are put in place by the creators, but the shape of the work is decided by the user at the moment of interaction.[30]

Harmony Bench explains it this way:

> Hyperdance is a kind of screendance that solicits user interaction and is in turn shaped by that interaction. In navigating a hyperdance, users generate their own choreographies for screen dancing images. Users are active participants in creating the work they see onscreen ... the work does not exist without their intervention. (2006: 2)

This form of the screendance stresses the excitement of discovery as much as it does performing and co-creating. Few instructions are typically offered, so the viewer/participant learns the choreography; each interaction is a type of 'rehearsal', but for a dance that is always different and never completed. The site http://www.du.ahk.nl/people/carolien/index.htm highlights *Trilogy* (2003), three interactive dances: 'The Elbow Room'; 'Me, My Bag, and the Car'; and 'Jump the Gun'. The site http://www.mulleras.com/index.html also offers three web works: *Mini@tures* (1998–2001), *Invisible* (2002–2005) and *96 Details* (2006–2009).

Figure 15: Katrina McPherson and Simon Fildes, *The Truth: The Truth* (2004)

The site http://hyperchoreography.org/index.html features three pieces by Katrina McPherson and Simon Fildes – *Big* (2002), *Ardnamurchan Zillij* (2004) and *The Truth: The Truth* (2004) – and links to other sites and projects (see Figure 15). How hyperchoreography will develop and contribute to our understanding and experience of experimental screendance (and dance in general) is yet to be determined. Remembering André Breton, just as screendance redefined and extended dance as a collaboration between film/video and choreography that was more than mere documentation, hyperchoreography should redefine and extend screendance as a collaboration between computer (user) and choreography that provides more than passive observation.

The above texts are some of those that have influenced me as I entered, and continue to investigate, the field. But more than just personal influences, these pieces can also provide a convenient (if culturally and regionally skewed) introduction to the exciting and always expanding arena of experimental screendances. A Study in Choreography for the Camera set the standard for future works, even though earlier but less dramatic examples exist. From Deren we inherited a hybrid form, not only of dance and cinema, but of dance, media and experimental art. Not everyone appreciates this interdisciplinary model,[31] but some basic questions incessantly drive us forward. How do these three areas unite in a way that recorporealizes the performer(s) in a unique screenic space? How can we manifest Dodds' various "bodies" and Greenfield's "third experience"? How do we produce works that force us to reconsider the idea of dance? How do we create and analyse screendances that challenge us aesthetically, culturally and ideologically? With 65 years of screendance history and the formation of a canon, how can we recognize and utilize intertextuality? What role will new technologies and methods of distribution and exhibition/interaction play in this discipline? And what role does music and sonicity play in our reception and interpretation of screendance? Each screendance answers these questions in its own way, some more fully and/or successfully than others. And with each answer, we move into deeper and richer waters that will eventually and precisely define the screendance and position it for further evolution.

Notes

1. As part of this archaeology it is important to document a brief biographical note. I have taught experimental film and video for 23 years. I've been fortunate to collaborate with and co-teach a Dance for the Camera course with a colleague, Professor Susan Mann from the Dance Department, for 18 years. We finished creating our first dance for the camera, Do You Like That?, in 2008, with an original score for the piece by William Kleinsasser, Professor of Music at Towson University.
2. Greg S. Faller is Professor of Electronic Media & Film and Associate Dean of the College of Fine Arts & Communication at Towson University, Maryland. He has co-taught an interdisciplinary Dance for the Camera class for 18 years. He was an essayist, advisor, assistant and associate editor of The International Dictionary of Films and Filmmakers (1984–2001) and has been published in Literature/Film Quarterly, Popular Music and Society, American National Biography, Film Quarterly, Media Criticism (Kendall/Hunt, 1992) and The Fifties: Transforming the Screen (Scribners, 2003). He co-chairs the Maryland Sister States and World Artists Experiences International Film Series which is an annual state-wide event.
3. I take this term from Doug Rosenberg (2000: 280) who defines it as "a reconstruction of the dancing body via screen techniques".

4. A panoramic frontal tableaux is an unedited single wide-shot recorded by a front and centre stationary camera that reveals the entire body and some of the stage.
5. See http://www.youtube.com/watch?v=4IbXitdg2GQ for Rachel Lopez's performance of Sherwood's restaging.
6. "Choreocinema" is ascribed to *New York Times* writer John Martin as quoted by Lewis Jacobs in 'Experimental Cinema in America, Part Two: The Postwar Revival', *Hollywood Quarterly*, 3(3), Spring 1948: "The beginnings of a virtually new art of 'choreocinema' in which the dance and the camera collaborate on the creation of a single new work of art" (p. 31).
7. The term "cine-dance" was employed by Peterson (1967) and Brakhage (1967).
8. https://en.wikipedia.org/wiki/Dance_film (accessed 23 September 2013).
9. https://en.wikipedia.org/wiki/Dance_film (accessed 23 September 2013).
10. https://en.wikipedia.org/wiki/Dance_film (accessed 23 September 2013).
11. https://en.wikipedia.org/wiki/Videodance (accessed 23 September 2013).
12. "A definition of 'videodance' is movement-based work that is conceived and/or choreographed for viewing on a single screen – be it a TV, monitor or by projection – and that exists as a work in its own right, i.e. it is not part of a live performance. Videodance can be based on already existing live dance works, but the work will have gone through a complete re-work to create a work unique to the screen. The vast majority of people making this kind of work are now doing so using digital video technology, at some, if not all of the production stages. However, the term 'videodance' does not exclude work that has been shot or even edited using a film format". http://www.makingvideodance.com/Writing.html (accessed 3 April 2015).
13. '(Hu)Manifesto: Possibilities for Screendance' (2006 Draft 2.0) (http://www.dvpg.net/screendance2006.pdf). This is not an attempt to define screendance or to suggest that there is one way to create a screendance. It is, instead, an attempt to open and enrich the discourse surrounding the field. In a humanifesto, content comes to the surface. This humanifesto asserts that screendance has the potential to articulate metaphor, express conceptual concerns and manifest thematic possibilities. Inherent in the proposition of screendance is the possibility that through an accretion of images of bodies in motion, a larger truth may unfold: one that is greater than the impact of each moment experienced in isolation; one in which sequential images in the context of dance on screen resonate with accompanying frames of reference to manifest a larger understanding of the world.

    In order to accomplish this, the screendance community must by necessity engage itself with rigorous critique that is grounded in both pre-existing and yet-to-be articulated methodologies. Inherent in this proposition is the understanding that the following issues are references that may exist in screendance. It is not an exhaustive list:

Form	Content	Technique
Gender	Ageism	Virtuosity
Semiotics	Meaning	Culture
Politics	Hybridity	Identity
Populism	Race	History

While all of these elements need not be present in a screendance, we propose that screendance be viewed through these and other external prisms in order to afford screendance a level of rigour equal to that of other art forms and to facilitate and stimulate informed critique.

14. "Screenic" was cited in Doug Rosenberg's 'Excavating Genres' (2010) and attributed to Harmony Bench and N. Katherine Hayles.
15. See Doug Rosenberg (2010), 'Excavating Genres'. He notes, "Given the evolution of theoretical discourse in the arts beyond screendance, however, it is no longer adequate to define a work for the screen by those formal qualities that simply imply that the work could not be created as a live event" (69).
16. See http://www.southeastdance.org.uk, http://www.dancecamerawest.org, http://www.dancefilmsassn.org or http://dancefilms.org, http://www.danceuk.org, http://www.contemporarydance.com.au, http://www.danceforthecamera.org and http://www.americandancefestival.org/projects/video-film-projects/
17. See http://www.rosas.be, http://www.ultimavez.com, http://www.dv8.co.uk, http://www.lalalahumansteps.com, http://www.mitchellrose.com and http://www.physicaltv.com.au.
18. See http://arts.brighton.ac.uk/projects/screendance/screendance-network, http://www.choreovideo.com, http://www.dancemedia.com, http://www.dance-tech.net/profile/MoveStream and http://www.dancefilms.org/festival/dance-camera-2015/.
19. *The International Journal of Screendance* was launched in summer 2010 at the American Dance Festival. Published by Parallel Press/University of Wisconsin-Madison Libraries (online and print) at http://journals.library.wisc.edu/index.php/screendance. The *Dance on Camera Journal* is published by the Dance Films Association.
20. Screendance programmes can be found at: University of Wisconsin-Madison, University of Utah, University of Illinois, University of Brighton and Dundee University.
21. A partial list of adaptations and/or narrative works could include: Pascal Magnin's *Reines d'un jour* (1996) and *Contrecoup* (1998), Annick Vroom's *Rest in Peace* (2001), Anne Teresa De Keersmaeker's *Achterland* (1994), De Keersmaeker and Thierry De Mey's *Rosas danst Rosas* (1997) and *Fase* (2002), David Hinton and Lloyd Newson's *Strange Fish* (1993) and *Dead Dreams of Monochrome Men* (1995), Newson and Clara Van Gool's *Enter Achilles* (1996), Newson's *The Cost of Living* (2005), François Girard's *Le Dortoir* (1991), Tom Cairn's *Alistair Fish* (1995), Édouard Lock's *Amelia* (2006), Wim Vandekeybus's *Roseland* (1990), *La Mentira* (1992), *In Spite of Wishing and Wanting* (2002) and *Blush* (2005), William Forsythe and Thierry De Mey's *One Flat Thing, Reproduced* (2000), Yvonne Rainer's *Trio A* (1978) and Laura Taler's *A Village Trilogy* (1995).
22. See, for example, Rabinovitz (1991), Nichols (2001) and Sitney (2002).
23. See, for example, Sitney (2002); Curtis (1971) and Anker et al. (2010).
24. See, for example, Rabinovitz (1991); Porter (2009); Curtis (1971) and Faller (2003).
25. See, for example, Vaughn (2002); Dodds (2001) and Porter (2009).
26. See, for example, Valliere, R. (1982); Szporer (2002) and Starr and Russett (1976).
27. See, for example, Haller (1997); Faller (2003) and Elder (1997).

28. See the Filmmakers' Coop catalogue description at http://film-makerscoop.com.
29. http://www.lizaggiss.com (accessed 23 September 2013).
30. http://hyperchoreography.org (accessed 23 September 2013).
31. Stan Brakhage said, "The cine-dance, this is at worst an attempt of one medium to put itself into another medium which will not meaningfully be put upon. At best, it is a gesture art lacking grammar ... I do not think there is, as of now, any cine-dance worth mentioning as such" (1967: 131–32). Sidney Peterson said, "If dancing were basket-weaving, there would be no problem about it being relegated to the role of subject matter in a cinematic or televised message. The main difficulty arises, I believe, because dance too is an art of the moving image. It does not relate to film as, for example, scene painting relates to theatre. It is, in effect, a competing medium" (1967: 75).

References

Anker, S., K. Geritz and S. Seid (eds) (2010), *Radical Light*, Berkeley and London: University of California Press.

Bench, H. (2006) 'Hyperdance: Dance Onscreen, Dance Online or, What Difference Does the Medium Make?', *Screendance: The State of the Art Proceedings*, 6-9 July, online at http://www.dvpg.net/screendance2006.pdf (accessed 23 October 2010).

Bench, H. (2010), 'Anti-Gravitational Choreographies: Strategies of Mobility in Screendance', *International Journal of Screen Dance*, 1(1), 53–61.

Brakhage, S. (1967), 'Film: Dance', reprinted in B. McPherson (ed.) (2001), *Essential Brakhage: Selected Writings on Filmmaking by Stan Brakhage*, New York: McPherson & Company, pp. 129–32.

Cannon, T. (2001), 'Sara Kathryn Arledge: *Introspection*', in B. Posner (ed.), *Unseen Cinema*, New York: Black Thistle Press/Anthology Film Archives, pp. 75–76.

Carroll, N. (2001), 'Toward a Definition of Moving-Picture Dance', reprinted in *The International Journal of Screen Dance*, 2010, 1(1), 111–25.

Croce, A. (1978), 'Dance in Film', reprinted in J. Porter (ed.) (2009), *Dance with Camera*, Philadelphia: Institute of Contemporary Art, University of Pennsylvania, pp. 146–57.

Curtis, D. (1971), *Experimental Cinema*, New York: Dell Publishing.

Dodds, S. (2001), *Dance on Screen*, New York: Palgrave Macmillan.

Elder, B. (1997), *Representations of the Body in Recent Films and Poetry*, Waterloo, Ontario: Wilfrid Laurier University Press.

Faller, G. (2003), 'Unquiet Years: Experimental Cinema in the 1950s', in P. Lev (ed.), *The Fifties: Transforming the Screen 1950-1959*, New York: Charles Scribner's Sons, 279–302.

Franko, M. (2001), 'Aesthetic Agencies in Flux', in B. Nichols (ed.), *Maya Deren and the American Avant-Garde*, Berkeley and London: University of California Press, pp. 131–49.

Geritz, K. (2010), 'Period of Invention: An Interview with Sidney Peterson', in S. Anker, K. Geritz and S. Seid (eds), *Radical Light*, Berkeley and London: University of California Press, pp. 48–51.

Greenfield, A. (2002), 'The Kinesthetics of Avant-Garde Dance Film: Deren and Harris', in J. Mitoma (ed.), *Envisioning Dance on Film and Video*, New York: Routledge, pp. 21–26.

Hale, C. (2001), 'Rosemary Lee Review', online at http://www.artsadmin.co.uk/projects/passage (accessed 17 November 2010).
Haller, R. (1997), *Intersecting Images: The Cinema of Ed Emshwiller*, New York: Anthology Film Archives.
Horak, J.-C. (1995), 'The First American Film Avant-Garde, 1919–1945', in J.-C. Horak (ed.), *Lovers of Cinema*, Wisconsin and London: University of Wisconsin Press, pp. 14–66.
Jacobs, L. (1948), 'Experimental Cinema in America, Part Two: The Postwar Revival', reprinted in E. Smoodin and A. Martin (eds) (2002), *Hollywood Quarterly: Film Culture in Postwar America, 1945-1957*, Berkeley and London: University of California Press, pp. 28–50.
James, D. (2005), *The Most Typical Avant-Garde*, Berkeley and London: University of California Press.
Lockyer, B. (2002), 'A New Place for Dancing', in J. Mitoma (ed.), *Envisioning Dance on Film and Video*, New York: Routledge, pp. 156–62.
Marks, V. (2002), 'Portraits in Celluloid', in J. Mitoma (ed.), *Envisioning Dance on Film and Video*, New York: Routledge, pp. 207–210.
McPherson, K. (2006), *Making Video Dance*, London and New York: Routledge.
Nichols, B. (ed.) (2001), *Maya Deren and the American Avant-Garde*, Berkeley and London: University of California Press.
Peterson, S. (1967), 'Cine Dance and Two Notes', reprinted in P. Sitney (ed.) (1987), *The Avant-Garde Film*, New York: Anthology Film Archives, pp. 74–79.
Porter, J. (2009), *Dance with Camera*, Philadelphia: Institute of Contemporary Art, University of Pennsylvania.
Posner, Bruce (2005), *Unseen Cinema: Early American Avant-Garde Film 1894-1941*, New York: Anthology Film Archives & Image Entertainment.
Rabinovitz, L. (1991), *Points of Resistance*, Chicago: University of Illinois Press.
Rosenberg, D. (2000), 'Video Space: A Site for Choreography', *Leonardo*, 33(4), 275–80.
Rosenberg, D. (2006a), 'Dancing for the Camera Catalog Essay', *Screendance: The State of the Art Proceedings*, 6-9 July, online at http://www.dvpg.net/screendance2006.pdf (accessed 23 October 2010).
Rosenberg, D. (2006b), 'Proposing a Theory of Screendance', *Screendance: The State of the Art Proceedings*, 6-9 July, online at http://www.dvpg.net/screendance2006.pdf (accessed 23 October 2010).
Rosenberg, D. (2010), 'Excavating Genres', *International Journal of Screen Dance*, 1(1), 63–73.
Siebens, E. (2002), 'Dancing with the Camera: The Dance Cinematographer', in J. Mitoma (ed.), *Envisioning Dance on Film and Video*, New York: Routledge, pp. 218–23.
Sitney, P. (1963–1964), 'Imagism in Four Avant-Garde Films', reprinted in P. Sitney (ed.) (2000), *Film Culture Reader*, New York: Cooper Square Press, pp. 187–200.
Sitney, P. (2002), *Visionary Film: The American Avant-Garde 1943-2000*, 3rd edn, Oxford and New York: Oxford University Press.
Starr, C., and Russett, R. (1976), *Experimental Animation*, New York: Da Capo Press.
Szporer, P. (2002), 'Northern Exposures: Canadian Dance Film and Video', in J. Mitoma (ed.), *Envisioning Dance on Film and Video*, New York: Routledge, pp. 168–75.

Towers, D. (2002), 'Fast Forward', in J. Mitoma (ed.), *Envisioning Dance on Film and Video*, New York: Routledge, pp. 189–92.

Valliere, R. (1982), *Norman McLaren, Manipulator of Movement*, Newark: University of Delaware Press.

Vaughn, D. (2002), 'Merce Cunningham's Choreography for the Camera', in J. Mitoma (ed.), *Envisioning Dance on Film and Video*, New York: Routledge, pp. 34–38.

From *Beat Street* to *Step Up 3D*
The Sound of Street Dance Films

Mary Fogarty[1]

While conducting an ethnography of the breaking scene in Edinburgh, I happened to see a screening of *Step Up 2: The Streets* (Chu, 2008) – a film about street dancing that I assumed might be of interest to participants in the local hip hop dance scene.[2] However, if the audience at the screening I attended was in any way typical, I was clearly mistaken. The cinema was packed with teenage girls and included only a handful of men (perhaps three, each a member of an older, heterosexual couple). Many of the female teenagers entered the cinema in groups of six to eight people, and proceeded to chat through most of the film, laughing at the dialogue and making jokes to amuse their friends.[3] When the final credits began to roll, the girls promptly got to their feet and left the cinema, even though the dancing on screen continued. They did not appear to be taking the film too seriously, and did not seem particularly invested in the dancing aspects of the film. While they were indeed an active audience, this activity involved conversations that took place either on top of the film's dialogue or in response to that dialogue. In other words, the film afforded an opportunity for a social event, one that produced a live crowd sound all of its own, characterized by volume, superfluous noise, fidelity and realism. Street dance films are not typically comedies, yet the audience in Edinburgh seemed to treat *Step Up 2* more as a comedy than as the musical melodrama its marketing proposed. And just as this audience did not seem to take the film very seriously, neither did the hip hop dancers in the Edinburgh breaking scene I spoke to – indeed, they tended to avoid films such as this entirely – despite the prominence given to dance performances by top hip hop dancers as extras in the films.

The relationship in street dance films between cinematic sound (including music, effects and dialogue) and dance moves reveals a tension between production and reception,[4] representation and labour. The film being exhibited always encounters the possibility of external sounds, especially those created by the cinema audience itself, resulting in the co-creation of an event, a temporal experience that sounds different each time thus never duplicated. Street dance films frequently include performances by top dancers in international street dance scenes whose cultural capital stands in some contrast to the status of the films themselves. That is to say, while hip hop music is now taken very seriously by fans, critics and scholars (Frith, 2007), street dance films, packaged as supposedly trivial forms of Hollywood light entertainment, are not taken seriously at all even with their documentation of the talents of top dancers. This may be further exacerbated by their contexts of viewing. Viewers may not necessarily watch these films in a focused way, and since they are available on DVD for home viewing, and often on internet sites such as YouTube, they may not even watch the entire film in one sitting. Thus particular scenes or 'moments' may be watched in a fragmented fashion or with inattentive or diffused interest, isolated from the rest of the film.

In the literature on popular dance there are two broad views of street dance films. On the one hand, the cycle is understood in terms of its social function in circulating the images and sounds of hip hop culture internationally. Many ethnographic investigations explain the central role that street dance films of the early 1980s had for the growth of the hip hop culture in various countries (Mitchell, 1996; 2001; Bennett, 1999; Shapiro, 2004; Condry, 2006). Here, particular b-films are acknowledged by participants for their cult status in hip hop culture, as important films for the circulation of the dance. As Sally Banes (1994) points out, the films have a range of production qualities and cover a range of dance styles, and in doing so, have an impact on the dancing itself (the way dance is presented and the dance styles embodied by active viewers turned dancers). On the other hand, these films are examined for their problematic representations of gender, ethnicity and sexuality (Dodds, 2001; LaBoskey, 2001; Blanco Borelli, 2009; Monteyne, 2013), since they highlight the significance of dance in young people's lives. The first approach centres on how people have used films in cross-cultural appropriation and development (sociological aspects), and the other on the role of scholarship as cultural critique and feminist intervention (involving textual and movement analysis).

Thus, it will be useful to understand the sociological aspects of these films first, before moving on to a more detailed analysis of sound in street dance films. The early street dance films helped the circulation of street dance practices worldwide. There are two aspects of this fact worth highlighting for my argument. First, the early street dance films were taken seriously by emerging dancers in various countries outside the USA who were trying to get access to the movement vocabulary of dance styles such as breaking or popping. In the beginning, pioneering b-boys[5] from various locales of the early 1980s described the impact of the movie *Flashdance* on their dance practice.[6] They would sneak into the cinema just to see the 30-second clip of 'street dancers' in the film, and then would meet up with rival crews outside the cinema and battle,[7] trying to emulate the dance moves they had just witnessed. Here, the dancers were not watching the films in their entirety but rather were focused only on those moments in the film where music and dance intersect in particular performances that create interest and intrigue, becoming informal educational tools for peer-to-peer learning about a dance style. Second, hip hop dancers do not take the later street dance films seriously. Although younger b-boys acknowledge that these early films influenced the pioneers in their various countries, they themselves are more likely to admit to being informed by different ways of accessing dance. One b-boy in his early twenties, who grew up outside of Glasgow, admitted to me that he had learned breaking originally from video games, which he confessed was judged by his peers and elders as an inauthentic way to learn. However, he defended his position by explaining this was his only access as a teenager. Many hip hop dancers who learned originally through mediated sources would choose instead to hide their "inauthentic" points of access to the local scene (Fogarty 2011). Another example, from an account by an Iranian-American b-boy, Justin Mashouf, addresses the significance of rapid mediatization that changed access to street dance representations beyond films for different generations of dancer-viewers:

> Well b-boying came to Iran in the 80s similar to how it came to other parts of the world, through the film [*Flashdance*], and also through the film [*Beat Street*]. With the movies and the music reaching Iran through the VHS tapes, people would share and flip around. Even my cousin, who's in his late 30s, early 40s remembers breaking in high school, initially all during Iran-Iraq war, which was unfortunate that b-boying came to Iran in such an awful time in Iran's history. American culture was definitely very restricted because of the political legacy between Iran and the US especially during the early days of the revolution. But now b-boying culture is really consumed and spread because of the Internet and cell phone videos.[8]

This account suggests a shift from b-films to the internet, in terms of younger generations of b-boys and b-girls accessing street dance culture. This perhaps explains how historical accounts continue to cite the 1980s films as significant to older generations, and the newer films such as the *Step Up* series are ignored. With the internet, dancers can access the culture through other forms of mediation and thus are less inclined to sit through a narrative to catch those fleeting moments of dance that may prove inspiring. Although in the case of *Flashdance*, the aspiring dancers who watched it largely disregarded the plot,[9] the film contained short moments of dance that related to a living culture, which many young people in the 1980s aspired to join. Since none of the accounts of these films to date have considered the significance of sound, for either the circulation of hip hop or the cultural critique of its representations, I will now consider what an analysis of the film cycle's use of sound may offer to screen dance analysis.

Since the turn of the twenty-first century, there has been a proliferation of commercial productions such as *Save the Last Dance* (Carter, 2001), *Honey* (Woodruff, 2003), *You Got Served: Take it to the Streets* (Pollina, 2004), *Stomp the Yard* (White, 2007), *Battle of the Year: The Dream Team* (Lee, 2013), and the series *Step Up 1* (Fletcher, 2006), *Step Up 2: The Streets* (Chu, 2008), *Step Up 3D* (Chu, 2010) and *Step Up All In* (Sie, 2014). Parodies have also appeared, such as *Kickin' It Old School* (Glazer, 2007) that featured iconic b-boys such as Jesse 'Caspar' Brown. Britain's entries into this cycle of street dance films include the film, *StreetDance* (Giwa and Pasquini, 2010), that was followed up with *StreetDance 2* (Giwa and Pasquini, 2012), which again featured a wide array of internationally recognizable dancers from both the hip hop community and reality television contests such as *Britain's Got Talent*.

As dramas centred on the theme of street dancers' lives, these feature films exist alongside independent works such as the film, *B-girl* (Dell, 2009) featuring real-life b-girl Lady Jules (Julie Urich), documentaries such as *The Freshest Kids: A History of the B-boy* (Israel, 2002), *Planet B-boy: Breakdancing has Evolved* (Lee, 2008), *Turn It Loose* (2009), as well as all of the 'underground' b-boy/b-girl videos produced by dancers for other dancers (see Fogarty 2012). Although independent and documentary videos are beyond the purview of this chapter, they contribute some of the conventions for understanding the codes of honour and competition found in street dance films. Feature-length street dance films and hip hop culture have always existed in a sort of uneasy relationship, perhaps a result of the problematic use of (now) legendary hip hop dancers in Hollywood productions such as *Flashdance* (Lyne, 1983), *Wild Style* (Ahearn, 1983), *Breakin'* (Silberg, 1984), *Breakin' 2: Electric Boogaloo* (Firstenberg, 1984) and *Beat Street* (Lathan, 1984). Whereas the older films from the early 1980s quickly earned their legacy in hip hop histories through their featured b-boys and impact on the global circulation of breaking, the more recent films are unlikely to be mentioned in accounts of hip hop dance and culture. The more recent street dance films have influenced public perceptions about the lifestyles and aesthetics of street dancers, even inspiring new generations of dancers, and yet these films are rarely acknowledged, or even watched, by key participants in various local hip hop and funk dance scenes.[10]

That these newer films do not 'speak' to the aesthetic preferences of many dancers is worth considering, because of what this lack of interest might reveal about the specific meanings and values of music in particular dance practices for participants. For example, the musical choices evident on their soundtracks differ significantly from the actual musical tastes of older dancers, and would be unlikely to be heard at live events in performances of the dance styles represented. Because musical taste is such a crucial aspect of hip hop dance culture, I address this question further below. It is also telling that historical and sociological accounts of hip hop culture tend to overlook these films. While the films do not have to reflect, represent or even resemble the 'authentic' lifestyles or musical tastes of b-boys, b-girls, poppers and lockers,[11] the films can nonetheless have ripple effects on new generations of dancers, affecting their tastes, their values, perhaps their senses of history. In other words, even if these films are widely dismissed or discredited by older participants, the films may matter to newer participants and audiences and thus merit our attention.

An examination of street dance films' production and reception can offer a new context for thinking about the relationship between sound and dance, particularly in terms of how sound works and how dance moves to meet the music in specific films. It also allows consideration of the impact that these sounds may have for non-dancers whose values may be distinct from those of dancers.

Dance scholars have typically focused on movement analysis as a means of cultural critique. For example, Melissa Blanco Borelli (2009) gives a critical overview of how the hips of the mulatta characters in street dance films are emblematic of a negotiated racial space between whiteness and blackness; a space that transforms over time and across the dance cycle. One of the first scholars to write about popular dance, Angela McRobbie (1984), analyses how, for the British white youth that she studied, dance plays the role of a social fantasy that is often racialized. Dancing, she suggests, is pleasurable for girls and women. Hip hop dancing has revealed just how many males participate in dance practices as well, although the viewing of street dance films, as indicated in my opening, remains a pleasurable practice dominated by female audiences at least in public places.

In the detailed analysis of *Step Up 3D* (Chu, 2010) that follows, I want to reflect on how sound contributes to an analysis of both movement and social fantasy: how filmic sound amplifies the embodied perspective of characters, adding racial identifications, sound tagging and dynamics to dance movement. Alongside these identifications, the ubiquitous presence of music in contemporary life is reflected in portrayals of the city in street dance films. The street dance film cycle consistently foregrounds both the public and the private (domestic) spaces of the city through sound. These spaces have their own sonic characteristics which help to dramatize the differing locations of street dance practice: street dance takes place both outdoors and indoors, imprinting a trajectory of spaces with the activities of individual and group practice, public performance and battling. Since these activities depend on music, the interactions of diegetic and non-diegetic musics with the various acoustic structures of the film's locations provide an additional layer of meaning, affecting plot, felt emotions and dance spectacle. The ways that the music and the sound of the location (whether included or excluded) are mixed thus help shape the meaning of dance on screen.[12]

In *Step Up 3D*, the sound of dance, music, crowds and the city shapes dance into a particular kind of sound experience. The use of 7.1 surround sound exemplifies recent trends in the mediation of dance on screen. For example, most of the sound mix supplies key identifications with specific dancers who find themselves the witnesses to new worlds of dance. Here, the psychological use of sound amplifies dance in curious ways and, I will argue, constructs the experience of dance as an individual engagement (with music) rather than a sonically social one (with people). This way of listening to dance owes much to the history of sound recording and multichannel audio techniques and has implications for future understandings of dance practices.

The opening scene of *Step Up 3D* demonstrates how film sound and music interact seamlessly to weave dance elements into the movie's storyline. In street dance films the dancing is presented in set pieces reminiscent of the dance sequences in classical Hollywood musicals. However, where Hollywood's dance sequences often underline the extraordinary or fantastic aspects of dancing, in street dance films dance appears as a central, all-consuming facet of the daily lives of the film's protagonists. The 'authenticity' of the dancers is asserted from the beginning of *Step Up 3D*, where a sort of a prologue in the form of a documentary, in video camera frame format, presents 'interviews' with the dancers where they explain their love of dance and how it has helped them face life challenges. In order to maintain this image of authenticity, the dancing in the film is fully integrated with the plot. This integration is maintained across the trajectory of performance locations; as we move from street to studio to warehouse, the film's sound design ensures seamless transitions, presenting dancers' relationships to music as both individual and social. In other words, dancing to music is not only represented as a collective experience, but also as a psychological one, informed by the interior life of the (white, heterosexual, male) dancer. This interior life is set up against the fantasy of the 'streets' that is Othered through sound and turned into a magical new world.

In *Step Up 3D*, the sound design helps to shape our experience of the dance, as well as underlining distinctions between how live dance competitions sound *in situ* and how they sound in the cinema with an audience. If the general sound mix of *Step Up 3D* sets up an individual and interior experience of dance practice, the crowd scenes, where dance crews compete, offer another perspective. I will argue below that the sound of the crowd, and its position and meaning, are particularly revealing.

Although *Step Up 3D* begins with a pseudo-documentary, featuring the actors who will appear in the film, the soundtrack for the prologue is not dance music but an orchestral score with an aspirational harmonic structure. It is quiet and unobtrusive, swelling at the end to emphasize the start of the film proper with a panoramic shot of New York City. As the camera descends over a couple of groups of people dancing in Washington Square Park, some dance beats are introduced into the score, not as actual music to dance to but as musical icons of the urban dancing that has just come into view. The camera moves past the circle of dancers and spectators to a close-up of the film's main protagonists, entering the park with a tour of NYU students, and the soundtrack fades out to the natural sounds of the city.

The score marks the transition from pseudo-documentary to fictional narrative by swelling to a climax/crescendo as we see the panoramic overhead establishing shot of NYC, and the sound design introduces all the main sound and music relationships to come. Thus the opening dialogue, of Moose (Adam Sevani) and Camille (Alyson Stoner) with Moose's parents (Kathy Najimy and Frank Moran) who have come to New York to help them settle in to college life, takes place against the soundscape of New York City. We hear the other voices of the crowds in the park, the sounds of birds, and off screen the sound of the traffic in the road beyond the park, punctuated by distant police sirens. The sound of the city is spread out beyond the confines of the family conversation and the visual domain, and the audio balance is clearly 'realistic' in that the voices of the actors have to compete with the surrounding city sounds to make themselves heard. There is no music, and this contrasts dramatically with the opening 'documentary' footage.

The transition that follows introduces some key elements of the film's use of sound and music. First, a passing stranger brushes against Moose. This touch, with its attendant and exaggerated sound of impact, triggers a swell of non-diegetic film music; we hear the significance of this moment. The sound of the touch is one of impact and contributes to a subtle effect as if the sound were experienced from the embodied point-of-view of the character, Moose. The music is orchestral and expectant, swelling as Moose follows the stranger, who will soon be revealed as the main lead character Luke (Rick Malambri), along the pathway of the park. It turns seamlessly into the pulse of dance music as a group of street dancers comes into view. The music is not just an aural sign of plot significance, but it changes the viewer's attention: we were in a big city with a diffuse attentiveness to crowds, dialogue, clock chimes, traffic and distant sirens. The music on the soundtrack shifts our focus, now aligning us with the internal state of mind of the principal character, enhanced by a newly reverberant acoustic space on the soundtrack. While the external world is signed as 'outside the frame' by its acoustic depth of field, his interior world is contained, and that containment reverberates. The outside world is still visible, but blocked from our hearing as the music swells. We are now meant to hear the music through the subjectivity of a dancer, and this helps us navigate the shift from non-diegetic to diegetic, that is, we are now listening like dancers. The music, which is beat-driven dance music, changes its orientation from non-diegetic to diegetic. The sound mix transforms so we start to hear the voices of the people in the circle around the dancers, and the music itself shifts its location to appear to be emanating from a boom box sitting on the pathway. Here music is very much the dominant element, however, and its appearance as diegetic is momentary and symbolic. As the dancing continues, the music swells and re-orientates, and suggests identification with the internal, embodied energy of the protagonists. This is the first appearance of a crucial method of sound manipulation that dominates the film: the tagging of the soundtrack as actually diegetic, even when it blocks out all other possible sound. This can be seen to represent the all-consuming power of the dance.

The seamlessness with which the music changes from orchestral commentary to dance beats, from non-diegetic soundtrack to diegetic incident, and almost from objective to subjective listening positions, is one of the ways that the transition from everyday movements to dance movements are enacted smoothly throughout the narrative. The whole opening sequence of *Step Up 3D* has to provide a convincing link between the banality of the characters' everyday lives and the transformative power of dancing; between the plot-driven, social interactions of the characters and the internal, individual experience of their dancer *personae*. This linking is achieved through sonic events which position sound, music and acoustics in ever changing relationships to the characters and the action. This then affects the actual musical moments, which can be represented in the dance sequences, where musical choices are an integral part of the image of street dance practice.

While the sound of the city is a recurring motif, *Step Up 3D* also emphasizes sound media and sound-related products that are featured visually throughout the plot and appear in the dialogue. For example, dancers are said to be 'b-fab', meaning they were 'born from a boom box'. These are articulations of hip hop's origins and relationship to the so-called ghettoblaster as an iconic marker of sharing sound in public spaces for the purpose of dancing.

Sound effects are used to dramatize the dynamics of the dance styles portrayed in the film's opening battle sequence, as moves by participants on the dance floor are emphasized via Foley sounds. Like the kung fu films of the 1970s, the soundtrack draws the viewer's attention to particular movements in the details of the dancing by means of Foleyed swooshing and impact effects. This can be heard as an extension of the technique used in the films of Fred Astaire, where the tap impacts were amplified in the post-production process. But where Astaire's exaggerated tap sounds resulted in a rhythmic music intended as a sort of hyper-realism, highlighting the interaction of feet and stick with the floor, in *Step Up 3D* the swooshes and impact sounds exist more explicitly in the world of fantasy. They give a sense of power, temporal form and comic-book energy to the movements of the dancers, and crucially present the movements as off-the-floor, as unleashed from the force of gravity. They are particularly evident in those moments in the film where the dance becomes pure spectacle. They contribute to what Michel Chion (1994) calls the "audiovisual illusion", in which sound, "enriches a given [film] image so as to create the definite impression, in the immediate or remembered experience one has of it, that this information or expression 'naturally' comes from what is seen, and is already contained in the image itself" (5).

Chion discusses in some detail the ways in which sound and movement come together in what he calls "temporal linearization", and he argues convincingly that the power of sound focuses our seeing the *temporal* aspect of an image. This use of sound to enhance the embodied experiences of movement gives particular focus to the dynamics of dance movements (acceleration, intensity, intention), where the quality of the gestures is crucial. Such heightened Foley sound in the battle sequences of street dance films have become as central to the meaning and visceral effects of these scenes as they have to the choreographed violence of kung fu films. Craig Reid suggests that, "the importance of sound effects in fight choreography cannot be overemphasized" (1994: 35) and the same can now be said for the additional Foley sound accompanying spectacular moves in twenty-first-century street dance films.

Different Worlds of Dance

In street dance films, classical music often accompanies the entrance of street dancers into the dance conservatoire, art school or opera house and is meant to connote the prestige, class and seriousness of these institutions, differentiating them from the everyday, ordinary and perhaps lowly world of the hip hop street. The British film, *Street Dance 3D*, actively frames this other dance world in the most sympathetic light. Here, the struggles of dancers in the ballet world are highlighted in both the narrative structure and in the choreographed sequences. The three main choreographers for the film, Kate Prince, Kenrick Sandy and Will Tuckett, come from a diverse range of dance backgrounds and collaborate on various scenes to feature the strengths of different styles. One effect is a 'jack of all trades, master of none' result, where ballet dancers perform poor breaking footwork, and the talents of the street dancers are generally altered, minimized or employed behind the scenes so as not to upstage the main actors. As a result, the musical selections of these scenes often function more effectively than the dance performances, such as the fusion of Sergei Prokofiev's signature melodies from *Romeo and Juliet* with hip hop beats to enhance the narrative surrounding two dancers from different dance worlds.

Street Dance 3D also features George Sampson, and crews such as Flawless, Diversity, Plague, and BirdGang who, as with the American dancers in street dance films, tend to be household names for the general public due to their success in televised dance competitions. This celebrity status is built into the film's narrative structure and thus increases the anticipation of the audience. For example, although George Sampson does not dance 'full out' until the climax of the film, his fans in the audience likely anticipate that moment, thus building some additional suspense beyond that provided by the narrative.

One of the major shifts from the early street dance films to the present ones is the shift of 'other' dance worlds portrayed that provide the motivation and inform the aspirations of the main characters. For example, early films often feature the conventional dance 'world' of Broadway (also known as legitimate theatre, to signal its higher cultural capital) as the ultimate goal. In later reversionings of this generic plot, in order to 'make it' in dance there are other avenues offered up. For example, in *Honey* (Woodruff, 2003), the main character aspires to work in music videos with artists such as Missy Elliot. Similarly, the characters in *Step Up 3D* aspire to win an international hip hop dance championship (this is a possibility that simply did not exist during the early representations of hip hop on film). Real-life choreographers who have worked with artists such as Missy Elliot for music videos and live performances, such as Nadine 'Hi-Hat' Ruffin, now create the choreographed sequences in street dance films with ambitions to fuse various street dance styles. This is an innovation by choreographers, marking these battles as distinct from most live battles in the actual hip hop scene. However, this is often regarded by b-boys and b-girls to be a blurring of important distinctions that separate their various dance styles and subsequent identity markers and subcultural capital (Thornton, 1995) associated with each style.

The impact of music can be seen in accounts of its use in the actual production techniques of filmmaking. In *You Got Served*, the narrative demanded that a particular crew could be seen to dance 'badly' at one point. In order to achieve this, the director removed the music to which the dancers had rehearsed the scene. Thus unfamiliar music was played quietly during the filming of this sequence, in the hope of throwing the dancers off their best performances and making them look 'authentically' bad for narrative purposes. In the commentary on the DVD (Stokes, 2004), the directors and cast explained how difficult it was to work with b-boys and b-girls who refused to mess up their dancing or to dance badly for the sake of the narrative. Rehearsals, and the production of performances for screen, reveal the tensions between cultural meanings around music subscribed to by actual street dancers and those created through the narrative. Playing the 'wrong' music seemed to be one technique employed by supervisors to produce dance engineered for dramatic effect rather than terpsichorean virtuosity.

There are several points to make about this. The first is that music in professional production practices *affords* dancers energy and inspiration. Second, street dancers, especially those who are trained in alternative, informal ways, often rely on music to enhance performance and this informs their transitions to professional contexts. Movement and music are inextricably linked. And finally, b-boys and b-girls' reputations rely on and are invested in performing to the best of their ability, whether on screen or off. The distinction of mediated or live formats matters little when a performer's 'authenticity' and legitimacy within a larger, international community of dancers are on the line. This has often made their transition to professional contexts, where they have little control over how their dance is represented, a tense one.

In an attempt to address issues of authenticity, street dance films often feature a scene where dancers discuss the moment when they first saw breaking and got into the dance, and in many cases this involves a mediated experience. For example, *Step Up 2: The Streets* (Chu, 2008) begins with a voice-over by the protagonist, Andie (Briana Evigan) narrating her first influences. While she is talking, video footage is shown of b-boy/b-girl events of the past (such as B-Boy Summit) featuring well-known b-boys and b-girls, such as Ken Swift, Kujo, Remind and Asia One. The b-boys, b-girls and events of the past are not named explicitly so this is situated more as a personal narrative than one of historical significance and legacy. The film then goes on to feature key dancers in the street dance scene such as Kejamel 'K-Mel' Howell, Donnie 'Crumbs' Counts and Jeffery 'Machine' McCann, many of whom made their names in the scene through winning battles at events shown but not named.

There are also a mix of fictional crew names such as 'Beat Street' (*Beat Street*), the 'Pirates' (*Step Up 3D*), the 'Surge' (performed by the group Flawless in *Street Dance 3D*) and the actual nicknames of real b-boys and b-girls being used in recent street dance films.[13] This adds to the blending of fiction with the real-life characters of hip hop culture, a blend that is continued through other aspects of the filming, such as b-boys and b-girls refusing to mess up moves just to serve the narrative function of the film (after all, they are being called by their real names, they are generally doing their own signature moves, and they are dancing in what resembles a 'public' forum). Dancing has a complex ontological status in fiction film – it is not really fictional since a dancer is really dancing (just as professional sports is non-fiction entertainment). Thus, the dancers I spoke with who appear in such films admit their nervousness about leaving the many takes of a dancing scene in the hands of the director and editor who then might be unable or unwilling to select the most flattering cut of their dancing for the final version.

One of the difficulties for filmmakers when casting dancers appears to be the issue that no street dancer is keen to look like a bad dancer for the sake of the narrative.[14] They certainly don't want to lose a battle, aesthetically, regardless of what the narrative demands. One *exception* to this rule is Leon 'Vietnam' Carswell, who appeared in *Step Up 3D*:

> The film sequences were challenging. We were asked to fly to NY and then did our scenes in water and concrete and astro-turf. It was very wet and cold. The film location was in a warehouse of some sort close to Wall St.
>
> In our battle scene (Battle of House of Gwai) we used a street stunt I learned from an acrobatic team called the Calypso Tumblers from Guyana ... I had to act like I fell though because we had to have a turning point in the scene. The main crew had to win. So I did a stunt fall from a handstand 12 feet in the air. Watch it in slow, it looks so real. (interview with the author, 2010)

In this account, an expert dancer fell out of a move for narrative purposes, and did not seem to mind this. From his perspective, this fall was a difficult stunt that involved a great deal of orchestration and risk, and was thus impressive in its own right. Here, his relating of acting the role of a dancer who made a mistake is seen within the trajectory of stunt doubling.[15]

He also points to the role of the crowd in the dance sequences: "It was a very reactive movie. During the viewing, the crowd was into it. 'Ohhhhs, ahhhs'. It was like they were at the battle!"[16] In a live battle, the vocal engagement of the crowd registers the quality of the dance moves. The crowd reactions chart the flow of the battle, and hearing this gives a cumulative impression of which dancers are winning or losing. From the evidence provided here, the crowd at the filming of this movie were involved in a similar way. But the audio mix of a movie such as *Step Up 3D* is complex. The battle scenes, where the crowd plays its part, have a particular, dramatized sound that moves the sonic action beyond the screen to include the cinema auditorium. Thus, in the final battle, the music begins with a brief diegetic tag, and then quickly becomes non-diegetic, filling the cinema with dance music as the dancers face the camera, as if performing directly for the cinema audience. From this perspective, the cinema audience is pushed from the role of passive spectators and are positioned so as to experience the dance from the point of view of the dancers' *opponents* in the battle. One quickly realizes that in street dance battles, the spectators with the best view in the house are the opponents and this is one avenue where film can improve upon the lived reality by offering a point of view that few witness live. The music thus becomes, in a sense, *diegetic* again, within the enlarged performance space of the screen plus auditorium. The enclosed space of the onscreen setting opens up to include the cinema auditorium, and the cinema audience within the arena of the dance. The physical presence of the dancers is now made almost palpable by the swooshes and impact sounds mentioned earlier, which effect a sort of contact between the dancers onscreen and the audience in the cinema, through sound. The cheering of the onscreen crowd is often mixed to produce a generic roar in the background, and is featured only briefly pulling the audience momentarily into the depths of the scene through both sound and image, forming a point of social contact between onscreen audience and cinema audience, to create a larger sense of engagement.

While potentially visually and musically involving for the cinema audience, this strategy at times makes the action difficult to follow or understand, and in *Step Up 3D* the director resorts to verbal announcements by the emcee to help make the ebb and flow of the final battle comprehensible: 'Samurai's [the name of the opposing crew] wiping the floor with these guys. It looks like it's over.'

The crowd noise, which would chart the success of the different stages in a real street dance battle, is obscured by the music and sound effects of the movement mixed high on the soundtrack to enhance the excitement of the event. Thus there are no social auditory cues to help convey and interpret the drama of the dance itself – who is winning and who is losing the battle according to the sounds of the crowd.

The agglomeration of dance styles represented in the battle adds to its confusion. All styles are blurred into a mix of street-style choreography that serves to dramatize the act of competition. This limits spectator understanding of real distinctions within street dance styles and their often distinctive relationships to specific musics. That said, some sympathetic directors do take a moment during many of the films to cite different dance styles, in a 'lesson' for newcomers to the culture. For example, in *Street Dance 3D*, the main protagonist verbally introduces the various street dance styles to the ballerinas, supplemented by short dance demos from her crew members, including popping, locking and breaking. The missing link, however, is the music. Again the musical accompaniment supports a narrative conceit, suggesting that all the various street dance styles are performed to the same musical selections. I argue that this downplays the significance of particular music for street dance styles, and, likewise, downplays the significance of musical tastes (and distinctions) and their centrality to b-boys and b-girls, as suggested by the quotations from various dance practitioners cited above.

In the film narratives themselves, music functions in a different way. In the battles between various crews for many of the street dance film portrayals, the music changes as each opposing crew steps forward to perform. This is a major distinction from the reality of street dance battles, where the DJ without the foreknowledge of the dancers chooses the music. For example, in b-boy competitions, Kevin 'DJ Renegade' Gopie was one of the first of the international DJs to keep the music track the same through the course of the two opposing crews' performances. This is essential, as music underpins and shapes perceptions of live performances, as much as it does for film performances and narratives. A change in track may unfairly advantage the crew who gets the stronger track to dance to. Another international figure, DJ Leacy, would scratch in new musical selections during battles by observing the dancers and where they were in their movement, to assign music accordingly, playing where possible to the musical tastes of the dancers themselves. This is one of the major distinctions with representations of b-boys and b-girls in the street dance film cycle, where the musical tastes of dancers are portrayed as inconsequential to the music that is selected for either the battles, or the soundtracks that are foregrounded in the montage sequences.

Yet *Step Up 3D*, and its use of stereo sound, contribute a unique sonic event, and a form of embodied citation, to the history of dance on screen that is also worthy of discussion. One dance scene that takes place on the street, 'Don't Dance', references Fred Astaire and Ginger Rogers. Unlike the battle sequences, where the use of multi-channel sound 'makes space' for the dancing, by emanating from the sides of the cinema, rather than the front, in this scene the sound emanates from behind the screen. This is now reminiscent of the sound of the cinema before stereo sound (and after silent cinema's live sound). For the cinema audience, during the battle sequences there is a strange effect as the sound is always pushing out from the sides, leaving the movement, as it were, centre stage. That's quite a strong effect for a dance film, and would not be possible without stereo – or indeed even Dolby Surround – which takes the sound right out to the sides and round the back of the spectator, leaving the audience with the dance moves foregrounded.

In the 'Don't Dance' sequence of *Step Up 3D*, Moose and Camille perform a dance sequence down the street, which is done in a long, one-shot take. Here the sound emanates from behind the screen, rather than utilizing the surround sound experience to the fullest. This resembles the earlier model of cinema sound, which again may be traced back to live theatre and vaudeville. The music is in front of us. And although the music is carefully tagged as diegetic, including an ice-cream truck driver's response: "What do I look like ... a jukebox?" as he turns up the song for the dance sequence to begin, this tagging serves to provide an entrance into a transgressive event where we are transported back in time to the world of Hollywood musicals, with props and fantastical opportunities for interaction with the life of the city street. This is made even more stunning by the single-shot long take, enabled by camera movement tracking down the street. Camille and Moose perform jazz steps, locking (a style that emerged in the 1970s) and fall over couches, fend off a woman's water hose with garbage buckets[17] and partner dance to demonstrate the reunion of their friendship after competitive dance got in the way; in the end, dancing brings them back together.

Conclusion

This chapter highlighted the role of sound in both a sociological and musical analysis of the street dance film cycle. From considerations of musical taste to the use of multi-channel sound to facilitate different icons and the tagging of screen dance history, sound has long contributed to embodied portrayals of street dancers' lives. In doing so, sound enhances the impact of dance for participants and spectators alike. Sound and music immerses listeners, just as dancing is a full-body experience, and together they amplify this all-encompassing experience.

These movies provide employment for professional street dancers[18] both in terms of the actual film performance and residual payments, and also in terms of potential future employment based on the reputations gained from their appearances in such films. This is a financial benefit to them, even though the narrative and scenic processes of commercial cinema may compromise the portrayal of the dance itself. The history of dance on film is riddled with similar cases, including the representations of lindyhoppers in films from the 1930s (Crease, 1995).

This account has also tried to demonstrate ways in which a sophisticated film sound design can help motivate and articulate the necessities of plot and dance, as well as creating a subtle and flexible bond between the onscreen dancing and the spectators, both casual and committed. These films are affecting and engaging as a cycle and as narratives that can cajole one into the perspectives of a danced drama (although this is not always the case). One can feel the youthful presentation of romance, with its second by second emotional pull, the anxieties of identities and their matching links to style of dress and style of movements. Of course there is also an older audience of street dancers, reading these films against a different set of criteria related to the issues of authenticity and critical reception. This mix of receptions is as fascinating as it is revealing of both the reflexive and hidden relationship between these popular, commercial movies and hip hop culture more generally.

This particular relationship, having been neglected in the scholarship of hip hop studies, helps reveal how *significant* the *trivial* can be.

Notes

1. Mary Fogarty is an Assistant Professor of Dance at York University, Canada. Her work about hip hop dance, film and video appears in the following anthologies: *The Routledge Reader on the Sociology of Music* (2015), *The Oxford Handbook of Dance and the Popular Screen* (2014) and *Ageing and Youth Cultures* (2012). She is the lead facilitator/lecturer for the Toronto B-Girl Movement, a community programme that mentors girls and women in hip hop culture (www.keeprockinyou.com).
2. I am a Canadian hip hop dancer, known as a 'b-girl' as I specialize in the style of dance known as 'breaking' or 'b-girling/b-boying'.
3. At a live theatrical performance of B-Boyizm Dance Company at the Harbourfront Centre in Toronto, Canada, the teenagers behind me, similarly, spoke and joked throughout the entire performance (13 April 2012).
4. Hip hop dance studies have considered early hip hop Hollywood films in relation to labour, as in the work of Thomas DeFrantz (2014) on the early 1980s 'break-sploitation' films.
5. A 'b-boy', within hip hop dance culture, typically refers to a male dancer who specializes in the dance style known as 'breaking', 'b-boying' or, in media accounts as 'breakdancing'. See Fogarty (2011) for a more detailed breakdown of this terminology as applied in various international contexts.
6. Interviews that I carried out with dancers from Los Angeles in 2007 and Erfurt, Germany in 2008.
7. A 'battle' is a formal or informal competition between two individual dancers or crews.
8. Online at http://www.elanthemag.com/index.php/site/featured_articles_detail/international_b_boy_justin_mashouf-nid263444173/ (accessed 21 December 2010).
9. According to interviews I conducted between 2007–2009 with b-boys who practised in the early 1980s in New York City, Los Angeles and Germany.
10. Gleaned from interviews and conversations with b-boys during my PhD research (Fogarty, 2011).
11. B-boys and b-girls are dancers that break, and are part of the dance style of 'b-boying'/'b-girling' or breaking, that can be distinguished from other dance styles such as locking (a funk dance that originated on the West Coast of the United States) and popping.
12. As Jane Feuer (2013) suggests, the film *Dirty Dancing* "gives us the impression that the dancing is diegetic, but the music is not" (61).
13. Donnie 'Crumbs' Counts is called 'Crumbs' by other characters in *You Got Served* and called 'Don' in *Step Up 2*. The character 'Lil' Steph' in *Street Dance 3D* from the real-life German crew, Flyin' Steps, is also called 'Lil' Steph' and likewise 'Brooke' from London is called by his real name.
14. Ascertained from correspondence with various street dancers, 2010.

15. Interestingly, Gene Kelly's character, Don Lockwood, has the *reverse* career trajectory in *Singin in the Rain*, from stunt double to dance star!
16. Interview with the author, 2010.
17. Reminiscent of Gene Kelly's trash can dance in *It's Always Fair Weather* (Donen and Kelly, 1955).
18. See Feuer (1993) on the difference between amateur and professional set-ups in dance films from Fred Astaire and Ginger Rogers to the present day. She notes that "there seems to be a remarkable emphasis on the joys of being an amateur" (13) in these films that also represent professional entertainment.

References

Banes, S. (1994), *Dancing in the Age of Postmodernism*, Middletown: Wesleyan University Press.

Bennett, A. (1999), 'Hip hop am Main: The Localization of Rap Music and Hip Hop Culture', *Media, Culture and Society*, 21(1), 77–91.

Blanco Borelli, M. (2009), 'A Taste of Honey: Choreographing Mulatta in the Hollywood Dance Film', *International Journal of Performing Arts and Digital Media*, 5(2-3), 141–52.

Chion, M. (1994), *Audio-vision: Sound on Screen*, ed. and trans. C. Gorbman, New York: Columbia University Press.

Condry, I. (2006), *Hip-Hop Japan: Rap and the Paths of Cultural Globalization*, Durham: Duke University Press.

Crease, R. (1995), 'Divine Frivolity: Hollywood Representations of the Lindy Hop, 1937–1942', in K. Gabbard (ed.), *Representing Jazz*, Durham: Duke University Press, pp. 207–228.

DeFrantz, T. (2014), 'Hip-Hop in Hollywood: Encounter, Community, Resistance', in M. Blanco Borelli (ed.), *The Oxford Handbook of Dance and the Popular Screen*, New York: Oxford University Press, pp. 113–33.

Dodds, S. (2001), *Dance on Screen: Genres and Media from Hollywood to Experimental Art*, New York: Palgrave.

Feuer, J. (1993), *The Hollywood Musical*, 2nd edn, Bloomington: Indiana University Press.

Feuer, J. (2013), 'Is *Dirty Dancing* a Musical, and Why Should it Matter?' in Y. Tzioumakis and S. Lincoln (eds), *The Time of Our Lives: Dirty Dancing and Popular Culture*, Detroit: Wayne State University Press, 59–70.

Fogarty, M. (2011), 'Dance to the Drummer's Beat: Competing Tastes in International B-Boy/B-Girl Culture', PhD dissertation, University of Edinburgh, available online: https://www.era.lib.ed.ac.uk/handle/1842/5889 (accessed 11 May 2012).

Fogarty, M. (2012), 'Breaking Expectations: Mediated Youth Cultures', in Special Issue: Mediated Youth Cultures, *Continuum: Journal of Media and Cultural Studies*, edited by A. Bennett and B. Robards, pp. 449–62.

Frith, S. (2007), *Taking Popular Music Seriously*, Aldershot: Ashgate.

LaBoskey, S. (2001), 'Getting off: Portrayals of Masculinity in Hip Hop Dance in Film', *Dance Research Journal*, 33(2), 112–20.

McRobbie, A. (1984), 'Dance and Social Fantasy', in A. McRobbie and M. Nava (eds), *Gender and Generation*, London: Macmillan, pp. 130–61.
Mitchell, T. (1996), *Popular Music and Local Identity: Rock, Pop and Rap in Europe and Oceania*, London: Leicester University Press.
Mitchell, T. (2001), *Global Noise: Rap and Hip-Hop outside the USA*, Middletown: Wesleyan University Press.
Monteyne, K. (2013), *Hip Hop on Film: Performance Culture, Urban Space, and Genre Transformation in the 1980s*, Jackson, MI: University Press of Mississippi.
Reid, C. (1994), 'Fighting without Fighting: Film Action', *Film Quarterly*, 47(2), 30–35.
Shapiro, R. (2004), 'The Aesthetics of Institutionalization: Breakdancing in France', *Journal of Arts Management, Law, and Society*, 33(4), 316–35.
Thornton, S. (1995), *Club Cultures: Music, Media and Subcultural Capital*, Cambridge: Polity.

Filmography

B-girl. 2009. Directed by Emily Dell. USA: Two Camels Films. 83 minutes.
Battle of the Year. 2013. Directed by Benson Lee. USA: Contrafilm. 110 min.
Beat Street. 1984. Directed by Stan Lathan. USA: MGM. 105 min.
Breakin'. 1984. Directed by Joel Silberg. USA: MGM. 90 min.
Breakin' 2: Electric Boogaloo. 1984. Directed by Sam Firstenberg. USA: MGM. 94 min.
Flashdance. 1983. Directed by Adrian Lyne. USA: Paramount Pictures. 95 min.
The Freshest Kids: A History of the B-boy. 2002. Directed by Israel. USA: QD3 Entertainment. 96 min.
Honey. 2003. Directed by Bille Woodruff. USA: Universal. 94 min.
Planet B-boy: Breakdancing has Evolved. 2008. Directed by Benson Lee. USA: Mental Pictures. 95 min.
Step Up. 2006. Directed by Anne Fletcher. USA: Touchstone Pictures. 104 min.
Step Up 2: The Streets. 2008. Directed by Jon Chu. USA: Touchstone Pictures. 98 min.
Step Up 3D. 2010. Directed by Jon Chu. USA: Touchstone Pictures. 107 min.
Step Up Revolution. 2012. Directed by Scott Speer. USA: Summit Entertainment. 99 min.
Step Up All In. 2014. Directed by Trish Sie. USA: Summit Entertainment. 112 min.
Stomp the Yard. 2007. Directed by Sylvain White. USA: Rainforest Films. 115 min.
StreetDance 3D. 2010. Directed by Max Giwa and Dania Pasquini. UK: Vertigo Films, BBC Films. 98 min.
StreetDance 2 3D. 2012. Directed by Max Giwa and Dania Pasquini. UK and Germany: Vertigo Films, BBC Films, British Film Institute. 85 min.
Turn It Loose. 2009. Directed by Alastair Siddons. Executive producer Georges Bermann. UK: Partizan Films. 96 minutes.
Wildstyle. 1983. Directed by Charlie Ahearn. USA: Wild Style. 82 min.
You Got Served: Take it to the Streets. 2004. Directed by Chris Stokes. USA: Sony Pictures. 95 min.

Space, Authenticity and Utopia in the Hip Hop Teen Dance Film

Faye Woods[1]

The hip hop teen dance film flourished in the 2000s. Drawing on the dominance of hip hop in the mainstream music industry, films such as *Save the Last Dance* (Thomas Carter, 2001), *Honey* (Billy Woodruff, 2002) and *Step Up* (Anne Fletcher, 2006) combined the teen film's pre-existing social problem and musical narratives. Yet various tensions were created by this interweaving of representations of post-industrial city youth with the utopian sensibilities of the classical Hollywood musical. These narratives celebrated hip hop performance, and depicted dance as a bridge between cultural boundaries, bringing together couples, communities and cultures. These films used hip hop to construct filmic spaces and identities while fragmenting hip hop soundscapes, limiting its expressive potential.

This chapter will explore the hip hop teen dance film's celebration of, yet struggle with, hip hop by examining the soundscapes of particular films: specifically the interactions between sound, narrative and form. It will engage with these films' attempts to marry the representational, narrative and aesthetic meanings of hip hop culture with the form and ideologies of the musical genre, particularly the tensions and continuities that arise from this engagement with musical utopian qualities as identified by Richard Dyer (1985). Yet, while these films clearly illustrate these tensions, they also demonstrate an effective, if partial, integration of hip hop soundscapes and the dancing body in their depiction of dance, highlighting both forms' aesthetics of 'layering, rupture and flow' (Rose, 1994: 22).

Drawing on Jane Feuer's construction of the American film musical as representing a cyclical development of the genre, rather than a linear evolution (1993: 129–30), I suggest that the history of teen film can be positioned as operating in a series of cycles. The "result of shifting industrial and audience patterns" (*ibid.*: 130), these cycles draw on and modify their predecessors and are informed by cultural, social and political contexts. Other writers – most significantly Timothy Shary (2002) – have positioned the teen film as a series of subgenres and, arguably, as a range of narratives: horror, musical and social problem/delinquent. However, positioning the history of the teen film as cyclic rather than a series of subgenres helps to illustrate the way a single film's success can snowball into a series of imitators, before fading away as another trend arrives, or coexisting with other cycles.

The hip hop teen dance film was catalysed by the success of *Save the Last Dance* in 2001 at the tail end of the 1990s teen film boom.[2] Up to 2010's *Step Up 3D*, it encompassed inter-racial romance, crime drama, sports movie hybrids, step dancing, breaking and ballet. It is part of the cultural landscape of teen musicals on both cinema and television screens, from *High School Musical* (Emile Ardolino, 2006) to *Glee* (Fox, 2009–2015) and sitting alongside blockbusting television talent searches (the *Idol* franchise, for example). This cycle draws on the ideologies and structures of the musical while centralizing hip hop dance and diverse, if not multi-faceted, racial representations, drawn from hip hop's move from youth subculture to mainstream cultural phenomenon in the late 1990s and early 2000s. The hip hop teen dance cycle draws on both social problem narratives (Shary, 2002; Lewis, 2002) of the 1990s 'hood' film and the utopian musical narratives (Feuer 1993) of the 1980s teen dance film.

The teen dance film cycle, instigated by the success of *Grease* (Randal Kleiser, 1978) and *Fame* (Alan Parker, 1980), included *Flashdance* (Adrian Lyne, 1983), *Footloose* (Herbert Ross, 1984) and *Dirty Dancing* (Emile Ardolino, 1987). These are female coming-of-age narratives, where personal fulfilment is achieved through a combined success in dance and romance. The cycle had strong links with the classical Hollywood musical, reconstructing its narratives and ideologies (Altman, 1987) in pastiche[3] fashion for the postmodern era (Feuer, 1993: 133). Yet significantly these films largely replace the diegetic 'number' with popular song sequences that blur classic diegetic boundaries in their relationship with dance and movement (*ibid.*: 130), representing changing relationships between narrative and song in line with the growth of the music video.

The early 1980s saw a brief wave of breakdance films that hybridized the teen dance film's concerns with a social problem narrative. *Wild Style* (Charlie Ahern, 1982), *Beat Street* (Stan Lathan, 1984) and *Breakin'* (Joel Silberg, 1984) chronicled and capitalized on the emergence of hip hop as an urban sub-culture. Their depictions of black and Latino youth's creative engagement with city spaces challenged the dominant media images of inner-city criminality (Bercov Monteyne, 2007: 96). These precursors to the hip hop teen dance film depicted a transformative power of hip hop that featured strong elements of the utopian sensibilities typically found in the classical Hollywood musical (Dyer, 1985). Both teen dance and breakdance films present dance as the means of social, financial and emotional escape from a life of limited, class-driven opportunity.

The hip hop teen dance film has strong connections with the 1980s teen dance film cycle, yet its hip hop soundtrack and depictions of urban youth and minor criminality also draw on the iconography and representations found in the 'hood' films of the early 1990s.[4] Films such as *Boyz n the Hood* (John Singleton, 1991), *Juice* (Ernest R. Dickerson, 1992) and *Menace II Society* (Hughes brothers, 1993) focused on the young working-class black male and his struggles with a controlling and violent society. These filmic ties between popular music, race and juvenile delinquency stretch back at least as far as 1955's *Blackboard Jungle* (Richard Brooks), yet this cycle is distinguished by its links with Gangsta rap – which dominated the late 1980s and early 1990s hip hop industry – in its narratives, representations and sounds. The cycle's social problem narratives arguably exploited the 1980s culture wars and what Craig Watkins identifies as Republican-fuelled moral panic over the young black male and the post-industrial ghetto (1998).

Yet Watkins suggests "the popular cultures of black youth operate as a complicated site of ideological struggle, commodity production and pleasure" (1998: 13). As part of contemporary political and cultural discourse, *Boyz n the Hood* and *Straight Outta Brooklyn* (Matty Rich, 1991) were both positioned as serious 'issue' dramas, drawing Oscar nominations and widespread critical praise. Yet, as Watkins demonstrates, cultural commentators argued the cycle's representations of young black men and the ghetto fed into the problematic political ideologies and delimiting representations of black life.[5] However, as the 1990s progressed, the range of representations and soundscapes were diversified by 'new black cinema': from the gravitas of Spike Lee to romances such as *Waiting to Exhale* (Forrest Whitaker, 1995) and *Brown Sugar* (Rick Famuyiwa, 2002), hip hop soundtracks began the return to neo-soul and old-school hip hop.

The turn of the millennium saw hip hop moving beyond the 'dangerous', marginalized associations with Gangsta rap to the centre of popular culture. In 1999 *Time* magazine celebrated hip hop's twentieth anniversary[6] with a cover story that suggested "we are living in the age of hip hop" (Farley 1999: 54). The article reported that hip hop outsold country music in 1998 and that Anglophone customers purchased more than 70 per cent of hip hop albums.[7] Pop-rap had always had chart success, but by the end of the 1990s, propelled by innovative record producers and significant record label investment, hip hop had fully crossed-over from a subculture of black youth to become *the* preeminent youth culture. For example, throughout 2004 every number one song in Billboard's Hot 100 was by a hip hop or R&B artist (Kitwana, 2005: 50). In 2005 rapper 50 Cent became the first artist to have four singles in the US top 10 at once since the Beatles, while white rapper Eminem's first three albums achieved combined sales of over 20 million (Hess, 2005: 385).

The move away from hyper-masculine Gangsta rap and the diversification of representation in new black cinema influenced the hip hop teen dance films' female-centred narratives and increasingly diverse hip hop soundtracks. Films such as *Save the Last Dance*, *Honey*, *Step Up*, *Stomp the Yard* (Sylvian White, 2007), *How She Move* (Ian Iqbal Rashid, 2007), *Step Up 2: The Streets* (Jon Chu, 2008) and *Step Up 3D* (Jon Chu, 2010) sought to replicate the crossover success of hip hop music, featuring multi-racial casts in narratives of hip hop culture transgressing social and cultural boundaries. These representations contrast with the white, middle-class spaces and stories of the preceding 1990s teen film and television cycle. However, it is undeniable that hip hop teen dance films focus predominantly on white experiences of black, urban, working-class spaces. *Save the Last Dance* has been criticized for its elision of political and cultural issues linked to representations of black dance and urban youth (Boyd, 2004; Gateward, 2005). While shifting racial divisions and barriers onto ones of class, the *Step Up* trilogy problematically transposes essentialized hip hop identity onto white protagonists living within black urban spaces.[8] With their working-class urban locations and racially diverse casts the cycle has links to the social problem film, yet these films remain dance fantasies, where "class and race are obstacles that exist only to be overcome in a dazzling display of teen spirit" (Harris, 2007: 78).

The cycle addresses social issues with differing levels of consciousness, but nearly always through their connection with performance. The films often present hip hop dance as a figurative and, at times, literal escape from the social problems of post-industrial city that 'realistic' 'hood' films depicted, however sensationally, with fatalism. The hip hop teen dance film can be read through Richard Dyer's argument that entertainment offers up temporary utopian answers to the inadequacies and tensions of society (1985: 227). In particular, the pleasure of communal or group dance connects with Dyer's utopian sensibility of community, which resolves the problem of "fragmentation", represented in those high-rise flats, ready-made for the post-industrial cities of the cycle (*ibid.*: 228).[9]

However, as Dyer argues, musicals are deeply contradictory, due to the distance between the 'representational' narrative and the 'unreal' number, which must be worked through and managed. The same is true of the hip hop teen dance film, in its hybridizing of the verisimilitude of the 'hood' film's iconography and dance fantasies of the teen dance film. As Dyer points out, the musical does not always succeed in managing its contradictions (*ibid.*: 229) and the tensions present in the hip hop teen dance film suggest that these contradictions remain.

Hollywood Fantasy Meets Urban 'Reality'

Adam Krims suggests that hip hop's focus on cultural ownership and 'realness' foregrounds issues of identity to a greater degree than other music forms (2000: 9). In blending the teen dance film's reconstructive pastiche with a culture built on 'authenticity' and depictions of struggle, the hip hop teen dance film created contradictions within its own structure. Like Krims, Alexander Riley emphasizes authenticity as one of the central tenets of hip hop where "authenticity means being 'the realist' or the one most in touch (through purportedly real life experience) with the agonistic, tragic rules of the subculture" (2005: 307). The 'hood' cycle films, urban youth predecessor to the hip hop teen dance films, were marketed and received as politicized, Oscar-worthy dramas (*Boyz n the Hood*) or tragic and brutally-violent action films (*Menace II Society*). Largely independent of major Hollywood studios, these nihilistic narratives and downbeat conclusions could preserve the ideologies espoused in their Gangsta rap soundtracks. In contrast the hip hop teen dance cycle was primarily produced by major Hollywood studios. While dysfunction, conflict and unhappy endings were common to many of the 'deconstructive' or critically reflexive (Feuer, 1993) musicals of the post-studio era – from *A Star is Born* (Cukor, 1954) to *New York, New York* (Scorsese, 1977) – this recent cycle instead continues the reconstruction of the tropes and themes of the classical Hollywood musical also found in the 1980s teen dance films (Feuer, 1993).

The hip hop teen dance film's focus on dance as performance and their narrative drive towards a climatic 'final show' connects the cycle with the backstage musical, while a celebration of the amateur performer and community links them with the folk musical (Altman, 1987). Yet the classical Hollywood musical's drive towards utopian resolution (Dyer, 1985) leads films in this cycle to attempt to recuperate and 'resolve' complex urban issues within the framework of a conservative narrative structure. Contrastingly, hip hop teen dance films can be seen to suffer from a representational burden. As Alan Light notes, by the very fact of its existence, hip hop has a political dimension, whether it is expressed topically or not, and the tensions within hip hop, between entertainment and politics, are ultimately irreconcilable (2004: 143–44). This is the burden of the hip hop teen dance film. Despite their position as Hollywood studio features and their links with previous dance fantasies, this burden of representation is not present in white teen dance films. Despite its commercial exploitation and movement to the mainstream, hip hop retains a minority, oppositional identity for many consumers and critics. Krims notes that "the touchstone of authenticity in public representations of hip hop culture and rap music has long been some notion of urban locality and ethnic and/or class marginality" (2000: 198).

Yet hip hop itself maintains a particular status as a form that allows both excess and entertainment to exist simultaneously with social comment. "[F]ramed more and more as fantasised and spectacular" (Krims, 2000: 83), hip hop repeatedly displays a delicate balance of authenticity and fantasy in narratives which combine stories of marginalized 'street' life with excess in consumption or violence. These narratives, ultimately, become difficult to translate within Hollywood musical structures. Discussing *Honey*'s storyline, that of a Bronx dancer's ascendancy from community dance teacher to Manhattan music video choreographer, Scott (2003) suggests it mirrors hip hop's contradictory "aggressive celebration of upward mobility and its simultaneous embrace of democratic, street-level authenticity". There exists no Hollywood filmic model for hip hop's kind of spectacularized social commentary, so the contradictory ideologies of hip hop combine with the musical's inherent contradictions (Dyer, 1985) to create tension upon tension within the hip hop teen dance film.

Like Krimms, Tricia Rose identifies hip hop's primary thematic concerns as identity and location (1994: 9–12) and views the culture as a reaction to the geographical and spiritual post-industrial destruction of community (*ibid.:* 34). The hip hop teen dance film draws on the pre-existing signifations of hip hop to demarcate narrative and geographic spaces as black and urban with the potential for performance, through the use of a hip hop soundtrack.

Defining and Delineating Space through Hip Hop

Throughout film and television, a hip hop soundscape often acts as shorthand for demarcations of youth space and black community – and, in the process, works to code urban space as unsettlingly unknown to a white perspective. From *The Blindside* (John Lee Hancock, 2009) to *Friday Night Lights* (NBC, 2006–2011) to *The Wire* (HBO, 2002–2008) it is the often threatening thump of diegetic hip hop bass that signifies a space as urban 'ghetto'. In the breakdance and 'hood' films hip hop tracks primarily emanate diegetically from speakers and car stereos to appropriate public space for their young owners. These diegetic soundtracks announce presence, control and, at times, threat. This construction of filmic space through sound is maintained in the hip hop teen dance film. Yet here hip hop is presented as progressive and exciting and a means of release for its primarily white protagonists. Dance locations become spaces of musical hybridity, creating community and combining high and popular culture.

A sequence early in *Save the Last Dance* features hip hop's coding of space during Sara's (Julia Styles) first day at her new – primarily black – school on the South Side of Chicago. The introductory sequences of the film present the contrast and culture shock of the ballet dancer's move to urban Chicago to live with her estranged father after her mother's death and her failed Juilliard audition. The school sequence and its sound are focalized through Sara as we follow her into the school. The soundtrack presents the experience as a sensory overload for this female, small-town and white character. Contrasts and oppositions are established through comparisons with her previous school, depicted in the film's opening montage in a series of short shots of yellow school buses, letterman jackets and spacious hallways (02:31–02:54). Musically, cultural differences are established through the absence of diegetic music in her former school. Sara's conversation with a friend is accompanied only by a light score to pull it into the montage (02:34–02:54), whereas diegetic music is present in non-scholastic spaces of her new school such as the steps and canteen.

At her new school the 'over-presence' of hip hop hits Sara and the audience as soon as she exits her father's car (and it could be said, 'white' space). A short series of shots shows black students outside the school, moving to the diegetic music, bobbing to their own headphones, greeting each other, smoking and shouting (09:09–09:30). The camera tracks Sara as she walks through them, standing out from the black-clad crowd not only in her red jacket and her whiteness but even in the smooth, long tracking shot. The music is given a diegetic source from a student's boombox, but its volume dominates the sound mix. This volume is an immediate and determined announcement of black culture and identity. As part of the intimidation of the unknown space, the beat is aggressive and the lyrics sexually provocative, but the drive of the rhythm is infectious. Sara leaves the music behind as she enters the school and is confronted with metal detectors and searches, then plunged into crowded hallways filled with jostling, shouting students (09:30–10:20). However, the same song re-appears in a later scene as Sara enters the cafeteria (13:06). Intimidated again, she is unsure of her place when faced with another rowdy, music-filled space, coded as unruly, black and youthful.

In its story of a Bronx hip hop dancer's work with local youth and her rise and fall as a Manhattan music video choreographer, *Honey* creates narrative distinctions between the 'authentic' hip hop space of the Bronx and the ultimately false glamour of the Manhattan music industry. These oppositions can be aligned with Dyer's utopian signifiers, with Honey's (Jessica Alba) localized and honest hip hop dance, read as 'transparency' and constructed in opposition to (and offering the solution to) the 'manipulation' of the white Manhattan industry executive Michael and his exploitation of the 'bling' and sexuality of hip hop (Dyer 1985: 227). However, the two New York boroughs are introduced through the mirroring of aerial establishing shots that utilize an aesthetic elsewhere limited to the film's depiction of hip hop music videos, thus constructing them as spaces of potential hip hop performance. The film opens with a fast-paced helicopter shot of night-time Manhattan (00:21–0:35), appearing as the rap vocal of the accompanying Mark Ronson hip hop dance track 'Oooh-Wee' talks of "night-time New York City" (00:21). Composed of a funky beat, tapping cowbell rhythm, layers of sampled strings, male vocals and a fast-paced male rap, it musicalizes a series of angular camera movements as the shot progressively rotates around and zooms in on the island, ultimately locating a downtown club within the cityscape. Each sharp zoom down into the island is accompanied by a non-diegetic 'woosh' on the soundtrack, incorporated into the song's layers. As the camera cuts down through the roof into the heaving club (00:40) the track becomes diegetic, yet still linked to the continually moving camera, down from the ceiling onto the bar in slight slow motion. Here a swift track and 'whoosh' along the bar (00:46) reveals an overhead shot of drinks, before a cut to a medium close-up of Honey bartending (00:50) with a shift to full diegetic sound – and the vocal hitting the word "honey" in its rap line, placing us within the narrative space. This opening seeks out Honey within the expanse of Manhattan, centralizing her as the narrative focus. Familiar and glittering, Manhattan is cast as a hip hop space. Tricia Rose argues that hip hop "replicates and re-imagines the experiences of urban life and symbolically appropriates urban space through sampling, attitude, dance, style, and sound effects" (1994: 22). Here hip hop "rupture and flow" (*ibid.*: 22) is evident as the conventional helicopter establishing shot of New York has been fractured by an angular and speeding camera. Flow here is created in the continuity between city skyline and club interior and the interplay between diegetic and non-diegetic music. A mirroring, circling, fast zoom-in offers our first view of Honey's neighbourhood, accompanied by an up-tempo, 'dancey' piano and snare-beat score whose constituent elements cohere with the pop hip hop that dominates the film's soundtrack (7:02–7:08). We circle overhead around a view of the sunlit project towers in golden brown hues, before zooming in to the neighbouring apartment buildings and street, then cutting to a long shot of Honey greeting neighbours. The sequence works to depict an aesthetically pleasing, community-centric scene, supporting the film's larger theme of community. This technique is used later in the film as single establishing shots to situate Honey within the expanse of Manhattan at a video shoot (26:28) and to later re-establish her within the Bronx street (53:13). This mirroring of the establishing shot also sets up both of the narratively oppositional locations (Bronx as community, Manhattan as industry) as hip hop spaces, allowing Honey's movement between the two worlds to occur smoothly, disguising the huge economic and social gaps between them.

Step Up, through its cross-class romance, presents dance as a site of cultural fusion, using hip hop music and dance to define identity and geographic space. After he is caught vandalising the Maryland School of the Arts (MSA), working-class teenager Tyler (Channing Tatum) serves his community service assisting the school's janitor. Classically-trained dance student Nora (Jenna Dewan-Tatum) notices his 'natural' hip hop dance ability and, with instruction from her, Tyler replaces her injured partner in her final performance at the school's showcase. As the narrative progresses it unites Nora and Tyler in dance spaces where they combine their disciplines, yet at the film's outset they are divided both culturally and spatially. Tyler is linked with the streets – we first meet him dancing at a house party and he ranges casually through the night streets with his friends. Nora is aligned with MSA and we, like Tyler, first see her in a dance class performing a fast-paced contemporary choreography to a strong and regimented rhythm (14:27). Their differences are demarcated spatially when Nora watches through a school window as Tyler dances for his friends around a stolen car outside of MSA, appropriating the city and school space with hip hop sound and dance (16:40–19:00).

In line with this cycle's demarcation of space through music, an upbeat hip hop track plays diegetically from the car stereo, built around a complex beat with a combination of staccato drum and loose, swooping rhythm, funk bass guitar sample and swift rap flow. Initially subsumed by the boys' conversation, the track rises in volume to dominate the space as Tyler displays his moves in response to his friends' teasing (16:48), then, in parody, performs imitations of the 'ballet' moves of the MSA dancers.[10] As he progresses to more spectacular leaps off the car and ground, Nora catches sight of him from inside. In one shot Nora is framed in the background through a window, while Tyler dances in the foreground, their divisions rendered spatially – him in appropriated street space, her within the confines of the school (18:20). Him defined through loose limbed, yet spectacular, improvised moves to flowing hip hop; her through dynamic yet sharply controlled choreography to her teacher's count. While the scene acts to demonstrate Tyler's dance abilities for Nora and to define their differences spatially it also presents Tyler's use of hip hop dance to mock the institution that has placed him in a menial role. Here, the street is constructed as a space of hip hop and spontaneous performance. The car stereo appropriates communal space, transforming it into dance space where Tyler parodically fuses high and popular art. In contrast to Nora's professional training, Tyler is positioned as the gifted amateur of the folk musical (Feuer, 1993: 13), appropriating space for his improvised performance.

Divided Soundscapes: Limiting Hip Hop

While the hip hop teen dance film celebrates hip hop in its narrative, the cycle tends to limit hip hop soundscapes to dance moments and the demarcation of youth spaces: cars, basketball courts and clubs. Like the breakdance and 'hood' films, they turn instead to the expressive capabilities of underscore and R&B

music for their interpersonal and dramatic action. Francis Gateward (2005: 177) and Jade Boyd (2004: 74) accuse *Save the Last Dance* of being a full-length music video; however its soundscape in fact limits hip hop primarily to diegetic use in youth spaces. Romantic and dramatic action are, instead, accompanied by a non-diegetic score, drawing on the conventions of Romantic tonality present in classical scoring (Gorbman, 1987). A score composed of flutes, horn, and sweeping strings in a minor tone accompanies an emotional moment between Sara and Derek (Sean Patrick Thomas) as she explains how her guilt over her mother's death prevents her from dancing ballet (55:47–58:30). The music's soft, plaintive tone draws the viewer into her sorrow and Derek's tenderness. A shift in emotion is signified by a rising horn motif as he encourages her to try again (57:50), moving into softly romantic strings as they embrace (58:22). The film leans closer to romantic drama than other films of the cycle, with their issue-led narratives of inter-racial romance, teen motherhood and gang violence. Its use of a more conventional score reflects its dramatic ambitions.

It is *Step Up* that most smoothly coheres its dance and narrative soundscapes, constructing continuities between its score and hip hop music moments. As a backstage musical, the romance between working-class Tyler and classically trained dancer Nora parallels the 'final show', with their romance expressing the film's themes of culture-clash and fusion. Nora is described by her friend Miles as "Old school, I ain't talking about Sugarhill Gang, I'm talking Vivaldi old school" while Tyler calls her choreography "stiff" and "boring". Yet his self-taught hip hop body cannot reproduce her disciplined lines and skilled movements. Through training and romance they create a dance piece that draws on a combination of their styles. This theme of creative fusion is reflected across the score, which features spare and sustained keyboard phrases with funk and soul guitar rhythms, often combined with classical phrasing and instrumentation.

This fusion is also figured through the character of Miles, a black MSA composition student who Tyler discovers comes from his neighbourhood. The music Miles creates combines classical music with hip hop beats and samples of soul and funk phrases. This music features diegetically as accompaniment to Nora and Tyler's emerging dance style, both in a studio practice, a nightclub's communal dance number and the final dance piece at the MSA showcase. This interweaving of musical genres continues in the tracks which non-diegetically accompany (yet bridge the diegetic gap in their alignment with dance movement) practice montages and teaching sessions, featuring a mix of hip hop beats and strings. Romantic moments are accompanied by soft soul and funk-tinged tracks that share tonal qualities with the score. As a result musical blendings and continuities spread out beyond the cultural fusions taking place in the dance spaces.

While the original *Step Up* film seemed to have resolved hip hop soundtrack divisions, these were then reinstated in its sequel. *Step Up 2: The Streets* followed Andie (Briana Evigan), a hip hop dancer from Tyler's neighbourhood who begrudgingly takes a place at MSA to avoid being sent out of town and leaving her local dance crew, the 410. When her studies interfere with her 410 rehearsals she is thrown out of the crew, only to form a new one from MSA's misfit students. They plan to compete at – and win – the climactic dance battle: The Streets. Although the film is centred around hip hop performance and its challenge to cultural divisions and hierarchies, hip hop tracks are once again limited to accompaniment of performance and youth leisure space. Instead an orchestrated score accompanies subplots featuring Andie's conflicts with her guardian and the school's director and her romantic moments with Chase (Robert Hoffman), a dancer at MSA.

The film concludes with a 'final show' at The Streets, showcasing spectacular dance performances to complex diegetic mashups of music genres and sound fragments. Yet, in contrast to these adventurous diegetic soundscapes, the final scene is scored by a series of orchestral crescendos as narrative resolutions and romantic moments unfold within the celebrating crowd (85:31–88:02). These culminate in a climactic harmonic, sweeping crescendo of strings and brass as Andie and Chase kiss, rising to a fanfare that is almost parodic in its imitation of a classical Hollywood score as the camera tracks back and upwards, losing them in a sea of dancing bodies (87:40–88:02). While this film showcases cutting-edge dance styles and flash mobs and social media's role in 'battles', it situates these elements of cultural vanguard within a classical score and divided soundscape, reflecting the underlying conservatism of the hip hop teen dance film.

Structure and Movement: Rupture and Flow

Having discussed how the cycle utilizes hip hop to define space yet delimits its presence within soundscapes, I now wish to consider the relationship between soundscapes, narrative and movement. The hip hop teen dance film often draws on a version of the backstage musical narrative with elements of folk musical. It primarily depicts three forms of dance 'number': the practice, the communal performance and the stage performance. The communal performance in the hip hop teen dance cycle is often circular, with relatively porous boundaries between audience and performer (Bercov Monteyne 2007: 92).[11] The stage performance is most often the 'final show', with a more conventional proscenium staging.

The hip hop teen dance film cycle interprets hip hop's primary properties of "flow", "layering" and "rupture" (Rose, 1994: 22) in a number of ways. The interrelationship between soundtrack, the dancing body and the musicalized image illustrate Rose's contention that "in hip hop, visual, physical, music and lyrical lines are set in motion, broken abruptly with sharp angular breaks, yet they sustain motion and energy through fluidity and flow" (*ibid.*: 38). The broken yet fluid line is seen in both the dance and aesthetic style of the film, with angular breaks and fluid flow found in dance and music, while the fragmented space and time of the practice montage is cohered into a narrative flow by its accompanying track. In all these films, the dancing body is primarily presented as an object of power (and at times physical threat), which physicalizes the often dense layers and fragments of accompanying hip hop tracks. DeFrantz suggests that "power in hip hop is most apparent in the aggressively layered, dynamic array of shapes assumed by the dancing body ... [the] assertive angularity of body posture and an insistent virtuostic rhythmicity" (2004: 71). This strength and power are showcased in the sharpness and controlled flow of the hip hop and fusion dance exhibited in these films. The multiple layers of rhythm and sonic textures present in the series of mash-ups that accompany the final performances of the 410 and MSA crews in *Step Up 2* allow the showcasing of varying speeds, junctures, shapes and forms in their combinations of dance styles and bodily movement. Andie's MSA crew performs their climactic 'battle' number to a mash-up of tracks heard at different points in the film (80:47–85:10). The number opens with a sequence of angular movements; elbows are thrust sideways, knees and torsos dynamically lower to 'impossible' angles, the movements visualizing the warped scratch and electronic crunch of the accompanying track. Later the sparse boom and echoing bounce of the rhythm refracts across their synchronized, undulating bodies, controlling them like a heartbeat (84:15). In these films, the flow and virtuosity of highly skilled hip hop movement, whose sharp changes in rhythm and direction are designed to impress, coalesces with the multiple layers and juxtapositions of contemporary hip hop music.

The dance montage, a shot series of spatial and narrative breaks cohered by the flow of the non-diegetic track, is prominent within this film cycle – just as the pop song montage was for the teen dance film cycle (Feuer, 1993: 132). While the diegetic 'number' features in the final show performances of *Save the Last Dance* and *Honey* or the series of dance battles of *Step Up 3*, the practice montage is also a recurring device. In these sequences music bridges the diegetic gap, as diegetic dance coordinates with non-diegetic music letting narrative and score coalesce. This follows the organization of the sound/image relationship that Feuer identifies in the 1980s teen dance film, where numbers were "structured around a non-diegetic popular song to which the characters dance or throughout which narrative segments of an episodic structure are rhythmically cut" (*ibid.*: 192). The practice montage works to demonstrate both the development of a performance and functions as a number itself, often serving to progress the interpersonal narrative, following the musical genre's convention of rehearsal numbers as courtship rituals (ibid.: 11).

In *Step Up 2*, the practice montages show the progression of a group of individuals towards a cohesive, utopian, community (Dyer, 1985). Andie's MSA crew begins as a collection of distinct individuals, with dance styles tied to their defined identity. This is illustrated in the practice montage set to the metallic tap, shuffling polyrhythms and brass fanfares of Missy Elliott's 'Shake Your Pom Pom' – a track about celebrating, displaying and challenging others with your spectacular dance moves (41:10–43:18). In the appropriated space of the out-of-hours MSA studio, Andie and Chase try to teach the disparate group choreography. A series of short, sharply edited shots displays the dancers arrayed around the studio performing their own devised moves or failing to grasp the choreography, to comic frustration.

As the montage progresses, the group celebrates the individual of each dancer. They display moves in dance circles and, in a series of shots where each dancer moves down the mirror, they begin to teach each other in paired mirrorings, reflecting a deepening social bond. The sequence illustrates DeFrantz's argument that "participation in the larger black culture involves the successful attainment of social dances and the invention of individual movement style as a marker of identity" (2004: 76). Here a montage structured by the beats of hip hop rhythm displays the signature moves of the individual in relation to the multi-racial community of the crew as it begins to coalesce.

Practice montages offer sequences where non-diegetic hip hop tracks structure both the filmic aesthetic and the flow of the musicalized body. Sequences set in the wide, open space of the MSA studio – also featured in Nora and Tyler's practice montages in the original *Step Up* – are notable for featuring a series of wide and full-body long shots, showcasing the performing body. Yet these dance movements still capture the rupture and flow of their hip hop soundtrack through bodily movement and the use of multiple camera angles, jump cuts and time ellipses to fragment the visual aesthetic of the practice montages. *Step Up*'s foregrounding of contrasts and connections – both aural and visual – between 'high art' and 'the street' are drawn out in the opening credit sequence that features the MSA studio. Introducing the film's thematic conflict, the sequence intercuts classical ballet dancers and hip hop dancers and is structured by the non-diegetic accompaniment of a multi-layered track which constructs a flow from fragments of orchestral and hip hop motifs (0:31–02:26).

The ballet dancers perform in the MSA studio, in its bright, open spaces, with its shafts of light and its pallet of pastels and soft browns. In contrast the hip hop dancers are in an industrial space at night, an urban space of dirty windows and police sirens, with a pallet of blacks, blues and reds. The sequence begins with wide, long shots of both spaces with their dancers, multi-racial, male and female, arranging themselves across the frame to diegetic sound, then the music track assembles as they begin to dance (00:31–00:50). Building up from a low bass refrain with brass tones, a hi-hat and drum beat are added, then a rattling, clapping rhythm which is accentuated by the jumping feet of both sets of dancers (0:53). Staccato strings add a motif before the male rap vocal completes the sonic layering.

The sequence presents hip hop's fracture, layering and flow read across classical dance. It cuts rhythmically, though not exactly to the beat, between the two spaces and routines, at points creating paired shots of both disciplines: both ballet and hip hop dancers jumping and criss-crossing their feet, both performing leg raises, dips and both pairing up in partner dance. At other moments the two forms are in contrast, creating distinctive shapes as the flow of ballet is cast against the sharp, angular beats of the hip hop dancers. While both sets of dancers are united in their exhibition of dexterity, skill and strength, the track's multiple layers align certain movements to different sonic elements, connecting non-diegetic soundscape with diegetic dance space as the structure of the edit bridges the diegetic gap. This bridging is seen as the swoop of the strings aligns with a sweeping ballet lift (1:23) or a spin or flowing arm of a hip hop dancer (1:49). At other times the prominent rhythmic beat or bass refrain syncopates to the thrown arms and beating steps of the hip hop dancers (1:22) or the defined placement of ballet dancers' legs and hands (2:20). This juxtaposition and alignment of the two dance styles with the blended layers of the accompanying track introduce the culture clash theme and the aesthetic distinctions that will become central to the film, while demonstrating that rhythm, flow and dynamic energy are defining qualities of both dance forms.

The hip hop teen dance film's melding of form, combining 'high' and 'street' arts, replicates how the classical Hollywood musical resolved tensions between classical and folk arts, where "the classical presence elevates the status of popular music just as jazz imbues concert music with humanizing folk qualities" (Feuer, 1993: 60–65). Additionally, it also reflects hip hop's culture of sampling, borrowing and layering and points to dance's borrowings from legacies of black movement, from the Lindy hop, to double dutch to stepping (Rose, 1994: 49). Thus the layering of sounds in the music accompanying *Step Up*'s opening credits replicates the constructions and borrowings that the film itself narrativizes through Tyler and Nora.

This analysis of the hip hop teen dance film cycle illustrates that music and dance, with long-held connections to minorities of the post-industrial city and their resistance to conservative forces, actually meet these conservative forces in the formulaic narratives and utopian pleasures of the classical Hollywood musical. In a cycle that capitalizes on hip hop's move to the mainstream, and mirroring the form's inevitable depoliticization and white 'appropriation', tensions are created when representations of black urban youth and social problem storylines combine with the utopian fantasies of achievement found in the 1980s' teen dance film. These films partially resolve some of these tensions through the relationship of sound and body in their dance numbers. These numbers are structured around the angular shapes and breaks being combined with a dynamic fluidity that is hip hop's 'rupture and flow'. While these numbers showcase the dynamism of hip hop dance and music, the limitations placed on hip hop in the overall soundscape and predictable narratives illustrate that the tensions remain and that there are problems incorporating the form wholly into Hollywood cinema, which means that, like its ancestor the 1930s backstage musical, the hip hop teen dance film remains, at present, sonically un-integrated.

Notes

1. Faye Woods is Lecturer in Film and Television at the University of Reading, UK. Her research interests include cultural representations of youth, popular music in film and television, feminist media studies and television industries. Her work has appeared in the journals *Television & New Media* and *Critical Studies in Television*, and edited collections *Television Aesthetics and Style* (2013) and *Shane Meadows: Critical Essays* (2013). She is currently writing a monograph on British youth television for Palgrave.
2. This boom saw a range of smaller and ongoing cycles including relocations of classic novels – *Clueless* (Amy Heckerling, 1995), *10 Things I Hate About You* (Gil Junger, 1999) – and teen horrors – *Scream* (Wes Craven, 1996) and *The Faculty* (Robert Rodriguez, 1998).
3. See Usha Iyer's chapter in this volume for an account of similar practices in Bollywood film.
4. Variously termed 'homeboy cinema' (Jones, 1991), 'the ghetto action film' (Watkins, 1998) and 'the African American crime drama' (Shary, 2001).
5. See Watkins's chapters 'Producing Ghetto Pictures' and 'The Ghettocentric Imagination' for further discussion of the representations, political and social contexts and aesthetic style of the cycle (1998).
6. Although this was actually that of its commercial exploitation as it marked twenty years since the release of 'Rapper's Delight', the first rap single.
7. Bakari Kitwana questions the veracity of this statistic and what he terms the "myth of hip hop's primary white audience" (2005: 81–106), suggesting that this works towards an "unspoken but growing trend among mass audiences to expunge Blackness from hip hop" (106).

8. All-black narratives are limited to films located in Historic Black Universities – the marching band of *Drumline* (Charles Stone III, 2002) and stepping in *Stomp the Yard* – or independent cinema with the Canadian *How She Move*.
9. The other social tensions and utopian solutions are scarcity/abundance, exhaustion/energy, dreariness/intensity and manipulation/transparency (Dyer, 1985: 228).
10. This is not a new activity: we can see here links to MGM's Freed Unit musical's parodic presentations of high-art's pretention in films such as *The Band Wagon* (Vincente Minnelli, 1953) (Feuer, 1993: 62).
11. Bercov Monteyne suggests that the circular nature of the breaking circle and the movements of performers between audience and performance space have close ties with the folk musical (2007: 92).

References

Altman, R. (1987), *The American Film Musical*, Bloomington: Indiana University Press.

Bercov Monteyne, K. (2007), 'The Sound of the South Bronx: Youth Culture, Genre, and Performance in Charlie Ahearn's *Wild Style*', in T. Shary and A. Seibel (eds), *Youth Culture in Global Cinema*, Austin: University of Texas Press, pp. 87–105.

Boyd, J. (2004), 'Dance, Culture, and Popular Film: Considering Representations in *Save the Last Dance*', *Feminist Media Studies*, 4(1), 67–83.

DeFrantz, T. F. (2004), 'The Black Beat Made Visible: Hip-hop Dance and Body Power', in Andrew Lepecki (ed.), *Of the Presence of the Body: Essays on Dance and Performance Theory*, Middletown: Wesleyan University Press, pp. 64–81.

Dyer, R. (1985), 'Entertainment and Utopia', in Bill Nichols (ed.), *Movies and Methods II*, London: University of California Press, pp. 220–32.

Farley, C. J. (1999), 'Hip-hop Nation', *Time*, 8 February, pp. 54–64.

Feuer, J. (1993), *The Hollywood Musical*, 2nd edn, London: Macmillan Press.

Gateward, F. (2005), 'In Love and Trouble: Teenage Boys and Interracial Romance', in M. Pomerance and F. Gateward (eds), *Where the Boys Are: Cinemas of Masculinity and Youth*, Detroit, MI: Wayne University Press, pp. 157–82.

Gorbman, C. (1987), *Unheard Melodies: Narrative Film Music*, London: British Film Institute.

Harris, S. (2007), 'Step Up', *Sight and Sound*, 17(1), 78.

Hess, M. (2005), 'Hip-hop Realness and the White Performer', *Critical Studies in Media Communication*, 22(5), 372–89.

Jones, J. (1991), 'The New Ghetto Aesthetic', *Wide Angle*, 13(3/4), 32–43.

Kitwana, B. (2005), *Why White Kids Love Hip-hop: Wankstas, Wiggers, Wannabes, and the New Reality of Race in America*, New York: Basic Civitas Books.

Krims, A. (2000), *Rap Music and the Poetics of Identity*, Cambridge: Cambridge University Press.

Lewis, J. (1992), *The Road to Romance and Ruin: Teen Films and Youth Culture*, London: Routledge.

Light, A. (2004), 'About a Salary or Reality? Rap's Recurrent Conflict', in Murray Forman and Mark Anthony Neal (eds), *That's the Joint: A Hip Hop Studies Reader*, New York: Routledge, pp. 137–45.

Riley, A. (2005), 'The Rebirth of Tragedy out of the Spirit of Hip-hop: A Cultural Sociology of Gangsta Rap Music', *Journal of Youth Studies*, 8(3), 297–311.
Rose, T. (1994), *Black Noise: Rap Music and Black Culture in Contemporary America*, London: Wesleyan University Press.
Scott, A. O. (2003), 'She's Aiming for the Stars, with Feet Planted in the Bronx', *New York Times*, 5 December, online at http://www.nytimes.com/2003/12/05/movies/05HONE.html (accessed 22 January 2015).
Shary, T. (2002), *Generation Multiplex: The Image of Youth in Contemporary American Cinema*, Austin: University of Texas Press.
Watkins, C. T. (1998), *Representing: Hip-hop Culture and the Production of Black Cinema*, Chicago: Chicago University Press.

The School and 'The Streets'
Race, Class, Sound and Space in Step Up *and* Step Up 2

Brian Su-Jen Chung[1] *and Afia Ofori-Mensa*[2]

Step Up (Anne Fletcher, 2006) opens with a scenic juxtaposition, a technique repeated throughout the film to highlight the distinction between the two settings of the narrative: the school and the streets. What appears first is a rehearsal space so quiet the viewer can hear pointe shoes clicking as ballet dancers walk in the room, bags and cardigans thudding softly as they hit the wooden floor. There is a low hum of conversation while the dancers stretch. The scene is lit in warm tones of sepia and pink. Bright backlighting enters from tall windows at the rear of the room. Then there is a cut to another location: tarmac pavement and chain-link fencing. In this scene, hip hop dancers shout greetings to one another while sirens wail in the distant background. This shot is darkly lit in cool blue and grey tones. The characters' faces are not visible when they get in position to dance.

As the opening credits begin, a second cut leads back to the indoor rehearsal space, where the ballet dancers warm up silently. The women are all in pink leotards and chiffon wrap skirts, their hair pulled back in low buns. The men wear tights and identical sleeveless white shirts. Another cut returns the film's audience to the dark outdoor space of the streets. No two dancers' outfits match. While the group inside the rehearsal room is primarily white, with a couple of black dancers, the group outside on the pavement is composed largely of persons of colour, with one or two white dancers mixed in.[3] Petey Pablo's 'Show Me The Money' begins to play over the scene. The song continues as the camera cuts back and forth between the school and the streets. The hip hop beat of Pablo's piece is infused with heavy, staccato string sounds, which lend a classical feel to the music. The ballet dancers' precise, synchronized movements in the indoor space of the rehearsal room echo that classical feel. On the other hand, the movements of the hip hop dancers do not line up precisely, nor are they intended to, as hip hop is a style of dance often much more extemporaneous than ballet.

This initial juxtaposition establishes a dichotomy between the school and the streets that gives meaning to the entire film. The dichotomy puts distinctions of race, class, style and sound at the centre not only of *Step Up* but also of its sequel *Step Up 2: The Streets* (Jon M. Chu, 2008). The first instalment of the series, *Step Up*, depicts the story of Tyler Gage (Channing Tatum), a teenager growing up in a turbulent foster home in a working-class neighbourhood of Baltimore, Maryland. Tyler's natural aptitude for hip hop dance sets him apart from his peers at local urban parties, but he is unmotivated to make further use of his talents. That all changes one night when a careless act of vandalism lands Tyler community-service hours cleaning the prestigious Maryland School of the Arts (MSA), a fictional Baltimore high school where young people train for professions in the performing arts. Through interactions with an MSA student named Nora Clark (Jenna Dewan Tatum), who becomes Tyler's dance partner and romantic interest, Tyler ultimately gains admission to MSA and training and validation as a dancer.

Where *Step Up* is about one dancer's journey from the streets to the school, the second film in the series, *Step Up 2: The Streets*, narrates a reverse journey. In the wake of her single mother's untimely death, Andie West (Briana Evigan), a neighbourhood acquaintance of Tyler, has lost much of her will to succeed. Like Tyler, though, Andie maintains her ability to dance. At Tyler's urging, Andie auditions for a spot at MSA. Bored of her ballet training in the dance programme there, she teams up with standout student Chase Collins (Robert Hoffman) to put together a hip hop crew of MSA students that will compete at a neighbourhood dance-off called 'The Streets'. Taken together, *Step Up* and *Step Up 2: The Streets* tell a story of social mobility through dance, amidst the urban decline of early twenty-first-century Baltimore. In their narratives, the *Step Up* filmmakers represent 'the streets' – the poor and working-class neighbourhoods of Baltimore and the hip hop dance competition held there – as noisy and chaotic. The school, on the other hand, is a space of classical learning, characterized by order and discipline and, above all, silence.

The purpose of this chapter is to illustrate relationships between race and social mobility in the early twenty-first-century urban United States of America, by examining how those two phenomena operate in the cinematic narratives of the popular hip hop dance films *Step Up* and *Step Up 2: The Streets*. Within those narratives, we analyse visual, verbal and aural components of the films – where 'verbal' refers to the content of what characters say in monologues and dialogue, while 'aural' refers to the sounds of characters' voices, music, ambient noises, and silence. A careful analysis of those components in tandem reveals how the films instruct audiences about race and social mobility through the discourses of colourblind meritocracy. Colourblind meritocracy refers to the evaluation of individuals on the basis of the quality of their performance and decidedly not on the basis of their race. Colourblind meritocracy's overwhelming emphasis on performance and aptitude serves to elide the structural workings of privilege, which produce uneven life chances across generations, based on social identity. Simultaneously, the notions of quality and aptitude are themselves not objective but rather designed to favour the racially privileged. The discourses of colourblind meritocracy at the heart of the narrative in *Step Up* and *Step Up 2: The Streets* present a fallacious moral lesson about urban cultures of the USA – that performance and aptitude, not race, determine social mobility.

In making sense of the workings of US culture in the early twenty-first century, it is particularly meaningful to focus on hip hop given its broad importance to youth and young adult cultures of that period. As hip hop music occupied its peak share of the US music market in the first few years of the twenty-first century (Rose, 2008), the rapidly growing culture of hip hop came to represent not only the black and Latina/o urban youth in whose communities hip hop culture originated, but also white mainstream consumers who listened to hip hop music, learned hip hop dance moves, and watched hip hop videos as well.

Given the popularity of hip hop cultural productions in that period, the first decade of the twenty-first century saw a sharp rise in the number of Hollywood films made about hip hop and other forms of urban dance. The first film of the period was the interracial, hip hop/ballet romance *Save the Last Dance* (Thomas Carter, 2001), which was followed by *Honey* (Bille Woodruff, 2003), *You Got Served* (Chris Stokes, 2004) and *Roll Bounce* (Malcolm Lee, 2005) in rapid succession, before *Step Up* was released in 2006. While *Save the Last Dance* remains one of the highest grossing dance films of the last three decades in the US, *Step Up* follows closely behind and further stands out as the only hip hop dance film of the period to generate four sequels, *Step Up 2: The Streets*, *Step Up 3D* (2010), *Step Up Revolution* (2012) and most recently *Step Up: All In* (2014), all with major box office releases (http://boxofficemojo.com/genres/chart/?id=dance.htm; accessed 26 January 2011).

Like others in the genre, the *Step Up* films present narratives about hip hop dance uniting young people across divides of race, class and place. Furthermore, the genre is characterized by plot elements validating hip hop dance as a form of expression that can discipline uncontrolled or unproductive individuals, and make them contributing members of their communities. However the *Step Up* narrative is distinct for two main reasons. First, where other hip hop dance films take place in a single segregated place, the narratives of *Step Up* and *Step Up 2* rely heavily on the geographical dichotomy of the school and the streets.[4] Second, and most notably, the *Step Up* films are the only ones in the genre that do not focus primarily on young persons of colour. Instead, they depict white, working-class protagonists with unusual aptitude for hip hop dance.

The success of the *Step Up* series, compared to other hip hop dance films, makes *Step Up* and *Step Up 2: The Streets* a particularly effective entry point for understanding which narratives of class and race most resonated with consumers of popular culture in the early twenty-first-century US. Tyler and Andie's whiteness is a standout feature in a genre dominated by protagonists of colour. Cultural critic Tricia Rose argues,

> The rise in rap/hip hop was driven primarily by the sale of images and stories of black ghetto life to white youth ... Indeed, between 1995 and 2001, whites comprised 70–75 percent of the hip hop customer base – a figure considered to have remained broadly constant to this day. (2008: 4)

Such a trend would seem to explain the commercial success of *Step Up* and *Step Up 2: The Streets*. As a combined narrative, the films present white protagonists, with whom a primarily white audience might identify, and accompanying depictions of 'black ghetto life'. Those are the two elements at the heart of the racialized dichotomy of the school and the streets, on which the narrative rests.

One key aspect of that dichotomy is the racialization of order and discipline at MSA as characteristics associated with whiteness. By 'whiteness', we do not refer merely to the racial designation of European-descended people. Rather, whiteness is a normative position within a system of racialized privilege. That system controls dominant values by associating positive qualities with whiteness and, in turn, representing qualities that have come to be associated with whiteness as positive. Whiteness is an unmarked category against which racial difference is constructed and judged in dichotomous terms of normal and aberrant. Whiteness is a lived and embodied set of social privileges *and* systematic institutional benefits, legitimated through its invisibility in discourse (Kobayashi and Peake, 2000; Lipsitz, 1998). In *Step Up* and *Step Up 2: The Streets*, the association of white characters with proper cultural values serves to justify those characters' access to resources, such as schools, employment, and subsequently, wealth accumulation. The narrative arc and moral transformation of the white protagonists rely upon "whiteness as the positive universal versus blackness as the negative particular" (Dyson, 2004: 108). The choices that the white protagonists make in *Step Up* and *Step Up 2: The Streets*, and subsequently how the audience evaluates those choices, have everything to do with not being black. On-screen, whiteness is a standpoint, a position of normalcy and moral superiority against which blackness is measured and stigmatized.

Both films suggest that their white characters can achieve social mobility if they simply commit to reforming their bad attitudes and eradicate the behaviours they developed while growing up amongst working-class persons of colour. This explanation, consistent with what Rose terms 'hyper-behaviouralism', (2008: 7–8) stands in for interrogations of how race and class operate structurally in creating unequal access to economic capital and political power within urban spaces. The effects of such a view go beyond mere substitution of one suggestion for another equivalent one, however:

> This hyper-behavioralism – an approach that overemphasizes individual action and underestimates the impact of institutionalized forms of racial and class discrimination – feeds the very systematic discrimination it pretends isn't a factor at all. (Ibid.)

The insidiousness of a hyper-behaviouralist approach lies not only in its racist caricatures of persons of colour as underachievers but also, and perhaps most importantly, in its obscuring of whiteness as, what sociologist George Lipsitz calls "an organizing principle in social and cultural relations" (Lipsitz, 1998: 1).

In the first two *Step Up* films, visual, verbal and aural elements of the narrative operate in relation to each other to obfuscate the structural workings of whiteness. *Step Up* visually and verbally represents camaraderie across a racialized binary that includes white Tyler and his black neighbourhood friends. Their friendship, coupled with Tyler's personal trajectory and achievements, suggests that the black characters would be as socially mobile as the white protagonist if only they would reform their own attitudes towards education, training and work. *Step Up 2: The Streets* appears to go beyond a black-white binary in its depictions of racially diverse dance crews in both the school and the streets. This multiculturalist take on urban social relations further lends credence to the notion that protagonist Andie's whiteness is irrelevant to her ultimate success.

In the *Step Up* series of films, sound serves to establish distinctions between white and nonwhite, and between the school and the streets. Michel Chion uses the term 'added value' to indicate the ways in which sound "enriches a given image so as to create the definite impression ... that this information or expression 'naturally' comes from what is seen, and is already contained in the image itself" (Chion, 1994: 5). In the case of the *Step Up* films, added value gives racialized meaning to the school, representing white bodies as though they 'naturally' produced discipline, training and silence. The aural contrast between the school and the streets creates a 'common-sense' backdrop for white protagonists Tyler and Andie's social mobility and the concurrent underachievement of friends of colour back home in their urban neighbourhoods. The sounds of glass breaking, punches landing and rap music blaring signal a lack of discipline, structure and productivity on the part of the neighbourhoods' primarily black and Latina/o residents, which ultimately leads to their lack of social mobility. In all of this, whiteness is hidden, so that Tyler and Andie appear to achieve solely by means of fortuitous happenstance and their own hard work.

By applying theories of race and added value to our analysis, we situate the films' interrelated narratives of sound, space and behaviour in a wider discursive context. The films' aural representations of racially differentiated bodies and spaces align with extant discourses about black noise as an example of 'cultural dysfunction'.[5] Such discourses allege that disorder and underachievement proceed 'naturally' from the bodies, behaviours and cultures of persons of colour. Our contribution to the scholarship on notions such as 'cultural dysfunction' and 'hyper-behavourialism' is to apply theories of sound in film to highlight how such notions are naturalized through sensory depictions that activate audiences' 'common-sense' understandings of a social world organized by invisible whiteness. Our contribution to scholarship on sound in film is to expand upon analyses of the relationship between the aural and the visual, by examining how added value takes on a complex racialized dimension in contemporary hip hop dance films. In what follows, we mobilize hip hop studies, African American cultural criticism and theories of sound in film, as lenses through which to read *Step Up* and *Step Up 2: The Streets*. We argue that the films use added value through sound to tell meritocratic stories of Tyler and Andie's transformation from illicit street dancers to disciplined students at MSA. We focus on the interplay between diegetic sounds or sounds that exist in the world depicted by the film, and non-diegetic sounds or sounds that the audience hears but the characters in the film do not. Through diegetic sounds of disorder, *Step Up* and *Step Up 2: The Streets* suggest that the underachievement of blacks and Latina/os who occupy segregated urban neighbourhoods is a 'natural' consequence of negative cultural attitudes and lack of personal responsibility. At the same time, the filmmakers demonstrate a preference for non-diegetic sounds, and underlying diegetic silence, in the predominantly white spaces of MSA.

The juxtaposition of the school and the streets thus reinforces the invisibility of whiteness by rendering structures of power and the workings of class and race privilege undetectable. Through its use of white protagonists as hip hop street dancers, the *Step Up* series presents the working-class, white, dancing bodies as unique in their ability to bridge the school and the streets. Their authenticity in both places represents all urban spaces (schools and neighbourhoods) as freely accessible to the city's inhabitants regardless of race and class. However, close analysis of the bifurcated soundscape of the school and the streets reveals how the use of sound enables whiteness, and its foundational impact on inequalities of class and race, to go unmarked in the films' narratives of social mobility.

The School

The first instalment of the series, *Step Up*, establishes the school and the streets as diametrically opposed spaces. The film depicts a story of personal triumph, as white, working-class teenager Tyler Gage dissociates himself from the self-destructive behaviours of the streets to become a scholarship student at the prestigious MSA. The sonic representations of Tyler's disorderly home neighbourhood contrast with the training and work ethic instilled in students at MSA. The notion of merit, on which Tyler's character development rests, operates in tandem with the cultural dysfunction overtly associated in the film with the black individuals amongst whom Tyler originally lives. That resulting narrative suggests that personal responsibility, rather than racialized privileges and inequities of power, allows Tyler to access the benefits of the school.

By showing Baltimore's poor and working-class neighbourhoods as populated by both white and black people, the film seems to debunk stereotypical imaginings of urban place and culture in the US. The story of foster child Tyler portrays poverty as knowing no colour lines: his foster family includes a black foster brother, a white foster sister and two white foster parents who live amongst black residents of dilapidated row houses. The residential mixing of differently racialized people in 'unexpected places' – a black son in a white foster family, a white family in a poor and working-class urban neighbourhood, and Tyler, a white hip hop dancer at an all-black party – destabilizes the audience's sense of race and reality.

However, the film nonetheless instantiates strict, 'common-sense' boundaries of race, culture and place. It does so through a sonic economy of meanings based on the racialized portrayals of the black streets and the white school as tightly contained places of disorder and discipline, respectively. Tyler is the only nonblack person at the local parties, and he and other members of his foster family are the only nonblack individuals who appear in their neighbourhood. In the film, Tyler's white racial identity goes unmentioned by his black peers in the neighbourhood, affirming the portrayal that conditions of urban life are purely based on cultural attitudes, rather than on racial privilege and the historical relationship between whiteness and wealth within the US.

The diegetic sounds of black space, emitted by characters themselves or as music played in the scene, reproduce the racialized distinctions that the film initially appears to critique. In *Step Up*, dancing exists as part of the everyday corporeal grammar that delineates 'appropriate' behaviour in distinct spaces. From the initial juxtaposition of dancers at the school and in the streets in the opening credits, the interplay between bodily movement and sound establishes how spaces should be understood and differentiated racially. Throughout *Step Up*, that interplay articulates the school and the streets as distinct spaces of racialized behaviour. When Tyler appears with his black friends, Mac (Damain Radcliff) and Mac's little brother Skinny (De'Shawn Washington), they are typically shown at leisure – going to parties, watching television or playing basketball. When they are engaged in any kind of labour, it is illicit work such as stealing cars for Omar, a local black thug played by hip hop artist Heavy D (see Figure 1). The film represents working-class white and black characters in 'the streets' as cultural equals, lacking the proper personal responsibility and cultural attitudes towards work that would help them improve their life chances.

The narrative of urban dysfunction begins in the first scene, in which Tyler, Mac and Skinny attend a party where everyone except Tyler appears to be black. Rap music blares throughout the row house as Tyler is shown dancing with a young woman. A nameless man approaches Tyler, pushing him away as he asks why Tyler is dancing with the man's girlfriend. When Tyler retorts that the young woman was clearly interested in him, a fight ensues between the two men. Sounds of punching and furniture crashing are audible over the loud conversations and hip hop music at the party. When Tyler's opponent pulls out a gun, Tyler, Mac and Skinny run out of the house, laughing about the altercation that just ensued.

Figure 1: Mac, his younger brother Skinny, and *Step Up* protagonist Tyler Gage walk leisurely through the streets of Baltimore, on their way to play basketball. The boys earned the money that Mac and Skinny hold by stealing cars for Omar, a neighbourhood thug played by hip hop artist Heavy D.

From the beginning, diegetic sounds produce a discursive relationship between rap music and cultural dysfunction in the form of masculine violence. That very relationship between black music and violence, cultural critic Robin D. G. Kelley notes, is a typical feature of misreadings and misrepresentations of the oral cultures of the black 'underclass' (Kelley, 1998). Rap music figures prominently in the scene as a natural part of the black neighbourhood and thus adds racialized value to the violence that ensues. Even with the rap music playing in the background, the sounds of fighting and crashing furniture are audible to the film's audience. The audience is made to understand this confluence of sonic and visual meanings of disorder to be 'reality' given extant discursive associations between cultural dysfunction and hip hop music. In the specific case of *Step Up*, Tyler's hip hop dancing body also figures into this portrayal of a chaotic, black, urban neighbourhood. As the catalyst for a violent altercation, his dance with the young woman is portrayed as irresponsible behaviour, and the convergence of sound and bodily motion is evocative of that.

Tyler's movement into an upper-middle-class white identity is facilitated, ironically, by his illicit act of bringing the disorderly behaviour of the streets into the school. The inciting moment of the plot of *Step Up* takes place when 'the streets' – represented by Tyler, Mac and Skinny – penetrate the school, as a can that Tyler throws at Skinny misses its target and goes through an MSA window instead. The sounds of their taunts and laughter, of cans and other rubbish hitting the ground, and, ultimately, of glass shattering as the can breaks the window exemplify the noise and disorder of the streets. With the barrier between the school and the streets literally fractured, Tyler, Mac and Skinny decide to go in after the can. When the three enter the school, it is silent. The only noise there is what Tyler, Mac and Skinny produce: their dialogue, their laughter, their lampoons of what they presume the space is typically used for. "Yo, we ain't got nothing like this in our school", Mac says, as he, Tyler and Skinny walk into the school's theatre; and Skinny responds, "That's because our school's broke". The difference in socioeconomic status between the school that the boys attend and the one in which they are standing becomes rationale for what follows. Skinny accidentally bumps into a prop, and just as they hear the sound of the ceramic crashing onto the stage, Mac sweeps by wearing a cape, wig and beard he has taken from a nearby costume rack. "Don't worry Skinny", he says in a deep affected baritone. "These rich kids can afford this". Then he begins to break other items on the stage, now intentionally.

Tyler, Mac and Skinny's vandalism of the theatre visually reproduces 'the streets' inside the school. This scene is dimly lit in cool tones and therefore recalls the opening shots of the dancers in the street. As Tyler, Mac and Skinny trash the theatre, they turn props and set dressings into rubbish, like the can originally aimed at Skinny that shattered the school window. The sounds of items breaking as they fall to the stage, and of the three boys sword fighting, jumping, and tapping on a nearby set of timpani drums, echo the noise and disorder of 'the streets' out of which the boys entered the school. That noise and disorder, so foreign to what is typical of the school, brings a security guard running into the theatre. The security guard initially grabs hold of Mac, but as the two struggle onstage, Tyler jumps into the security guard's grasp, displacing Mac and allowing him to run away.

The motion of Tyler substituting his white, working-class body in place of Mac's black, working-class body sets up the plot of the rest of the film, and indeed, of *Step Up 2: The Streets* as well. Tyler is ultimately the one apprehended, the one punished, and the one whose punishment – 250 hours of community service cleaning the MSA building he had vandalized – gains him access to the resources of the school. There is no mention in the film at all of Tyler being white, nor of the role that his whiteness plays in his ability to transition from janitor to student at a predominantly white school. Such choices illustrate Lipsitz's argument that, "as the unmarked category against which difference is constructed, whiteness never has to speak its name" (Lipsitz, 1995: 369). Instead, the MSA director's decision to take Tyler on as a student is depicted as a natural response to Tyler's outstanding hip hop dance abilities. And his resultant social mobility is depicted as proceeding solely from changes in Tyler's cultural attitudes and in his approach to his own education, not from privileges afforded to him by whiteness.

Just as whiteness is unmarked race, so silence is unmarked sound, especially when set against the audible and visible representations of black, urban disorder that appear in *Step Up*. As Tyler makes the journey each day from the streets to the school, the diegetic sounds that accompany the disorder of black urban space give way to the cinematic silence of MSA. Silence, in this case, does not mean the school's classrooms are devoid of sounds entirely. Instead, as Chion argues:

> The impression of silence in a film scene does not simply come from an absence of noise. It can only be produced as a result of context and preparation. The simplest of cases consists in preceding it with a noise-filled sequence. So silence is never a neutral emptiness. It is the negative sound we've heard beforehand or imagined; it is the product of a contrast. (Chion, 1994: 5)

In *Step Up*, the silences of the school are presented as such, primarily by contrast with the noise of the streets. Various scenes cut quickly from a loud moment on the streets to a quiet one at the school, repeating the kind of juxtaposition that opens the film. In addition, as Chion suggests, subtle noises can create the impression of silence. When the film's audience can hear the light tap of pointe shoes as ballet dancers walk across a wooden floor, it produces the sense that the space is otherwise so soundless; a noise that would usually be subsumed by music or conversation is the most audible sound in the room (Chion, 1994: 57). A third way in which the *Step Up* filmmakers produce a sense of silence in the MSA scenes is through the use of non-diegetic sound. As is typical of the hip hop dance film genre, hip hop and rhythm and blues (R&B) music accompany the characters as they dance. What is notable in *Step Up*, though, is that when characters dance in the rehearsal spaces of MSA, the music they dance to is non-diegetic, thus maintaining the impression that those spaces are silent within the world of the film.

Through the interplay of diegetic and non-diegetic sound, and of noise and silence, the film centres Tyler's transition from a disorderly body to a disciplined body. Representations of Tyler's time at the school – first as a janitor and later as the dance partner of white, upper-middle-class star student Nora – are offset by the disorderly sounds of 'the streets' he leaves each day to go to MSA. In that transformation, his dance partner, the director of MSA and the criminal 'justice' system all enable Tyler to understand the benefits of personal responsibility. The narrative of Tyler's social mobility relies on sound, which produces added value to the film's depictions of race and class. The diegetic and non-diegetic sounds give meaning to the visual narrative, marking the school as upper-middle class and 'the streets' as working-class and poor, and creating the sense that white persons naturally belong in the former space and persons of colour in the latter. Sound frames Tyler's white body as racially unmarked, based on the kinds of behaviours – danced, and otherwise – that he is trained to undertake.

At a particular turning point in the film, hyper-behaviouralism manifests when Tyler suggests to Mac that their cultural attitudes towards work are holding them and, presumably their community, back. Tyler, Mac and Skinny are all watching a basketball game on television at Mac and Skinny's house, the night after Tyler failed to show up for a dance rehearsal with Nora. Though slated to be Nora's partner in her senior showcase performance, Tyler has decided he no longer wants to participate. Still torn between his obligations to Nora and his identification with the lifestyle in which he grew up, Tyler turns to Mac, who is criticizing a basketball game being aired on television. Tyler asks Mac why he never tried out for a basketball team and Mac responds:

> *Mac:* Look, look! Weak crossover.
> *Tyler:* Yeah, you think you're as good as these guys?
> *Mac:* Please.
> *Tyler:* Why don't you try out?
> *Mac:* For the And1 team?

> *Tyler:* Mm-hm.
> *Mac:* Why would I need to do that for?
> *Tyler:* I don't know; I always thought you should play for the school team.
> *Mac:* The school team? Yeah, right. They suck. Never.
> *Tyler:* Maybe they wouldn't suck if you played.
> *Mac:* Man, what, is this part of your community service? What you gonna say next? 'This is your brain on drugs'? Man, forget with that.
> *Tyler:* I'm just sayin'...
> *Mac:* All right, man. Just drop it. Don't see you out tryin' to do nothin'. You quit everything you start, and you know it. (*Step Up*, 2006)

In this verbal exchange between Mac and Tyler, the two characters appear to have equivalent attitudes towards productivity. At first, Tyler's suggestions that Mac use his basketball skills productively as a member of a team are met with Mac's resistance to those suggestions, making Tyler appear to be more motivated than Mac. Mac's final line of the scene, though – placed at a moment in the film when audiences have just witnessed Tyler's decision not to fulfil his commitment to Nora – serve as a reminder that Tyler, too, is resistant to using his skills productively as a member of a team. Neither of them, it would appear, is "out tryin' to do nothin'".

Certain visual elements of the scene reinforce Tyler and Mac's similarity and the parity of their cultural attitudes as well. They sit side-by-side on a sofa facing the television. They are dressed similarly, each with oversized, short-sleeved t-shirts that are layered over light, neutral-coloured long-sleeved t-shirts and baggy jeans. Even their haircuts look alike, with their hair trimmed short and their hairlines shaped in similar ways. The verbal and visual likenesses give hyper-behaviouralist meaning to this moment in the film. The two characters appear to start from a similar position and therefore are represented as having the same opportunity to take advantage of their talents. Two scenes later, though, Tyler chooses to return to rehearsals with Nora at MSA, a decision that leads to him earning official admission and a scholarship to MSA.

The exchange between Tyler and Mac relies on a denial of racialized privilege by shrouding that privilege in the language of merit – who does and does not deserve opportunities based on individual work ethic. Tyler's entrance into MSA, ultimately in a productive capacity, enables the film's discourse of social mobility by way of personal responsibility, while Mac and Skinny's continued problems in the streets seem to result from their own inherent lack of motivation.

Further, visual cues operate together with the aural elements of the scene to enforce a hyper-behaviouralist reading. The visible presence in the setting of black characters Mac and Skinny, and earlier in the scene of their black mother as well, remind the audience that despite white character Tyler's presence, this is a black home. The noises from the basketball game and the crinkling of a packet of corn chips that Tyler has just handed to Skinny give added value to the association between leisure and this black space. In other words, by way of sound, the leisure is racialized as black, just as by way of the visibility of the black characters, the space is racialized in the same way.

Though Tyler's whiteness goes unmentioned in the scene, as it does throughout the film, subsequent scenes depicting Tyler's return to predominantly-white MSA as Nora's dance partner associate him visually and aurally with whiteness, just as he disassociates himself from Mac's cultural attitudes. To prove his trustworthiness and his commitment to being Nora's partner, Tyler is shown in a children's ballet class that Nora is teaching, where – unlike in Mac and Skinny's home – everyone present appears to be white. The only noises there are the sounds of productivity: Nora's didactic voice, the tinkling piano music that guides the tempo of the dancers' movements, and the shushing coming from the young dancer in front of Tyler who takes it upon herself to police his behaviour and uphold the relative silence of MSA. Just as the space of Mac and Skinny's home and the leisure enacted there were racialized as black, the space of MSA and the work conducted there are racialized as white, a socioeconomic and cultural reality that facilitates Tyler's belonging at the school and his access, and to the social mobility his education there provides.

The transitional moment when Tyler, sitting on Mac and Skinny's sofa, changes his mind and decides again to be Nora's dance partner is pivotal. As the camera zooms in on his contemplative expression, and Mac and Skinny are pushed outside the frame, Tyler is represented as an exception: as a young, white man from 'the streets', it is as though he alone in that community comprehends why personal responsibility matters. And as his body is disciplined through classes and rehearsals with Nora, his ability to be authentic as a trained dancer at the school is represented as exceptional as well.

The final scene of *Step Up* emphasizes the film's hyper-behaviouralist narrative of meritocracy, again, by essentializing white identities as capable and therefore deserving of opportunities for advancement. The scene is the quintessential dance movie climax: a big production number, wherein the dancers display what they have been learning throughout the narrative for audiences both within and watching the film. The scene takes place in the very auditorium that Tyler, Mac and Skinny trashed at the beginning of the film, marking the restored space again as the gateway for Tyler between the streets and the school. The plot device to showcase the dancers' talents is, in this case, just that: a showcase – an annual event at MSA in which graduating seniors perform for the public in hopes that recruiters in attendance will choose the dancers to audition for reputable professional companies.

Though it is ostensibly Nora's career on the line, it is Tyler whose dancing is highlighted primarily in the showcase scene. The combination of music, dance, lighting, scenery and audience serves as a backdrop for Tyler to prove his merit. To open the dance sequence, music student Miles (Mario) – a black character whom viewers learned earlier in the film grew up in the McCullough Homes housing project where Mac and Skinny currently live – drops a beat on a computer. It is quickly revealed, though, that Miles will simultaneously be conducting a full orchestra, which provides the music for Tyler and Nora's dance. Miles's mixing of hip hop music and classical symphonic conducting at the school showcase produces the hybridized musical sounds that parallel symbolically his social mobility from his origins in the Baltimore projects to being a legitimate student at MSA (see Figure 2). Yet Miles is not the focus of the scene, nor has the audience learned much about his background during the film. Quickly the camera pans up from Miles's position in the orchestra pit to the dance action on the stage above. There, the scenic backdrop, depicting tall windows topped with half-circle arches, recalls the dance rehearsal room, the space that has come to stand in for the school throughout the film. On

Figure 2: Miles, played by R&B singer Mario, conducts an orchestra of MSA students during the dance showcase at the end of *Step Up*. He uses the DJ equipment in front of him to produce a mash-up of hip hop and classical sounds, which mirrors the hybridized choreography Tyler and Nora perform onstage.

the other hand, the stage is lit in red and blue tones, not unlike the hip hop dance scene on the pavement with the chain-link fence that appeared in the film's opening juxtaposition. Combined with the diegetic sounds of music that is at once hip hop and classical – which also function non-diegetically for the audience watching the film – sound and image enable a reading of Tyler's performance as an achievement of personal responsibility. The streets must visually and sonically be present to mark the narrative not as one of whiteness but rather as a story of merit – that anyone, no matter the background, can achieve social mobility in the same fashion as Tyler.

At the end of the scene, Mac greets Tyler backstage, offering congratulations for his performance. Tyler responds to Mac saying, "C'mon, man. You seen me dance before", and Mac, genuinely impressed, responds, "Yea, but not like that. I never saw you dance like that". Pointing to Nora to indicate the person responsible for the change in his dancing, Tyler says to Mac, "Well, that's her". Indeed, it is primarily through Nora's efforts – her instruction during the pair's afterschool practices and in the youth ballet classes she compelled Tyler to attend – that Tyler's body has been disciplined in a manner observable by the director of the school and suitable to effect Tyler's belonging at MSA. The school's director, herself a white woman, further legitimates Tyler by introducing him to a curious dance recruiter as a new MSA student. Thus the director not only solidifies Tyler's position in the MSA student body, but she also solidifies the position of Tyler's dancing body itself in the white upper-middle- and upper-classes represented by the school itself.

The visual and aural portrayals of Tyler's white body as a realization of both the school and 'the streets' reaffirm essentialist notions of racialized difference. In spite of being from the same neighbourhoods as black characters, Tyler's recognition of the opportunities for him at MSA, juxtaposed against his black friend Mac's indifference to his own situation, secures the hyper-behaviouralist idea that whites and blacks have different cultural attitudes and priorities that individually and collectively affect their relationships to productivity and thus their potential for social mobility. *Step Up* portrays Tyler's body as visually and aurally authentic in both the school and 'the streets'. That dual authenticity instantiates meritocracy through and against the existing discourses of black sounds. By way of added racial value, the *Step Up* filmmakers create the illusion that there is a 'natural' or 'common-sense' association between the black characters in the film and the leisure, disorder and lack of discipline in which they are depicted as living. At the same time, there appears to be a 'natural' or 'common-sense' association between white Tyler and his socially mobile trajectory.

However, a close analysis of the relationship among the visual, verbal and aural elements of the film reveals that it is not just Tyler's personal attitude but in fact white privilege that facilitates both his authenticity and his social mobility. White privilege acts as a foundational structure of the social worlds of both the film's characters and its audiences. This racialized privilege organizes those worlds in such a way as to align whiteness with opportunities for advancement, like those provided by Nora and the MSA director to Tyler but not to black dancers with similar aptitude. Additionally, whiteness operating in a capitalist framework privileges certain markers of merit, such as enrolment in a predominantly white private institution like MSA, over others, like beating neighbourhood contenders in a street basketball game. Thus the behaviours labelled as 'cultural dysfunction' are racially stigmatized, in contrast to those behaviours that are aligned with whiteness and labelled as 'success'.

'The Streets'

The sequel to *Step Up* furthers the hyper-behaviouralist narrative of the series, drawing 'common-sense' connections between race and success while masking the workings of whiteness. *Step Up 2: The Streets* closely reproduces the storyline and moral argument of *Step Up*. The portrayals of racialized space in the sequel follow the dichotomy established in the first film between discipline and chaos, and whiteness and blackness, respectively. The MSA is again depicted as a place with a white director, a predominantly white student population, and a white star student, Chase (Robert Hoffman), who facilitates white protagonist Andie's entry into the space of order, discipline and productivity through dance. The sounds of MSA, juxtaposed against 'the streets', again add racialized value to the visual and verbal narrative of white achievement and black cultural dysfunction. The first film achieves that dichotomous contrast and its arguments about colourblind meritocracy through a racialized binary, wherein all characters are either white or black. The second film, on the other hand, argues for colourblind meritocracy by depicting a multiculturalist vision of a racially diverse urban landscape. In *Step Up 2: The Streets*, the hallmarks of multicultural ideology – mutual recognition of ethnic cultural difference or the rhetoric of sameness based on the notion that everyone has 'ethnic cultures' – are conspicuously absent. Instead, multiculturalism exists in a shallow, visual depiction of white, black, Latina/o and Asian bodies dancing together in a single MSA Crew, against the protestations of black characters in 'the streets' who would seem to prefer that the city and its youth cultures remain segregated by race and class (see Figure 3).

Figure 3: Members of the MSA Crew walk, smiling, through the streets of Baltimore after a dance rehearsal. A multiracial crew, the small group of students creates an illusion of racial and ethnic diversity at mostly-white MSA.

In *Step Up 2: The Streets*, the white protagonist Andie again lives in an urban neighbourhood in Baltimore, where she appears as the racial exception given that her guardian is black and the leaders of the 410 Crew, which Andie identifies as a sort of surrogate family, are black as well. When Andie ultimately makes her way to MSA, she is disowned by Tuck (Black Thomas) and Felicia (Telisha Shaw), the leaders of the 410, who reject Andie's social mobility as a betrayal. As Andie and Chase build a racially diverse crew of MSA students to participate in a hip hop dance competition called 'The Streets', the filmmakers construct a racialized debate about the 'ownership' of hip hop. On one side of the debate are the 'self-segregationist' tendencies of Tuck and Felicia, who reject any dancers associated with the school. On the other side are the apparently colourblind, meritocratic efforts of Andie and Chase, who assert that hip hop belongs to whomever is best at it and cares about it the most. Through the depiction of a successful, racially diverse hip hop dance crew, and the subtle demonization of the most vocal of the black characters in the film, the filmmakers align themselves – and in turn the film's audience – with a colourblind, meritocratic vision of hip hop.

By representing the white-led MSA Crew as authentic in both the school and 'the streets', and the black-led 410 Crew as ultimately untenable in either space, *Step Up 2: The Streets* makes the hyper-behaviouralist assertion that the self-segregationist attitudes of poor and working-class hip hop dancers limit those characters' mobility, legitimacy and success. In this second film, the presence of dancers of various racialized backgrounds in the MSA Crew even further obscures the role that whiteness plays in social and geographical mobility. It is not only the white protagonist Andie who can be authentic in multiple spaces in the urban setting of Baltimore, the film suggests; it is her entire multicultural crew. The diegetic sounds of anger and violence emitted by the 410 Crew and its black leaders add racialized value to that narrative. The tones of those characters' voices, and the noises of their disorderly behaviour, create the illusion that black cultural dysfunction and self-segregation keep individuals like Tuck and Felicia from having the freedom of movement through urban space that Andie and her MSA Crew enjoy. In reality, though, the same race and class privilege that undergirds the story of Tyler Gage's social mobility, and adheres to institutions like MSA, gives the MSA Crew and its white leadership the power to access the resources of the school at the same time that they can dominate the competition in 'The Streets'.

From the first scene, *Step Up 2: The Streets* offers a revision of hip hop culture's origins, wherein white characters like Andie fit authentically on the basis of their merits in hip hop dance. In the opening sequence of the film, archival footage, diegetic silence and non-diegetic narration operate in tandem to create the sense that the film's narrative of urban social mobility and colourblind meritocracy is part of actual hip hop history. Following the opening titles, the first image visible to the film's audience is footage of breakdancing competitions and exhibitions, featuring the legendary Rock Steady Crew – a hip hop dance group of black and Latino men that originated in the Bronx, New York in the late 1970s. The footage has been stripped of diegetic sound, leaving aural space for an alternative history to be superimposed on the images. The only thing the audience hears as the film opens is non-diegetic sound. A light orchestration of a single piano with violins and timpani drums lends a solemn feel to the voice of Andie, who recounts a history of The Streets dance competition. The non-diegetic narration provides a fictional account that recasts the audience's understanding of what appears on-screen:

> I remember the first time I saw someone move like they were from another planet. I couldn't keep my eyes away. I was little; my mom took me to watch a jam session in the neighbourhood. (*Step Up 2: The Streets*, 2008)

Andie's narration aligns with the images on-screen such that it appears as though the jam session of which she speaks is the one in which the Rock Steady Crew appears. The silencing of the archival footage means that the first sound the film's audience hears is Andie's voice speaking the personal pronoun "I", which links the white protagonist to the visual depictions of hip hop dance. The past-referential phrases "I remember" and "I was little" further serve to collapse her personal history of childhood with the history depicted in the footage. The effect of making Andie's fictional story seem as though it were a part of a nonfictional history is produced by the interplay of verbal and visual elements. The aural composition of the scene adds value, creating a sense of reality that lends credence to the meritocratic bent of the narrator's words:

> Soon some of the best dancers around were showing up to compete in something they eventually called 'The Streets'. It became a hub, and I got a front row seat to history. I wanted to glide and spin and fly like they did, but it didn't come easy. My mom would tell me, 'Don't give up. Just be you. 'Cause life's too short to be anybody else'. (*Ibid.*)

The use of archival footage that is manipulated to seem even more 'historical' serves to legitimate the images and the narrative layered upon them, as authentic productions of the urban streets. The Streets dance competition, a fictional event, becomes a historical reality through the juxtaposition of the grainy footage and Andie's non-diegetic retelling of the story behind those images. The colourblind meritocracy undergirding Andie's commentary, and the film as a whole, is thus presented as a historical reality as well. The aphorism "just be you" suggests that Andie, as a white woman, 'deserves' the same access to hip hop as the dancers of colour on the screen, without having to change who she is. Thus, the meritocratic argument the filmmakers present from the beginning is that it makes sense that a young, white woman should be narrating hip hop history over images of black, Latino and Asian street dancers, because, though "it didn't come easy", she never gave up.

Andie's fictional account of The Streets serves as a moral lesson about racial segregation in urban spaces. Through the logic of colourblind meritocracy, Andie's narration frames white individuals like herself as authentic to hip hop in the same way that persons of colour can be authentic to traditionally white spaces of the city, such as private schools, as long as they apply themselves through hard work. The film's introduction represents urban cultures and spaces as having been always integrated, at least since the advent of hip hop. The voice of the white protagonist stitches together images of black, white, Latina/o and Asian bodies dancing together on the pavements of urban streets. Andie closes her narration, though, by saying, "Everything changed". Her regretful statement taken together with the representations that follow in the film, of The Streets competition where Andie and her white collaborator Chase are now unwelcome, instil in the audience the idea that segregation is irrationally self-imposed by members of minoritized communities.

Even though individuals of various racial backgrounds participated in hip hop from the time it originated, that diversity did not equate to the colour-blind meritocracy that Andie touts. In actual histories of hip hop, black and Latina/o youth created 'families of resemblance'[6] based on their spatial awareness of how race affected their experiences of political, economic and social disenfranchisement. Whereas Andie's narration, and the narrative of *Step Up 2: The Streets* at large, represents the rifts in hip hop culture that happened when "everything changed" as though they produced urban inequality, instead those involved in hip hop from its beginnings were aware of how racism and racialized social policy produced those inequalities. As journalist and music critic Jeff Chang (2005) comprehensively documents in *Can't Stop, Won't Stop: A History of the Hip-hop Generation*, the effects of white flight in urban spaces – the state-directed disappearance of high-wage manufacturing jobs and the elimination of social welfare services – disproportionately affected working-class black and Latina/o communities. In the name of 'urban renewal', the levelling of city blocks in their neighbourhoods in favour of public and privately funded development elsewhere, further reflected in the built environment what black and Latina/o youth understood as their racialized second-class status. In some instances, those youth formed collectives of break dancers, b-boys and music producers or DJs, out of a consciousness of their shared fate of institutionalized ghettoization.

For them, hip hop culture did not represent coming together as the elimination of racial difference. Rather, collective participation in hip hop, in certain cases, represented some individuals' attempts at coming together to deal directly with the realities of race and racism that manifested in black and Latina/o neighbourhoods. Andie's introduction to *Step Up 2: The Streets* creates lines of sameness through her meritocratic suggestion that anyone can have access to hip hop, and by extension to all urban space, if they just "don't give up". On the other hand Crazy Legs, a member of the b-boy group the Rock Steady Crew featured in the archival footage in that same opening sequence, draws lines of sameness between blacks and Latina/os based on shared marginalization: "[Y]ou were either Black or Puerto Rican. The bottom line is what it really comes down to. We all lived in the same ghetto. There weren't too many differences. We were all on the same welfare, and we lived in the same projects" (http://www.daveyd.com/crazylegsinterview.html; accessed 19 February 2010). Andie's narration of urban solidarity bears only a superficial resemblance to the shared race and class struggles to which Crazy Legs refers. Instead of the universal values of meritocracy, Crazy Legs favours an understanding of cultural proximity between blacks and Latina/os, produced by the structural conditions that brought those communities together, and also contained those populations within particular city streets, block parties and residential projects.

Step Up 2: The Streets' revisionist narrative of hip hop history obscures how racism operated through policies of urban development. The film's focus on legitimizing white characters as 'authentic' to hip hop, and therefore deserving of entrance to certain areas of Baltimore where hip hop dancers reside, draws attention away from how whiteness creates the conditions of spatial segregation. An early scene in the film takes place at one such segregated urban dance space The Dragon, which is desegregated by the two films' white protagonists, Andie and Tyler Gage of *Step Up*. The Dragon is an urban locale where hip hop dancers and break dancers, or b-boys, battle for the respect and acclamation of an on-looking crowd. There, Andie runs into Tyler, who encourages her to attend MSA. To combat Andie's initial resistance, Tyler suggests they have a dance-off. The wager between them sets Andie on a path of social mobility that mirrors Tyler's from *Step Up*: if Tyler wins, they agree, Andie will audition for a spot in the dance programme at MSA.

Before the two begin dancing, the film's audience learns that Tyler's time at the school has facilitated his entry into the professional dance world: he and Nora are going on tour. Nora – who never actually appears in the second film – continues to enable Tyler's social mobility and his legitimization as a trained dancer. In addition, there is another kind of legitimization from which Tyler benefits in informal urban dance spaces like The Dragon. The club is loud and raucous, with the line between dance floor and audience blurred by a crowd that consists primarily of black and Latina/o persons. Yet upon Tyler's entrance, the space grows quiets enough so that the characters at The Dragon and the film's viewing audience can hear the master of ceremonies, DJ Sand, say, "We got royalty in the house! Tyler Gage is here! Clear the dance floor!" Quickly, the crowd pushes to the perimeter of the room. Panels in the floor of the club open to reveal trampolines, and Tyler and Andie flip, jump and dance until one of Tyler's dance moves proves so impressive that the crowd's screams declare Tyler the winner of the battle and of his wager with Andie.

DJ Sand's designation of Tyler as "royalty" of Baltimore street dancing, the insistence that the dance floor clear, the compliance of the crowd, the unexpected appearance of trampolines in the floor that had not been made available to other dancers, and, above all, the sound of the crowd's cheering in response to Tyler's dance, all legitimate Tyler as an authentic presence in 'the streets', just as his tour with Nora legitimates his professionalization as a dancer. For his ability to move between the two spaces, the school and 'the streets', Tyler credits MSA. His role in the film is to facilitate Andie's access to the same range of authentic identities and the same variety of urban spaces from which he benefited. When he goes to the house of Andie's guardian, Sarah (Sonja Sohn), to convince her to let Andie audition for MSA, Tyler argues that Andie's entry into the school is "the one shot she needs to take all that anger she's got and be able to put it into a structure". In this final moment of his appearance in the film, Tyler thus passes on a lesson of the series: the need for Andie's white, working-class body to submit to "structure" or discipline, in order that she be able to function authentically in both the school and 'the streets'.

As the story unfolds in *Step Up 2: The Streets*, it is revealed that The Streets competition – originally open to anyone with the proper skills – has become, without reason, restricted to participants who learned hip hop dance outside of formal spaces of instruction. For those who control participation in the competition, the school is a place that, because of the race and class privilege with which it is associated, is not as authentic as 'the streets'. Furthermore, the organizers of this now exclusive competition have also drawn firm but imaginary boundaries across the city. The boundaries determine who is and is not allowed to enter certain neighbourhoods based on this unexplained emergence of hip hop authenticity. The seemingly arbitrary nature of urban social conflicts presented in *Step Up 2: The Streets* sutures together two otherwise unrelated phenomena: urban racial segregation and debates about hip hop authenticity. Through this suturing, *Step Up 2: The Streets* equates freedom to participate in The Streets hip hop dance competition with freedom to occupy any given space in the city. By doing so, the film obscures how race and class have been instrumental in producing institutional segregation and inequality within urban space, and substitutes, in place of that reality, a fiction of colourblind meritocracy.

Whereas colourblind meritocracy in *Step Up* is presented along a black-white binary, the sequel makes a meritocratic argument about its protagonist's success by representing even greater racial diversity in the dance crews of which she is a part. The narrative of the film operates as a multiculturalist call, which derives hyper-behaviouralist meaning in opposition to the 'self-segregating' politics of black characters in the 410 Crew. For example, Tuck and Felicia force Andie out of their group once they find out she has other obligations and aspirations at MSA. Instead of embracing her attempts to improve her life chances, the 410 Crew is repeatedly shown denouncing Andie for failing to stay loyal to the class and geographic self-segregation of the 410 Crew affiliation.

Once again, the restricting of non-diegetic sounds to the school adds value to the perception of the streets as a place of cultural dysfunction. The sonic representation of the incessant leisure of the 410 Crew – sounds of video games, television and chatter at Tuck's house – is juxtaposed against the diegetic silence and non-diegetic sound of scenes that take place at the school. The journey from leisure to quiet gives meaning to the transformation of Andie from a character who is 'of the streets', to a dancer who can perform hip hop better than her black peers because she has not only been disciplined by the school, but also has embraced colourblind meritocracy. In *Step Up 2: The Streets*, the selective visibility of Tuck and Felicia follows these logics of whiteness, which flatten histories of anti-black racism to mere cultural attitudes of personal residential preference. As is the case in *Step Up*, black characters are presented as the ones who are unwilling to desegregate and who irrationally refuse to accept the school as a place where everyone can pull themselves up by their bootstraps.

Step Up 2: The Streets utilizes the same sonic conventions of *Step Up* to facilitate the audience's understanding of white space as quiet and disciplined, and working-class, black spaces as noisy and disorderly. Aural cues instruct the film's audience to recognize productive versus non-productive behaviours and identities. When Felicia calls Andie, repeatedly, to hang out at Tuck's house during one of their crew's enforced bonding sessions, Andie is shown quietly sleeping on her bed at home on a school night, with a book opened up across her chest and her mobile phone ringing softly in the foreground. This is in stark contrast to the activities at Tuck's house where Tuck is shown playing video games amidst the raucous sounds of his crewmates' laughter and play. The juxtaposition of quiet and noise makes sense to the audience as an economy of sound that guides how we evaluate white and black spaces. The leisure of Tuck and Felicia is continuously framed by the race and class segregationist culture with that of the 410 Crew. Through added value, the filmmakers' sonic choices instruct the audience to denounce that culture as irrational, prejudiced and socioeconomically limiting.

The dichotomy of leisure and discipline justifies to the audience the workings of whiteness through visual, verbal and aural portrayals of black cultural dysfunction. Similarly, whiteness is legitimated through another dichotomy of cultural dysfunction and normative behaviour: the 410 Crew's violent and senseless protection of their turf against the MSA Crew's unconditional acceptance of difference. When Chase, the white co-leader of the MSA Crew, is shown walking home from a neighbourhood party to which the whole crew had been invited, Tuck and two other members of the 410 Crew, one black and the other Latino, accost Chase. They warn him to stay away from Andie, from The Streets competition, and from 'the streets' – their designation of the urban neighbourhoods in which upper-class white individuals like Chase do not belong:

> *Tuck:* Just 'cause you hangin' with 'D' [Andie] don't mean you got what it takes. She don't know where she came from.
> *Chase:* You don't know anything about her.

> *Tuck:* Now you defending her?
> *Chase:* Yes, I am. See you at The Streets.
> *Other black male member of 410 Crew:* At The Streets? You in the streets now! (*Step Up 2: The Streets*, 2008)

Tuck's initial line in the exchange serves as a challenge not only to Chase's authenticity but also to the system of colourblind meritocracy in which Chase, as a protagonist of the film, operates. The formulation of "Just 'cause ... don't mean", indicates Tuck's belief that Chase may think associating with Andie is enough to demonstrate the unspecified "what it takes". Tuck disagrees, however, not because spending time with Andie does not on its own provide sufficient hip hop dance skills. Instead, the positioning of the statement, "She don't know where she came from", immediately after Tuck's initial assertion, demonstrates that "what it takes" does not have to do with skill at all. Rather, the word "where" denotes place, and thus Tuck's 'self-segregationist' argument is that "what it takes" derives from location – social location as well as geographic location – not merit.

The focus on location continues as the other member of the 410 Crew turns Chase's words back on him, by conflating The Streets dance competition with 'the streets', a synecdochical reference to Baltimore's working-class and low-income neighbourhoods. The nameless black male's switch from "at The Streets", the competition, to "*in* the streets", a racialized geographic identity, substitutes the spaces of hip hop dance for the spaces of the city at large, just as the film represents segregation in hip hop as though it were formative of segregation in urban space.

Immediately following the line, "You in the streets now!" the three 410 Crew members take physical action to reproduce the segregation of 'the streets' by violently threatening Chase. Visually, the audience can see the racialized difference between the perpetrators and victim of the violence. Two black and one Latino man push white Chase up against nearby chain-link fencing and begin to pummel him. Diegetic noises of violence – punches and kicks to Chase's face and body and the sound of the fence collapsing as the three young men slam Chase against it – are the most prominent sounds of the scene. Along with those sounds, the words of the three members of the 410 Crew make the 'self-segregationist' argument that Chase, presumably because of his intersectional identity is an upper-class, white male, school-trained dancer, should not share the spaces they occupy. The sounds of violence add value to commonly held stereotypes of cultural dysfunction and self-segregation that are enacted in *Step Up 2: The Streets*. The film portrays Chase and Andie as unfairly excluded from both The Streets and 'the streets', by black and Latino men who violently police the boundaries of those spaces. The 410 Crew's verbal and physical assault on the protagonists, which is both seen and heard by the film's audience, unfavourably represents urban communities of colour as not wanting to integrate with the rest of what is perceived to be a multicultural America.

In fact, the key departure of the second *Step Up* film from the first is that *Step Up 2: The Streets*' racially diverse MSA Crew represents the benefits of hard work in a multicultural America. In stark contrast to the black cultural dysfunction of the 410 Crew, which ultimately leads to its demise at The Streets competition, the misfit MSA Crew's students of colour exude the promise of colourblind meritocracy as intrinsic to the collective good. The presence of black, Latina/o, Asian and Asian American individuals in the MSA Crew, led by white students Andie and Chase, reinforces the colourblind meritocratic rhetoric that moving beyond racial difference will naturally lead to social and economic sameness.

The film inhibits a discussion about the materiality of racial difference by further coding the MSA Crew's racial diversity as a narrative of social and school outcasts coming together. In the final scene, the MSA Crew shows up at The Streets dance competition, which is being held at an open-air warehouse. As DJ Sand cues the music for the next set of competitors, Andie intrudes on him and asks to make a plea to all present at the competition to allow the MSA Crew a chance to dance.

> The streets are supposed to be about different people coming together … We're all here because we have this thing we do; we dance … And it shouldn't matter what we wear, what school or what neighbourhood we're from. Because the best part about The Streets is that it's not about what you've got. It's what you make of what you've got. (*Step Up 2: The Streets*, 2008)

During Andie's impromptu speech, the camera cuts to Tuck and Felicia scowling at her in disapproval. By the end of Andie's plea, however, the rest of the crowd is cheering. Andie's use of the collective pronoun 'we' interpolates members of the MSA Crew, members of the 410 Crew and all those in the racially diverse crowd into a single homogenous group. She uses phrases like "We're all here because … we dance" and "it shouldn't matter" to emphasize further the group's sameness. The crowd's audible acceptance of the MSA Crew's race, class and geographic difference – just as they had done for Tyler and Andie at The Dragon earlier in the film – indicates to the film's audience that neither race nor class are organizing principles in regard to who is allowed to access different residential and educational spaces of the city.

Set against Tuck and Felicia's seemingly irrational interest in protecting their turf, the sounds of applause together with the visual array of differently racialized bodies privilege the idea that white students, and Andie in particular,

The School and 'The Streets'   103

are authentic to 'the streets'. Here it is important to note that even given the context of her statements, it is not possible to determine definitively whether she is referring to The Streets or 'the streets'. Andie's assertion that "it's what you make of what you got", immediately following the ambiguous mention of "the streets", elaborates the point that her argument about merit is not confined to performances of hip hop at the dance competition. Her argument is also, more broadly, about individual attitudes towards social mobility in the city. Andie's comments frame Tuck and Felicia's identity politics as harmfully confining the 410 Crew to 'the streets', far from the benefits of the school. With Andie restoring The Streets to the inclusive, desegregated space she presented in her opening narration, the film comes full circle. Together, sounds, sights and words lend common-sense authority to a hyper-behaviouralist narrative that valorizes Andie's position and contains the problems of The Streets/'the streets' to black cultural dysfunction.

After the onlookers give the MSA Crew approval to participate, the crowd and the crew suddenly change locations to the outside of the warehouse, shown by a mob of people exiting through an opened chain-link fence, and literally into the street. It begins to rain, and the lights that were on earlier are completely shut off. Bystanders turn their car lights on, and one person pops open the boot of his car to reveal an extensive sound system to provide music. The diegetic sound of the music, to which the MSA Crew performs, also operates non-diegetically as no other sounds can be heard from the crowd. This seeming absence of sound, typically associated with scenes set at the school, operates in this final scene to distinguish the MSA Crew from the noise that typically accompanies and defines the 410 Crew. The music also functions diegetically, through added value, to alert the film's audience that the representations and moral argument of the narrative operate in the audience's own 'real world' and not just in the film.

At the end of the performance, diegetic sounds of the crowd roaring in approval officially announce the MSA Crew as the winners to the dismay of Tuck, Felicia and the rest of the 410 Crew. New MSA headmaster Blake (Will Kemp), who has temporarily traversed the boundary between the school and 'the streets' in order to watch the MSA Crew perform, is impressed and congratulates Andie and Chase. As Blake reverses his earlier expulsion of Andie from the school and welcomes her back to MSA the following Monday, Andie's and Blake's dialogue reminds the film's audience that she will again be making the journey that lies at the heart of the *Step Up* series narrative – from 'the streets' to the school. And Tyler Gage's success, of which the viewer is made aware at the beginning of the film, is a reminder that the school can train a dancer to be marketable, to go on tour and to make money. The filmmakers of *Step Up 2: The Streets* suggest that the school can effect social mobility by disciplining the dancing body to be productive under capitalism. For the 410 Crew, this is not the case. They are of 'the streets', they claim to represent 'the streets' and therefore their brown and black bodies are limited to 'the streets'. The plot and dialogue of the film would suggest that what limits them are their own desires not to achieve, their poor attitudes towards spaces of instruction and discipline like MSA and their inability to embrace the rhetoric of colourblind meritocracy.

Andie's ultimate acceptance of what Blake, and by extension MSA, has to offer shows that she has distanced herself from the negative attitudes of 'the streets' – a euphemism for black cultural dysfunction – even as she has demonstrated herself to be authentic and successful at The Streets. Thus, The Streets operates as a metonym for the desegregation of urban space, and Andie's story operates as an allegory of how meritocracy leads to social mobility. This heavy-handed theme of merit operates through representations of white work ethic and perseverance, which leave the legacies of whiteness obscured. However, *Step Up 2: The Streets* should instead be read through a lens that centres the historical realities of how racialized urban policies have created segregated urban spaces and limited the access of minoritized communities to the most privileged of those spaces and the resources that adhere to them. Through such a lens, it comes into focus that the headmasters of MSA in both films are white characters, that those white characters control Andie and Tyler's access to the resources of a predominantly white institution, and that Tyler himself introduces white protagonist Andie to the school in the first place. From that perspective, it is clearly whiteness that undergirds the segregation of urban spaces. Therefore white privilege, not simply hard work, offers characters like Andie and Tyler the ability to move through multiple urban spaces and be accepted as authentic, and even outstanding, in them all.

Blake's validation of Andie's dancing in the final scene of *Step Up 2: The Streets* reiterates the moral argument of the *Step Up* series: merit, not privilege, leads to social mobility. The films' portrayals of Andie and Tyler as authentic, first in 'the streets' and then at the school, allows for a celebratory narrative of personal triumph based on their individual merits. Both films show their white, working-class protagonists gradually recognizing the benefits of MSA training as they distance themselves from the unproductive lifestyles they once lived in 'the streets'. For Tyler and Andie, access to the school facilitates changes in their work ethics and in their cultural attitudes towards personal responsibility. This celebratory narrative, however, relies on portrayals of black cultural dysfunction, articulated through the soundscapes of both films. The films' use of the diegetic sounds of urban space portrays underachievement as confined to the interiority of the black and brown characters who are 'of the streets'. This visual and aural representation of black cultural dysfunction, set against Tyler and Andie's apparent merit, obscures the reality that the power and privilege that structure whiteness are at the core of the white protagonists' success.

Tyler and Andie's social mobility in the film is built upon an ahistorical account of contemporary racial dynamics. This hyper-behaviouralist discourse, expressed through the interplay of aural and visual representations, signals to audiences that the conditions of urban poverty are based on black cultural dysfunction and individual attitudes towards work. The sounds of violence, vandalism and leisure seem to emanate naturally from black characters in 'the streets'. The use of diegetic sound aids the audience in making false meaning out of harmfully racialized images. Such meaning-making perpetuates discourses of cultural dysfunction that place wrongful blame on poor and working-class people of colour for their own oppression, undermine the historical specificity of black and brown expressive cultures in the US, and minimize the tremendous value of black and brown cultural productions in contemporary urban life.

Notes

1. Brian Su-Jen Chung is an Assistant Professor of Ethnic Studies at the University of Hawaii at Manoa. His current work focuses on suburban landscape design, public cultures, and Chinese global capital in the making and cultural memory of the region known as Silicon Valley.
2. Afia Ofori-Mensa is Director of Undergraduate Research and Visiting Assistant Professor of Comparative American Studies and Africana Studies at Oberlin College, Ohio. Her work engages with narratives and cultures of communities of colour in the twentieth- and twenty-first-century US. Her primary research interests are in ethnic studies, American studies, women's and gender studies, and popular culture studies. Her current book project, *How to Win a Beauty Pageant*, examines relationships among femininity, race and US national identity using beauty pageantry and princess culture as case studies. She is also a photographer; her piece 'The Winner' was exhibited at Oberlin College in 2012.
3. We use 'black' throughout this chapter rather than 'African American' to refer to the phenotypic racialization of characters in the films. Although the films we examine take place in the United States, it is not always clear in the films' narratives what the ethnic backgrounds of black-appearing characters are. Thus 'black' serves as a racial designator for persons who may be ethnically Afro-Caribbean, Afro-Latina/o or African immigrant, not necessarily African American. We use 'African American' when referring to the field of study or forms of expressive culture particular to that ethnic group. When referring to black individuals together with Latina/os, persons of Asian descent, or other non-white characters, we employ the more general term 'people of colour'.

4. Though we recognize the place of *Step Up 3D* and *Step Up Revolution* in the genealogy, these most recent *Step Up* films depart from the first two, because the third and fourth films take place in New York City and Miami, respectively, and thus erase both MSA and the streets of Baltimore from the narrative. As our argument is primarily concerned with sonic depictions of the school and the streets, and their relationships to race privilege and myths of meritocracy, we do not examine *Step Up 3D* or *Step Up Revolution* alongside the other two films in this chapter.
5. By 'cultural dysfunction', we refer to the conceptual frameworks used to justify the idea that racism no longer exists. Commonly referenced to describe the allegedly pathological lifestyles of black urban neighbourhoods, 'cultural dysfunction' as a discourse of social mobility obscures the workings of government policy and the flight of capital in creating black urban poverty. Simultaneously, these perceptions of black cultural dysfunction have been used to influence government policy and the distribution of welfare resources. Beginning in the 1980s and intensifying in the 1990s and into the first decade of the twenty-first century, right-wing political pundits have represented rap music as the unmediated voice of those black communities trapped in ghettos and perpetuating this cultural dysfunction of unbridled violence, drug abuse and welfare dependency. Scholars and cultural critics of hip hop culture point out that this belief fails to recognize historical conditions that have given rise to the limited content of rap, which include the deregulation of broadcasting corporations and the corporate restructuring of the music industry to streamline its content to that which is most profitable and most desired by its consumers. For more information on the relationship between race, consumerism and debates about black cultural dysfunction see Rose 2008, Kelley 1998 and Tanz 2007.
6. George Lipsitz invokes the term "families of resemblance" to describe how oppressed communities "seek to make alliances with other groups by cultivating the ways in which their particular experiences spoke with special authority about the idea and alienations felt by others". We draw from this term to show how racial commensurability is centred on "oppositional groups united in ideas and intensions, if not experience." See Lipsitz 1986.

References

Chang, J. (2005), *Can't Stop, Won't Stop: A History of the Hip-hop Generation*, New York: Picador Press.

Chion, M. (1994), *Audio-Vision: Sound on Screen*, translated by C. Gorbman, New York: Columbia University Press.

Dyson, M. E. (2004), *The Michael Eric Dyson Reader*, New York: Basic Civitas Books.

Kelley, R. (1998), *Yo Mama's Disfunktional!: Fighting the Culture Wars in Urban America*, New York: Beacon Press.

Kobayashi, A., and Peake, L. (2000), 'Racism out of Place: Thoughts on Whiteness and an Antiracist Geography in the New Millennium', *Annals of the Association of American Geographers*, 90(2), 392–403.

Lipsitz, G. (1986), 'Cruising around the Historical Bloc: Postmodernism and Popular Music in East Los Angeles', *Cultural Critique*, 5(2), 174–90.

Lipsitz, G. (1995), 'The Possessive Investment in Whiteness: Racialized Social Democracy and the "White" Problem in American Studies', *American Quarterly*, 47(3), 369–87.

Lipsitz, G. (1998), *The Possessive Investment in Whiteness: How White People Profit from Identity Politics*, Philadelphia: Temple University Press.

Rose, T. (2008), *The Hip Hop Wars: What We Talk about When We Talk about Hip-hop – and Why it Matters*, New York: Basic Civitas Books.

Tanz, J. (2007), *Other People's Property: A Shadow History of Hip-Hop in White America*, New York: Bloomsbury.

The Essence and Momentum of *Honey*
An Interplay of Sound and Movement

Diane Hughes[1]

Hip hop[2] emerged through the cross-cultural creative expressions of the Hispanic, African-Caribbean and African-American youth (Rose, 1994: 60) in the localized Bronx area of New York City. As a "permeable art form, hip hop reflects and reinterprets the world around it" (Uno, 2006: 304) and yet, due to inherent cultural traditions and diverse forms of expression, hip hop is a complex term to define. Tanz (2007) discusses its complexity in relation to hip hop being a signifier and suggests that hip hop is "a mode of being" (Tanz, 2007: ix). In a broad context, hip hop includes "graffiti writing, DJ-ing, break dancing, MC-ing (rapping), street language, clothing, and defiant-and-sexual-attitudes" (Donalson, 2007: 3). In a musical context and as a "collective term" (Toop, n.d.), hip hop represents a musical genre that is rhythmically driven. It often features sampled and looped sounds. In its purist form, hip hop provides a voice for the oppressed through "rhyming lyrics and a multi-textual collage style composition" (Perry, 2004: 8). It is therefore a genre in which mechanical beats and spoken words are often interwoven, and through which artists reflect and express urban life. For those receptive to its rhythmic conventions, hip hop music can induce a range of dance movement including breakdancing, freestyle and acrobatics. As an expressive art form that originated in the streets, hip hop also denotes urban trends, particular fashions and specific vernacular.

From its Bronx origins, hip hop now transcends demographics of race, gender and social status (Potter, 1995: 10). The transition from localized urban expression to a globalized and often mainstream commodity is well documented (Dimitriadis, 2004; Mitchell, 2001; Perry, 2004). Murray (2004) discusses the "transnational" conversion of hip hop that has spawned music and culture and "gained a lasting foothold in the market economy" (Murray, 2004: 5). Within popular culture, hip hop is represented in music, dance, film, gesture, vernacular and fashion. Since the 1980s, hip hop commoditization has been evidenced in film production and is typically seen through the expressions of "graffiti writing, break dancing, and rapping" (Donalson, 2007: 3). In the ensuing decades, the Hollywood film industry has embraced hip hop and it has "assumed a fundamental role as the interpreter of the youth movement" (Donalson, 2007: 5). Hip hop is now represented in different types of films such as "pseudo-biographical films, 'hood' films, and hip hop documentaries" (Stewart, 2009: 49). It is also represented in films that follow in the tradition of the dance film (Donalson, 2007: 12) or the popular dance film (Boyd, 2007: 75). With its embedded hip hop traits, *Honey* (Woodruff, 2003) is representative of the dance film genre and is clearly produced to suit mainstream teen appeal.

Hip Hop Traditions and Traits

The following discussion focuses on the ways in which hip hop culture and traditions are interpreted and crafted within *Honey*'s interplay of sound and movement to form the essence and momentum of *Honey*. In this context, and for the purposes of this discussion, "essence" is defined as the central core or the feature that affords the film its "identity" (Sinclair, 2006: 481) and provides the progressive "impetus" (Robinson, 1996: 883) or the momentum that culminates in a highly energized dance finale. Essential to the momentum are pervasive rhythmic beats and corresponding synchronized movement.

Synopsis

Throughout the interplay, the character of Honey Daniels (Jessica Alba) strives to succeed as a dancer/choreographer. Working as a part-time bartender, retail salesperson and hip hop dance teacher at a neighbourhood centre in the Bronx, Honey is spotted by music video director Michael Ellis (David Moscow) and subsequently rises from obscurity to the seemingly lucrative arena of music video production. Honey's transformed life is somewhat compromised as she struggles between the industry shallowness she encounters and her philanthropic desire to help the neighbourhood youth which is largely represented through the characters of Benny (Lil' Romeo) and his younger brother Raymond (Zachary Isaiah Williams). Honey's best friend Gina (Joy Bryant) and Honey's boyfriend Chaz (Mekhi Phifer) provide grounding influences against the superficial, and at times salacious, nature of Honey's industry involvement.

While *Honey* incorporates hip hop traditions, it does not represent hip hop as a youth subculture *per se*. Rather, *Honey* celebrates the energy of hip hop and explores aspects of it, albeit in a somewhat saccharined approach. *Honey* is essentially the portrayal of a formulaic "kind of hip hop rags-to-riches-to-reality story"[3] in which hip hop is used to explore themes of exploitation, culture, relationships and trust. The production team of Andre Harrell, together with Marc Platt, was keen to work on a project that Platt described as "exciting, exhilarating and hopeful".[4] In its realization, elements of the 'hood' and a low socio-economy are introduced and then, to some extent, sanitized. The character of Chaz escapes being a stereotypical hood gang member by inheriting a barber shop; Benny leaves juvenile detention and abandons a defiant attitude after receiving a visit from Honey. Even a dance benefit concert that comes together quickly and effortlessly attracts seemingly lucrative philanthropic interest that provides the film's magical conclusion.

From its inception, *Honey* drew together a production team of recognized industry professionals to provide a credible and relevant foundation for a film ostensibly aimed at popular consumption by a teen/hip hop audience. As the spectator observes the world of commercialized dance (Boyd, 2007: 78) and behind-the-scenes video making, *Honey* finds its integrity in the purposeful crafting of what is, at times, a 'backstage' dance film. The term 'commercialized dance' helps to elucidate styles of dance such as hip hop that are transformed into "an entertaining component of popular culture" (Boyd, 2007: 78). Experienced in music video direction that features commercialized dance, Billie Woodruff (director) was appointed[5] to lead *Honey*'s creative nexus. Formidable industry choreographer (Searle, 2010) LaurieAnn Gibson (choreographer), together with music producer Rodney Jerkins (executive music producer) whose professional credits included working with "hip hop icons",[6] completed the creative team. The potential credibility that such a creative team offers is reflected in the specific inclusion of aspects of the contemporary music industry. Woodruff explains:

> We talked about ways to keep it [*Honey*] realistic, given my background in the world of music videos, hip hop and rock. So we included things that can happen, given the real world that comes into Honey's story.[7]

Certainly there are elements of Woodruff's professional practice evident in *Honey*. The filming and camera angles utilized in *Honey*'s dance segments are similar to those in the group dance segments of Britney Spears's video 'Born to Make You Happy' (Woodruff, 1999)[8] and in the nightclub scenes of R. Kelly's video 'Ignition' (Woodruff/Kelly, 2003).[9] The purposively crafted music video sets and featured choreography also aid the veracity of *Honey*'s production. This is reinforced by the inclusion of cameo roles of artists such as Missy Elliott, Tweet, and Ginuwine. While the inclusion of hip hop artists, and more specifically rap artists, has been a tradition in hip hop featured films since the 1980s (Donalson, 2007: 141–53), the inclusion of hip hop artists in *Honey* further legitimizes the narrative focus around creating dance videos. Consistent with gender stereotypes evident in much popular music (Hobson and Bartlow, 2007: 2), *Honey*'s commercialized representation of video production includes the image of the female dancer as a sexualized commodity and, within this commercialized representation as female dancer/choreographer, Honey is expendable.

Hip hop traits in *Honey* are also evident in its urban focus. This is enhanced by the pre-production research into costume and set design with hip hop elements reflected in the myriad of street-style clothing, football-styled sneakers, jerseys and bling. While these elements are prominently displayed they are never overtly referred to (with the exception of the scene where the sneakers are stolen), reinforcing the entrenched hip hop culture. Hip hop culture is also evident in the constant incorporation of vernacular into the dialogue, such as "homegirl" and "hood rat". The set designs of urban scenes and video production are purposefully contrasted with each other to provide a stark difference between "real-life texture"[10] (Stefanovich, production designer) and the artificially constructed music video sets. Somewhat incongruous to the production team's premise to signify hip hop is the actual casting of Alba in the lead role.[11] However, Blanco Borelli (2009) attributes the casting of Honey's mother, Lonette McKee, as providing relevance through her "filmic history for African American audiences" (149). It is therefore this casting that underpins the role of Honey as a mixed-raced or "mulatta" genesis (Blanco Borelli, 2009).

The Constructs of Sound and Movement

Methodology

Throughout the analyses, the interplay between the constructs of sound and movement were determined. In the following discussion, and before focusing on the interplay, the constructs and methods of analysis are discussed separately. The methodology draws on sound aesthetics as defined by Bordwell and Thompson (1985). Sonic components and dimensions are identified which subsequently enabled discernment of the perceptual function of sound in *Honey*. The quality of sound represented by speech, noise and music was analysed in relation to the specific components of loudness and timbre. The temporal relations of sound onsets were determined and the sonic texture identified within the dimensions of rhythm (patterns and tempo), fidelity and space. The incorporation of music was also contextualized in relation to the use of pre-existing tracks, specifically composed tracks, additional composition and sound bridges. Waveforms of the overall soundtrack were examined for visual patterning of rhythmic sequences, accented beats, and to identify changes in decibel levels. The analysis of movement identified cinematographic techniques, including camera angles and variations in film speed, which impacted on the perception of movement in the film. The function and type of embodied physical movement was identified. Specific dance movement was analysed for style and rhythmic complexity. Synchronized group moves (Holman, 2004: 37) and solo moves, including elements of breakdancing, such as headspinning and acrobatics, were noted.

The Soundscape

The music in *Honey* is carefully constructed to provide the spectator with an aural perspective of the hip hop genre in which the relevance of technology and sampling cannot be ignored. Rose (1994) suggests that the use of sampling in hip hop gives voice to African-American approaches to "sound, rhythm, timbre, motion, and community" (Rose, 1994: 84). Describing rap as "a complex fusion of orality and postmodern technology" (Rose, 1994: 85), Rose views the incorporation of technology in hip hop music as embedded expression rather than an extension of hip hop. However, the use of technology in sequenced sounds and looped effects also facilitates the creation of tracks where the emphasis is not on lyrical content. Warner (2006) explains:

> The growing absence of lyrics in modern dance music hints at a form of narration that is non-text based. The concrete nature of images and sampled sounds tend [sic] to make lyrics redundant and require [sic] the perceiver to arrive at a narration through sound, supplemented by moving images, rather than words. (179)

This is particularly evident in *Honey* when the low decibel level of some synchronized music results in the lyrical content being somewhat indistinct while contemporaneously the beats remain audible. When the lyrical content is purposely audible, it is expressed either as rap with an emphasis on rhythm or as song with an emphasis on melodic and lyrical content. Whether rhythmic or melodic, the orientation of the vocals is composed or selected to suit the context in which it is used. The incorporation of both commercially produced tracks and purposively composed tracks provide the spectator with a smorgasbord of sampled sounds, textual timbres, rhythmic patterns and varying tempos. While the rhythmic pattern of accenting the second and fourth beats of common time is apparent in much of *Honey*'s music, accented hand claps and basketball taps are also evident. Adding to accented beats are looped rhythmic patterns and driving bass lines.

From the outset, the music in *Honey* was to play a key role and its relation to movement is clearly evident in its intent, as producer Marc Platt elucidates:

> The music in this movie is a character and it tells part of the story. The feel of the music, the sensibility of it, the lyrics, all go hand-in-hand with the dance and the movement, the characters, the drama and the story.[12]

Executive music director and composer of sixteen of the film's songs, Rodney Jerkins, aka Darkchild (Massey, 2009: 264), notes that he was drawn to the project in part by the emphasis on the characterization, role and intent of the music.[13] The realized intent is that Jerkins's music prominently features throughout *Honey* and the melodic content heard in many of Jerkins's tracks is, at times, contrasted by accented rapped lyrics. Representing a range of hip hop nuances and sounds, the film credits over thirty music tracks incorporated into *Honey*'s soundscape. The selected and expressly crafted music is also reminiscent of "realistic motivation" (Smith, 1998: 183) as the tracks are either reflective of hip hop nuances or allude to narrative constructs.

Honey's comprehensive sound channel (Chion, 2009: 228) is an interchange of music, performed sound and sound effects. In this context, the music ostensibly follows "traditional functions, including establishing mood and supporting the film's construction of formal unity" (Smith, 1998: 155). Typically diegetic and non-diegetic music, together with selected sound effects, provide sound bridges to enable score continuity and sinuous scene segues. These include scene transitions that are, at times, crafted using soft onsets of diegetic sound. In these instances, the onsets occur earlier than their related image and are therefore examples of "displaced diegetic" sound (Bordwell and Thompson, 1985: 198). Diegetic sound can also function by alluding to the "spatial depth absent in the image by the creative manipulation of tone-colour and volume" (Cooke, n.d.). This technique is repeatedly utilized in *Honey* and aids in maintaining production "fidelity" (Bordwell and Thompson, 1985: 190). For example, the beats from the boom box become audibly louder as the local kids enter Honey's dance class.[14] Similarly, in a later scene when Honey is talking in Gina's apartment, the reflected room sound is heard in Honey's affected vocal tone and, as the camera moves closer to Honey, the room ambience is negated and Honey's voice becomes clearer. The panning of sound effects is also used to enhance fidelity such as the 'ringing' phone heard through one side as if emanating from the sound source itself.

The original score by Mervyn Warren underscores the narrative action and, in conjunction with other sound components, is consistently implemented at varying degrees of loudness. At times, increasing levels of volume are used to change images or to provide a focus for subsequent visual images. Contrasts in the texture and timbre of sound provide ambient settings in ways that complement the narrative. For example, the inclusion of the soulful track 'Know Your Way' (Alleyna and Taylor, 2003),[15] that features acoustic guitar and the rich vocal tone of Ebony Alleyna, provides a contrast in its real instrumentation and melodic reflective quality to underscore Honey's uncharacteristic disillusionment. Even the contrasting vocal timbre and patterns of speech between the lead characters creates another level of sonic texture. Honey's light and often upbeat vocal tone is contrasted by the deep timbre and slower pace inherent in Chaz's vocal delivery.

Movement

Aiding the perception of pace and momentum are effects such as the inclusion of passing traffic or the movement of a train. However, it is the choreographed synchronized dance sequences that are integral to building the film's energy. Gibson's choreography incorporates hip hop moves, and while elements of breakdancing are seen mainly in relation to the gang of local kids, the incorporation of call and response techniques is apparent in the competitiveness of the "battle dancing" (Perry, 2004: 83) in the nightclub scenes. This is particularly evident at the nightclub, the Overdrive, where Honey works. It is here that Katrina (LaurieAnn Gibson) strives to "outdo" Honey where seemingly freestyle, or improvised movement (Hebdige, 2004: 226), is executed. Camera angles draw the spectator into the dance scenes as figures are shot, at times, from behind the eyeline of the characters (see Figure 1) or from above. Varying camera angles and strategic editing are also used to ensure that lead dancers are the focal point in sequences. At other times, filming focuses on the movement of dancers' feet or on the isolations in dancers' movement. Also evident in the choreography are the influences of double-dutch jump roping which, as Holman (2004) explains, was an influence on female breakers of the late 1970s (Holman, 2004: 37). Similarly, repeated basketball motifs are used.

Figure 1: Spectator perspective [02:48[16]] (*Honey*, Woodruff, 2003)

In the video scenes, Gibson's choreography is clearly connected to the pulse and accents of the musical beats and is characteristic of the synchronization required in commercial dance videos. In video production, as Warner (2006) discusses, the music is typically produced before the image. The influence of musical tempo on dance movement is therefore seen in images that reflect "specific rhythms and timbres" (Warner, 2006: 173). In an interview conducted in 2010, Gibson explains this influence in relation to her choreography:

> Music is the other thing, that in tandem, works with my gift [dance]. It speaks to me and tells me what to do where. The music has the other element, the balance for me. (cited in Searle, 2010)

While in reality much hip hop movement is performed by untrained 'street' dancers, Gibson's technique and choreographic demands led to months of preproduction rehearsals and fitness strategies.[17] While Gibson also credits Alba as possessing "natural lines that are similar to a trained dancer",[18] the preproduction strategies of preparing Alba for dancing in the lead role, together with what are carefully constructed and edited dance sequences, enabled Alba to appear as a credible and engaging dancer.

The Interplay of Sound and Movement

Preceding the opening scene and underscoring the Universal logo, *Honey* begins with a commercial track, 'Ooh Wee' (Hobb, 2003),[19] performed by Mark Ronson that features rap artists including Ghostface Killah and Nate Dogg. With references to the hood in the rapped lyrics that are heard over the accented second and fourth beats of each bar and sampled cowbell and string sounds, 'Ooh Wee' simultaneously establishes a contemporary urban and dance focus. The track then provides a sound bridge to a night-time panoramic view of the New York city skyline which is synchronized to related New York city lyrics. The macro aerial view that passes over Manhattan and ends outside the nightclub (the Overdrive) where Honey works, coupled with the soundtrack, immediately signifies the essence and momentum that spearheads the production.

The cinematographic technique of utilizing varying film speeds, including fast-forwarding and slowing down, to emphasize a focal point that is characteristically synchronized to the soundtrack, typifies how the movement in *Honey* is not always physically embodied. In the opening minute of *Honey*, the spectator is taken over the Manhattan skyline initially with intense speed that slows to coincide with a change in focal point to a vertical view over a Manhattan street before progressing to focal points both outside and inside the Overdrive. These initial changes in focal points are accompanied by momentary sampled sound effects at increased volume levels. These audible volume changes, including the decreased volume level that coincides with the scene change from inside to outside the nightclub, is clearly evident in the corresponding waveform. Changes in track levels are also heard as the visual focus changes at 00:41, 00:44 and 01:04 respectively. This interplay is musically rhythmic which aids in its momentum.

The narrative begins with the macro aerial view of the New York skyline that zooms and narrows to the location of the nightclub where Honey works. Underscoring the nightclub scenes is the sound of energetic, scratching hip hop beats that decrease in volume as the dialogue begins. Inside the Overdrive, physically embodied movement is clearly apparent both in the purposeful dance moves and in idiosyncratic responses to the audible dance beats. Patrons at the bar are seen nodding in time to the beats while waiting for their drinks. Honey, together with another bartender, visually responds to the beats while serving drinks behind the bar. Gina similarly responds to the beat as she waits for Honey to finish her shift. In contrast to the patrons who move with individual style and intensity are the black and silver costumed dancers strategically positioned on a stage and on various podiums. Patrons in the DJ booth including the DJ, while overlooking the dance floor, are seen to be pulsing to the beats.

Honey proceeds to the dance floor to the track 'Gimme The Light' (Henriques and Remi, 2002)[20] and the increase in musical tempo of 12 bpm[21] from the previous track helps build momentum. When making her way to the centre of the dance floor, Honey stops to watch Katrina as she displays her dance prowess (see Figure 1). Moving away from Katrina, Honey gestures to the DJ who by seemingly scratching a turntable, changes tracks to 'React' (Sermon, Smith and Noble, 2002).[22] A corresponding waveform clearly reveals different accents in the preceding rubbing and scratching and the accentuated second and fourth beats of the subsequent track. Honey begins to react to these beats and is seen to attract onlookers as they encircle her and cheer her on. The reduction in tempo of 16 bpm from the previous track underpins the subsequent focus on Honey and her capacity to dance. The perception of her ability is aided through editing techniques and by incorporating camera angles that concentrate on Honey's 'abs', body rolls and floor work. Honey emerges as a talented dancer who is popular with the patrons (see Figure 2). It is in this sequence, as Katrina looks on, that the competitiveness and encircling formation (Shloss, 2006: 413) of the breakdancing tradition are apparent.

As the action transcends to outside the nightclub, Honey and Gina find a group of local kids ensconced in beatboxing and breakdancing. Rhythmic

Figure 2: Honey and crowd gestures evocative of hip hop traits [03:59] (*Honey*, Woodruff, 2003)

clapping is supplemented with vocalizations and accented phrases of 'huh huh', as well as the repetitive and percussive phrases of 'hey hey hey' and 'go Benny'. As the tempo changes throughout the segment, so do the styles of movement. The syncopated rhythmic patterns are interpreted through a variety of movements including headspinning, popping, locking and acrobatics (see Figure 3). Graffiti is also evident on the surrounding walls. Slightly incongruous to the back alley location and the surrounding graffiti is what appears to be a strategically placed floor mat.

The scene and mood change as an instrumental track provides a sound bridge and underscores an aerial view of the Bronx-style housing projects. The film then speeds forward to a view of Honey walking to the neighbourhood centre where she teaches hip hop. Inside the centre the sound of players' shoes on the basketball court, together with the basketball as it bounces on the timber floor, provide percussive elements synchronized to the instrumental track. This unique interplay of sound and movement is contrasted by a few seconds of musical silence before Honey introduces a dance track, a remix of loops, to her dance class. The dance class is interrupted when the local kids enter while 'grooving' to music from their boom box. The kids are moving in freestyle that is in contrast to the choreographed movement of the dance class. Diegetic sounds simultaneously emanate from the class CD player and the boom box, and their overlapping adds to the tension and suggestion of 'battle' between the class and the kids. As the kids try to learn the choreography, the sound of sneakers hitting the timber floor provides a percussive element that again emphasizes rhythmic patterns and accents. This is particularly evident in the section where there is no music and the percussive footwork patterns are heard.

Figure 3: Breakdancing [05:12] (*Honey*, Woodruff, 2003)

Later, and having missed an open dance call, Honey's disappointment at not being able to audition is juxtaposed with the vibrancy of colour, sound and movement of the subsequent scene at Michael's video production office. In this later scene the spectator is confronted by multiple television screens all playing videos of nightclub dancers. The sounds of telephones ringing and the movement of office workers stop the moment Michael asks who Honey is and her image appears on the screen. The track used to underscore this on-screen image provides a sound bridge to the next scene at the Overdrive. It is in this subsequent scene that Michael introduces himself to Honey and offers her the chance to dance in a Jadakiss video. As Michael and Honey talk over the sound of a somewhat indistinct dance track, there is an audible emphasis on the second and fourth beats and a creative use of mirror-ball affected lighting as shards and colours move across the patrons while they dance.

The collocation of physical movement and diegetic sound is also seen in the portrayal of Honey's hip hop classes and the movement of the basketball players practising on the court below. Both are striking representations of embodied movement. The intense momentum is complemented by the heavily accented and driving dance music, together with the sound of the basketball as it bounces again on the timber floor. The initial part of the scene provides a stark contrast to the section of the scene where only low-level ambient noise is audible as Honey talks to Raymond and reflectively states that, lucky for him, she is "not goin' anywhere". The disappointment evident in Honey's statement and vocal tone, together with the essence of the subsequent scene, encapsulate initial disillusionment followed by later acceptance. A sound bridge into the next scene is created by the effect of music from a car being initially prominent and then less audible as it drives by the location of the neighbourhood 'Discount Center' where local 'drug' dealers hang out. Ambient hip hop music is audible in the background as gang members watch for prospective deals and potential threats.

Figure 4: Hip hop gesturing [22:41] (*Honey*, Woodruff, 2003)

Honey is eventually booked by Michael to dance in a Jadakiss video in which the track 'J-A-D-A' (Jerkins, Phillips and Jacobs, 2003),[23] featuring Jadakiss and Sheek, is synchronized. The prominent dirt, graffiti and colour of previous scenes are replaced by a high-gloss black and white set, symmetrical patterns and choreography. The gesturing moves of the rappers are contrasted by the fluidity of the dancers (see Figure 4). In addition to the physical movement, the interplay of sound and movement in this scene is aided by the rhythmical patterns of the stage lighting and a pyrotechnics display that are set against the musical beats. The stereotypical choreography of commercialized dance is again emphasized in the video shoot that features the track 'Sexy' (Jerkins et al., 2003).[24] Filming with angles sighted below other female dancers allows voyeuristic images that are reminiscent of the nefarious images in 'booty videos' (Murray, 2004: 6). Honey's body rolls against the seated singer as he reaches out towards her 'booty'.

During a break on the next video shoot, Honey is seen to draw choreographic inspiration from street basket-ballers and from girls who are skipping rope. While hip hop dance moves traditionally draw on real-life experiences, this choreographic inspiration is somewhat exaggerated. The underscore of synthesized strings to hip hop beats highlights the images of Honey copying basketball moves and girls skipping rope. As the scene segues from Honey practising the predictively inspired moves to rehearsing the moves with the dancers, the images are momentarily superimposed (38:11). The track used for this video shoot, 'Honey' (Jerkins et al., 2003),[25] is heavily sequenced with repetitive looping that lends itself to accented poses. These are translated into the choreographic formations evident in Figures 5 and 6.

Figure 5: Shooting hoops [38:37] (*Honey*, Woodruff, 2003)

Figure 6: Skipping rope [38:43] (*Honey*, Woodruff, 2003)

An interesting musical inclusion in *Honey* is Mary J. Blige's track 'No More Drama' (Harris, Lewis, DeVorzon and Botkin, 2001)[26] which samples 'Nadia's Theme' (DeVozron and Botkin, 1971) from the television series *The Young and the Restless* (ABC). At this point the pace of the film slows and the music, through its difference in vocal tone and slowing tempo, aids in highlighting the abuse of Benny. The piano sampling provides an ambient underscore as Honey and Raymond set out to find Benny. Blige's reflective vocalizations reveal a "grain" (Barthes, 1977: 188) that seems to express what Frith (1998) denotes as a singer's "deepest feelings" (Frith, 1998: 192). There is little interplay with movement other than walking through the streets where, at times, Honey's steps are synchronized to the beats of the tracks. The repetitive motif of the basketball bouncing, this time on the street, is also synchronized to the timing of the track.

In the ensuing 'Hypnotic' (Jerkins *et al.*, 2003)[27] video shoot, Tweet's sweet vocal tone is in contrast to the heavy accented hip hop beats. In this scene, the interplay of sound and movement is clearly evident. Also in contrast are the graceful, almost ethereal, moves as Tweet descends while other dancers 'fly' across the set. The subsequent locking moves of the dancers, synchronized to syncopated beats, are again contrasted by Tweet's graceful gestures and the stillness of the male dancers. The convincing crafting of Tweet's video set, complete with boom cameras and monitors, is shown in Figure 7. The silhouettes of Benny and Raymond are highlighted in the shaft of light.

Figure 7: Tweet's video scene [43:50] (*Honey*, Woodruff, 2003)

The mood changes with the track 'It's a Party' (Savage, J. Campbell and W. S. Campbell, 2003)[28] and provides an underscore to the black and white party that Honey attends with Michael. As Honey finds a quiet room to call Gina, the reduced audible level of the track helps to distance Honey from the party. As Honey talks on the phone, the movement of the water in the lit swimming pool evokes a somewhat reflective ambience that is interrupted as Michael enters the room. The movement of the water becomes more noticeable as the tension between Michael and Honey intensifies. Honey rejects Michael's affection, and walks out. The introduction to 'Hot' (Jerkins et al., 2003)[29] provides a sound bridge into the street scene where Honey's dancers rehearse with Ginuwine. The momentum increases with the inclusion of some acrobatic moves and a pied piper effect is created as Ginuwine moves forward through the dancers. The simplicity and innocence of the choreography is juxtaposed with Michael's retaliation against Honey through firing her young dancers and instructing a replacement choreographer, rival night-club dancer Katrina, to make the choreography more 'sexy'. The rejected and despondent young dancers leave Ginuwine's video shoot.

A sound bridge of keyboard and strings leads into the scene where Benny is back with a gang and the sound of a train arriving at the platform is heard. This sound sequence ends with the squeal and release of a train's brakes as it moves into the platform. This is an interesting scene as the sound of the boys walking in the train is both rhythmic and percussive. The next sampling and rhythmic pattern begins after the boys have stolen a pair of shoes and the film goes to black. The following sequenced underscore becomes increasingly audible and, as the boys run up the station stairs with the stolen shoes, the film immediately cuts to Honey's next dance audition scene. This is an example of the masterful crafting of the interplay as the sequencing at this point is also reminiscent of the sound of a train moving quickly. The use of Knoc-Turn'Al's 'The Way I Am' (Harbor and Storch, 2001),[30] with its heavily accented beats and rapping style of metered rhyme, provides the underscore to Benny's subsequent arrest for drug dealing. It is in the train, and during the subsequent arrest scene, that the tempo of composed musical interlude increases to highlight critical narrative events.

As Honey prepares to hold the benefit concert, the track 'Rule' (Orzabel et al., 2001),[31] performed by hip hop artist Nas, underscores the distribution of promotional posters, dance rehearsals and requests for donations. The lead into the finale begins in the rehearsal process and an instrumental section of 'I Believe' (Jerkins et al., 2003),[32] written specifically as the theme for *Honey*, is heard. Benny works a sleight-of-hand trick, that he learned while in juvenile detention, into the choreography. The finale begins with contrasting ballet and acrobatic movement (see Figure 8) set to a pop-influenced track and, as the finale builds momentum, larger groups, more hip hop in style, fill the stage. The second and fourth beats of each bar are also accented through clapping and, when the tap dancers appear, syncopated rhythms are audibly apparent. The sequence of three male dancers accenting the beats and jumping on to the toes of their sneakers provides heightened momentum. The overall vitality and focus of all the dancers is underscored by the convincing recorded vocal delivery of Yolanda Adams and the repetitious lyrical motif of 'I believe'. *Honey* concludes with an appearance by Missy Elliott who introduces Honey to a girl band 'Blaque' at the 'Bronx Dance Center' founded by Honey Daniels and funded by philanthropic interest. As the credits roll, Blaque transforms from choreographic rehearsal to video where the repeated rhythmic basketball motif is again evident and a percussive element utilizing tin garbage cans and lids is introduced.

Figure 8: Contrasting styles [80:18] (*Honey*, Woodruff, 2003)

Conclusion

While the preceding discussion has included some undeniably superficial representations of hip hop traditions, *Honey* does indeed challenge certain stereotypes. Honey's refusal to be submissive refutes the gender power play and exploitation often depicted in mainstream interpretations of hip hop culture. The inclusion of the "mulatta" (Blanco Borelli, 2009) female lead who struggles on a number of levels and then triumphantly emerges may actually provide inspiration to some audiences. The strength of Honey's character lies in her resilience and determination and in her portrayal as "an independent and ambitious mulatta [who] does not specifically rely on male patronage – black or white" (Blanco Borelli, 2009: 149).

The recurrent theme of high art (ballet) verses popular culture (hip hop), evident in instances where Honey's mother encourages Honey's cultural pursuits through ballet and travel, culminates in the dance finale where balletic poses are simultaneously contrasted by breakdancing moves. These balletic inferences are conceivably poignant inclusions set to challenge the traditional concept of cultural capital. Perhaps their juxtaposition is to highlight hip hop's "socio-political relevance and pop-culture cool" (Murray, 2004: 8). Chang (2007) elucidates:

> hip hop culture has become one of the most far reaching arts movements of the past three decades. The best artists share a desire to break down boundaries between "high" and "low" art – to make urgent, truth-telling work that reflects the lives, loves, histories, hopes, and fears of their generation. (Chang, 2007: 60)

While Rose (2008) bewails the "dumbing down" (3) of hip hop imagery where positive traits and a sense of community are marginalized, Honey's community is consistently and coherently portrayed. It is, however, other expressions of hip hop culture, and elements of the narrative, that are somewhat diluted in their representation. A stronger hip hop affiliation may have been possible, although within any mainstream aesthetic it is conceivably "a stretch to incorporate the ideology of 'keeping it real'" (Arnold et al., 2006: 306). Perhaps if hip hop affiliation was further implemented in *Honey*, a different audience demographic would likely have been targeted.

It is through the creative platforms and professional experiences of Woodruff, Jerkins and Gibson that *Honey* finds its intensity and focus. From the film's outset, the crafting of macro visual to micro action, together with the manipulation of volume levels and film speed, typifies the interplay of sound and movement. Just as musical tracks provide the impetus for synchronized movement, other elements within the sound channel, such as musical beats, crowd noise, or even the sound of a basketball hitting the ground, are used to focus attention on movement in its various contexts. The interplay between sound and movement also has, at times, the ability to convey narrative without reliance on spoken or sung words. So while *Honey* may be described as a formulaic dance film, it is within its shaping and production that an undeniably symbiotic relationship between sound and movement is expended.

Notes

1. Diane Hughes is Senior Lecturer in Vocal Studies in the Department of Media, Music, Communication and Cultural Studies at Macquarie University, Sydney. Her research interests include the singing voice, pedagogy, film and sound, recording practices, the music industries and popular music. She is the President of the Australian National Association of Teachers of Singing (ANATS Ltd).
2. In the literature the unhyphenated 'hip hop' and hyphenated 'hip-hop' are used interchangeably as both an adjective and noun. This discussion draws on the work of leading hip hop researcher, Tricia Rose, in which the unhyphenated 'hip hop' is used as both an adjective (e.g. Rose, 1994: ix) and noun (e.g. Rose, 1994: 23). It is therefore used as such throughout this article, and this volume.
3. The official website for *Honey* includes a section called 'Production Notes' (2003). This provides insight into the creative direction and nexus of the project from its inception through to its realization. This quote is attributed to Andre Harrell (producer), in 'Production Notes', http://www.honeymovie.com/main_pop_up.html?deeplink=howdTheyDoIt (accessed 16 January 2011).
4. This quote is attributed to Marc Platt (producer), in 'Production Notes', http://www.honeymovie.com/main_pop_up.html?deeplink=howdTheyDoIt (accessed 16 January 2011).
5. 'Production Notes' (2003), http://www.honeymovie.com/main_pop_up.html?deeplink=howdTheyDoIt (accessed 16 January 2011).
6. 'Production Notes: Finding the Right Sound' (2003), http://www.honeymovie.com/main_pop_up.html?deeplink=howdTheyDoIt (accessed 16 January 2011).
7. This quote is attributed to Bille Woodruff (director) (2003), in 'Production Notes', http://www.honeymovie.com/main_pop_up.html?deeplink=howdTheyDoIt (accessed 16 January 2011).
8. See 'Britney Spears – Born to Make You Happy', http://www.youtube.com/watch?v=Yy5cKX4jBkQ (accessed 25 March 2012).
9. See 'R. Kelly – Ignition', http://www.youtube.com/watch?v=y6y_4_b6RS8 (accessed 25 March 2012).
10. This quote is attributed to Jasna Stefanovich (production designer) (2003), 'Production Notes: Keepin' it Real', http://www.honeymovie.com/main_pop_up.html?deeplink=howdTheyDoIt (accessed 16 January 2011).
11. It is rumoured on various websites that Aaliyah, an African-American artist who died in 2001, was originally cast in the role of Honey Daniels; see, e.g., http://au.complex.com/music/2011/08/10-facts-about-aaliyah-you-might-not-know/ (accessed 27 October 2015).
12. This quote is attributed to Marc Platt (producer), in 'Production Notes: Finding the Right Sound', http://www.honeymovie.com/main_pop_up.html?deeplink=howdTheyDoIt (accessed 16 January 2011).
13. Rodney Jerkins (executive music producer) (2003), 'Production Notes: Finding the Right Sound', http://www.honeymovie.com/main_pop_up.html?deeplink=howdTheyDoIt (accessed 16 January 2011).

14. A counterpart to this creation of fidelity is the false construction of musical dominance and power within spaces. For example, the small ghetto blasters repeatedly used (and visually depicted) in Honey's dance class manage to produce huge, bass-filled sounds.
15. All tracks discussed in this article contain information listed as they appear on the rolling credits at the end of *Honey* (Woodruff, 2003) and as listed at http://www.imbd.com/title/tt0322589/soundtrack (accessed 1 October 2011). 'Know Your Way' written by Ebony Alleyna, Richard Taylor. Performed by Ebony Alleyna. Courtesy of New Vision Arts Management.
16. The frame examples (Figures) incorporated in the discussion are indicated with their relevant cue points. These figures and cue points were taken from the DVD release of *Honey* (Universal Studios, 2004) that was manufactured, sold and distributed under exclusive license by Universal Pictures (Australasia) Pty Ltd.
17. Included in a bonus feature of 'Behind the Groove: The Making of *Honey*', on the DVD release of *Honey* (Universal Studios, 2004) by Universal Pictures (Australasia) Pty Ltd, were a selection of production and artist interviews. Alba talked about going to the gym to increase her fitness level in preparation for *Honey*.
18. Included in the bonus feature, 'Behind the Groove: The Making of *Honey*', Gibson credits Alba as having "natural lines".
19. 'Ooh Wee'. Written by Bobby Hobb. Performed by Mark Ronson (featuring Ghostface Killah, Nate Dogg, Saigon and Trife Da God as Trife). Courtesy of Elektra Entertainment Group. Contains a sample of "SCORPIO". As recorded by Dennis Coffey. Licensed courtesy of Avant Garde Enterprsies Inc./Interior Music Corp.
20. 'Gimme The Light'. Written by Sean Henriques. Performed by Sean Paul and Toni Remi. Courtesy of VP Records/Atlantic Recording Corp. By arrangement with Warner Strategic Marketing.
21. This measures the tempo of a musical work in beats per minute or bpm.
22. 'React'. Written by Eric Sermon, Justin Smith and Reggie Noble. Performed by Eric Sermon. Featuring Redman. Courtesy of J Records. Redman appears courtesy of Def Jam Records.
23. 'J-A-D-A'. Written by Rodney Jerkins, Jason Phillips and Sean Jacobs. Produced by Rodney Jerkins for Darkchild.com. Performed by Jadakiss and Sheek. Jadakiss appears courtesy of Ruff Ryders/Interscope Records; Sheek appears courtesy of D-Block, Inc./Ruff Ryders Records/Interscope Records.
24. 'Sexy'. Written by Rodney Jerkins, LeShawn Daniels, Fred Jerkins, Kenneth Pratt and Shawn Desman. Produced by Rodney Jerkins for Darkchild.com. Performed by Shawn Desman. Courtesy of BMG Canada/UOMO LLC.
25. 'Honey'. Written by Rodney Jerkins, LeShawn Daniels, Fred Jerkins and Kenneth Pratt. Produced by Rodney Jerkins for Darkchild.com. Performed by 3rd Storee. Courtesy of Edmonds Record Group/Def Soul Records.
26. 'No More Drama'. Written by James Harris III, Terry Lewis, Brian DeVorzon and Perry Botkin. Performed by Mary J. Blige. Courtesy of MCA Records. Under license from Universal Music Enterprises.

27. 'Hypnotic'. Written by Rodney Jerkins, LeShawn Daniels, Fred Jerkins and Kenneth Pratt. Produced by Rodney Jerkins for Darkchild.com. Performed by Tweet. Courtesy of Goldmind Inc./Elektra Records.
28. 'It's A Party'. Written by Tamara Savage, Joi Campbell and Warryn S. Campbell II. Performed by Tamia. Courtesy of Elektra Entertainment Group. By arrangement with Warner Strategic Marketing.
29. 'Hot'. Written by Rodney Jerkins, LeShawn Daniels, Fred Jerkins and Kenneth Pratt. Produced by Rodney Jerkins for Darkchild.com. Performed by Ginuwine. Courtesy of Epic Records.
30. 'The Way I Am'. Written by R. Harbor and Scott Storch. Performed by Knoc-Turn'Al. Courtesy of Elektra Entertainment Group. By arrangement with Warner Strategic Marketing.
31. 'Rule'. Written by Roland Orzabal, Ian Stanley, Chris Hughes, Nasar Jones, Jean Claude Oliver, Samuel J. Barnes and Amerie Mi Marie Rogers. Performed by Nas (as NAS) featuring Amerie. Courtesy of Columbia Records.
32. 'I Believe'. Written by Rodney Jerkins, LeShawn Daniels, Fred Jerkins, Kenneth Pratt and Dominic Durham. Produced by Rodney Jerkins for Darkchild.com. Co-produced by Fred Jerkins III, Dominic Durham for Darkchild.com. Performed by Yolanda Adams. Courtesy of Elektra Records.

References

Arnold, E., Raimist, R., Epps, K. and Wanguhu, M. (2006), 'Put your Camera Where my Eyes See: Hip-hop Video, Film, and Documentary [roundtable chaired by E. Arnold]', in J. Chang (ed.), *Total Chaos: The Art and Aesthetics of Hip-hop*, New York: BasicCivitas, pp. 306–320.
Barthes, R. (1977), 'The Grain of the Voice', in *Image, Music, Text*, translated by Stephen Heath, New York: Hill and Wang, pp. 179–89.
Blanco Borelli, M. (2009), 'A Taste of Honey: Choreographing Mulatta in the Hollywood Dance Film', *International Journal of Performance Arts and Digital Media*, 5(2&3), 141–53.
Bordwell, D., and Thompson, K. (1985), 'Fundamental Aesthetics of Sound in the Cinema', in E. Weis and J. Belton (eds), *Film Sound: Theory and Practice*, New York: Columbia University Press, pp. 181–99.
Boyd, J. (2007), 'Dance, Culture and Popular Film', *Feminist Media Studies*, 4(1), 67–83.
Chang, J. (2007), 'It's a Hip-hop World', *Foreign Policy*, 163, 58–63.
Chion, M. (2009), *Film, a Sound Art*, translated by C. Gorban, New York: Columbia University Press.
Cooke, M. (n.d.), 'Film Music', *Grove Music Online. Oxford Music Online*, Oxford University Press, http://www.oxfordmusiconline.com/subscriber/article/grove/music/09647 (accessed 7 January 2011).
Dimitriadis, G. (2004), 'Hip-hop: From Live Performance to Mediated Narrative', in M. Forman and M. A. Neal (eds), *That's the Joint! The Hip-hop Studies Reader*, New York: Routledge, pp. 421–36.
Donalson, M. (2007), *Hip Hop in American Cinema*, New York: Peter Lang.

Frith, S. (1998), *Performing Rites: Evaluating Popular Music*, Oxford: Oxford University Press.

Hebdige, D. (2004), 'Rap and Hip-hop: The New York Connection', in M. Forman and M. A. Neal (eds), *That's the Joint! The Hip-hop Studies Reader*, New York: Routledge, pp. 223–32.

Hobson, J., and Bartlow, D. (2007), 'Introduction Representin': Women, Hip-hop, and Popular Music', *Meridians: Feminism, Race, Transnationalisation*, 8(1), 1–14.

Holman, M. (2004), 'Breaking: The History', in M. Forman and M. A. Neal (eds), *That's the Joint! The Hip-hop Studies Reader*, New York: Routledge, pp. 31–40.

Massey, H. (2009), *Behind the Glass Volume II*, Milwaukee: Backbeat Books.

Mitchell, T. (ed.) (2001), *Global Noise: Rap and Hip-hop outside the USA*, Middletown: Wesleyan University Press.

Murray, D. (2004), 'Hip Hop vs. High Art: Notes on Race as Spectacle', *Art Journal*, 63(2), 4–19.

Perry, I. (2004), *Prophets of the Hood: Politics and Poetics in Hip Hop*, Durham and London: Duke University Press.

Potter, R. (1995), *Spectacular Vernaculars: Hip-hop and the Politics of Postmodernism*, Albany: State University of New York Press.

Robinson, M. (ed.) (1996), *Chambers 21st Century Dictionary*, Edinburgh: Chambers.

Rose, T. (1994), *Black Noise: Rap Music and Black Culture in Contemporary America*, Middletown: Wesleyan University Press.

Rose, T. (2008), *The Hip Hop Wars: What We Talk about When We Talk about Hip Hop – and Why it Matters*, New York: BasicCivitas.

Schloss, J. (2006), 'Like Old Folk Songs Handed Down from Generation to Generation: History, Canon, and Community in B-Boy Culture', *Ethnomusicology*, 50(3), 411–32.

Searle, D. (2010), 'LaurieAnn Gibson – a Passion and a Calling', *Dance Informa*, 6 March 2010, online at http://www.danceinforma.com/magazine/?tag=laurieann-gibson.

Sinclair, J. (ed.) (2006), *Collins Cobuild Advanced Learner's English Dictionary*, Glasgow: HarperCollins.

Smith, J. (1998), *Sounds of Commerce: Marketing Popular Film Music*, New York: Columbia University Press.

Stewart, J. (2009), 'Reel to Reel: Filmic Constructions of Hip Hop Cultures and Hip Hop Identities', *Interdisciplinary Humanities*, 26(2), 46–67.

Tanz, J. (2007), *Other People's Property: A Shadow History of Hip-hop in White America*, New York: Bloomsbury.

Toop, D. (n.d.), 'Hip Hop', *Grove Music Online. Oxford Music Online*, Oxford University Press, http://www.oxfordmusiconline.com:80/subscriber/article/grove/music/46869 (accessed 17 January 2011).

Uno, R. (2006), 'Theatres Crossing the Divide: A Baby Boomer's Defence of Hip-hop Aesthetics', in J. Chang (ed.), *Total Chaos: The Art and Aesthetics of Hip-hop*, New York: BasicCivitas, pp. 300–305.

Warner, T. (2006), 'Narrating Sound: The Pop Video in the Age of the Sampler', in P. Powrie and R. Stilwell (eds), *Changing Tunes: The Use of Pre-existing Music in Film*, Aldershot: Ashgate, pp. 167–79.

Gone in a *Flash(dance)*
The Estrangement of Diegetic Performance in the 1980s Teen Dance Film[1]

Kelly Kessler[2]

The American film industry of the late 1970s and 1980s embraced the economic potential of cross-marketing and musical tie-ins as it capitalized on the rise of the mall-bound multiplex and a new youth-oriented take on what had been the waning musical genre. Just as teens had swarmed to drive-ins to escape – or transcend – their new suburban homes and parents in the 1950s, the babies of the boomers now rushed to the mall. Filled to the brim with food courts and new-fangled video game arcades, these shopping paradises rose as a sign of the American teen's economic cache. After shopping and playing a round of Pac-Man, restless teens could then scurry to the mall's great contribution to teen culture (and one of the saviours of the Hollywood money train): the multiplex.[3]

Concurrently, the motion picture industry was toying with increased horizontal integration and honing its cross-marketing and cross-promotion skills. Following early leads of counterculture darlings *Easy Rider* (Dennis Hopper, 1969) and *The Graduate* (Mike Nichols, 1967), mainstream blockbusters of the seventies and eighties like *Saturday Night Fever* (John Badham, 1977) and *Grease* (Randal Kleiser, 1978) brought together youthful characters, (minor) social dissent and a large volume of music. Hollywood and record producer bigwigs snapped at their chance to capitalize on an emerging trend in recent breakout soundtrack hits from the aforementioned films and a captivated and spatially wrangled teen market. The eighties' filmmaking strategies would not only naturalize the notion of the tie-in soundtrack album, but also encourage visual stylings commensurate with the new and omnipresent musical beat (Wyatt, 1994: 36–47).

Although by no means the only vehicles marketed through their music, a revised version of the Hollywood musical found a quite profitable home in this economic and artistic environment. The American motion picture industry had all but abandoned the integrated musical by the early 1980s, with 1983 being the last year to see the release of more than one such vehicle until 1996 (Kessler, 2010: 168–69). Teeming with youthful stars and filled with an angst that could only be resolved by dancing it out to jamming underscored beats, non-integrated dance musicals such as *Flashdance* (Adrian Lyne, 1983), *Footloose* (Herbert Ross, 1984) and *Dirty Dancing* (Emile Ardolino, 1987) helped the otherwise lacklustre musical take hold in the eighties. Focusing on the three aforementioned dance films, this chapter examines both the visual and aural trends in these films and how they ultimately come into play with – and largely eschew – the norms and perhaps resultant ideological goals of what I will term the more classical song and dance Hollywood musicals which found greatest prominence prior to the mid-sixties.[4] While these later films all present feuding social groups which ultimately find some kind of musical and communal harmony – a trait common to the films of Gene Kelly, Fred Astaire and Rogers and Hammerstein – their combination of visual and aural choices work against that narrative project. Perhaps made more to benefit the soundtracks and music video tie-ins than their films' narratives, these stylistic choices produce a disconnect between the aural and visual tracks that works against the creation of an image of gracefully or passionately dancing bodies and the utopic possibilities described by many film musical scholars as implicit in the more classical Hollywood musical.[5]

Through the interrogation of various visual and aural trends common to the earlier or here termed *classical* song and dance driven musicals – spontaneous performance of integrated song and dance and a visual projection of full bodies in motion or multiple bodies in union – and those of these later teen dance films – largely underscored music, a lack of diegetically performed song, and camerawork that fractures the dancing bodies rather than showing the visual union or choreographed whole – I will highlight ways in which this later musical trend strayed from earlier norms. While these shifts imply neither substandard filmmaking, a deviant split from the musical genre, nor all-in-all markers of *bad* films, they do highlight ways in which this subgenre sidesteps formal choices often highlighted by scholars as the ones more defining of the classical musical's utopic spirit.[6] Whereas scholars such as George F. Custen (1997) have pointed to these earlier song and dance musicals as cultural salve or ideological reinforcement of hegemonic norms, the later dance films' visual and aural characteristics highlight, instead, their roles as the source material for cross-promotion, a fast-paced and growing music video industry and teen target audience.

Dancing into the Multiplex

By the mid to late 1970s Hollywood was turning its sights onto both a new and younger audience and a flashier style of filmmaking. Studies showed that by 1977, 87 per cent of movie tickets were purchased by patrons under forty, 57 per cent were bought by those under twenty-five, and the twelve to twenty group was thriving (Hoberman, 2004: 322). Thomas Schatz and Justin Wyatt discuss this demographic and the industry's formal turn towards 'New Hollywood' or 'high concept' fare respectively. They both argue this stylistic shift sacrificed narrative complexity in favour of a stronger focus on image and affect, and what Wyatt (1994: 22) highlights as high concept's tunnel vision focus on "the look, the hook, and the book". This new style of filmmaking privileged products that could be sold across platforms – soundtracks, tie-ins, video games – and embraced internationally because of their striking images and lack of complex culturally specific narratives. Similarly, New Hollywood turned away from the edgy filmmaking of the late sixties and early seventies, and towards a form "more exciting than interesting, more style than substance" (Schatz, 1993: 19). More plot driven than character driven, these films lacked the level of social and individual complexity often attributed to the New American Cinema, but were nicely positioned to target the youth audiences that were peopling the increasingly omnipresent mall-bound multiplexes.

Simultaneously, the small screen had found a new way to draw the same desirable demographic. MTV launched in 1981 and by 1983 the cable music channel had penetrated most major markets. Prior to the music channel's 1983 penetration of New York and Los Angeles, Saul Austerlitz argues, "the channel was, more than anything, starved for product to fill the gaping holes in its schedule" (2007: 32). J. Hoberman argues, however, that:

> Within two years, rock videos rejuvenated the moribund record industry (saving it from the threat of video games) and made the leap to network television. The often derided MTV aesthetic had already spawned two Hollywood blockbusters (*Flashdance* and *Purple Rain*) as well as at least one television series (*Miami Vice*). (2004: 330)

Along with providing a shot to the system of the recording industry, this new, lucrative television outlet would redefine the television–film–music relationship and open up a space of economic and cinematic viability for what was then an atrophying musical genre.

R. Serge Denisoff and George Plasketes (1990: 258) position *Flashdance* as one of the "progenitors" of the MTV–Hollywood marriage that would transform blockbuster moviemaking in the 1980s. In their study of synergy in 1980s filmmaking they question whether those at the helm of the film foresaw the potential power of the MTV connection or lucked into it. Regardless, the film would open in April of 1983, hit the Billboard charts with its soundtrack on 30 April, release its first music video into MTV rotation on 11 May, and hit soundtrack gold on 17 June (and multi-platinum the following year). *Footloose* and *Dirty Dancing* would follow suit releasing multiple songs from their soundtrack-heavy films into the MTV rotation, reaching number one on the charts, and acquiring multi-platinum status.[7] Despite critical responses deriding *Footloose* as "a seriously confused movie that tries to do three things, and does all of them badly" (Ebert, 1984) and *Dirty Dancing* as merely having "some nice dance sequences" and Patrick Swayze's character being "too soft to be convincing" (*Variety*, 1986) the audiences came to the video screens, the movie theatre and the record stores in droves.

Dancing across Big and Small Screens

Flashdance, *Dirty Dancing* and *Footloose* surely bring back good feelings and romance akin to the more traditional days of the musical, but the differing aesthetics between the music video and the classical Hollywood musical lead to starkly different final products. The largely non-diegetic music and quick-paced and discontinuous editing of the newer films foster musical projects that visually and aurally eschew the often theorized musical utopias of the classical musical that relied on the diegetic unification of sound, song, body and dance. Contrary to J. P. Telotte's (2002) assertion that the non-integrated musicals of this period (specifically *Saturday Night Fever*, *American Hot Wax* [Floyd Mutrux, 1978] and *Footloose*) illustrate the *narrative's* inability or unwillingness to produce a utopic conclusion, I argue that the stories addressed here do include narrative resolutions similar to those idyllic ones often associated with the more classical musical.[8] After all, welder/dancer Alex (Jennifer Beals) and her boss-man (Michael Nouri) (*Flashdance*), rebellious city boy Ren (Kevin Bacon) and preacher's daughter/townie Ariel (Lori Singer) (*Footloose*), and experienced and sultry Johnny (Patrick Swayze) and sheltered and repressed Baby (Jennifer Grey) (*Dirty Dancing*) ultimately find each other in loving embraces – and two of the three couples in the throes of a dancing embrace – at their films' end. Although these narratives project an idealism common to the genre, their MTV-inspired (dis)integration of sound, music and movement – where the song and dance elements project some kind of temporal, sonic, narrative or spatial break from the film's ongoing diegesis – stylistically project something contrary to the type of utopia theorized by scholars such as Richard Dyer (2002) and Rick Altman (1987).

This separation of song, music and movement from the depicted diegetic action avoids and alters what scholars have identified as the bedrock of the genre. In the old days of the classical musical (and occasionally more recently), music – seemingly unmotivated by diegetic action – appeared to propel the townspeople of *Oklahoma!* (Fred Zinnemann, 1955) or *The Music Man* (Morton DaCosta, 1962) into simultaneous song and dance. Suddenly everyone was thrust into performance as they were overwhelmed by an often sourceless music that led friends, lovers and townspeople to burst into unified song or communal dance as their regular mundane lives were taken over by a new musical one. As music with no apparent diegetic source begins in *The Music Man*'s 'Marian the Librarian' (01:01:20), for example, the town's boys simultaneously march in lockstep to the beat. The rhythm of life – Marian's date stamp or marching boys' and girls' pseudo-choreography – then follows the sounds of the music as the characters' actions and the newly emerging music integrate to project a cohesive world where song, dance and music seamlessly blend.

The camera captures the reciprocal relationship fostered between the music, which has encroached upon the diegetic world, and the movement of the body that now reflects the elevated and utopic sense of reality fostered by the invasion of such a musical interlude into life's everyday acts. While the music may have started as non-diegetic, its integration into and motivation for diegetic action shifts its position. Such an elevation of dance, sound and song is common across the classical stage of the genre, whether with *Singing in the Rain*'s (Stanley Donen and Gene Kelly, 1952) Don (Gene Kelly), Cosmo (Donald O'Connor) and Kathy (Debbie Reynolds) exploding in an exuberant performance of 'Good Morning, Good Morning' or Busby Berkeley's high spectacle and dancing camera capturing a bevy of bathing beauties in *Footlight Parade*'s (Lloyd Bacon, 1933) 'By a Waterfall'. In each of these cases – one fully integrated and one a show number – a sense of temporal continuity links diegetic sound and diegetic movement.

Such continuity underscores the arguments of scholars such as Dyer, Jane Feuer and Altman who identify these performative moments as the catalyst for the successful narrative resolution of the companionate romance and bonded community, as well as that of the extra-cinematic sense of social cohesion produced by the classical song and dance musical. Dyer (2002: 20) argues that while musicals fall short of actually presenting utopic worlds, their integration of the soothing or encouraging sounds and visuals of song and dance into the story world create a utopic *sense*. The audience merely *feels* – after seeing the flood of hoofers and hearing the syncopated sounds of their voices and dancing feet – that the utopia is possible. Through the simultaneously passed-along song or communal dance, Feuer (1993: 3, 13) argues, the diegetic community emerges as a united one that can encourage a similar feeling in the viewing audience.

Altman (1987) argues that a similar utopian space and feeling of community emerge through a reversal of the traditional sound–visual hierarchy in the musical. While commonly the visual track guides or provides causality for the onscreen action, the musical often reverses this as images or actions are "'caused' by the music rather than some previous image" (69). As the pseudo-diegetic music – unrealistic to the real world, but seemingly responded to by those who live within the film's diegesis – moves the characters into action, a magical transformation occurs. Music and dance – integrated into or sharing the space of the previously fraught world – unite to provide heretofore unheard-of possibilities. Altman notes, "In leaving normal day-to-day causality behind, the music creates a utopian space in which all singers and dancers achieve a unity unimaginable in the now superseded world of temporal, psychological causality" (*ibid.*). This magical aural transformation allows everyone to march to the same drummer: a drummer not often heard in the dance films which commonly evade integrated song and such displays of spontaneous performance linked to emerging diegetic music. While not impacting the entertainment value of these films, these deviations from musical integration surely place the teen dance films outside the formal realm common to many earlier musicals.

The transition from the integrated musical to a more MTV-styled form disrupts the utopic affect implied by Dyer, Altman and Feuer. The music video – contrary to the visual/aural fluidity of the classical song and dance musical – often projects a discontinuity between the sonic and visual. Richard Gehr (1983: 39) describes the new televisual form as one where "gestures, actions, and intentions are nearly always divorced from systematic content", a trend illustrated through the spate of music videos created from footage pulled from the three films addressed here. The video for Eric Carmen's 'Hungry Eyes', for example, maintains a consistent audio track while indiscriminately shifting between disassociated visuals. As Carmen sits in an isolated screening room he views images from *Dirty Dancing*, of himself singing to himself, and of a seemingly random sexy blonde. He suddenly appears in an alley where he sees similar footage of the film and the woman.[9] Such disjointed and narratively disconnected images deny the co-presence of sound and bodily performance (whether through song or dance), as the sequences devolve into a nearly incoherent presentation of visual and aural excess that distances any fluid story from the sound or visual track.[10] Marsha Kinder (1984) argues that the aural continuity that does exist within the new television form simply serves to distinguish a given video "from the chains of similar images in the video clips that precede and follow this particular musical text" (3).

Some videos presented much more narratively and visually fluid storylines. Lionel Ritchie's 'Hello', for example, crosscuts throughout to depict changes of place and time as it unravels a romance between professor and student. Simultaneously, it maintains a stable narrative as it presents song through a combination of onscreen singing and voiceover. Although here presenting a more cohesive visual story than Carmen's 'Hungry Eyes', the 'Hello' audio track still emanates from various and disconnected sources: voiceover Ritchie the singer and diegetic Ritchie the professor. Both forms – Carmen's narratively fractured and Ritchie's temporally/spatially discontinuous – are reflected in the visual stylings of the dance films, creating a disjunction between musical performance (aural or choreographic) and the transcendent musical cure hypothesized by Dyer, Altman and Feuer.

As this new musical form embraces both the narrative style of the classical genre and visuals and aural choices more akin to that of the music video, the estrangement of song, dance and music from the films' fluid narratives appears through three different means, all antithetical to the classical musicals' described utopic affect and reflective of the new relationship between musicals, the record industry and music television: (1) through non- or quasi-diegetic music tied to non-dance focused montages; (2) through filming and storytelling styles that better suit their conversion to music video than the portrayal of the diegetic dancing body; and (3) through diegetically performed song and dance that narratively project a lack of enjoyment, communal unity, or soul. In all three cases, the diegetic or emotional division maintained between the magical musical world and the mundane reality of the non-musical realm stunts the hypothesized utopic affect of the musical, while aiding in the production of the economic windfall tied to the soundtrack and music video tie-in.

I Can Hear the Music But I'm Not Dancin'

In all three films, the music's narrative function differs – at least formally – from the curative integrated one common to the more classical musical. Whereas Altman's aforementioned quasi-diegetic tune thrusts the integrated musical hero into dance, love and communal performance, these films include a preponderance of music that lacks any solid diegetic function, and instead is often relegated to aurally underscoring the action occurring on screen. In contrast to the integrated musical, these musical moments lack any direct connection to the diegesis or the physicality of the characters involved. The music does not drive their bodies into action. Instead, it often merely serves as a secondary – and redundant – non-diegetic reflection of the action through lyric or rhythm, or as Jeff Smith (1998: 164–65) asserts regarding scoring, a "quick-and-dirty means of establishing or reinforcing traits of a character".

Within both *Footloose* and *Flashdance*, songs that would come to define the films emerge through underscored (and therefore aurally non-diegetic) montage. Distanced from moments of diegetically live song or dance, these pseudo-musical numbers float in the background in sequences that depict romance or intense action, separate from the larger dance-driven conflicts. Underscoring either dynamic visuals (for example, quick and disjointed cutting which often obscures the actual action) or dramatic narrative action, songs such as 'Holding Out For a Hero' and 'I'm Free' (20:53 and 01:30:00, *Footloose*) or 'What a Feeling' and 'I Love Rock n Roll' (00:17 and 24:48, *Flashdance*) circulate outside of the larger musical narrative. Characters remain physically and psychologically disconnected from the music as the blending of splintered visuals and non-diegetic songs creates its own small film-bound music videos. Instead of creating an elevated and idyllic sense of reality through the spontaneous performance of song and dance, the music and associated visuals in these films serve more directly as source material for video tie-ins.

Maintaining a distance between the music and the diegetic woes of the respective films' narratives, non-diegetic moments of dramatic underscoring provide aural accompaniment to the action, but fail to bring the characters into that aforementioned middle ground where the idealism evoked by the music naturally blends with the lives of the characters. Instead, the burst of musical energy that emerges remains outside the diegetic world, rendering the once theorized transcendent quality of the music impotent. The characters themselves never transcend the realm of the everyday for that of the integrated musical world. Bonnie Tyler's 'Holding Out For a Hero' surely found a degree of commercial and cultural cache in the wake of *Footloose*, charting at number 34 two months after the film's opening, but within the narrative it merely functions as a non-diegetic soliloquy to the game of chicken occurring between the tractor-riding protagonist Ren and antagonist Chuck on the screen.[11]

As is often the case in *Footloose*, 'Holding Out For a Hero' begins as a piece of diegetic music blaring through the speakers of the romantic rival's boom box. The song ultimately – like with Sammy Hagar's 'The Girl Gets Around' (06:21) and Shalimar's 'Dancin' in the Sheets' (11:19) earlier in the film – exceeds (through volume) its actual sound source to largely engulf the aural realm of the scene. Unlike the trend Altman (1987: 66–67) identifies, where the movie musical includes a diegetic accompaniment that ultimately transcends its diegetic source (music box, guitar, and so on) to provoke integrated sung performance or instigate dance, this music does not join with the onscreen action. The music pouring from the radio does not become more closely related to the action – driving those in proximity to suddenly burst into communal performance; rather, the music seems to go from quietly diegetic to wholly non-diegetic as its volume denies any sense of aural fidelity. Instead of becoming part of the diegetic action, it runs parallel, and through its relegation to the non-diegetic realm merely narrates or describes – rather than creates or participates in – what occurs within the lives of the characters.

'Holding Out For a Hero' underscores the underdog narrative as Tyler's husky voice growls out a lament for the loss of good men and decries, "where's the street-wise Hercules to fight the rising odds" (Steinman and Pitchford, 1984). However, the song remains external to the embodied narrative. Unlike past musical underdog narratives where the embodiment of the music and song directly leads to the characters' burst in confidence (e.g. *The Sound of Music*'s [Robert Wise, 1965] 'I Have Confidence' or *The King and I*'s [Walter Lang, 1956] 'Whistle a Happy Tune') these music-heavy dance musicals often integrate the music in such a manner that it falls short of Dyer's utopic possibilities. While Dyer (2002: 20) describes the musical as in fact creating a utopic *feeling* rather than any promise of actual utopia (through the sounds of dance, the energy of performance, the burst of colour), these films relegate these building blocks of feeling to the outside or non-diegetic frame of the narrative, never merging diegetic music and dance with the actual narrative flow or characters' actions.

All three films utilize the technique of underscoring action with non-diegetic pop songs that would later appear on MTV or on the tie-in soundtrack. *Flashdance* begins with a totally non-diegetic rendition of 'What a Feeling'. The heroine Alex hops on her bike and rides through the industrial streets of Pittsburgh. Almost immediately the scene shifts to images of steel workers, backlit heavy machinery, and a lone welder (Alex) whose face is hidden by his or her mask. These same images – bicycle, city, steel mill, welding – would, along with a string of equally striking montage elements, form the basis of both of the film's popular music videos, 'What a Feeling' and 'Maniac'. Rather than creating a seamless musical world, as is the case with Marian the musical librarian, the *Flashdance* opening distances aural production from diegetic action. Instead the musical number serves mainly as underscoring for salient visual contextual cues, a soft setup for the continued co-presence of music and manual labour within the narrative, and an extremely useful catalogue of somewhat disparate but high-style shots from which later videos could emerge. *Dirty Dancing*'s 'She's Like the Wind' (1:23:27) and 'Overload' (40:07) both serve as non-diegetic brooding music for Johnny as they briefly underscore the angsty action when he finds himself locked out of his car and without a job. Across all three films, this musical presence – or rather lack thereof – allows for a kind of half-step towards integration. While simply doubling or rearticulating the diegetic action or tone, the music remains a half-step away from actual contact with the story or its moving bodies.

Video Killed the Dancing Star

The musical distanciation or apparent lack of musical embodiment comes not only from the separation of music and dance, but also through the cinematic choices made in the presentation of dance. Of course these three films welcome the inclusion of dance, and each embraces fleeting moments of more classical presentation of choreography, distanced from the quick-paced editing of music video and more reflective of the filmed choreographic work of the likes of Michael Kidd (*Seven Brides for Seven Brothers* [Stanley Donen, 1954]), Gene Kelly (*Singin' in the Rain* [1952]) or Hermes Pan (*Top Hat* [Mark Sandrich, 1935]). Such choreographers – combined with their respective cinematographers and editors – highlighted floor coverage, the entire body or multiple bodies in fluid movement, and the overall shapes and patterns of the dance. *Footloose* follows this trend as it features its teen hoofers at the prom (1:39:45 in a near communal folk dance). *Flashdance* concludes with a hybridized ballet/breakdance/ aerobics performance to 'What a Feeling' (1:26:49) that evokes the visuals of an Astaire or Kelly number that pulls back to capture floor coverage, body shapes and the overall flow of the dance, as erotic dancer Alex auditions for a classical dance school. *Dirty Dancing* includes a flashy performance by Penny and Johnny (10:21) on the ballroom dance floor, Johnny and Baby's out-of-town mambo (47:06) and a final large group number to '(I've Had) The Time of My Life' (1:30:19). More commonly, however, the films' dance sequences forego, both visually and aurally, projecting dance as something so overtly connected to sound, bodies and personal freedom, as neither the bodies nor the sounds they produce – taps, shuffles, and so on – emerge as central to the cinematic image/soundtrack. These more classic moments emerge as the exception rather than the rule.

The video-era dance film – and many of the more integrated musicals to come – more commonly fractures the body through quick-paced editing and a close-up heavy cinematographic style, rather than depicting dance's fluidity, its movement, and the joining of lovers and community in a visual union. Many of the most central dance numbers of *Dirty Dancing*, *Footloose* and *Flashdance* employ shooting-styles that drive wedges between the visual projection of the dancing body and the seamless union of song and dance. Much like the aforementioned non-dance-oriented musical montages, many of the dance sequences present an aesthetic more akin to the music video – or more easily integrated into one – than a style focused on capturing the individual or group in the throes of dance. Not only has the aural-visual link been severed through the repeated integration of non-diegetic music, but also the visual projection of the community or lovers united in transcendent movement fades as the camera repeatedly obscures the body in favour of a series of sexualized close-ups rife for transfer to music video.

Throughout the films, dance sequences themselves emerge as near videos, often presented in a non-linear or fractured temporal form. Many of these numbers appear as traditional 'we're getting better' or 'I've got to dance it out' montages: 'Let's Hear it For the Boy' (59:40, *Footloose*), 'Never' (35:30, *Footloose*),

'Maniac' (13:34, *Flashdance*), 'Hungry Eyes' (35:58, *Dirty Dancing*) and 'Wipe Out' (34:00, *Dirty Dancing*). These numbers suggest the trend towards underscoring addressed in the previous section, but use the underscoring to link a series of temporally disparate or visually fractured dance-related interludes. In each case, non-diegetic music (or music that begins as diegetic and then transcends its compositional motivation and becomes underscoring) creates a sense of non-diegetic aural continuity that the images themselves deny or undermine.

Numbers such as 'Never' and 'Maniac' depict one singular instance of dance, while presenting isolated moments of choreography in a montage form that condenses the time taken to depict the dance. Both privilege visually dynamic screen compositions that may or may not best feature the dance itself. 'Maniac' occurs as Alex works out in her loft. Although very little dancing actually transpires, the film's narrative frames her as dancer as she runs in place, stretches her legs, moves her head around and flexes her butt. The camera obscures the lack of actual dance as a series of close-ups (CUs) that feature isolated body parts to the rhythm of the music. The pulsating synthesized beat begins with a CU of Alex wrapping the balls of her feet as she flexes her toes and ultimately runs in place to the non-diegetic beat. Within the first ten seconds of the song, the montage includes a CU of Alex's running feet, a CU of her intensely exhaling as she sweats and runs in place, a CU of her leotard-ed buttocks and swinging arms (lit so the rest of her body disappears into darkness), another CU of her running feet, and a return to her buttocks and arms. That initial ten seconds of song/dance reflects the pace of editing and type of framing used throughout the number: quick, close and to the beat of the non-diegetic music. The number continues in a similar vein, adding recurring CUs of her swivelling hips and neck, recurring medium long shots of stretches, a couple seconds of balletic bar work, spinning buttocks, and a CU of her dog. The number then ends abruptly as the song stops and the scene shifts to Alex gulping a post-workout glass of water.

In 'Maniac' the visual splintering of the image and/or the flow of dance reflects a trend in these films, ones in which the *idea* or plot-driven presence of dance or the visually stylized framing of non-dance movement as dance eclipses the actual presentation of choreography or diegetic engagement with the music. Music and dance no longer unite to serve as the mythical social glue or siren song to young lovers. Instead they comprise a diegetic plot-point, and its fractured images (and the disembodied sounds of music) function more effectively as extradiegetic merchandising. *Footloose*'s 'Never', although displaying more full-body shots of dance, embraces a style similar to that of 'Maniac'. The number occurs over pseudo-diegetic music (as Ren puts in a cassette tape to simulate a source for the musical montage). His tantrum or choreographed response to the town's rejection of his big city ways emerges through a montage that combines dance, gymnastics, low-key lighting, short shot length and temporal disjointedness with inserts from previous scenes depicting Ren's social downfall. In both of the aforementioned cases – 'Maniac' and 'Never' – the dance itself appears disjointed, separated from motivated aural production and often obscured from clear view; however, the shots and built-in cuts create a kind of pre-packaged catalogue of images to be mixed and matched as they construct the tie-in music videos.

Along with the montages that connect a somewhat temporally localized performance moment with a piece of pseudo-diegetic music, these films also favour the 'we're working on it' montage sequence that illustrates a build in technical skill. *Footloose*'s 'Let's Hear it For the Boy' shows hayseed Willard's struggle to overcome an unabashed lack of rhythm as he combines Ren's dance advice with gymnastics, wrestling and good old-fashioned stomping. *Dirty Dancing* uses two major montage sequences to illustrate the increase in Baby's dance skills, her transition into womanhood, and the budding relationship – from adversarial to seductive – between Baby and Johnny.[12] 'Wipe Out' and 'Hungry Eyes' accomplish this most fully.

'Wipe Out' chronicles the first major series of dance lessons and shows Baby becoming a real contender – choreographically and sexually. Costume changes denote the passage of time. Unlike *Flashdance*'s and *Footloose*'s 'gotta dance it out' numbers, this one provides major compositional motivation, as Baby's success in mastering the mambo will prevent Johnny and pregnant Penny from losing their moonlighting job at a neighbouring hotel. The music of 'Wipe Out' fades up and down as moments of dialogue and action interrupt the more fractured shots of Baby repeating the same steps over and over and over. The camera vacillates between medium close-ups (MCUs) of the dancers and CUs of Baby's inept footwork. More directly motivated than in the previously discussed montage sequences, the camerawork directs the viewer's attention to salient images and depicts narrative progression (while also providing clean pre-isolated shots to comprise accompanying music videos). The 'Hungry Eyes' montage – with the music functioning mainly as underscoring, but at times briefly appearing to possibly penetrate the diegetic action – accomplishes the same task, as repeated CUs of feet, medium shots (MS) of Baby's and Penny's legs, and MCUs of hands on hips and torsos project both Baby's burgeoning skills and the rising intimacy between the dance partners. For both of the aforementioned numbers, lyrics, camerawork and the strategic pairings of lyrics and onscreen action allow the largely non-diegetic accompaniment to parallel or retell the splintered choreographic and narrative action. Nonetheless, the songs and singers remain outside of the action and deny the union of song and body, as the voices of Eric Carmen and the Surfaris emerge rather than those of Baby and Johnny.

Beyond the montage moments of dance, even those numbers presented in relative real-time abandon the visual and aural connection common to the more classical musical in favour of the discontinuity of the music video. In these moments, the diegetic music accompanies a dance sequence presented with a sense of temporal and spatial continuity. While not necessarily shown with a sense of visual continuity – or fluidity or a sense of wholeness – the film presents the dance number (at times from beginning to end) in one continuous moment. Although closer to building a direct connection between music and movement, these routines still highlight a disjointed sense of bodily movement as the camera tells the story more than the dancing body.[13]

Real-time numbers in both *Dirty Dancing* and *Flashdance* render actual bodily movement secondary to that of the movie camera and choices in editing. As was often common in Berkeley's visual dazzlers, the camera tells the story – rather than the dancer's body. Repeated quick cuts, extreme camera angles, CUs or extreme close-ups (ECUs) of dance moves or non-dance-related bodily movement define how the dance will visually emerge as the camera only fleetingly captures the entire body in movement. Rather the music drives the camera, as the visual power of the camera supersedes the storytelling power of the dancer. Visually similar to the music video, these numbers present disjointed visuals in conjunction with a continuous music track to evoke a *feeling*. The depiction of the actual dance itself emerges as inferior in the creation of narrative meaning – as its actual movement, spatial sense and relationship to the music appear secondary to the story told or feeling created by the camera.

Dirty Dancing first introduces the sultry world of the staff dancers through a combination of The Contours's 'Do You Love Me' (14:45) and Otis Redding's 'Love Man' (18:15). The camera draws Baby through the room and between the bodies of numerous dancers. Shifting from CU to MS and Baby's point of view (POV) to a more objective POV, the camera only momentarily captures any whole pictures of the dance.[14] Instead it shifts from the faces, butts, hips, torsos and feet of coupled but nameless dancers, those who form Baby's early education in the sensuality of dance. Rather than highlighting the interaction of the couple, or even the dynamic of the community, the film foregrounds the non-dancing Baby reaction shots and a disjointed interaction between the camera and various dancers: one couple's swivelling hips to a tilt shot that frames a woman's boobs as she does a backbend, to a tilt highlighting another male dancer's squat to his partner's crotch. The at-times quick, often limited, shots of bodies mirror the heterogeneous and decontextualized style prevalent to the music video (and a style that would then be mirrored by similarly-styled dancers in the Jennifer Warnes/Bill Medley '[I've Had] The Time of My Life' music video). The sultry chorus visually exists as an aura of horniness outside the aforementioned (and often similarly fractured) dances of the romantic couple; as isolated individuals and sexualized CUs overwhelm the visual space they obscure the larger communal response to the music.[15] As with 'Maniac', the continued focus on the highly edited pieces of the choreographic whole take the fore, leaving the performances or affect of the larger diegetic (or by proxy, theatrical) community to fall to the wayside.

A similar music video style drives the visuals of *Flashdance*'s flash-dancers, one where the shooting style of the individual dance connotes more than the dance itself. Kathryn Kalinak (1984) describes the film's dance style as "a kind of non-dancing, an abandonment to self-expression" (3) captured through a frenetic camera style similar to Berkeley. All of the numbers in Mawby's Bar/Alex's dance club – Alex's 'He's a Dream' (04:20) and 'Imagination' (52:10) and Tina Tech (Cynthia Rhodes)'s 'Manhunt' (33:09) – depict the movement of a single dancer and single choreographic moment. The over-presence of the camera, however, detracts from the performance (or self-expression) of the individual, while instead focusing on an overall high-concept visual style. Incorporated into the videos for both 'Maniac' and 'What a Feeling', the resulting visuals of these dance numbers perhaps illustrate their primary logic being something other than clear communication of the narrative.

The highly stylized costumes, sets and choreography of these numbers disrupt rather than meld with the narrative. Mawby's appears as something just one step above the film's other strip club: the trashier nudie bar Zanzibar. Despite this and with little resistance from the bar's patrons, Alex's performances emerge as something artsy rather than sultry. Both of her numbers include concept-heavy costumes and less than erotic movement – much in contrast to those of Tina Tech. Alex's first dance – remembered mostly for the iconic image of water pouring down on her as she arches over a chair – shifts between banging on a chair and exuberant marching. Adrian Lyne shoots the scene largely in stark silhouette. Alex enters the stage wearing a full 1980s pantsuit with big shoulder pads. She quickly removes the suit – which then appears to stand on its own – and rolls it off the stage. While bereft of the salacious movements expected for such a club and present in Tina's more animalistic crawling and slithering in 'Manhunt' (shot in CU and at a low camera height), 'He's a Dream' functions nicely in the two tie-in videos with its striking imagery and repetitive splashes of water on Alex's eventually scantily-clad body.

Alex's kabuki-esque makeup, forced-perspective setting, turquoise toreador pants and strobe lights in her 'Imagination' number again seem incompatible with the expectations of the bar's audience. The shape of her stylized robe casts voluminous shadows onto the checkered, forced-perspective façade. She then strips away her robe to reveal a red 1980s power suit and then skin-tight toreador pants and a scoop-neck t-shirt. She flails in the corner of the room as strobe lights and a canting camera project her frantic image. As with 'He's a Dream', the striking images make little sense within the context of the story, but blend fluidly with the 'Manic' music video (as her odd performance partially tells the story of a "Maniac on the floor" who's "dancin' like she's never danced before") (Matkosky and Sembello, 1983).

Even when these films do embrace actual performance of dance, they simultaneously allow external stimuli – camerawork, sound editing, soundtrack and video tie-ins – to take precedence over the actual dance itself. As the non-dance underscored montage sequences sever the connection between music and diegetic performance, these choreographed moments – montage or real-time – weaken the narrative-linked communicative power of dance and the aural/visual co-presence of the choreographic vision, dancer and voice. In most cases, these visual/aural/choreographic discontinuities – while perhaps preventing the once common utopic communal cure of performance – fold nicely into economically beneficial and industrially desirable music videos. In short, the dancing may not quite *tell* the story, but it helps *sell* the story.

I Can Hear the Music but I Just Don't Feel Like Dancin'

In both of the aforementioned patterns – underscored non-dance montage and music video styled moments of dance – the once close relationship between sound and body gives way to a primary concern with the camera and its relationship to elements other than synthesized diegetic music and dance. Underscored and visually stylized storytelling and the lucrative music video become the primary motivators for song and dance as the seamless blending and mutual diegetic embodiment of the two fade. Just as telling, however, is the limited and connotative place of 'realistically presented' diegetic song and dance. Moments that present non-soundtrack-bound singing voices or dance that exists outside the realm of the video-bound image project a hollowness of music in these diegetic worlds that foreground the mechanical production of sound and movement.

Braudy (1976: 155), Feuer (1993: 10–11) and Altman (1987: 63–67) each attribute energy and passion to communal dance – whether Gene Kelly's energy lured others to participate or the group spontaneously intuited each other's movements. In these newer dance films, moments where the community joins voices and bodies in song and/or dance – unaided by the moments of quick-paced editing, highly sexualized CUs or the piped-in sounds of chart-topping pop tunes – fall flat. These less-mediated moments project the lack of skill, passion and energy of the group. Strangers, resort goers, church members and the like, do not suddenly possess the acumen of a powerful gospel choir, modern dance troupe or rock group. Rather, their sounds and movements emerge as hollow. Their lack of energy and pizzazz only highlights the denigrated position of performative integration – or the magical blending of music and body. The substandard performances that occur in everyday life simultaneously stress the projected significance of those performative moments that rely more fully on the camera or pre-recorded soundtrack tunes than the everyday folks within the narratives themselves.

Both Dirty Dancing and Footloose create worlds where song and dance performed by ordinary people or captured in a style contrary to the music video falls short. Throughout Dirty Dancing, song and dance performed outside of the realm of the video-esque identifies people as passionless, visionless or frivolous. The sultry, temporally and visually disjointed and highly sexualized dance occurring inside the staff barracks and between Baby and Johnny stands in stark contrast to other moments of performance that set the rest of the resort employees and patrons apart from those the narrative frames as valid and impassioned. Guests participate in a frivolous bunny hop (1:06:31) and show their lack of performance skills at a dance class (04:35) led by Penny (Cynthia Rhodes) (at which Baby must asexually partner with an elderly woman). Throughout the narrative, Neil Kellerman (Lonny Price) (the resort owner's smarmy nephew) attempts to seduce Baby with his awkward dance steps (10:21), which juxtapose strongly with the graceful and seductive movements of Johnny. Once no longer part of this inept crowd – and now defined by the sexualized dances and camerawork related to the *real* dancers – Baby emerges in stark contrast to her previous self and her incessantly naïve sister, Lisa (Jane Brucker), who continues to follow the path of the backward resort performances.[16] Not until the end of the film will the average people find the passion embodied by the dirty dancers. Also at that moment, they too take on a toned-down version of visual and aural distanciation as '(I've Had) The Time of My Life' aurally absorbs the scene and quick camerawork invades the dance floor. Like Baby and Johnny before them, everyone has become the protagonist in the music video: a place where dancing passion resides outside the realm of aural and visual continuity and authenticity.

Flashdance and Footloose reflect a similar trend, as the presentation of the Zanzibar (1:14:48) strippers highlights their soulless performances as the relatively still camera focuses in on their dead eyes and monotonous movements. Diegetic – and non-recording based – music only appears in Footloose through the quiet, unprofessional and narratively oppressive voices of the churchgoers. These same folks who oppress Ren and ban rock 'n' roll and dance from the town meekly sing 'What a Friend We Have in Jesus' (04:42). These fleeting moments that present aurally, temporally and spatially congruous song and dance often compound the ideological underpinnings projected through the more mechanized and deconstructed moments of performance throughout these films, as these 'real' moments of song and dance emerge through inept and soulless performances. When real folks sing (or dance) in real time and space, it does not produce the narrative impact implied within the more classical musical. In such a space, both types of visual and physical performance – highly mediated/disjointed and objectively and narratively presented – project something that stops short of glorious synthesis of voices and bodies that welcomed the utopic possibilities or the transcendent state once promised. Either through a growing rift between aural, physical and visual performance or a stunning narrative devaluation of more naturalized moments of song and dance, these qualities fade.

The Fading Echoes of the Hoofers

This visual and aural distanciation that defined the teen dance films of the 1980s did not exist in a vacuum. They existed as part of emergent generic mores from the sixties, seventies and eighties that ushered in a somewhat darker musical, eschewed narratively integrated and bodily produced instances of song and dance, highlighted the economic possibilities of the blockbuster and capitalized on its affinity for high-concept visuals and quick-paced editing. The early 1980s bust and millennial boom of integrated film musicals bookend this period of the teen dance film. Even as a new integrated phase of the genre would gain some economic and critical viability a decade after the dance films, the visual, aural and economic trends entrenched in the eighties would continue (Kessler, 2010: 186–88).

As the musical finds its footing again at the turn of the century, performative estrangement comes to define the genre. The chart-topping hits of Madonna, Beyonce, Christina Aguilera and Queen Latifah underscore the new musical's performance-light visage, continuing the diminution of the visual and ideological connotative power of a once seemingly organic combination of physical performance, narrative and communal utopia. Blockbuster musical hits and misses such as *Evita* (Alan Parker, 1996), *Moulin Rouge!* (Baz Luhrmann, 2001), *Chicago* (Rob Marshall, 2002), *Rent* (Chris Columbus, 2005) and *Dreamgirls* (Bill Condon, 2006) reflect the same tentative relationship with presentation of performance as did the earlier teen dance films. While these films embrace the notion of spontaneous performance through song, their affection for heavy-handed camerawork and underscored musical montage means they continue to highlight a mechanized sense of performance rather than one that glorifies the transformative potential of blended bodies, voices and stories (Kessler, 2010: 185–91). Perhaps American filmmakers simply fear the audience response to old-school styles of visual and aural performance. Perhaps the continued yen to court the teenage audience or maintain over-the-top visual stylings that sell well internationally drive the aesthetics of contemporary musicals.

Regardless of impetus, these new films continue to bear the markings of the musical hybrid teen dance film that straddled the ideological, aesthetic, narrative and aural qualities of the emergent music video and the more traditional Hollywood musical.

Notes

1. The general concept for this chapter was inspired by minor points raised in the "Epilogue" of *Destabilizing the Hollywood Musical: Music, Masculinity, and Mayhem* (Kessler, 2010). I would like to thank Michael DeAngelis for his gracious advice and support through this project.
2. Kelly Kessler is an Associate Professor of Media and Cinema Studies at DePaul University, Chicago. Her work largely engages with issues of gender and genre in American television and film. Kessler's book, *Destabilizing the Hollywood Musical: Music, Masculinity, and Mayhem*, explores the gendered ramifications of the genre's shift in the latter part of the twentieth century. Her work can also be found in journals and anthologies such as *Television and New Media*, *Cinema Journal* and *Feminism at the Movies*.
3. William Paul (1994) interrogates this shift from single-screen theatres to multi-screened, mall-bound structures. He notes that the move towards the multiplex escalated in the 1980s, producing some theatres "so large that they became malls unto themselves" (491). According to an article in *Variety* (Tusher, 1984) published the year of *Footloose*'s release, that year's boom in film screens – at an all-time high since 1948 – was largely due to newly built multiplexes. These same mall-bound structures would provide teens with easy access to both films and their music tie-ins.
4. While the form of the musical was never a wholly stable one, prior to the mid-sixties, musicals where song, dance and music united within the diegesis and led to the eventual resolution of a blended community and companionate romance dominated the genre. For more on this, see Rick Altman's (1987) *The American Film Musical* or Kelly Kessler's (2010) *Destabilizing the Hollywood Musical*.
5. For the purposes of this chapter, I intentionally sidestep the less economically successful and/or less dance-oriented films that targeted the same teen demographic through similar means: *Breakin'* (1984), *Breakin 2: Electric Boogaloo* (1984), *Beat Street* (1984), *Purple Rain* (1984), *La Bamba* (1987), among others. Simultaneously, I eschew discussions of films that placed equal or added focus on marketability through video and soundtrack tie-ins but made no attempt to narratively embrace the norms of the musical through a focus on song and/or dance: *Top Gun* (1986), *Batman* (1989), *Cocktail* (1988), among others. Although such films share characteristics with the three films that comprise my study, because of lack of video presence or lack of physical performance, they less effectively reflect the burgeoning norms this chapter interrogates.
6. Please note, this is not presented as a piece on media reception. Instead, its focus lies on formal shifts that occur between the classical integrated musical and the

teen dance films of the eighties and how their visual/aural tendencies reflect conflicting ideological and industrial concerns.
7. All *Billboard* information in this chapter comes from Joel Whitburn's (1996) *The Billboard Book of Top 40 Hits* (singles) or his (1996) *Top Pop Albums: 1955-1996* (albums).
8. Scholars such as Rick Altman (1987: 63–67), Jane Feuer (1993: 10–11) and Richard Dyer (2002) point to the utopic possibilities projected through the Hollywood musical. Whether through the utopic feelings conjured through dance, colour and rhythm or the idyllic communal unification evoked through climactic weddings, passed-along songs or folk dances, such scholars contend that the genre itself has historically projected an image of endless possibility and potential social harmony. I do not claim, however, that early musicals did not include moments of more fraught social tensions. For more on social unrest in the Hollywood musical see Kelly Kessler's *Destabilizing the Hollywood Musical* (2010). Further, for this chapter, the term 'integrated' will refer to the practice of characters spontaneously bursting into song and dance. In these moments, song and dance become one with the narratives, blurring the lines between the non-musical world and the perhaps more perfect musical one. For more on musical integration, see the work of Jerome Delameter (1981) and John Mueller (1984).
9. Similar diegetic/non-diegetic discontinuity exists in Patrick Swayze's 'She's Like the Wind' video, which depicts a non-filmic Swayze thinking of the diegetic Baby (through what seems like memories seen through a rippling water surface). *Footloose* and *Flashdance* stick to diegetic images, but pull shots from all over the films' narratives to best visually punctuate their videos. For example, the 'Footloose' music video uses over 80 shots from the opening credit sequence, over 40 from the 'Never' dance montage, nearly 20 from Willard's 'Let's Hear it For the Boy' montage, and countless others from musical and non-musical moments from the film.
10. Although the film musical may commonly include montage from one choreographed moment to another, the music video commonly joins visually fractured moments that neither retain temporal, spatial or aural unity. Whereas *The Sound of Music*'s Maria and the children sing 'Do-Re-Mi' over a period of time and across Saltsburg, they together diegetically sing the number, linking them to their world and to the actual performance.
11. Notably, the music video for 'Holding Out For a Hero' did not include content from the film, but rather an odd Western motif which begins with Tyler escaping from a burning house. 'Holding Out For a Hero' was also the film's lowest charting song, with songs such as 'Footloose' and 'Let's Hear It For the Boy' hitting number one and 'Almost Paradise' topping out at number seven.
12. The type of romance narrative projected through the Baby/Johnny montage sequences mirrors the narrative trajectory typified by Fred Astaire and Ginger Rogers. In his description of the fairytale musical, Rick Altman (1987: 63–67) discusses the duo's relationship emerging through events such as the "challenge dance" and the "romantic dance". Through these numbers their personality conflicts emerge and find resolution. While Johnny and Baby's romance similarly emerges

through dance in *Dirty Dancing*, it often crops up between the lines of montage, rather than through individual, isolated numbers.
13. Sherril Dodds's (2005: 68–69) *Dance on the Screen* examines the styles and challenges present when the traditionally live art of dance transfers to the screen. She highlights the difficulty experienced by choreographers and directors as they transfer dance to the television screen and tackle the challenge of maintaining the spirit of dance in a context where the medium compromises the sense of live-ness and the overall visual composition. She further examines the rise of "video dance", a genre of screen dance that overtly – through its choreography – explores the complex relationship between dance and video.
14. Shots that capture more of the dancing bodies occur when Johnny and Penny enter and become the centre of attention or when Johnny approaches Baby.
15. The film continuously frames these nameless dancers in a similar fashion: opening credits, the aforementioned scene, the quasi-dance scene when Baby arrives with Penny's abortion funds, and the final dance number.
16. Ironically, her stilted performances directly mirror the kinds of integrated musical numbers these dance films abandon, as she ruminates about warbling 'I Feel Pretty' (*West Side Story* [Jerome Robbins and Robert Wise, 1961]), only to ultimately sing a kitchy Hawaiian song (01:12:42) in theatrical costume.

References

Altman, R. (1987), *The American Film Musical*, Bloomington and Indianapolis: Indiana University Press.

Austerlitz, Saul (2007), *Money for Nothing: A History of Music Video from The Beatles to the White Stripes*, New York: Continuum.

Braudy, L. (1976), *The World in a Frame: What We See in Films*, Garden City, NY: Anchor Press.

Custen, G. F. (1997), *Twentieth Century's Fox: Darryl F. Zanuck and the Culture of Hollywood*, New York: Basic Books.

Delameter, J. (1981), *Dance in the Hollywood Musical*, Ann Arbor: UMI Research Press.

Denisoff, R. S., and Plasketes, G. (1990), 'Synergy in 1980s Film and Music: Formula for Success or Industry Mythology?', *Film History*, 4(3), 257–76.

Dodds, S. (2005), *Dance on the Screen*, New York: Palgrave.

Dyer, R. (2002), 'Entertainment and Utopia', in S. Cohan (ed.), *Hollywood Musicals: The Film Reader*, London and New York: Routledge, pp. 19–30.

Ebert, R. (1984), Review of *Footloose*, *Chicago Sun-Times*, 1 January, online at http://rogerebert.suntimes.com/apps/pbcs.dll/article?AID=/19840101/REVIEWS/401010339/1023.

Feuer, J. (1993), *The Hollywood Musical*, 2nd edn, Indianapolis and Bloomington: Indiana University Press.

Gehr, R. (1983), 'The MTV Aesthetic', *Film Comment*, 19(4), 37–40.

Hoberman, J. (2004), 'Ten Years That Shook the World', in T. Schatz (ed.), *Hollywood: Critical Concepts in Media and Cultural Studies*, vol. 1, New York and London: Routledge, pp. 315–32.

Kalinak, K. (1984), 'Flashdance: The Dead End Kid', *Jump Cut*, 29 (February), 3–5.
Kessler, K. (2010) *Destabilizing the Hollywood Musical: Music, Masculinity, and Mayhem*, London: Palgrave-MacMillan.
Kinder, M. (1984), 'Music Video and the Spectator: Television, Ideology and Dream', *Film Quarterly*, 38(1), 2–15.
Matkosky, D., and Sembello, M. (1983), 'Maniac', EMI.
Mueller, J. (1984), 'Fred Astaire and the Integrated Musical', *Cinema Journal*, 24(1), 28–40.
Paul, W. (1994), 'The K-Mart Audience at the Mall Movies', *Film History*, 6(4), 487–501.
Schatz, T. (1993), 'The New Hollywood', in J. Collins, H. Radner and A. Collins (eds), *Film Theory Goes to the Movies*, New York: Routledge, pp. 8–36.
Smith, J. (1998), *The Sounds of Commerce: Marketing Popular Film Music*, New York: Columbia University Press.
Steinman, J., and Pitchford, D. (1984), 'Holding Out for a Hero', CBS Records.
Telotte, J. (2002), 'The New Hollywood Musical: From *Saturday Night Fever* to *Footloose*', in S. Neale (ed.), *Genre and Contemporary Hollywood*, London: BFI, pp. 48–61.
Tusher, W. (1984), 'US Exhibs Showing New Growth', *Variety*, 28 November.
Variety (1986), 'Review: Dirty Dancing', *Variety*, 31 December, online at http://www.variety.com/review/VE1117790446.html?categoryid=31&cs=1&query=dirty+dancing#ixzz14p3UVMdz.
Whitburn, J. (1996a), *The Billboard Book of Top 40 Hits*, 6th edn, New York: Billboard Books.
Whitburn, J. (1996b), *Top Pop Albums: 1955–1996*, Menomonee Falls, WI: Record Research, Inc.
Wyatt, J. (1994), *High Concept: Movies and Marketing in Hollywood*, Austin: University of Texas Press.

'Anything but Ballet'
Individuality, Genre-Bending and Sexual Expression in Center Stage

Gillian Turnbull[1]

In a pivotal scene in the 2000 ballet film *Center Stage*,[2] main character Jody Sawyer (Amanda Schull) enters a Broadway dance studio with trepidation after a long day of ballet rehearsals. "Do you have a 5:30 class?" she asks the receptionist. "What kind would you like?" asks the receptionist. "Anything but ballet", replies Jody. She dresses for class in the corner of a bustling room, where dancers chat excitedly with each other, and snack on muffins before class begins. A far cry from the silent, critical and competitive atmosphere of Jody's classes at the fictitious American Ballet Academy, the jazz-oriented Broadway class transforms Jody's concept of who she is as a dancer, thus beginning a coming of age story that is becoming increasingly common to dance films. This dance class sets Jody on a course of finding romance, rejecting the strict confines of ballet life, and embracing an individual style that utilizes her ballet training, but adapts to a contemporary approach to ballet that is intent on breaking down its elitist barriers. Music is at the centre of this struggle, employed in *Center Stage* as the device with which dancers and choreographers alike forge subversive artistic identities.

In this chapter, I will argue that the employment of popular music throughout *Center Stage* functions to break the impenetrability of ballet, securing its place within a more commercial (or lowbrow) mainstream, while elevating popular music to the role of reconstructing ideas about classical dance. I will also explore how genre determines individual and sexual expression, manifested in the overt declaration of masculine and feminine identities in movement and in the use of alternative gestures in classical ballet, which similarly disrupt conventional notions about ballet traditions. Rock and pop music further enable the characters in *Center Stage* to use alternative gestures in order to disentangle the standard gender roles that still dominate ballet.

Center Stage is a prime example of the continual tension between high and low art. The American Ballet Academy, where the characters are studying, is a typical ballet school, at which students lament the high expectations and competitive nature of their environment while trying out 'new' forms of dance such as salsa and jazz during their spare time. The implication that classical music and dance evoke true beauty and otherworldly qualities counteract young choreographer Cooper Nielson's (Ethan Stiefel) desire to create a dance that is "as real as it can be". Music is used as the freeing force by which dancers may discover their true dance desires. Against tracks by Michael Jackson, the Red Hot Chili Peppers and Jamiroquai, dancers employ what Garafola (1998) terms the open-ended rhythmic gesture, that which does not rely on mime gestures fixed in meaning and shape. Pop song choices such as these foster a shift away from the pose-heavy choreography of the classical ballet pieces, highlighting the high–low art undercurrent of the film. Ballet technique is simultaneously valorized, as when Cooper's piece ends with a 20-*fouetté* and double *pirouette* sequence performed by Jody; it is this conflict that points to an effort to recognize the omnivorous tastes of a new middle-class audience (van Eijck, 2001), which currently characterizes many mainstream dance films.

Reinforcing and Rethinking Gender Roles

Ballet is a ripe area for the investigation of gender relations. Scholars have examined the ways in which traditional gender roles are reinforced in narrative, during performance, and backstage, often citing Romantic-era ballets as the origin of these ideals. Since the contemporary ballet repertoire is largely dominated by works from the Romantic canon, such as *Giselle*, *La Sylphide* and *Swan Lake*, images of the delicate, passive, distinctly feminine ballerina have dominated not only the persona attributed to female dancers, but have also dictated the trajectory of dance training, body shapes, and expectations of the professional dancer's submissiveness to the choreographer throughout twentieth-century ballet. In her exposé of the ballet world, *Off Balance: The Real World of Ballet*, Suzanne Gordon notes:

> The mould female dancers must fit is a peculiar idealization of the feminine. Onstage, ballerinas appear to be perfect women: delicate, graceful, slender, yet well rounded and well proportioned. Like so much on stage, this is no more than an illusion ... women are supposed to be placid, passive, and cooperative. This applies not only to their conduct, but to their appearance ... this surface layer of sweetness seems to be one of the identifying marks of the ballerina. (1983: 91)

Cordova notes that the era of Romantic ballet that provided the majority of works now anchoring the dance canon saw the separation of female and male roles, which was partially determined by the advance of pointe work, performed exclusively by females. Moreover, an art form that had previously seen low female participation, ballet opened up to include female travesty roles and the supportive body of the corps de ballet, which led to its eventual identity as a feminine art form (Cordova, 2007: 121). In contemporary performance and on film, the gendered traditions of ballet prevail, largely because the canon of works presented, or from which new works are drawn, valorizes the passive female or heroic male characters.

As such, *Center Stage* portrays the fictitious American Ballet Company (ABC) as one that is, like many of its counterparts, dependent on philanthropic donations, fundraising and ticket sales. It must therefore stage classics such as *Swan Lake* and *Romeo and Juliet* in order to guarantee a return audience, although another seemingly favourite performance among audience members is the final student workshop, at which many of the Academy students show off their technique for scouts from other companies. It is this final workshop around which tensions circle, culminating in a climactic routine performed by Jody, Cooper (stepping in for the injured Erik [Shakiem Evans]) and Charlie (Sascha Radetsky). This routine, choreographed by Cooper, ABC's star dancer, has been seen in rehearsed segments throughout the film.

The dance illuminates the multiple storylines that guide the film's plot: Cooper has staged a ballet showdown between Erik (himself) and Charlie, "the director of a ballet company" (meant to be ABC director Jonathan Reeves, played by Peter Gallagher), the winner of which will supposedly receive Jody's (meant to be ABC principal dancer Kathleen Donahue, played by Julie Kent) affections. The final dance sequence additionally brings the film's love triangle between Jody, Cooper and Charlie to the stage. At the heart of this routine, however, is the film's ultimate, and relatively obvious, dilemma: for whom should one dance, and to what extent should the dancer's dedication to her art be taken?

The final routine begins with a ballet class in progress. Charlie, as the company director, claps his hands and yells out counts to his class of female students, all moving into formed positions of *écarté*, *effacé* and fifth, in unison to the music of *The Nutcracker*. This is interrupted by a change in music to Michael Jackson's 'The Way You Make Me Feel' (1987) and Cooper roaring onstage on his motorcycle, dismounting to twirl Jody. He chases Jody among the dancers, who continue to perform *port de bras*, *tendus* and *battement frappés*. Cooper then displays his masculine magnetism through a series of leaps and multiple *pirouettes*, and joins Jody in a brief *pas de deux* while the corps watches in mimed positions of horror.

The following *pas de trois* is set to 'If I Was the One' (2000) by R&B duo Ruff Endz. It mostly conforms to the typical structure and movement patterns of a traditional *pas de trois*, although Cooper's solo display for Jody is marked by jerky movements, turned-in legs and flailing arms, as if to demonstrate why he is the more modern, appealing choice compared to the 'dull' conservatism that Charlie offers through his more conventional movements. At the end, still clearly torn between the two, Jody dances several *pas de boureés*, pausing in a fourth position on pointe, as the music transitions to a new track, Jamiroquai's 'Canned Heat' (1999). Jody's choice of her true love, dance, is reinforced by the lyrics sung, "Dance/Nothing else I need to do/But dance/All these bad times I'm going through/Just dance" as she pushes the men away and starts a solo dance backed by the corps. In this final moment of the routine, Jody continually evades the men as they chase her around the floor, preferring instead to lead the corps. At one point, the two men corner Jody and she disappears beneath them, offscreen, returning in a line of dancers with their hands splayed across each other's hips as they step forward, thrusting their pelvises. As the dance culminates with Jody's *fouetté* sequence, performed alone while the corps poses in a tableau of restraining the men, it is clear that she has chosen her dance over a man, a choice that might resonate with many dancers who are forced to choose between a career or a relationship.

This final dance sequence both reinforces and challenges the fixed gender roles so often found in the ballet world and the plots seen onstage. Gordon notes:

> Fearful and obedient, they [women] are indeterminate creatures of indeterminate sexuality, adolescents frozen on the border between childhood and adulthood ... In most companies, dancers, like the swans and their consorts, are controlled by choreographers, who are nearly always older men ... He decides how they are to look, feel, act, and think. He influences their decision whether to marry, whether to have children. (1983: 111)

The final dance is not only a multilayered reflection of the love triangles in the film, but also a commentary on the contemporary ballet world, and it sees Jody choose a solo life in a rare show of feminine strength not typically displayed in traditional ballet plots. This plotline contrasts with ballets like *Giselle*, where wilis, the ghosts of unwed women who force Loys/Albert to nearly dance to his death were:

> girls 'who loved to dance too much', and who, it was imputed, died 'on their wedding's eve, at the height of unconsummated sexual arousal' ... For some, loving to dance too much connoted sexual promiscuity, while dying from dancing signified orgasm as in 'la petit mort'. (Cordova, 2007: 115)

Were the final dance of *Center Stage* part of a Romantic ballet, Jody would likely face death rather than a fulfilling life of lead roles and dedication to her art.

The transformation of Jody from pretty ballerina that is gazed upon to a strong-willed young woman who chooses dance as her life partner additionally subverts the customary ballet narrative. In rejecting the romantic offerings of the male hero, Cooper, as well as the choreographic directions of Charlie, Jody reclaims an artistic identity and reformulates a gendered one. This action brings attention to the manipulation of the ballerina in ballet narratives and in the hierarchical structure of ballet companies, where her status falls below director, choreographer, coach, and often her male partners. However, although the transformation of Jody challenges the fixed position of the ballerina, the final routine itself falls short of the potential that parody and re-workings offer. For example, Susan Foster's work *The Ballerina's Phallic Pointe* shifts the audience's gaze to a "new language of desire ... not based in scopophilia, in which the process of looking arouses sexual stimulation and objectifies the person looked at ... [but] a fluid and unruly female image" (Midgelow, 2007: 88). Dressed in a bright red leotard, skirt and shoes, with dark eye makeup and red lips (see Figure 1), using sexualized movements such as thrusting hips and spine contractions, Jody becomes a mature dancer with heightened sexual appeal, especially when compared to her earlier persona in the routine and to the typical childlike young ballerina. Of course this artistic and sexual maturation is intended to be doubly true offstage. She becomes an available, yet unattainable character, flitting just out of the male protagonist's reach, titillating the ogling males' desires (Cordova, 2007: 124). This presentation of Jody, while rooted in her taking control of her self-presentation and allure, serves to stimulate a gaze that is entrenched in the objectification of the female body, thus sustaining the gendered conflict the routine purports to overturn. Similarly to Romantic ballet, which "repressed the erotics of the body's staging even as it participated in the commodification of the object of desire: the dancer herself" (Cordova, 2007: 119), the reinscription of the feminine on her sexually mature self may not actually deautomatize the audience's reaction to her, and thus may not require a full dismantling of the ballet and the ballerina (Midgelow, 2007: 86). The audience may be left feeling uncertain as to Jody's choice and the consequences of it: despite encouraging erotic creativity in female performance, "ballerina's bodies specifically are saturated with sex" (Midgelow, 2007: 82). Perhaps the suggestion by Claid that "female bodies have re-emerged as seductive performers", while being full agents in their awareness of who is being seduced and why (Claid, 2002: 41), is true of Jody at the end of her performance.

Figure 1: Cooper, Jody and Charlie in the final dance, *Center Stage* (Nicholas Hytner, 2000)

Movement and Musical Choices in Center Stage

Early in the film, Jody and her friends decide to escape ABC by going to a salsa club. Here, acoustic guitar melodies answer the vocal lines of Elvis Crespo, and long notes on the horns guide a relatively controlled duet between Charlie and Jody (see Figure 2). The dance's control, punctuated by elaborate lifts and dips, is called into question by Eva (Zoë Saldana) and Erik as they get up to join in and show them 'real' salsa. The implication that the two non-white characters (Eva is purported to be of mixed or possibly Hispanic heritage and Erik is African-American) can legitimately perform a Latin dance while Jody and Charlie, both white, are hampered by their repressed Western European bodies, is evident as the focus shifts to the formers' freer movements. This scene culminates in the song 'Come Baby Come', performed by Crespo and Gizelle D'Cole, where the couples dance more elaborately. The registral hiccups and moaned phrases from D'Cole heighten the *Dirty Dancing* inspired moves, such as Eva and Erik's entwined legs and Jody's shaking shoulders as Charlie follows on his knees. The excitement brought about in the dancers by this liberating experience is captured in Jody's statement as she and Charlie slow dance: "Why can't all dancing be this fun?"

156 Movies, Moves and Music

Figure 2: Charlie and Jody salsa

Her discovery of the pleasure of non-classical dance leads Jody to the Broadway studio. The class's central routine is performed to the Red Hot Chili Peppers' version of 'Higher Ground' (1989), a cover of Stevie Wonder's original from 1973. It opens with a pounding, slapped bass riff played by Flea (Michael Balzary). Its ostinato recurs throughout the entire song, with the exception of short bridge sections and the chorus, which are similarly syncopated. Compared to the bass in Wonder's original, Flea's bass pulses in the foreground, jarring against the drums when they enter with a strong backbeat, whereas Wonder's version spreads the bass riff across a clavinet and a mellower sounding bass played on a Moog synthesizer. Guitarist John Frusciante employs a similar rhythmic pattern to Flea, using a distorted timbre in the grumbling lower section of the riff and finishing with a treble-string jangle every two measures. During the chorus, Frusciante follows the vocal melody sung by Anthony Kiedis for the first half of each phrase, then alternates to correspond with Flea's descending bass line for the second half, finishing the chorus with two resonating chords that underpin Kiedis's final two lines.

That Frusciante doubles Kiedis's vocals in the first halves of the phrases is key to the dancers' engagement with the music. In particular, the first phrase of the chorus is marked by the dancers, separated into a male and female group who each perform the sequence, slapping their hips and moving them in a circle with arms up in the air as they gaze longingly at themselves in the studio mirror. Kiedis's voice increases in volume at this point, highlighting the transition and the key words of the chorus: "I'm so darn glad he let me try it again/'Cause my last time on earth I lived a whole world of sin". In earlier sections of the song, the dance appears to be structured around Kiedis's vocal phrases. His voice soars over the instruments in the opening phrases of the verses, while the dancers thrust their heads and arms back or step into multiple spins that last the length of his notes. During sections where Kiedis is not singing, the dancers shuffle quickly across the floor, highlighting the rhythmic backdrop of the song. This type of action is further expanded when the dancers kick-ballchange against Kiedis's rhythms into positions facing different directions as the chorus begins. The raw energy of the Red Hot Chili Peppers' arrangement is paralleled in the dancers' fascination with their bodies. They stare at themselves in the mirror, wrap their arms around their bodies in rhythmic patterns and repeatedly touch certain body parts seductively, each point like this a brief pause in the overall rapidity of the routine (see Figure 3).

Figure 3: Jody and Cooper lead the Broadway studio routine

The class and its central routine, while likely a common experience for the majority of the dancers, appears to be a collectively freeing moment. The opening bass riff stirs up claps and cheers from the dancers, and when the drums enter, the dance begins simultaneously with a vigorous kick forward. The groups waiting at the side cheer on their dancing classmates, and the routine has a markedly looser feeling than those seen previously in the film. While there are obvious stylistic reasons for this – *pirouettes* and *retirés* are performed in parallel positions, and energy and individual style are privileged over conformity; traits more common to jazz or modern dance – it is implied that the music heard here stimulates such flexibility in the general aesthetic. There is a variety in the upper body stiffness of Jody's fellow female dancers, and there is discernible difference in performance style based on each dancer's individual body shape. Arms and legs move freely and the perfectly formed shapes of ballet are discarded in favour of a continuous flow of movement.

Returning to the final dance sequence at the end of the film, these same rock music-influenced moves are found. Jody employs a variety of non-balletic gestures, including toe taps, flexed hands, parallel *retirés*, and hips swivelling side to side while on pointe. These are juxtaposed against more conventional ballet steps such as *posé temps levé* in *arabesque, grand jetés* and *sissones*. At other points, conventional steps, such as *pas de bourrée* and *relevés*, are mixed with unconventional hand and arm gestures: circling at the wrists (thereby cutting short the extended line so desired in ballet), shooing the men back, or waving above the head. This method of 'rockifying' the ballet, where modern moves are designed to distract from the strict and often stiff poses of the genre, extends the dancers' movements and parallels the freedom that the music is supposed to enable. In 'The Way You Make Me Feel', the strong backbeat on the snare drum dictates the corps movements, while they had been more pronounced on the first and third beats of the bar during the Tchaikovsky segment. During the synthesizer wash that concludes the introduction, Jody twirls to reveal the red outfit and in their brief duet, Jody and Cooper quickly drop out of posed positions in *attitude* and *arabesque* and arch their backs in sudden contractions to accent Jackson's words. Jackson's lyrics complement Cooper's attempt to woo Jody: "I feel your fever from miles around/I'll pick you up in my car and we'll paint the town". Jody teases Cooper, swaying through walks on pointe while he grasps at the hem of her skirt. Jackson's timbre, strained and raspy at times, signifies not only the longing conveyed by the lyrics, but Cooper's feelings of ecstasy at the sight of his desire. When the music changes to a more lilting feel in the chorus, with the backup vocals providing a continuous flow against the punctuated beat, Jody and Cooper break into sideways gallops. Overall, the electronic eighth-note syncopated beat and the horn punctuations in the verses provide an energetic mood that is mirrored by the dancers as they circle around the stage in traditional ballet steps such as *posé temps levé* in *arabesque*.

In 'Canned Heat', the first shout of "Dance!" is accompanied by a dreamy look on Jody's face, then a self-satisfied smile as she pushes the men away into a *retiré* position on pointe. The synthesized string punctuations and riffs accompany the upward hand flicks as she brushes the men's advances back, and she is joined by three corps dancers who mimic her movements to the funk guitar and syncopated bass. Although the female dancers still employ the posed positions seen earlier in the 'class', they drop out of them quickly to transition into runs and leaps that take them across the floor. Meanwhile, the men race in and out of the picture, gazing intently at the new Jody, while she alternates between a dreamy expression and fierce, knowing glances during lyrics such as: "It's just an instant gut reaction that I got/I know I've never ever felt like this before" and "Dance!/All the nasty things that people say/Dance!", which have symbolic meaning beyond Jody's onstage character, signifying her newfound artistic identity. As Jody turns her back to the audience in a twisting movement, Jay Kay (lead singer of Jamiroquai) sings "Got canned heat in my heels tonight".

After a brief section where Charlie, Cooper and Jody dance more conventional steps such as *sissonnes* and *grand jetés* accompanied by a flourish of strings, she again pushes them away to join the chorus in a line. As the girls thrust their hips forward on pointe, all of the instruments drop out with the exception of a highly syncopated fuzz bass and drums, accenting the rhythmic nature of their moves. The men jump and flail behind the line of corps dancers as Jody breaks away. The final *fouetté* sequence is set to a loop of Jay Kay's voice singing "dance", which not only regulates her *relevés* and landings through the *fouettés*, but reinforces without question what her ultimate desire is.

The routine, by parodying a ballet class, and by enabling Jody's on- and offstage secession from the ballet world, calls attention to the unchanging, rigid nature of the genre under critique. Cooper's choreography uses these images, "transforming and inverting them in such a way that the viewer is made aware of their sociological implications" (Midgelow, 2007: 94). When the steps and poses of the onstage class are then seen in combination with unconventional jazz and modern movements, against rock songs, the audience is forced to reconsider what should be regarded as high-art dance (*ibid.*: 92). Parody relies on the assumption that the viewing audience is familiar with the codes, narratives and performance practices of the subject being critiqued. In *Center Stage*'s final dance, a typical ballet audience would not only recognize the source genre, but would also enjoy its reworking as a humorous rejection of familiar symbols. Passive consumption is challenged in such a context, and the viewer is made aware of their previously unquestioned enjoyment of a largely unchanging form (*ibid.*: 90).

Ballet Technique in *Center Stage*: Changing High Art

The conflict underlying the film, one that arises in attempting to modernize classical ballet gestures, performance and technique, is exemplified by the final *fouetté* sequence performed by Jody, who has been described as imperfect in technique throughout the film. This rather difficult sequence consists of two *fouettés* in *retiré*, one *à la seconde*, and a double *pirouette* to close it; this is repeated five times in its entirety and is showcased as the routine's (and thus the film's) technical climax. This one step embodies the struggle that is never quite resolved in dance films; although Jody performs it perfectly and goes on to feature as a principal in Cooper's new ballet company, her supposedly poor technique and newfound disdain for the dance form she once cherished, while providing her with a satisfying artistic identity, effectively lock her out of the traditional ballet world permanently.

The incorporation of such a difficult step in the final routine, while a climactic point in the narrative (manifesting as the difficult routine in dance film), may in fact be a commentary on the dance vocabulary itself, one that simultaneously highlights and undermines the elitist nature of the genre (Midgelow, 2007: 60). The film audience may feel it is possible to participate in ballet when contemporary dance moves are incorporated, thereby decreasing the gap between practitioners of the art and the everyday person. Meanwhile, the final *fouetté* sequence maintains the spectacular aspect of the art that dancers and their audiences alike valorize. Part of ballet's identity as a highly technical, professionalized genre of dance emerged from the Romantic era, when its performers expanded the vocabulary and raised the standards to a nearly unachievable level. Cordova agrees:

> The requirements of its technique ensconced the separation of social and theatrical dance so characteristic now of Western societies ... Even as it evoked the social within its own performance, romantic ballet set itself apart from the traditions of French courtly dancing and demarcated social dancing from theatrical dance, the social event from the spectacle. (2007: 119–20)

Gordon comments on the powerful possibilities provided by modern choreography:

> Modern choreography also places far less emphasis on homogenization. Classical ballets depend on corps works – on regimented rows of female dancers, all of whom look, dance, and act alike. Modern technique does

the opposite: It releases the individual from the mass. In great part, modern dance is a conscious feminist revolt against ballet. (1983: 212)

Midgelow agrees, noting that the recoding of the dancing body through changing the dance vocabulary itself allows for a reconceptualization of the performing body, and thus gender: "'Reworked' dancing bodies enter into a dialogue with their predecessors and with history to create dynamic bidirectional duets, full of interconnections, echoes and contrasts" (Midgelow, 2007: 39). While Romantic ballets continue to be loved for their traditional representations of an essential femininity or masculinity, mirroring the "gender conventions which surrounded the emergence of the bourgeoisie's ideologies of gender and sexuality" (Cordova, 2007: 122), the contemporary dance film privileges the desires of an individual who potentially subverts a gendered identity, reflecting the 'be yourself' theme that pervades popular culture. The reverence with which star dancers are held, which becomes manifest in Jody's final performance against the corps, while attractive to audiences that believe in the power of individual will, also reinforce beliefs about social stratification and power relations that descend from the Romantic era (*ibid.*: 120). Jody's last line to her superiors when they call her to a meeting to decide her fate with the company not only panders to the notion of individual agency, but also destroys those power dynamics quickly:

> I'm not perfect, I'm just me ... and I'm starting to think I like that even better ... If you're not going to offer me a place in the company, then I don't want to hear it. And if you are, I might not have the strength to say no. And then I'd be spending my best dancing years in the back of a corps, waving a rose back and forth, and I'm better than that. So, thank you, Jonathan, for turning me into the best dancer I can be. I appreciate it more than I can say, really, because the best dancer I can be is a principal in Cooper Nielson's new company. (*Center Stage*, 2000)

Dance films such as *Center Stage* highlight the fulfilment that art forms such as ballet can elicit in its practitioners and the impossibly high standards that barricade participation by 'normal' folk. Dancers too may feel this conflict. In her ethnographic study of the Royal Swedish Ballet, Helena Wulff makes the following comment about the tensions experienced by dancers:

> Dancers think of themselves primarily as artists, not as participants in the 'high culture' of front stage. Although dancers want as many people as possible from all walks of life to come to see them dance, they also want their audience to react to what they see, to be 'touched', 'mesmerized' and 'to go home and really remember'. There is a fear in the ballet world that such experiences of ballet art will not come about if ballet people cooperate too closely with the market, turning ballet into light entertainment. (1998: 161)

The impenetrability of ballet as an art form is partially disabled by a film such as *Center Stage*. By using rock and popular music as a soundtrack to the rejection of its immutable nature, an audience familiar with such music gains access to ballet. In the rock dance sequences, the foundational steps and patterns are maintained, but they are disrupted by movements that a mainstream audience understands and could conceivably perform themselves. The audience is no longer confounded by the classical music and perfect technique of the dancer; they are now taking an active part in its modernization by mapping their own experiences of imperfection, isolation and difficult decision-making onto the performance.

Recent studies in taste shifts have revealed that those who previously consumed exclusively highbrow forms of art, such as classical music, opera and ballet, are increasingly turning to middlebrow and lowbrow art forms (see, for example, Peterson and Kern, 1996; Katz-Gerro, 1999; van Eijck, 2001). According to Peterson and Kern, middlebrow genres of music include easy-listening, musicals and big band, whereas lowbrow includes genres such as country, blues and rock. While such distinctions remain subjective, pairing a traditionally high art form (ballet) with a commercial, popular one (rock) may well be jarring to the typical ballet audience. However, as Peterson and Kern have shown, audiences of traditionally highbrow art forms are now opening up to different genres and are expanding their taste to become more 'omnivorous' in their consumption (1996: 900–904). These studies suggest that the way in which artistic products are understood, that is, as objects for intellectualized appreciation, helps to eliminate the uncomfortable realization that one may be delighting in the previously derided products of popular culture (*ibid.*: 904). As such, to use the well-dressed, largely white, middle- and upper-class audience shown at the final workshop in *Center Stage* as an example, the recognition that they are watching a parodic commentary on the elitism of the ballet world eases the horror that might accompany viewing a ballet set to rock songs.

The reverse pyramid discussed by van Eijck (2001), wherein members of higher-status groups appreciate a broader range of art forms, whereas lower-status groups tend to have more restricted taste, equally applies to *Center Stage*. How can the contemporary audience for ballet increase if it is not made accessible to a wider range of experience? As discussed above, the 'average' viewer might enjoy the satisfaction with which Jody rejects the status-driven ballet world, and might appreciate the fusion found in the film's choreography. The 'new' middle class that van Eijck discusses is one that consists of:

> younger, well-educated, often upwardly mobile persons whose lifestyles might be characterized as postmodern because their consumption patterns encompass leisure activities and preferences that seem

incompatible from a traditionalist point of view, such as visiting
amusement parks and museums or listening to classical and pop music.
(2001: 1167)

This class comes from a socially heterogeneous background and continues to operate in such a context, where traditional markers of class and ethnicity are not so easily displayed in one's artistic preferences. In a context such as this, the prioritizing of Jody's individuality may be the ultimately appealing element of *Center Stage*, since the plotline affirms the ideology on which most of this new class thrives.

Conclusion

Garafola discusses the 'new ballet' laid out by choreographer Michel Fokine in 1914, one that disposes of conventional gesture and fixity in favour of a "mimetic of the whole body" (Garafola, 1998: 4). The idea that a flow of movement would be more natural and compelling than the pantomime of Romantic ballet underpinned a new expressive language for the genre. In *Center Stage*, while conventional movement gestures and patterns are still valorized, not only in the 'rock' ballet sequences, but in the myriad ballet excerpts shown, the rhythmic gesture is privileged. When they first appeared in ballet, these open-ended gestures "acquired meaning from the musical and dramatic contexts in which they appeared" (*ibid.*: 5), but were also abstract enough to encourage audience interpretation. While pop songs are used both diegetically as the accompaniment to the characters' innovative choreography, and non-diegetically, dropping in subtly to enhance the characters' gradual rejection of classical ballet norms and gender roles, in both cases, these songs serve to continually remind the audience of the central contradictions of the film. The juxtaposition of jazz and popular dance against traditional ballet in the final dance sequence of *Center Stage* has the same effect. These movements are driven by the music to which they are choreographed, and have the final result of popularizing the ballet for a contemporary audience, while symbolizing Jody's artistic journey and secession from the confines of her chosen art. Jody's sexual maturation, although corresponding to artistic growth, is seemingly available for display only as she discards the opportunity for romance in favour of dance. Privileging dance might be most obvious in the choice of songs such as 'Canned Heat', but the same sensibility is present in the act of alternating pop songs with classical tracks, showing the dancers' ability to retain the traditions of ballet while challenging them. Ultimately the narrative reinforces the traditional gender inscriptions found in ballet, but it simultaneously satisfies the individual agency and omnivorous tastes of the audience to which *Center Stage* appeals.

Notes

1. Gillian Turnbull holds a PhD in ethnomusicology from York University, Canada. Her research focuses on Western Canadian roots and country music, and issues of independence, western identity and community. She is the author of the forthcoming book, *Roots Music in Calgary, Alberta*, co-editor of the forthcoming anthology, *Grassland Sounds: Popular and Folk Musics of the Canadian Praries*, edits the *Canadian Folk Music* bulletin, and teaches at Ryerson University in Toronto.
2. *Center Stage* (2000), Nicholas Hytner, Columbia Pictures.
3. All terms taken from Grant (1982).

References

Claid, Emilyn (2002), 'Playing Seduction in Dance Theatre Performance', *Discourses in Dance*, 1(1), 29–46.

Cordova, Sarah Davis (2007), 'Romantic Ballet in France: 1830–1850', in Marion Kant (ed.), *The Cambridge Companion to Ballet*, Cambridge: Cambridge University Press, pp. 113–25.

Garafola, Lynn (1998), 'Dance, Film, and the Ballets Russes', *Dance Research: The Journal of the Society for Dance Research*, 16(1), 3–25.

Gordon, Suzanne (1983), *Off Balance: The Real World of Ballet*, New York: Pantheon.

Grant, Gail (1982), *Technical Manual and Dictionary of Classical Ballet*, New York: Dover.

Katz-Gerro, Tally (1999), 'Cultural Consumption and Social Stratification: Leisure Activities, Musical Tastes, and Social Location', *Sociological Perspectives*, 42(4), 627–46.

Midgelow, Vida L. (2007), *Reworking the Ballet: Counter-Narratives and Alternative Bodies*, New York: Routledge.

Peterson, Richard A., and Kern, Roger M. (1996), 'Changing Highbrow Taste: From Snob to Omnivore', *American Sociological Review*, 61(5), 900–907.

Van Eijck, Koen (2001), 'Social Differentiation in Musical Taste Patterns', *Social Forces*, 79(3), 1163–1185.

Wulff, Helena (1998), *Ballet across Borders: Career and Culture in the World of Dancers*, Oxford: Berg.

Appendix I
Table of Dances

Dance Routine	Music	Chapter Number
1. Salsa routine	'Eres Tu', Elvis Crespo	10
	'Come Baby Come', Elvis Crespo and Giselle D'Cole	12
2. Jody's non-ballet class (inside Broadway studio)	'Higher Ground', Red Hot Chili Peppers	14
3. Final routine		
a. Mock ballet class	*The Nutcracker* (Dance of the Reed Flutes)	24–25
b. *Pas de trois*	'If I Was The One', Ruff Endz	26
c. Final sequence	'Canned Heat', Jamiroquai	27

Appendix II
Glossary of Terms[3]

À la seconde: To the second. A term to imply that the foot is to be placed in the second position, or that a movement is to be made to the second position *en l'air*.

Arabesque: A position of the body, in profile, supported on one leg, with the other leg extended behind and at right angles to it, and the arms held in various harmonious positions, creating the longest possible line from the fingertips to the toes. The shoulders must be held square to the line of direction.

Attitude: A position on one leg with the other lifted, the knee bent at an angle of 90 degrees and well turned out so that the knee is higher than the foot.

Battement: Beating. A beating action of the extended or bent leg.

Battement frappé: Struck battement. An exercise in which the dancer forcefully extends the working leg from a *cou-de-pied* (instep) position to the front, side or back.

Écarté: Separated, thrown apart. One of the eight directions of the body. The dancer faces a corner; the leg nearer the audience is pointed in second position, the torso is held perpendicular and the arms are held in *attitude* with the raised arm being on the same side as the extended leg.

Effacé: Shaded. The dancer stands at an oblique angle to the audience so that a part of the body is almost hidden from view, or, to qualify a pose in which the legs are open (not crossed).

Fouetté: A term applied to a whipping movement. The movement may be the sharp whipping around of the body from one direction to another.

Grand jeté: Large *jeté*. In this step the legs are thrown to 90 degrees with a corresponding high jump. It is done forward to *attitude*, *croisée* (crossed) or *effacée* and to all the arabesques.

Pas de bourrée: Bourrée step. *Pas de bourrée* is done *dessous, dessus, devant, derrière, en avant, en arrière*, and *en tournant en dedans and en dehors*, on pointe or demi-pointe.

Pas de deux: Dance for two.

Pas de trois: Dance for three.

Pirouette: Whirl or spin. A complete turn of the body on one foot, on pointe or demi-pointe.

Port de bras: Carriage of the arms. A movement or series of movements made by passing the arm or arms through various positions.

Poser: To place the foot on the ground.

Relevé: Raised. A raising of the body on pointe or demi-pointe.

Retiré: Withdrawn. A position in which the thigh is raised to the second position *en l'air* with the knee bent so that the pointed toe rests in front of, behind or to the side of the supporting knee.

Sissonne: A jump from both feet onto one foot with the exception of *sissonne fermée* (closing), *sissonne tombée* (falling) and *sissonne fondue* (melting), which finish on two feet. May be performed petite or grande.

Temps levé in *arabesque*: Time raised, or raising movement. This is a hop from one foot with the other raised in *arabesque*.

Tendu: Stretched. As, for example, in *battement tendu*.

Zoot Suit Mayhem
Swing Dance and the Skewed History in Steven Spielberg's 1941

Philip Hayward[1] *and Jon Fitzgerald*[2]

Introduction

After working in television drama production since the late 1960s, Stephen Spielberg established an international reputation with two highly effective genre films, the aquatic horror feature *Jaws* (1975) and the science-fiction thriller *Close Encounters of the Third Kind* (1977). These films were high box-office performers, *Jaws* achieving an international gross return of US$470 million on a production budget of US$12 million and *Close Encounters* returning US$337.7 million on a budget of US$20 million (2010 figures[3]). The two films were also notable for establishing an enduring partnership between the director and composer John Williams,[4] who won Grammy awards for 'Best Album of Original Score' for both features and 'Best Instrumental Composition' for *Close Encounters*. Spielberg and Williams's third collaboration was on *1941* (1979), a major budget production that confused critics and performed far less impressively at the box office than its predecessors (returning US$94.8 million on a budget of US$32 million[5]).

1941[6] was a period piece set in California during the opening phase of US involvement in World War Two. The topic was one that reflected a broader process of national retrospection in which the trauma of the (later) years of the Vietnam conflict and the ignoble spectacle of the Watergate saga triggered a nostalgia for the 1940s, and particularly its culture and fashions, that were regarded – somewhat paradoxically – as signs of a less politically compromised and more glamorous social moment. This was particularly apparent in a vogue for swing-influenced music and 'retro' glamour stylings that emerged in New York in the early 1970s associated with the city's gay and disco scenes. Bette Midler's 1972 debut album *The Divine Miss M* pioneered this with a version of vocal trio The Andrews Sisters' 1941 hit 'Boogie Woogie Bugle Boy' that became a top ten single for Midler in the US. Vocal quartet The Manhattan Transfer also became proponents of this style from 1973 onwards,[7] most notably on their high-profile eponymous 1975 album, which opened with a version of the Glen Miller Band's 1941 hit 'Tuxedo Junction' that substituted the horn parts of the original arrangement with vocal parts. This interest in swing-era music and glamour was also expressed in cinema, most notably in the form of Martin Scorsese's *New York, New York* (1977), which starred Robert de Niro as a saxophonist and Liza Minnelli as a singer who meet on 2 September 1945 – VJ (Victory over Japan) Day. Set to the music of the Tommy Dorsey Orchestra, the film charts their tempestuous relationship against the events of the immediate post-war era. While this 1940s' vogue did not precipitate a return to swing dancing, whose routines required far more partner co-ordination and rehearsal than the relative 'free styles' of disco, elements of swing-era dance did resurface in New York dance venues in the form of a new partner style often referred to as the 'New York' or 'Spanish' hustle (celebrated in the name of the Fatback Band's 1975 hit single).

Along with the accomplished nostalgia of the acts and film discussed above, one of the most inventive engagements with the musical, sartorial and stylistic heritage of the swing era arose from the work of Dr Buzzard's Original Savannah Band, an ensemble led by Haitian Americans August Darnell and Stony Browder Junior. The band released its first (eponymous) album in 1976, mixing elements of swing, Latin American and disco music in a lushly orchestrated and theatrical manner. Opening with the declaration "Zoot suit city", the album combined ballads and swing-inflected disco numbers – most notably on 'I'll Play the Fool for You' – and attracted a cult following around New York. While the band was notable for its adoption of 1940s 'zoot suits' (discussed further below) its influences and motivations for engaging with the music were markedly different from those of Scorsese or The Manhattan Transfer. As journalist David Nathan explained in 1976, "The original Dr. Buzzard was a practitioner of voodoo" who instructed band member Stony Browder Junior "about the magical influence that clothes can have" (Nathan, 1976: online). Elaborating on the band's 'style politics', Browder identified that:

> This country is built on decadence... it just shot up and America has the nerve and sassyness and brattiness to walk around, sticking our noses in other people's business and daring anyone to sass us back! So we wanted to reflect that attitude. It's like being teenagers amongst gangsters ... Swing music – from which jazz came – was the most expressive style, the ultimate rebellion. (*Ibid.*)

This description of zoot suit styles as transformative, of zoot suiter style as assertive and confrontational, and its identification of zoot suiter "attitude" as "rebellious" is relevant to both the *pachuco* style politics discussed below and the "sassy", "brattish" irreverence core to *1941*'s project and production team.

Returning to the lacklustre response to *1941*, one of the principal problems for the marketing of the film was its generic complexity. The film project arose from a script for a WW2 period project entitled 'Tank' proposed to writer/director John Milius in 1975 by two young writers, Robert Gale and Robert Zemeckis. Reportedly admiring their sense of "social irresponsibility" (DVD interview), Milius invited them to pitch another project. Interested in their idea for a feature representing the invasion threat panic that occurred in Los Angeles in February 1942, Milius suggested that they combine this element with a feature project he was developing on WW2 military leader General Joseph Stillwell. Gale and Zemeckis began developing a project, initially entitled 'The Night the Japs Attacked', by conducting extensive research on California in the early 1940s. After MGM declined the project, Milius recommended it to Spielberg, who took up the script and embarked upon extensive revisions during an extended production process and re-titled the project as *1941*.

The film's subject was a highly unlikely one for a Hollywood production. Prior to the Al-Qaeda attacks on continental American targets on 11 September 2001, the Japanese attack on Pearl Harbor on 7 December 1941 represented one of the most traumatic moments in recent US history, revealing the superpower's vulnerability to surprise attack.[8] While there were 38 years between the Japanese attack on Hawai'i and the film's release, this represents a relatively short period in generational terms. It is pertinent to contemplate, in this regard, what the acceptable period might be between the Twin Towers attack and a future comedy that satirizes post-9/11 anxieties. In political terms, *1941* was conceived and produced during the presidency of Democrat leader Jimmy Carter (1976–80), an interregnum in Republican Party rule that followed the tainted presidency of Richard Nixon (1969–74) and his hapless successor Gerald Ford (1974–77) and which preceded the national lurch to the right that typified the years of Ronald Reagan's presidency (1981–89). While Carter's presidency is primarily recalled as a period of high inflation rates and low economic growth peppered with national crises such as the Iranian hostage stand-off (1979–81) and the Three Mile Island nuclear accident (1979), it was also one in which comedy and satire proliferated. In the wake of Nixon's disgrace and Ford's grey mediocrity, political satire and boundary-pushing irreverence flourished in American popular media, exemplified by the success of NBC's weekly show 'Saturday Night Live' (which commenced in 1975) and, in particular, the anarchistic energy and charisma of its most prominent actors, John Belushi and Dan Ackroyd – stars of 1978's hit US movie *Animal House* (John Landis), an anarchic 'frat house'[9] film that generated US$115 million internationally from a production budget of US$2.7 million.

Combining the scale of big-budget Hollywood productions, the irreverent and resourceful inventiveness that typified 'Saturday Night Live' and the late 1970s revival of interest in swing and the 1940s, Spielberg's film is a big-budget, multiple character, slapstick comedy with an elaborate central dance sequence. Set in and around Los Angeles, the film gleefully riffs on the interconnected historical themes of war panic[10] and the intense social friction and conflict between groups of predominantly Mexican and, to a lesser extent, African-American youth who were distinguished by their flamboyant clothes and mainstream society. Male youth, who largely defined the subculture, wore distinctive 'zoot suits' – highly stylized outfits with baggy trousers tapering to a narrow ankle-cuff and jackets with flamboyantly wide lapels, together with accompanying accessories such as wide-brimmed hats, bold ties, watch chains and so on. These youths' fascination with fashion, dance music and a general pursuit of hedonism grated on the sensibility of Euro-American society at a time of national military mobilization and perceived threat of Japanese attack and invasion. Resultant tensions provoked a series of violent backlashes by gangs of (predominantly) white service personnel and civilians in California and other parts of the US in 1943–44. The history of this period and, in particular, of the arbitrary and frequently brutal action taken against the Hispanic *pachuco* youth subculture who embraced 'zoot suit' style, was 'buried' for much of the 1960s and 1970s but regained currency through the work of dramatist Luis Valdez in the late 1970s. Valdez began a career in politically-activist drama by founding the Teatro Campesino company in 1965 during a period of industrial action by Mexican-American farm workers in California. Interested in the form of distinctive, contemporary, hybrid Hispanic-US identity referred to as *chicano*, he went on to research, write and stage a representation of *pachuco* culture and oppression in the 1940s, entitled 'Zoot Suit', that opened in Los Angeles in 1978 (which he later adapted into an eponymous feature film version [1981]). The play and film featured a predominantly Mexican-American cast and included dance sequences and musical accompaniment. In an interview published in 1982, Valdez characterized his motivation for resurrecting the problematic aspect of American history in terms of the *pachuquismo* sensibility and subculture being:

> the direct antecedent of what has come to be termed "Chicano consciousness". In the 1940s pachucos were caught between two cultures, viewed with suspicion by both conservative Mexican-Americans and Anglos. The pachucos were the first to acknowledge their bicultural backgrounds and to create a subculture based on this circumstance. The Anglo establishment, caught up in its "war-time hysteria" labeled the pachucos "zoot suiters" after their most flamboyant fashion. They were highly visible and easy targets for the U.S. Servicemen in Los Angeles in 1942. The pachuco emerged as a cult figure for he was the first to take pride in the complexity of his origins, and to resist conformity.
> (in Morton, 1982: 75)

As Clayton and Specht have identified, *pachuco* youth looked outside of the more conservative tastes of their parents and, instead, their musical tastes included "boogie, mambo, lindy hop, rumba, jump, blues, swing and early rock and roll" (2005: 165). The style of music most closely associated with *pachuco* culture is often referred to as *pachuco* boogie. However, this style actually dates from the late 1940s, initiated by Don Tosti's track 'Pachuco Boogie';[11] and the music most often associated with early 1940s' *pachuco* culture was the swing jazz style typified by bandleaders such as Cab Calloway. Despite their embrace of a number of African-American musical styles, Aragon has emphasized that the *pachucos*'

> acculturation of the black zoot aesthetic was, as Pagán notes, more than an act of "mere imitation" (Pagán, 2003: 11). It was adopted and adapted, mixed with elements of Mexican culture, to suit their own particular sensibilities and social needs. (2007: 16)

Amongst the "particular sensibilities" were *pachuco* perceptions of appropriate gender styles. Aragon has identified that

> [v]aluing a more reserved masculinity, Mexican American boys wore a more subdued version of the zoot-suit, eschewing the rainbow colors favored by African Americans. (*Ibid.*)

Along with their clothes, zoot suiters were often associated with particular dance styles. Here, again, there were differences between African- and Mexican-American youth. The dance most often associated with the former was the Lindy hop. This style was developed by African-American performers such as George 'Shorty' Snowden and Frankie Manning in the 1930s at venues such as New York's Savoy Ballroom.[12] The dance was an energetic (and often acrobatic) variation on previous male/female partner swing dances, and the Charleston in particular. By the mid-1930s its acrobatic element had expanded to encompass so-called 'air steps', when (usually) the female partner would be swung past the hips of the male and/or be rolled over the male's arched back, and floor slides of various kinds. The most successful dancers would perform these moves in tight synchronization with the dynamic emphases of the music. As this description suggests, the style was often performed competitively, either as an intrinsic aspect of social dancing and its spectatorship or else in formally constituted contests. While the pioneers and leading exponents of the form were African American, the form's popularity also extended to European-American youth.[13]

Pachuco dancing (in California at least) was significantly different from either East Coast Lindy hopping or West Coast 'smooth' swing dance styles. As Aragon characterizes it (drawing on the 2001 'Zoot Suit Riots' episode of PBS's *The American Experience*[14]), *pachuco* cultures:

associated the flashy, energetic dance steps of the Lindy Hop with femininity and the Pachuco Hop instead consisted of the males standing aloofly on the dance floor while their partners danced around them. (*Ibid.*)

Macias (2008: 83) has described the dance style as deploying the male dancer essentially as a "stoic" and directorial figure who struck a pose and acted as a pivot for his female dancer to spin around, without exerting any of the effort required by East Coast Lindy hoppers to throw their partners into the air and catch and direct their descent.

While *1941* draws on the social friction between zoot suiters and military personnel in California during the war years, it de-racializes the historical 'awkwardness' of this conflict by marginalizing the *pachuco* identity central to Californian zoot suit culture and by representing its main deviant zoot-suiters as white Americans performing (African-American originated) swing dance styles. Indeed, Hispanic characters are largely absent from the film.[15] As such, the film is a significantly revisionist work that constructs a primarily Euro-American historical fiction out of an Hispanic experience of oppression. Set in Los Angeles and weaving around the (actual, geographical) Hollywood (the central American icon that a Japanese submarine crew are determined to attack), *1941* is steeped in both mid-twentieth century and more recent Hollywood history. Ultimately, the film is an irreverent, gleeful and affectionate skit on white California and its all-American values that plays fast and loose with its history and liberally laces its special effects slapstick and comedy with subtler textual pleasures for aficionados of cinematic style.

Sonic and Stylistic Orientation

1941 opens with a title frame and scrolling text that details the war panic that gripped California immediately after the Japanese attack on Pearl Harbor on 7 December 1941, accompanied by an orchestral sequence that communicates a sense of threat. While snare drum rolls, brass stabs and a march rhythm immediately suggest military associations, a number of elements give it an indeterminate complexity. Short, repeated-note patterns on strings (highlighting minor third and diminished fifth intervals) add to the sense of drama. Williams also creates a sense of unease and agitation by placing the brief musical utterances in an irregular and unpredictable sequence, and by including moments of silence to enhance the tension. There is also a distinct feel to the piece that Williams has characterized as an infusion of "swagger" and "impudence" into a "typical WW2 American march", as a result of "the accent" being "tilted" and "the synch-ups" being "a little off" (DVD interview).

The first image of the film is of a stretch of coastline introduced with the caption "The Northern California Coast. Saturday December 13th 1941 7:01 am", which leads into a sequence that directly alludes to Spielberg's earlier work. A young woman parks a car by the shore on a deserted beach, disrobes, runs into the waves and swims out into deep water. Suddenly, the water around her begins to churn. The allusion here is to the scene in *Jaws* where a young woman is attacked by a shark that propels her through the water before dragging her beneath the waves. While observant viewers may be able to identify that both women are played by the same actress (Susan Backlinie), the clearest reference to the earlier film is conveyed through the score, with Williams reprising his familiar two-note *Jaws* motif. The ominous semitone (half-note) motif emerges subtly – heard first on strings at low volume and with irregular, rhythmic patterns – before it crescendos and accelerates dramatically to become a foregrounded motif with an insistent, repeated rhythm and dissonant harmony. Although cued to expect horror by the motif and locale, the audience is jolted into a less predictable response as a submarine periscope rapidly rises between the swimmer's legs and lifts her high above the deck of the surfacing vessel. The woman's screams are cleverly blended into the dramatic musical score to resemble a vocal climax within an operatic aria, at the same time underlining the obvious phallic/sexual nature of the visual symbolism. Oblivious to the naked (and now silent) woman suspended above their heads, the submarine's crew emerge and are revealed to be Japanese, led by their captain (Toshiro Mifune) and accompanied by a German officer (Christopher Lee). Identifying that they are close to Los Angeles, the captain asks an aide, "Is there anything honourable to destroy in Los Angeles?" to which the aide replies "Hollywood". After some discussion about Hollywood's location and the crew's navigation skills, the captain orders the crew to set course for Los Angeles.

Shortly before the submarine descends, the aide casts a last look around before closing the hatch. As the submarine begins to submerge he glances up to see the naked posterior and cascading blond hair of the suspended swimmer (who has remained silent while the crew are on deck). Captivated with the spectacle before him he yells "Hollywood!" (or, rather, "Horrywood!") and points up to her. Baffled as to the sailor's suspension in the open hatch as water begins to pour down, his colleagues drag him inside, shut the hatch and slap him as he continues to blissfully intone the name of the 'dream factory' the naked blonde typifies for him. As the submarine sinks, the swimmer dismounts and swims to shore to warn of the submarine's arrival.

Performance Tensions

The next scene is introduced by another watery image, this time of plates being slapped into a sink over the opening bars of a big band rendition of 'In the Mood', perhaps *the* iconic swing tune from the early 1940s and one that Spielberg could be confident would immediately convey the era in question. Closely associated with the dapper and patriotic figure of Glenn Miller, leader of the Army Air Force Band in 1943–44, the instrumental was written in 1930 by Joe Garland and Andy Razaf and arranged into an enduring hit by Miller in 1939. Miller's recording of 'In the Mood' was specified by its arranger as a foxtrot, a dance rhythm that features six counts over a 4/4 rhythm, suitable for both foxtrot and Lindy hopping. Miller's hit arrangement, closely imitated by the recording featured in *1941*, is built on a classic big band groove with swing rhythm on hi-hats and a walking, four-to-the-bar string bass. The first section (after the introduction) is built on a twelve-bar blues pattern and has a simple melody (an arpeggiated motif that changes to fit the prevailing chord). Saxophones support this melody in a seductive, close-harmony style that sets the tone for Miller's arrangement – which is characterized by smooth sound blends, relatively mild and predictable timbral, textural and dynamic contrasts and restrained instrumental solos. All these elements make the number a rather stylized and smooth pop offering, particularly in comparison with the style of big band instrumental arrangements that East Coast Lindy hoppers regularly danced to, featuring more complex melodies and chord sequences, stronger dynamic contrasts and more adventurous solos.

Despite the number's (now) iconic association with a white band leader and US military activity, which might be perceived as antithetical to *pachuco* and African-American zoot suit culture in the early 1940s, Miller was part of the musical scene they identified with. After performing as a trombonist, arranger and band-leader for over a decade without achieving major success, Miller developed a particular sonic signature, based on unison clarinet and tenor saxophone melodic leads backed up by close harmonizing saxophones. This trademark was introduced in 1939 and rapidly attracted attention, with his band securing packed houses for gigs at New York venues such as the Meadowbank Ballroom and Glen Island Casino, which helped promote his breakthrough record 'Tuxedo Junction' in 1939. Hollywood interest developed and Miller and his band appeared in Twentieth Century Fox films *Sun Valley Serenade* (1941, Bruce Humberstone) and *Orchestra Wives* (1942, Archie Mayo). On the back of this rise in popularity, tracks such as 'In the Mood' appealed to a wide audience in the early 1940s, including zoot suiters.[16]

'In the Mood' occurs as diegetic accompaniment to a sequence set in a cheap diner where a kitchen hand, Wally (Bobby di Cicco), is practising dance steps for a dance contest that evening at the Crystal Ballroom in central Los Angeles that offers the prize of an RKO Pictures[17] contract for the winners. In addition to practising steps using numbered cues pasted to the floor, he performs his kitchen duties in synch with the track, flicking plates and cups across the room to his colleague, Herbie (Eddie Deezen), catching them in perfect synch to the track's rhythmic accents and phrase beginnings (examples of the former occur at 6:49 and 6:52 and the latter at 6:55 and 6:58). Establishing a combination of dance moves and choreographed action that recurs in the film's central ballroom sequence, the kitchen interaction sees Wally break open and drop eggs onto a griddle in synch with the music (7:00) and perform an impromptu, 'tuned' percussion version of part of the main melody on a line of saucepans (7:15). Engaging as this is, it is shown to be detrimental to his culinary focus as he knocks bottle tops onto the griddle as the frying continues. The music drops in volume during subsequent dialogue sections before Wally, summoned to deliver coffee to a table of soldiers in the dining area, led by Sergeant Tree (Dan Ackroyd), dances in (to a now-louder underscore) and performs a spin and knee drop followed by a handclap behind his back after placing the coffee pot on the table. Provoked by this display, and by Wally's gaudy Pearl Harbor themed Hawaiian shirt, Corporal Sitarski (Treat Williams) first berates him for his flippancy and demands to know why he isn't in uniform, before tripping him up and eventually striking him when Wally spills egg on his uniform. This brief interaction summarizes the tension between military personnel and zoot suiters in California and the propensity of the former to assault the latter. The very final bars of 'In the Mood' are cleverly used to underscore a statement that becomes a recurring, ironic, 'hook' in the movie, as Sergeant Tree intones, "If there's one thing we don't want it's seeing Americans fighting Americans".

The interaction between Wally and Sitarski in the diner also establishes the duo's oppositionality, with Wally defined by his dress and dance obsession and Sitarski by his alpha-masculinity and readiness to resort to violence. This tension is principally played out through the men's competition for the affection of Wally's dancing partner Betty (Dianna Kay). Kay is introduced in the subsequent scene where a group of young women are being briefed on how to behave as dance partners at United Services Organization (USO) functions.[18] Interspersed with other narrative threads, and numerous comic turns, the early part of the film charts Wally's efforts to gatecrash the contest, which has become restricted to service personnel as a USO function. Eventually gaining access dressed in a stolen naval uniform, Wally grabs Betty from Sitarski's arm on the way in and the film's main dance scene commences.

The USO Centrepiece

The film's central dance sequence is a 'relic' of what Spielberg has identified as his initial vision for the film, namely an "old-fashioned Hollywood musical" with "eight song and dance numbers all based on big band music ... Tommy Dorsey ... Benny Goodman ... and that sort of feel of the big band era" (DVD interview) but which he lacked confidence to pursue in the late 1970s (*ibid.*). Indeed the music originally envisaged for the key dance sequence (and used for pre-camera rehearsals for it) was Benny Goodman's extended 1938 in-concert recording of Louis Prima's 1936 composition 'Sing, Sing, Sing (with a Swing)',[19] a track that the film's composer John Williams has identified as of particular cultural significance since it closed the first ever big band jazz concert at Carnegie Hall in January 1938 (*ibid.*). While classic Hollywood musicals may have been an inspiration for the director, the swing dance styles chosen for the central choreographic routine (and its preceding narrative foreshadowing) were a long way from the smooth couple dance routines associated with Hollywood musical stars such as Fred Astaire and Ginger Rogers.[20] Indeed, the most obvious film/dance precedent was H. C. Potter's rather different filmic adaptation of the Broadway musical *Hellzapoppin'*, made in 1941. Potter's film prefigured *1941* in a number of ways, including spectacular special effects and inter-textual references to other contemporary films (such as Orson Welles's *Citizen Kane*, also made in 1941[21]) and dance sequences featuring top New York ensemble White's Lindy Hoppers and Dean Collins. Collins was a white New York dancer who relocated to California in 1938 and became the leading swing dance teacher and promulgator of the style on the West Coast. Surviving footage of Collins dancing in the early 1940s with his regular partner Jewel[22] so closely resembles scenes featured in Spielberg's film that they suggest themselves as choreographer Paul de Rolf's prime choreographic reference – along with the dynamic swing dance routine performed by White's Lindy Hoppers represented as an impromptu musical jam in *Hellzapoppin'*.[23] The latter routine, in particular, illustrates the appeal of East Coast (rather than *pachuco*) swing dance for the film's writers and director; its intense energy, flamboyance and athleticism provide a dramatic contrast to the attenuated social focus of the war years.

1941's choreographic centrepiece at the USO dance commences with Wally watching from outside. The dance contest and associated fight sequences are preceded by a further nod to 'classic' music of the big band era. Before Wally and Betty dance together we see and hear a female vocal trio singing (miming to) the Andrew Sisters/Glenn Miller band song 'Down By the Ohio' (1940),[24] which functions as a relatively sedate, moderate-tempo accompaniment to initial dance action that gives little sense of what is to follow. This early dancing is relatively restrained and only begins to become animated as Sitarski does rough, forceful steps with a reluctant (and stiff) Betty, while

Wally looks on through the window in an increasingly distressed state. Wally ultimately finds his way into the dance hall after having dropped a gun-shell on a military policeman's head in order to steal his uniform. In a 'cute' piece of sound design, at the very instant when the shell strikes the MP's head in a back alley the visuals shift to the dance hall, where the drummer has crashed his cymbals loudly to draw attention to the MC, who then announces that the jitterbug[25] competition is about to begin. The crowd counts down from ten to zero, accompanied by increasingly loud brass chord stabs before the competition dance tune begins.

The music changes dramatically as the contest begins. The new big band composition is considerably faster than 'Down By the Ohio', suggesting that the ensuing dance action will be highly energized. Williams acknowledged the close connection between his composition and Prima/Goodman's original in the title of his composition ('Swing, Swing, Swing') and he includes numerous musical references to the former, such as its very fast tempo, brass growls, clarinet solo and tom-tom interludes. The competition music features strong melodies and syncopated brass stabs and includes frequent changes in dynamics, musical textures and instrumental timbres. 'Primitive' elements (such as brass growls and tom-tom rhythms), associated with so-called 'jungle' music,[26] help accentuate the wild energy of the competition scene. Given the synchronization of music and movement during the early 'In the Mood' scene, it comes as no surprise that these elements are also closely matched during the jitterbug competition. Midway through the dance, for instance, as the intensity of the track subsides, the individual social dance styles of the dancers give way to a group choreography sequence. In this, the male dancers face out in a circle and swing their partners between their legs in unison, causing them to meet in a briefly-held star position in the centre of the floor, before embarking on a series of other synchronized geometric patterns. As Erikson and Trainor (1980: 66) confirm, the choreography was originally arranged to produce the type of geometric patterns revealed by Busby Berkeley's overhead camera set-ups in a series of MGM musicals in the 1930s and 1940s but technical difficulties prevented an overhead camera being mounted in the studio.

In addition to the choreographed dance moves, numerous elements are carefully aligned with the music. For example, Wally does an acrobatic, wall-climbing move and somersault that perfectly meshes with an ascending and descending chromatic trumpet line (1:12:55), while jungle tom-tom patterns are used on several occasions when Sitarski stalks Wally (e.g. 1:10:57, 1:11:03). A raunchy brass growl motif coincides neatly with the moment when Sitarski suddenly finds his face in the crotch of an upside-down female dancer (1:11:03), while the sudden cessation of the music after Wally is punched in the face by Sitarski (1:13:55) effectively heightens the dramatic impact of this moment.

The latter action underlines the manner in which the dance sequences are interwoven with extended stunt routines, as made clear in script supervisor Marie Kenney's shot notations for the climax of the dance contest:

> *Wally and Betty are really cooking, doing jig-walks and 'round the backs!*
>
> *Sitarski dumps Maxine in a trashcan, then wades back toward Wally – and Wally doesn't see him because he's too absorbed in the number – as Sitarski is about to nail him, Maxine dives on his back! Then they drop out of sight into the crowd!*
>
> [cuts briefly to exterior scene]
>
> *Everyone is watching Betty and Wally now – there can be no doubt about that they're the best dancers here! Wally sends Betty between his legs, then into a spin-out and another spectacular 'round the back! The audience is going wild! A crazy variation of the 'Shorty George' then leads Wally into a back flip – he whirls around and*
>
> BLAM! Right into SITARSKI'S FIST!
>
> (reproduced in Erikson and Trainor, 1980: 63)

At this point, the dance choreography gives way to an extended fight routine, as soldiers and sailors line up facing each other and then, cued by the noise of a breaking bottle, set to fighting and trashing the venue, accompanied by a group of *pachucos* who gain access to the venue in the confusion.

After spilling out onto the streets, and expanding as fresh batches of servicemen arrive, the fighting is interrupted by the arrival of Captain Tree in a tank. After firing his machine gun in the air, he subdues the rioters with a speech that begins with earnest patriotism:

> *What the Hell do you think you people are doing? You're acting like a bunch of Tojo's stooges. What do you want to do, put Yamamoto in the White House? The Axis is crawling like a slime all over Europe. I can't believe that Americans are fighting Americans.*

He then shifts to a more parodic tone as he describes the possible impacts of Japanese invasion, whilst gesturing to the Christmas decorations that line the street:

> *Look at Santa Claus, isn't he cute? Do you think that the Japanese believe in Santa Claus? Well, instead of turkey for your Christmas dinner how'd you like to eat raw fish heads and rice?*

He then adopts cinematic references:

> *Do you think the Krauts believe in Walt Disney? Well, was that Mickey Mouse I saw blitzkrieging across France? Pluto in Poland? Donald Duck at Pearl Harbour?*

Having gained control of the situation, the tank crew is faced with a fresh challenge as air-raid sirens blare. In response, Captain Tree begins shooting out the streetlights and illuminated signage before being knocked unconscious by a large Santa decoration that his tank collides with. At this point Wally is mistaken for an actual officer. Co-opted as commander of the tank crew, Wally (now flushed with patriotic pride) continues to shoot the lights out, rescues Betty from Sitarski's clutches and commands the tank crew to head for the ocean to take on another enemy, the Japanese submarine that has been sighted offshore. Dressed in 'manly' military garb and assertive in combat, Wally's problematic zoot suiter identity and predilection for dancing are resolved and his archetypal American masculinity restored.

Reflecting on the film's under-appreciation by US critics and audiences (in contrast to its warmer reception in Europe), Spielberg has characterized the film as "a blast in the face, of imagery and sound and crazy people, over-the-top performances ... a clash of cultures and ideals and revisionist history" (DVD interview). Reinforcing this view, co-writer Robert Gale has described the manner in which the film "combined a number of historical incidents into one big mess" (*ibid.*). The prolonged development process for the project and the combination of "incidents" in its final "revisionist" historical "mess" led to a de-ethnicization of the central friction between (primarily) *pachuco* zoot suiters and service personnel that Gale identified as one of the most significant findings during his initial research for the project, which he has described in terms of the "huge element of racism involved" in Los Angeles at that time (*ibid.*).

While it is perhaps unsurprising that such a contentious and problematic element of history was excised from a big budget comic extravaganza such as *1941*, the retention of a conflict between (Caucasian) servicemen and (Caucasian) zoot suiters as a key narrative element serves to downplay and diminish the oppression endured by the *pachuco* in the period. It also operates to efface the precise subcultural tensions and assertions that Louis Valdez's *Zoot Suit* stage drama highlighted in California as *1941* was in production. Similarly, the absence of African-American composers' work from the score and African-American dancers from the screen obscures their role in the development of Lindy hop dancing in the mid-late 1930s.[27] If only by default, these elements allow the film to posit the dynamic styles and performance of Wally and the other featured dancers as (implicitly) white swing styles. In this manner, the film's production processes can be seen to have 'bleached' its roots, as its final text emerged out of a production process that Milius has compared to "a snowball out of control" (DVD interview), at multiple removes from its original research and its grounding in the actuality of 1940s Los Angeles. Indeed, *1941*'s writers and director have acknowledged and celebrated its deliberate "social irresponsibility" and "political incorrectness" (DVD interviews); with Milius identifying the production team's proud Latin motto as *Civitas cena prudentia* ('Citizenry without prudence'). Central to their perception of the historical revisionism that alienated critics – and caused actor John Wayne to attempt to dissuade Spielberg from making the film at all (DVD interview) – was its representation of American panic and confusion at the early stage of the war. As one of the film's most apt lines of dialogue, voiced by the stoic General Stillwell (Robert Stack), has it, "this isn't the state of California, it's a state of confusion". Nowhere in the reflections of the production personnel some 16 years after the film's initial highly negative media reception is there any sense of what other political 'incorrectnesses' and offences might have been caused by its re-imagination of American cultural history through a primarily white lens. As this chapter has argued, perhaps the film's most striking aspect is its relegation of *pachuco* and African-American society and culture to the research back block of its gleeful historical fantasia. As dazzling as its dance sequences, stunts and comic interactions may be, its marginalization of key cultural stakeholders casts a notable shadow over the overall project.

Notes

1. Philip Hayward is an Adjunct Professor in the School of Communication at the University of Technology Sydney, and a member of audiovisual ensemble The Moviolas.
2. Jon Fitzgerald is Adjunct Associate Professor in the contemporary music programme at Southern Cross University, Australia. His doctoral thesis examined the development of popular songwriting in the early 1960s, and he specializes in the musical analysis of popular music. He is also an experienced performer, composer and recording artist.
3. Data taken from 'The Numbers' website: http://www.the-numbers.com/movies (accessed October 2010).
4. John Williams trained at New York's prestigious Juilliard School of Music in the mid- to late 1950s where he became acquainted with the origins of the classic style of Hollywood neo-romantic scoring analysed by Flinn in terms of its nostalgicism (1992) and also worked as a jazz pianist and session musician for film score composers such as Henry Mancini. Arriving in Hollywood in 1958 he connected and worked with a number of key composers from the 'Golden Age' analysed by Flinn, such as Bernard Herrmann, Franz Waxman and Alfred Newman, and renewed his association with Mancini, working on the composer's scores for *Peter Gunn* (1959) and *Charade* (1963). Drawing on his familiarity with Herrmann's oeuvre he wrote the distinctive theme (and much of the incidental music) for the popular science-fiction series *Lost in Space* (1965–68). Williams began to secure critical recognition in the late 1960s for scores for films including *Valley of the Dolls* (1967) and *Goodbye Mr Chips* (1969) and was employed by Irwin Allen for his trilogy of disaster films

The Poseidon Adventure (1972), *Earthquake* (1974) and *The Towering Inferno* (1974). In between his work on Spielberg's second and third features, Williams contributed a rousing orchestral score for George Lucas's *Star Wars* (1977) that remains the composer's best-known work.

5. Data taken from 'The Numbers' website: http://www.the-numbers.com/movies (accessed October 2010). *1941*'s lower-than-expected box office return raised questions about Spielberg's durability as a high-profile director that were spectacularly overcome with the success of the director's subsequent *Raiders of the Lost Ark* (1981), which won Williams his third 'Best Album' Grammy award.
6. All times referred to in the text below refer to the 1995 'Director's Cut' DVD version of the film and all quotations from production personnel are sourced from the 'Making Of' documentary included on the DVD, and are referenced as 'DVD interview'.
7. The band formed in 1969 and acquired a significant swing orientation as a result of band member Tim Hauser's interest in the style in a revised line-up that commenced in 1973 and rose to prominence in 1975 after signing to Atlantic Records and gaining a weekly show on CBS TV.
8. Although, as Stephan (1984) emphasizes, 'surprise' is perhaps an inappropriate word given the lengthy discussion of the merits of such an attack in Japan during the 1920s and 1930s.
9. Frat(ernity) houses are accommodation blocks for students at colleges and universities who belong to particular fraternities. The name 'Animal House' indicates the particular character of the fraternity to which the Belushi and Ackroyd characters are associated.
10. Inspired by an actual West Coast wide panic occasioned by a Japanese submarine firing torpedoes at the coast near Santa Barbara in February 1942.
11. See the 2002 compilation CD *Pachuco Boogie* for a selection of late 1940s *pachuco* tracks.
12. See Engelbrecht (1983) for further discussion.
13. Such as Sol Ruddosky (who adopted the stage name 'Dean Collins' in the late 1930s) whose work in California is discussed further below.
14. Drawing on material presented in the 2001 US Public Broadcasting Service programme 'The American Experience Zoot Suit Riots' (directed by Joseph Tovares).
15. The sole character assigned a Hispanic identity is the dancehall MC Sal Stewart (played by Joe Flaherty) who reveals in an aside that his character's real name is Raul.
16. Reflecting this, Luis Valdez specifies the track as 'incidental music' in a scene from the script of his drama *Zoot Suit* ([1978] 2004: 126).
17. RKO Pictures was a leading Hollywood studio in the 1930s, known for a series of successful dance films starring Fred Astaire and Ginger Rogers.
18. The USO (United Services Organization) was a recreational organization established in partnership with the US Ministry of Defense in 1941 to boost (male) military morale, and civilian women were encouraged to attend USO dances to that end.

19. First recorded by Goodman's band in 1937, the track was notable for its length, 8 minutes 43 seconds, extending across both sides of a 12" 78 rpm record.
20. Arguably best exemplified by their virtuoso performance of 'Waltz in Swing Time' from *Swing Time* (George Stevens, 1936).
21. In the form of a visual gag referencing the 'rosebud' sledge that burns at the end of Welles's film.
22. See, for instance, http://www.youtube.com/watch?v=PDeJHvEwUIE (accessed October 2011); and the dance sequences featured in Robert Mamoulian's film *Rings on her Fingers* (1942).
23. Choreographer Paul de Rolf is deceased and does not appear to have been interviewed about his work on the film. We are therefore unable to substantiate our contention but research for a big budget film such as *1941* would, in all likelihood, have included scrutiny of archival dance film sequences such as those discussed.
24. Before Miller's band became popular in its own right it regularly accompanied the Andrews Sisters (who came to prominence in 1937 through recordings and radio broadcasts).
25. 'Jitterbug' was a term used in the 1940s and 1950s to refer to both Lindy hopping and other swing dance styles.
26. Duke Ellington, along with trumpeter Bubber Miley, pioneered this 'hot', 'jungle' style at the Cotton Club (Harlem) during the late 1920s and early 1930s.
27. Indeed, it is significant that the only representation of African-American performance culture in the film is in the musical sequence 'When I See an Elephant Fly', performed by African-American ensemble Cliff Edwards and the Hall Johnson Choir, featured in the 1941 Disney feature *Dumbo* that General Stillwell is shown as watching in a cinema while the dancehall riot breaks out. The onscreen performance forms part of a sequence where besuited crows, speaking in exaggerated African-American accents, mock Timothy Mouse and Dumbo. (The sequence has been much debated in terms of its racist stereotyping; see, for instance, Wainer 1994.)

References

Aragon, M. (2007), 'Brown Youth, Black Fashion and a White Riot', Goldsmiths, University of London Centre for Community and Urban Research Occasional papers.

Clayton, L., and Specht, J. W. (2005), *The Roots of Texan Music*, Galveston: Texas A&M Press.

Engelbrecht, B. (1983), 'Swinging at the Savoy', *Dance Research Journal*, 15(2), 3–10.

Erikson, G., and Trainor, M. E. (1980), *The Making of 1941*, New York: Ballantine Books.

Flinn, Caryl (1992), *Strains of Utopia: Gender, Nostalgia and Hollywood Film Music*, Princeton: Princeton University Press.

Macias, Anthony (2008), *Mexican Mojo: Popular Music, Dance and Urban Culture in Los Angeles*, Durham: Duke University Press.

Morton, C. (1982), 'An Interview with Luis Valdez', *Latin American Theatre Review* (Spring), 73–76.

Nathan, David (1976), 'Really Something Else', Soul Music website 'Classic Interview', http://www.soulmusic.com/drbuorsaba19.html (accessed September 2011).
Pagán, E. O. (2003), *Murder at the Sleepy Lagoon: Zoot Suits, Race, and Riot in Wartime L.A.*, Chapel Hill: University of North Carolina Press.
Stephan, J. (1984), *Hawaii under the Rising Sun: Japan's Plans for Conquest after Pearl Harbor*, Honolulu: University of Hawaii Press.
Valdez, L. [1978] (2004), *Zoot Suit*, Houston: Arte Publico Press.
Wainer, Alex (1994), 'Reversal of Roles: Subversion and Reaffirmation of Racial Stereotypes in *Dumbo* and *The Jungle Book*', *Sync: The Regent Journal of Film and Video*, 1(2), http://www.ferris.edu/news/jimcrow/links/reversal.htm (accessed 16 October 2015).

Across the Universe and Nostalgia
Re-presenting the Beatles through Moving Images and Dancing Bodies

Colleen Dunagan[1] and Roxane Fenton[2]

In her 2007 film *Across the Universe*, director Julie Taymor combines a simple narrative of youthful love with a complex layering of visual and aural elements. The sophisticated interplay among the music of the Beatles, film work (camera and editing), dance and other visual elements makes the film a rich site for the investigation of ways in which movement, music and movie-making work together. Through close readings of several songs/scenes from the movie, we argue that the merging of sound and image in *Across the Universe* activates nostalgia (both for the US in the 1960s and for the mythology of the Beatles) in order to create a visual and aural tribute to the philosophical outlook conveyed in the Beatles catalogue. Or, to put it differently, the film argues that the pop music of the Beatles (a commercialized and commodified form) offers larger philosophical lessons relevant to American history. It suggests that love, both romantic and within a community of friends, provides an answer both to the turbulence of the 1960s and the unsettled world of the post-9/11 era of the film's release.[3]

Across the Universe combines song and dance, but it is neither a traditional film musical nor a straightforward dance film. It combines aesthetic choices about the image–sound relationship from different genres: film musicals, music videos, screendance and narrative dance films, making it a truly hybrid film and in places calling to mind the innovations of experimental and avant-garde cinema. This hybridity provides an opportunity to re-examine Andrew Goodwin's influential theory about the role of synaesthesia in the musicology of music video imagery (1992: 49–71). Music videos no longer hold the same place in media culture that they did in the 1980s when Goodwin developed his ideas, but in many ways the aural and visual conventions of the form have become part of the fabric of contemporary media culture, particularly in the US. Through our examination of *Across the Universe*, we consider both what Goodwin's ideas offer outside the strict context of music video and also ways in which those ideas fall short.

Dance plays many roles in music videos, just as it does in narrative films and film musicals, and the function of the dancing shapes the theoretical perspectives brought to its analysis.[4] In both filmed and live performance contexts, dance scholars have analysed the role of dance in the construction of subjectivity or identity, the ways in which dance participates in ideological discourse, and the ways in which choreographic structure contributes to both of these.[5] In *Across the Universe*, dancing sometimes communicates information about a character's feelings or about the general situation, but the characters do not use dancing to experience the world or construct their identities. Instead, dance is part of the visual language employed in the production of meaning across the film as a whole.

This use of dance as a visual language is, perhaps, best explained by the conventions of screendance, a genre of dance re-designed for or originally envisioned as film. These works highlight the ways in which film can be conceived of choreographically and the ways in which dance can be reimagined within the film medium. Screendance, as a form, blends the conventions of stage dance with those of cinema to create a cinematic form that strictly follows neither the conventions of narrative film, nor those of dance, but rather blends the two. However, unlike film musicals, which weave in and out of a narrative structure, screendance lives in a space that is never quite truly narrative in its structure and logic.[6] Recognizing a similar strain of hybridity in *Across the Universe*, we employ choreographic analysis, considering both dance specifically and the choreography of movement generally in relationship to other visual layers and to the music.

Across the Universe simultaneously provides a nostalgic tribute to the Beatles and uses their music to tell a love story set against the backdrop of one of the most turbulent moments in twentieth-century American history. The songs advance and reinforce the narrative action and also contribute to character development. The film includes songs that span much of the Beatles' career, and lyrics from the songs often appear as dialogue. Thus, the world of the film is seen through the words of the Beatles quite literally and pervasively. Further, the major characters' names are drawn from Beatles' songs: Jude (Jim Sturgess), Lucy (Evan Rachel Wood), Max (Joe Anderson), Prudence (T.V. Carpio), Sadie (Dana Fuchs) and Jo-Jo (Martin Luther).

The film plays on the popularity and enduring fame of the Beatles, not primarily as a band or as individuals, but as *the* icon for a generation and an era. Consequently, it treats the individual members of the band, their musical compositions and their philosophical perspectives as parts of an ideological construct signified by the band's name. Further, it treats this construct nostalgically, subtly rewriting the history of the band and its members at the same time as it draws upon that history. Just as the history told by nostalgia is always simpler than the events of the past, the construct of the Beatles evoked by the music and referenced in the story ignores the complexities of creative authorship, philosophical perspective and interpersonal dynamics among John Lennon, Paul McCartney, George Harrison and Ringo Starr over the course of the 1960s. Our analysis necessarily focuses on this nostalgic version of 'the Beatles' created by the film. Therefore, though most of the songs in the numbers we discuss are from the Lennon/McCartney catalogue, and the philosophical perspectives we discuss come from Lennon and Harrison, we talk about them as representative of 'the Beatles', arguing that this is part of the film's construction of nostalgia.

The plot of the film spans roughly two years, beginning early in 1967 and ending in the fall of 1968. Well-known historical events anchor the film in time and space: race riots in Detroit; the assignation of Dr Martin Luther King Jr; student protests and the occupation of buildings at Columbia University; an anti-war protest in Washington DC, and finally the Vietnam War. By this time, the Beatles were established as a musical phenomenon in both the UK and the US, and they were producing songs that diverged from the standard pop forms and that reflected a growing investment in Marxism/socialism, psychedelics and Indian philosophy (Baur and Baur, 2006). The songs in the first third of the movie (with one exception) come from 1963–65 and represent both the straightforward love song that was the band's speciality in those early years, and the early stages of their move away from the standard Brill Building pop song structure of the day (Covach, 2006: 37–39). The use of 'Let It Be' (1970) at the 33-minute mark signals a change, and for the remaining two thirds of the movie the songs (again with one exception) are drawn from the band's final years, 1968 to 1970. Through this structure of songs, the film duplicates in symbolic (and simplified) form the trajectory of the band's career and philosophical development.

The philosophical voice of the film is most clearly expressed through the character Jude, a working-class bloke from Liverpool who takes a job aboard a merchant ship in order to travel to America and meet his WWII soldier father. He jumps ship and decides to stay in America after joining up with Max, a disillusioned Ivy League student, and Lucy, Max's younger sister. Various allusions are made in the film, particularly in the beginning, that connect the character of Jude to John Lennon.[7] However, the key to Jude as the Beatles/Lennon is that his character most fully embodies the philosophical perspectives of the Beatles presented through the structure and lyrics of their songs and the evolution of that philosophy over time (Baur and Baur, 2006; Womack and Davis, 2006).

Fittingly, Jude is the only character who is not American by birth. This allows him to present an outside perspective on the historical events within the narrative by embodying the philosophy of the Beatles. While Max, Lucy, Jo-Jo and Sadie live American cultural history in varying ways, Jude only lives in the UK. While he is in America, he takes a more removed philosophical stance, rejecting consumerism and violent protests and achieving transcendence through his art, recreational drug use and, finally, love. He provides a kind of critical view on the historical and cultural events despite being a central character in the narrative.

The film thus presents two perspectives on this period in American history. On one hand, the narrative reminds us of student opposition to the Vietnam War via Lucy's involvement with student activism, protest and radicalism. Along the way, the film comments briefly on the psychedelic drug scene and the gurus who arose within it. The central characters are also part of a positively depicted counter-cultural world in Greenwich Village. On the other hand, the Beatles' songs are used to present a philosophical perspective of hope via love that has been attributed to the Beatles by several of the cultural theorists whose work we reference in our analysis (Zigler, 2006; Crooks, 2006).[8]

For example, in 'Take a Sad Song and Make it Better: The Beatles and Postmodern Thought', James Crooks argues that over the course of their career as a band, the Beatles produced a "meta-narrative of postmodern thought" through their music. Further, he maintains that their "critique of culture is grounded and framed on all sides by an enduringly *naive* celebration of love" (Crooks, 2006: 184; emphasis original). Just as Crooks traces the philosophical progression of the Beatles catalogue from postmodernism through deconstruction and poststructuralism to transcendence-through-love, *Across the Universe* marks a similar trajectory both through the character of Jude, as the representative of the Beatles, and through its pairing of Beatles songs with narrative and visual choreography (both of images and of dancing bodies).

The images stand in the middle between the larger narrative, which provides cohesive structure, and the selections from the Beatles catalogue which contribute to the narrative, but which also convey the philosophical perspective. Thus the Beatles catalogue itself, for which the songs in the movie stand, provides a key structure to the film. This use of the Beatles' music shapes the relationships among sound, image and narrative within the film. The images (including dance) sometimes link the two structures, while at other times they work more with one perspective than the other or highlight the tension between the two. Ultimately, the film merges the linearity of the classic realist film narrative with the nonlinear narrativity of the music video form (Goodwin, 1992: 74–85).

However, songs are frequently shortened, with verses, choruses or reprises eliminated when they do not contribute to the narrative or philosophical needs of the film. Instrumental sections are extended, and arrangements often use different tempos and instrumentation than the originals – they are also sung by the actors themselves. These alterations contribute to the film's generic hybridity. They refuse to recognize the dominance of song that Andrew Goodwin identifies in his theory of the "musicology of image", discussed below. (The changes also resist the conventional divide between narrative and number, characteristic of film musicals, a point to which we will return.)[9] Thus, *Across the Universe* highlights the complex possibilities in the image–sound relationship, simultaneously evoking and exceeding Goodwin's theory.

Analysing the mixed-genre conventions used in the film allows us to explain the ways in which the narrative and music push and pull at one another. This hybridity results from four basic strategies used to integrate sound and image. First, rather than each song matching one scene or location within the film, the instrumental music and songs often bleed over from one scene into the next. Second, the relationship between diegetic and non-diegetic sound often changes over the course of a given song. Third, as a result of the way the numbers are filmed, the inclusion of dance in the film aligns more closely with its roles in music videos and screendance, despite the fact that many of the numbers draw on choreographic conventions made popular in film musicals. Finally, the film combines the structure of narrative film, developed through dialogue and images, with that of a music video, in which the song itself provides the coherence of the work. However, the film structure exceeds that of a music video, since it uses not one song, but a collection of many songs by the same group.

Musicology of the Image

When Goodwin constructed his theory of the musicology of the image in the early 1990s, he was responding to the work of scholars on music videos – work that tended to characterize the form as postmodern. This argument was supported through analyses that emphasized the visual images, rather than the sound or the relationship between the two. Goodwin attributed this trend to the inappropriate application of film theory to music videos. To counter this, Goodwin argued that an accurate analysis of the structure and content of music videos must look at the images from within the conventions of popular music. Rather than read the music like a film soundtrack, he set out to demonstrate "exactly how we might invert the position of film studies, by demonstrating exactly how the visuals *support* the sound track" (Goodwin, 1992: 70; original emphasis). Further, the musicology of the image demonstrates "a close connection between visual and musical/lyrical elements in the music video text, encompassing forms of bodily movement that include dancing" (*ibid.*). Thus, when read from a musical perspective (recognizing both that music video images are constructed in relationship to the music and that the videos began as promotional items for that music) "music videos may be simultaneously non-realist and highly ordered/rational" (ibid.: 74).

Goodwin's central idea is that the structure of a music video ultimately comes from the music itself and not from an outside source. The music can provide structure in a variety of ways, he argues: through visualization of musical elements (synaesthesia), through dance, through the use of direct address, and through the repetition of known organizational and harmonic structures and conventions across multiple hearings, songs and media (ibid.: 60–85). Music videos duplicate the direct address of popular music, in which the 'story' of the lyrics is understood as being sung directly to the listeners, even when the singer speaks in the third person (ibid.: 75). Further, this mode of address was and is common in television (it is therefore widespread) and originates in the live performance of music (ibid.: 77). Thus, Goodwin argues that while music videos may seem to lack *narrative* closure, they still possess coherence, closure and stability (ibid.: 78–85).

Goodwin goes on to note that visual structure in music videos may come from outside the songs themselves, while still being driven by or created in relationship to the music. The images might simply provide an alternate way to understand the lyrics, or they may extend or even disrupt them. The goal of the video may be to encourage repeated viewing through the creation of pleasure, or to promote films and commodities other than the music. Further, videos present performers in ways that contribute to their larger public personas and stardom (ibid.: 85–86). Finally, Goodwin argues that videos provide visual pleasure through three visual hooks: close-ups of the performer's face, a scopophilic (voyeuristic and therefore objectifying) gaze, and emotionally or associatively evocative images that are linked with recurring musical elements (ibid.: 92–94). These conventions are different than those of the classic realist narrative conventions of cinema, not because they are postmodern or fragmented but because they arise out of a different medium – one governed by aural/musical principles rather than visual ones.

However, *Across the Universe* is unlike a music video in key ways. Music cannot provide the whole structure in the same way because it is feature-film length and uses many songs rather than just one. Second, as we mentioned, the songs have been reshaped (shortened, extended and given new musical arrangements) to fit the narrative needs of the film. Further, as in both narrative films and integrated film musicals, the songs often contribute to character development and forward the narrative action; however, in this film, the visual images often serve to recontexualize the lyrics of already well-known songs (see below). Because the characters are not the original performers of the songs, Goodwin's visual hooks work differently as well. In this case, the close-ups blend film and music video functions. They serve as a hook by allowing the viewer to connect emotionally with the characters (thus drawing the viewer into the narrative) and by more closely wedding the music and the film by suggesting the actors are 'authentically' singing the lyrics (rather than lip-syncing to their own voices recorded separately.) Scopophilic pleasures may likewise extend to the actors' vocal performances, but do not otherwise differ substantially from those in other film contexts.

On the other hand, the film uses a different kind of hook in that it contains a collection of songs written by one band; a band with both a deep and well-known cultural mythology and with songwriters who explored cultural, religious and philosophical ideas in their music. Therefore, it matters greatly to the meaning of the film that the music is all by one particular band, the Beatles. While a similar project could be undertaken with music by other artists (Bob Dylan, for example), it would not result in the same narrative. Most importantly, as we have suggested, the histories of the Beatles and their song catalogue provide a philosophical journey that runs parallel to the narrative of the film.

As useful as Goodwin's ideas are for understanding the role of music in *Across the Universe*, his efforts to reinforce the centrality of the music in his theory tend to slight the array of live, *visual* performance forms upon which television and film musicals draw. Further, as he admits, his analysis of the role of dance in music video images provides only one way to consider that relationship (*ibid.*: 68). Importantly, it is not only music videos that employ conventions other than those of classic realist narrative cinema, and thus the key to reading *Across the Universe* lies in understanding how the film joins conventions from music videos via the musicology of the image with those of film musicals, screendance and narrative film.

'I've Just Seen a Face'

'I've Just Seen a Face' (1965) provides a good example of this blending of conventions and performance modes. Overall, it most closely resembles a film musical number, yet it includes elements more common to music videos. The lyrics of 'I've Just Seen a Face' deal with love (or at least initial attraction) in a straightforward way that primarily aligns with standard pop music conventions of the 1950s and 60s. Within the film, this number is transitional, occurring at a point just prior to significant changes in the development of the major characters. The song allows Jude to express his initial interest in Lucy, while Max expresses his desire to go to New York, and before the song ends we see the view out the windshield of the car as Max and Jude drive towards the city.

The number takes place after a querulous family dinner during which Max announces he is dropping out of Princeton, when Lucy and Max take Jude to a bowling alley to hang out. Both the setting and the song signal the characters' relative lack of worldly experience. In combination with the use of film musical conventions, playful dancing and a bright colour scheme, the upbeat tempo and bluegrass feel of the song work to convey good wholesome fun and young love in a light and upbeat manner. Eventually, the number will stand in contrast to the counter culture in New York, with which first Jude and Max, and then also Lucy become involved, and later in contrast to the loss of innocence caused by the war, the race riots and the anti-war protests. In addition to representing a transition within the narrative, the number illustrates the ways in which Goodwin's "musicology of the image" is transformed by the influence of film musical and narrative film conventions.

The scene opens with a shot of a bowling ball as it rolls down the lane to strike the pins. The viewer hears the diegetic sounds accompanying this action. The crash of ball against pins triggers the onset of the song. Diegetic sounds continue as Jude begins to sing. This progression follows the standard transition into a film musical number identified by Rick Altman, a progression that he argues moves the number into a "supra-diegetic" space in which the reality of the film narrative is blended with the space of the imaginary. This space is governed by the logic of the song, rather than the logic of the narrative, and allows the characters to express themselves in ways that exceed what is acceptable in everyday interaction. The privileging of song in music video parallels and draws on this earlier convention. In the classic film musical number, diegetic sounds do not return until the end of the number and the transition back into narrative film space (Altman, 1987: 62–74). In *Across the Universe*, however, the narrative film space often remains a stronger presence as diegetic sounds continue through the number. Sometimes dialogue intrudes, temporarily returning the song to a background role more characteristic of the soundtrack in narrative cinema.

In 'I've Just Seen a Face' Jude sings through the basic structure of the song (AABAB). Throughout we continue to hear the sounds of balls striking the alleys and pins, as well as the laughter of Max and Lucy as they tease one another. As the song moves to the instrumental solo, Max and Jude discuss what to do now that Max has dropped out of college. The instrumental section is extended through the conclusion of the dialogue and into the dance sequence that follows, and this replaces the partial reprise of the basic song structure in the original.

Following the dancing, Jude repeats the bridge, "Falling, yes I am falling" (Lennon/McCartney, 1965), twice. The second time, the camera cuts to him and Max in the car on the highway headed to New York. The vocals disappear, the volume of diegetic driving sounds increases, and the instrumental ending becomes a soundtrack as Max tells Jude that Lucy has a boyfriend. Jude replies, "That's okay. I've got a girlfriend". The flippant nature of Jude's comment reinforces the light-hearted sense of the dance number and song. The music finally comes to an end as the New York City thruway sign fills the image. Using a song from a musical number as a transition between scenes in the narrative is not part of the standard form of film musicals and differs from music videos because it manipulates the song to accommodate dialogue and diegetic sound. The nature of the transition serves to further blur the distinction between genres and also to ground the film, overall, in narrative cinema conventions.[10]

The general structure of the number, along with the presence and nature of the dancing during the instrumental section, place it in the mode of the film musical number. However, the mode of address employed in Jude's performance combines styles from music videos and film musicals. Film musicals and some music videos have tended to use a direct form of address drawn from live music and dance performance. In addition to the form of direct address identified by Goodwin, performers typically direct their energy and attention outward, either directly towards the camera and the audience or towards another character but including the camera and audience. Common in music videos, this bodily type of 'live performance' address even occurs sometimes in classic narrative music and dance films, particularly when the band, singer or dancer are shown in performance settings.[11]

However, music videos also make use of a different address in which performers sing while remaining within 'natural' behavioural norms. 'I've Just Seen a Face' is one instance within the film where a character presents such a 'naturalized' performance.[12] When Jude first begins singing, he does not look directly at the camera, though it does position him in the centre of the frame. Further, his performance of singing stays within the realist conventions of narrative film; he does not appear to project or present the song for the viewer. Instead, he sings as though he were singing to himself, giving much the same bodily and vocal inflections that he would if he were speaking to himself. Camera movements and shot composition further position him in a naturalized music video mode. In the first shot the camera slowly makes a steady arc around the front of his body, and in the second shot the camera tracks backward as he walks towards it. Both compositions highlight Jude as the focus of not just vocal sound and lyrics in the scene but also of the visual logic. This shot choreography further calls to mind common scenes of singers in music videos, and the focus on the character's face provides one of Goodwin's visual hooks.

Jude's mode of address changes, however, when he reaches the bridge of the song and becomes more directly focused towards the viewer. He is filmed from above as he appears to slide down one of the lanes on his back. He looks into and sings for the camera as it tracks above him. He also addresses the camera directly after his discussion with Max, just before the scene switches to the car. These moments of direct address work to align the scene with that of the film musical number, as well as with many music videos.

As in the classic film musical number, dancing in 'I've Just Seen a Face' marks the farthest reach into the space of the imaginary.[13] Dance in *Across the Universe* includes carefully planned and sometimes stylized pedestrian movement, as well as more generally recognizable dance movement that requires specialized training. This mixing of movement styles reflects historical and cultural trends in film and dance across genres, including that of film musicals, avant-garde cinema, screendance and contemporary concert dance.[14] The use of movement in this film simply expands upon the rich history of choreographed motion in cinema and dance.

As Jude begins to sing, the movement around him remains largely pedestrian. It starts to look noticeably choreographed at the end of the second verse, as we see the teens bowl in sequence, starting at the back, and proceeding towards the camera in a wave effect that ends with Jude, Lucy and Max. The dance section is interrupted as Jude sings the bridge while sliding down the lane and as Max and Jude discuss the future. The end of Max's speech about how great New York will be provides the transition into the heart of the musical number. While speaking he jumps up, runs and slides on his feet, surfing down the bowling lane. The lighting changes dramatically from pedestrian to theatrical, and the instrumental music swells to dominate aurally as clearly choreographed action overwhelms pedestrian movement.

Teens, including Jude, Lucy and Max, run and 'surf' down the lanes and slide on their knees. Pairs of young men and women jump in unison over benches in modified leaps with both arms and legs bent at ninety degrees. Though mostly built on pedestrian movements appropriate to the context of the bowling alley, the action reads as dance because of the spatial and timing organization of the movement, particularly the use of unison, which creates clear visual designs and corresponds with the tempo and rhythm of the music. The vocals return with a shot of Lucy running and sliding down a lane, first facing the camera and then turning mid-slide to face Jude with one arm outstretched as he slides down the same lane towards her. The overall presentation of the dancing bridges the outwardly directed, visually spectacular musical production number and the situationally appropriate and youthfully energetic movement of the narrative dance film.

While 'I've Just Seen a Face' sets Max and Jude on their way to New York, 'Come Together' (1969) serves as the musical vehicle by which the remaining central characters literally come together in the Greenwich Village apartment of the Janis Joplin-like Sadie, who seems to rent out every available space within it, including a set of rooms to Jude and Max. This scene uses song, dance and organized pedestrian movement to complete the creation of this community. During 'Come Together' the viewer follows the Jimi Hendrix-like Jo-Jo as he arrives in New York City and makes his way to Greenwich Village where he auditions for Sadie at Cafe Huh? – a reference to the real Cafe Wha? – and then joins the communal apartment. He will become Sadie's guitar player and boyfriend. At the end of the song, lesbian Prudence, whom the audience has already met, comes in through the bathroom window.[15]

'Come Together' originally began as a campaign song for Timothy Leary's run for Governor of California with the slogan 'Come Together. Join The Party'. Its eclectic array of lyrics creates both an extremely laid-back rallying call and nonsensical rambling. While the lyrics contain many allusions (to hippies, a Chuck Berry song, and Yoko Ono), the most coherent statement is the call for union around an individual. By pairing this song with pedestrian-influenced choreography, the film draws upon the history of dance as a cultural unifier within the community, calling to mind the history of movement choirs, folk musicals and, most recently, flash mobs.[16]

'I Want You (She's So Heavy)'

One of the songs in the film that most clearly moves from the realist space of the narrative film into a space governed by song and dance similar to that seen in film musicals is 'I Want You (She's So Heavy)' (1969). Like a film musical number, it lacks diegetic sounds for much of the scene. It relies on large group unison and an emphasis on visual design in the choreography, and incorporates spectacle through dance, production elements (costumes, set and props) and film editing.[17] Yet it also enters a space of abstract and symbolic meaning more closely associated with screendance (see Brannigan, 2011: 100–111) or contemporary concert dance and serves an important role in character and narrative development.

During the song Max reports to the induction centre as directed in his draft letter. Song and dance combine to further the narrative while creating a surprising juxtaposition at the level of surface appearance. Lyrics about sexual desire contrast with choreography of images and bodies depicting Max's forced bodily submission to a kind of commodification, the somewhat rote preparation of interchangeable soldiers to supply a war. Notably the lyrics and music exist within two narrative contexts – Max's army induction and love interests among his housemates. The film increases the disparity between the two contexts by elevating the level of spectacle in the first, taking the time to develop a longer production number with a greater emphasis on dance and choreography. At the same time, the visual images and narrative reveal within the lyrics a deeper philosophical censure of or ambivalence towards desire.

As Max walks up the steps to the front door of the draft building, each step happens on a heavily emphasized beat of the music. Once he is inside, the lyrics begin and the Uncle Sam posters come to life, singing 'I Want You!' (Lennon/McCartney, 1969) and gesturing towards him. From this point on, the film image shifts completely over into the imaginary and symbolic world of the dance number. Here, choreography and film editing take the dominant role in meaning-making, so that dance conveys the homogenization of the individual through the conformity of military life. The choreography illustrates how the physical training of the body both shapes individual identity and defines the individual as a member of the larger socio-cultural body in ways that reflect a given moment within cultural history.[18]

Two soldiers grab Max and push him through a doorway into a long hallway bordered on each side by a line of soldiers. They have been rendered nearly identical looking with cartoonishly strong jaw lines created by mask-like prosthetics. All of them are noticeably taller and more muscular than Max, and when standing at attention, they create the effect of two impassive walls. Max is pushed onto a conveyor belt running down the centre of the hallway. As he rides along, the soldiers pull off his clothes until he is wearing only his white boxers. They remove his pants by manipulating him into a somersault. The film cuts to Max exiting the hallway to arrive in a line of other draftees, also in nothing but white underwear. Their scrawny, flabby or pasty chests stand in stark contrast to the exaggerated masculinity of the soldiers' appearance.

Max watches a sea of soldiers (wearing the same, nearly-identical latex faces) arranged in rows as they begin to sing and dance. Moving from a tight focus on the soldiers' chests, the image expands as the camera dollies back and rises, revealing the group choreography. The sharp actions derived from military gestures and forceful movements performed in unison embody their social role. Just as a given dance technique participates in the construction of social roles, such as gender, these movements enact a particular concept of what it means to be a male body, as well as a particular social body. Thus, the film presents the military as a cultural body that values aggression, order, symmetry, subordination and homogenization over other values, such as peace, freedom, equality and difference.[19] The camera cuts to a low diagonal shot as we see cubes lowering from the ceiling. Another cut reveals the recruits being carried towards the soldiers on a set of conveyor belts as the soldiers continue to dance.

Recruits and soldiers are paired together and boxes are lowered from the ceiling to settle around each pair, creating small identical rooms, each containing a desk and chair. A 'lid' slams down on each one to make them appear to be wooden boxes rather than rooms. At this point the image leaves the space of the real completely and is consumed by interlocking boxes (digitally created and manipulated) with sides that seem to slide or open up and out to reveal Max's body in fragmented pieces as various parts of him are poked and prodded and examined by doctors.

When this section ends, the film cuts back to the physical warehouse space in which soldiers and recruits dance. In a partnering sequence the soldiers manipulate the recruits, sending their bodies through a series of actions loosely resembling those of basic training. The choreography clearly emphasizes the role of the soldiers as active manipulators and the recruits as passive receivers. The sequence ends when the soldiers draw the recruits into a ballroom embrace, flip them into a side lift and then lay them down on their backs on the conveyor belts, which carry the recruits across and out of the room as both soldiers and recruits salute.

Throughout this part of the scene, the choreography redirects the meaning of the lyrics from sexual desire to the government's need to mass-produce expendable soldiers. The choreography's use of traditionally gendered partnering roles (active/male vs. passive/female) is here redirected by aligning the active role with the military and the passive role with the recruits in order to highlight the imbalance of the power dynamics within the drafting process, rather than that of romantic relationships.[20] However, the partnering also calls to mind the homo-social nature of the military and the sometimes extreme demands made in the name of 'love' of country. This redirection of traditional partnering and its gender associations is furthered by the fragmentation of Max's body within the digitally manipulated images, which calls to mind the horrors of war through its visual allusions to dissection and its literal reduction of Max's image to a series of body parts. Despite the sombre subject of the number, this scene does not quite take itself or the situation seriously. Dancing bodies and humorous elements, such as the exaggerated facial features, intersect with the choreography to soften the political message. The scene is critical of the draft, but Max has not yet been personally affected by the war. He is upset and anxious about being drafted, but the experience remains somewhat unreal.

The film cuts from Max saluting at the end of the choreography to a (digital) shot of a war-torn land with scattered trees and billowing smoke. The camera swoops in, and the trees are revealed as miniatures when a leg and boot come into view and crush some of them. The recruits sing 'She's So Heavy' (Lennon/McCartney, 1969), and the camera cuts to a shot of them in their underwear working as a group to carry the Statue of Liberty through the muddy wasteland. The camera booms up to reveal an overhead shot of the statue, the music disappears temporarily, and the film cuts back to the 'real' world as Max places a miniature Statue of Liberty on the desk of an induction officer. This Statue of Liberty sequence literally embodies the 'She's So Heavy' sequence from the song, creating narrative meaning that extends the lyric to provide political commentary on the war and the burden placed on the recruits by patriotic Cold War rhetoric about American involvement in Vietnam.

As the music resumes in the background, the camera cuts to Max at home once again, talking to his roommates about his experience. His movement through the apartment allows us to see Sadie and Jo-Jo dancing closely as she sings 'I Want You' (Lennon/McCartney, 1969) to him, sliding her hips against his pelvis seductively. The camera angle changes to show Prudence sitting on the board that bridges two windows of the apartment. She watches Sadie and Jo-Jo dance as she sings "I want you ... I want you so bad" (Lennon/McCartney, 1969) directed at Sadie. What began as an extra-diegetic number hovering somewhere between film musical number and screendance has transformed itself into something more closely resembling narrative cinema with its mix of soundtrack and diegetic song.

Prudence's inflection of the lyrics indicates the pain she feels because she desperately wants someone she cannot have, and calls to mind the song's origin as an expression of John Lennon's overwhelming desire for Yoko Ono. The pairing of these two interpretations of the lyrics forces the viewer to confront the danger that personal desire may become self-destructive when it is all-consuming. This echoes an Indian philosophical principle in which "desire and attachment are frequently viewed as problems in themselves" (Calef, 2006: 83), and, we maintain, this echo calls to mind the Beatles' incorporation of Indian philosophy into their lyrics.

Scott Calef draws on the Indian philosophy referenced in lyrics from Beatles songs in order to look specifically at their relationships to consumerism. He notes that for George Harrison, the principle translates to a concern more with "inordinate desires and overindulgence than with desire itself", and that for Paul McCartney "wanting the *wrong* things (and taking what he doesn't want) is clearly the problem, not desire itself" (Calef, 2006: 83; original emphasis). We see these same general philosophical principles arising within the songs that appear in *Across the Universe* and participating in the sound–image relationship. In the case of 'I Want You (She's So Heavy)', Lennon's perspective on the consuming nature of his desire seems ambivalent, and the film uses this ambivalence to highlight the way in which the military participates in the value system of capitalism by literally treating the recruits as valuable commodities for which it has an overwhelming need/desire.

Thus, the scene is a prime example of the ways in which the sound–image relationship creates multiple parallel meanings. By splitting the song over two locations and situations, the images juxtapose two very disparate interpretations of the lyrics, both of which contribute to the narrative action. The use of dance to generate symbolic meaning provides critical commentary on military culture, the draft and the war. The ambivalence towards desire expressed in the performance of the song, both in the dance number and by Prudence, and the juxtaposition of those seemingly disparate situations, construct for viewers one aspect of the Beatles' intellectual and spiritual journey.

'Strawberry Fields Forever'

The film's treatment of 'Strawberry Fields Forever' (1967) borrows heavily from music video conventions, to the extent that if it were removed from the film, the scene could easily be mistaken for a music video. Other scenes that primarily or very strongly resemble music videos include 'Because' and 'Across the Universe'. However, 'Strawberry Fields Forever' goes furthest in its adoption of music video genre conventions. In this scene, the choreography is entirely of images, rather than of bodies. In addition, it is the best example of the fragmentation of the image and the reliance upon music to provide structure and coherence that Goodwin addresses in his text.[21]

Much of the early writing about music videos focused on their fragmented images, claiming them as the icon of the form's inherent postmodernism. Goodwin countered this trend, arguing instead that the extreme fragmentation of images allows (and calls upon) the music to provide structure and coherence, instructing the viewer in how to read the relationships among the various images (Goodwin, 1992: 74–85). In 'Strawberry Fields Forever' various filmic components create this fragmentation: frequent use of close-ups, superimposition or a layering of images, use of dissolves, creation of and movement between multiple physical locations, the intermixing of documentary footage with film footage, and use of pastiche to create fantastical images in which elements from one location seemingly take an active role in another. The music and lyrics frame the images, aligning shifts in both to coincide with cuts between images or camera movement and offering images that provide a tangible embodiment for the abstract ideas found in the lyrics.

The music begins during a series of close-ups alternating between Jude smoking, the strawberries in the bowl, and Jude singing. Jude then begins pinning strawberries to a canvas in straight lines, as bright red juice drips down like blood. As he sings the first verse, "Living is easy with eyes closed" (Lennon/McCartney, 1969), he contemplates his completed strawberry composition as Lucy watches from afar. The mix of lyrics and images conveys both that Lucy does not really see him and that he finds it increasingly difficult to maintain his sense of self as he becomes disillusioned and grows disconnected from her.

The opening images are complemented by those at the end of the scene. Sounds of war fade out as the sound of a washing machine fades in, accompanying the visual transition. An extreme close-up of Lucy's eye in red is covered by a full-screen wash of red that suggests churning blood until the camera and colour retreat to reveal water and white sheets seen through the window of a washing machine. These images, which frame and enclose the scene, link the strawberries with blood and the blood with both Lucy and the mundane activity of daily chores. They provide a reference to the war and her preoccupation with it and a foreshadowing of the violent anti-war protests that follow.

The juxtaposition of and travel between multiple locations begins with the second chorus as Max starts singing. He and his unit are fighting in Vietnam. They are first shown within the frame of the television set, as if part of the news report, and then the image increases to fill the screen. From this point, the images alternate between shots of Max singing, of Lucy watching and of Jude either singing or painting, jumping back and forth from Vietnam to New York. The frequency of these cuts increases and images from one location are superimposed onto those of another, constructing an imaginary space that holds the various meanings of the scene.

The blending of locations and images gradually evolves into a pastiche that completely exceeds physical reality. The mashed strawberries and splashes of red paint – part of art in Jude's environment – become blood stains when transparently layered over Max's face. Film images are overlaid on or blended with documentary footage from the war to create a sense of extreme contrast. Jude angrily throws strawberries that become bombs landing in the jungle. Flaming strawberries rain down on images from the Vietnam War, emphasizing both its unreality and absurdity. This depiction of war is made all the more poignant because it subverts the longing of the lyrics and melody, such that 'strawberry fields' refers both to the land littered with dead bodies and the nostalgia that transforms places from our past into idyllic spaces. This complex interplay of images, music and lyrics illustrates the way in which the number both evokes Goodwin's theory of the music as structural device and exceeds his work as the film's images rewrite or revise the viewer's understanding of the song.

Unlike the other numbers we have analysed, 'Strawberry Fields Forever' lacks literal dancing bodies. This absence coincides with a key moment in Jude's philosophical evolution as he further removes himself from the American political and social unrest, questioning the viability of the choices that exist. His ambivalence towards, or rejection of, the available social causes leads him to distance himself from Lucy (even as she unwittingly distances herself from him) and delve deeper into his art.

'Revolution'

The tension that has been building between Jude and Lucy spills out as they argue in the laundromat: about Jude's attitude towards Paco (Logan Marshall-Green), the leader of the student protesters at Columbia; Paco's intentions towards the many women with whom he works; what Lucy sees as Jude's lack of social and political engagement; and the value of his art. Lucy ends the fight by walking out, but Jude has more to say. He follows her to the student protest office and expresses his perspective and his anger.

Jude is not in favour of the Vietnam War, but he rejects the increasingly radical ideas about ending it endorsed by Paco, Lucy and the student protesters. He expresses this rejection through his performance of 'Revolution' (1968), a song that has been widely interpreted as a statement of John Lennon's own political views. Steven Baur suggests that this song, when looked at in relationship to other work late in the Beatles catalogue, is evidence of Lennon's belief in Marx's theories of false consciousness and the need for radical shifts in ideology in order to create a more "equitable society" (Baur, 2006: 101). He argues, "When Lennon sang, 'we all want to change your head', he was, like Marx, trying to promote a new kind of consciousness – one that prioritized communal well-being over individual success" (ibid.: 101). However, the song also shows that Lennon was uncomfortable with the assumption within Marxism that violence was a necessary part of social progress (ibid.).[22]

Jude's performance of 'Revolution' at the protesters' headquarters supports Baur's reading of the song. He identifies and points out for Lucy and the viewer the very thing that she fails to see – the destructive nature of Paco's perspective. Having rejected the violent revolution (of Marxism or of radical war protest), but without any other option to present, he is left with nowhere to stand, no place from which to take action. In the scene he sings at Lucy, not to her, and he hovers, leaves and re-enters, pacing between desks, restless in his inability to take a stand and his inability to communicate with her. The use of a steadicam to film the scene enhances this restless quality by inserting small movements of the camera that match the unsettled aspect of Jude's movement. This is a very subtle choreography of the image that enacts one form of the concept of stylization discussed by Brannigan (2011) in her analysis of screendance and its influence on and place within cinema history. In essence, Jude's movement demonstrates a choreographic approach that minimizes the distance between choreography and naturalized gestures in acting (119–24). This simple stylization of natural movement allows the number to subtly reinforce how, at this moment, Jude's philosophy has alienated him from Lucy, and how this philosophical distance needs to be crossed in order to reunite with her at the end of the film.

This scene not only conveys a key moment in Jude's philosophical journey (as the stand-in for the Beatles), but it also most effectively demonstrates the way in which the film plays with forms of address and the way they work in various genres. Although he is singing, Jude delivers the song like a monologue, drawing on conventions of acting performance rather than musical performance. Despite the fact that people do not usually sing in a context like this, Jude combines vocal delivery with pedestrian actions in a seamless manner, allowing his presentation of the song to remain within the narrative, rather than escaping to a supra-diegetic space removed from reality.

'All You Need Is Love'

Jude and Lucy are further separated when Jude is deported to England after being arrested at a protest where he was trying to reach her. Helped by Max's reminder in 'Hey, Jude' to "Let her into your heart, then you can start to make it better" (Lennon/McCartney, 1968), Jude returns to the US after realizing the importance of his love for Lucy. Max has arranged for Lucy to attend a rooftop performance by Sadie and Jo-Jo (reunited after Sadie's brief sojourn as solo artist) on the roof of the building that houses her new record label. This moment in the film calls to mind the Beatles' own performance on the roof of the Apple Building, home of their production company, Apple Records. Within the narrative, this performance brings the central characters back together, re-establishing their community and resolving the various plot threads.

In addition to re-uniting the film's characters, the performance serves as another key moment in which the film partly re-writes the history of the Beatles, who were on the verge of falling apart at the time of the rooftop concert. The film calls to mind that historical moment of the dissolution of the Beatles as a band, while at the same time focusing on the enduring nature of the Beatles as a cultural phenomenon (and as a commodity). Furthermore, the performance of 'Don't Let Me Down' (1969) morphs into Jude (eventually joined by the others) singing 'All You Need is Love' (1967) as the final statement of the film. On one level, this is addressed to Lucy and their relationship, and on another to the community of main characters, but as the conclusion of the philosophical message, it also presents love as the answer to everything, and that as the enduring message of the Beatles' music.

By shifting the import of the historic Apple Building concert, the film minimizes the fact that the band members were moving increasingly in their own directions in order to present a coherent philosophical message. At this moment, despite the heavy reliance upon the Lennon/McCartney catalogue to represent the Beatles as a band, the film argues for a philosophical stance more closely aligned with George Harrison's contributions to the Beatles catalogue (particularly his later work). Reading through the lens of Harrison's exposure to Hindu philosophy, philosopher Ronald Lee Zigler argues that the lyrics of George Harrison's 'Within You Without You' (1967) address both personal and cosmic love. He makes a case for the lyrics as instructions for how to achieve transcendence by way of Indian philosophy: "By surrendering to the void, we encounter a spiritual revelation of life's fundamental reality through an experience of transcendence" (Zigler, 2006: 142). Here reality is no longer the mundane reality of the physical world as brought to us through our senses. Instead, transcendence comes from escaping the limitations of the physical, enabling a state of being/knowing in which we comprehend the truth of existence – as a reality governed by unity, rather than the distinction of separate 'things'. In Harrison's song, personal love (love for another individual) becomes a path to cosmic love (awareness of the unity of everything). In the film, personal love becomes a path to community, and by extension to global peace. In this final scene, the film reunites the Beatles, nostalgically, through this philosophy of love.

While "Within You Without You" does not appear in *Across the Universe*, the philosophy that Zigler reads in its lyrics is evident in the film and is conveyed through the collection of songs and their collaboration with the dance, narrative and image. The film's ultimate stance is the resolution to have faith in (personal) love and through it to hold onto the possibility of humanity one day reaching unity (cosmic love). Thus, Jude and Lucy's story is not only a standard Hollywood love story (though it is that), but also a philosophical lesson. It is interesting to note that the song Zigler calls "the clearest expression of John Lennon's take on Maharishi's many discourses on *The Bhagavad-Gita*" is also the title of the film (2006: 147–48). The title represents both Jude's philosophical journey as he twice crosses the Atlantic from Liverpool to Lucy, as well as the philosophical and spiritual journey embodied in the Beatles catalogue. As a result, the film ultimately participates in the construction of both the mythology of the Beatles and nostalgia for 1960s America as a time that embodied our potential for change. In its overall construction, both in this final scene and throughout, it reimagines possibilities for joining sound, moving bodies and moving images across genre conventions.

Notes

1. Colleen Dunagan is an Associate Professor of Dance at California State University Long Beach. Her writing about dance in television advertising and film has

appeared in *Dance Research Journal* and *The International Journal of Arts in Society*. She has contributed to *The Oxford Handbook of Dance and the Popular Screen* (with Roxane Fenton) and *The Oxford Handbook of Dance and Theatre*. Her current book manuscript examines the discourse of dance within television advertising.
2. Roxane Fenton received her PhD from the University of California Riverside. Her other work on dance films has appeared in *The Oxford Handbook of Dance and the Popular Screen* (with Colleen Dunagan). She has taught dance history and appreciation at a number of colleges and universities.
3. For this chapter, we have deliberately chosen not to concern ourselves with the authorial intentions of Julie Taymor or other creators of the film. We recognize that our conclusions, with regard to both the philosophical message of the film and the effect of various performance and genre choices, may in fact be opposite to what Taymor herself has stated about her intentions.
4. For examples of analysis considering other uses of dance in dance film, see Dodds (2004) and Dunagan and Fenton (2014).
5. We are referring to a large body of dance scholarship; however, examples of this work that speak to the kind of analysis we do in this chapter include essays in the following: Foster (1995), Morris (1996) and Desmond (1997).
6. For a more developed treatment of these ideas, see Brannigan (2011: 100–124) and Faller (this volume).
7. Like Lennon, Jude is from Liverpool and has a father he does not know well. Lennon's father was a sailor, while Jude's was an American GI. Jude becomes an artist, and Lennon was an art student. The song for which Jude is named was written for John Lennon's son Julian, who was named for Lennon's mother, Julia. Jude is deported for a visa violation, and the Nixon administration tried to deport Lennon.
8. Other authors who have written about the Beatles and love in similar ways include Held (2006) and Arp (2006).
9. Altman (1987) and Feuer (1993) provide widely recognized analyses of the conventional structure of film musicals, including the distinction between narrative and number, as well as the modes of transition between the two.
10. This type of transition is used frequently within *Across the Universe*, contributing to the film's generic hybridity.
11. Examples of songs used within a performance setting in the manner that often appears in narrative film include 'Don't Let Me Down' (1960) and 'Why Don't We Do It in the Road' (1968), both performed at Cafe Huh?, as well as 'Hold Me Tight' (1963), performed simultaneously in England and America at a nightclub and a prom.
12. Naturalized performance of songs is also present in 'Revolution' (1968), 'Girl' (1965), at the end of 'I Want You (She's So Heavy)' (1969), and at the beginning of 'Dear Prudence' (1968).
13. For more on the space of the imaginary in film musicals and the use of dance to signal the move to this space see Altman (1987), Feuer (1993) and Rubin (1993).

14. Both Dodds (2004) and Brannigan (2011) discuss the use of stylized gestural movement as choreography in film forms. While their arguments differ at points, we draw on and reiterate their recognition of this trend within the dance-film relationship. *Across the Universe*, like many of its predecessors, emphasizes the structure and visual design of movement over that of dance per se. This emphasis on motion has been wedded with the acting conventions of film to produce within screendance a tendency to create choreography through the stylization of pedestrian movement. However, contemporary stage dance, such as the work of Pina Bausch, also utilizes a stylized gestural vocabulary (Brannigan, 2011: 94–98).
15. The reference to the Beatles song 'She Came in Through the Bathroom Window' (1969) is reinforced when Sadie walks into the room and asks, "Where did she come from?" Jude responds, "She came in through the bathroom window".
16. Dance has been used both to create (through participation) and evoke (through performance) the concept of community. For our purposes, the relationship between dance and community within the film musical genre is most salient. In his genre-based analysis of the film musical form, Rick Altman argues that the folk musical, one of the three main sub-genres of musicals, employs dance specifically as a vehicle for creating, maintaining and representing community. According to Altman, the creation of community through dance participates in the production of a utopic space of expression and union within the musical form (1987: 124–27). A similar expression of community and communal expression as utopic is evident in the more recent cultural phenomenon of the flash mob.
17. For detailed discussion of film musical conventions and the production of spectacle see Altman (1987), Dyer (1992), Feuer (1993) and Rubin (1993). This employment of dance as spectacle, with a large chorus serving as one aspect of an elaborate production, is dominant in much of film musical history; however, it also has a history within concert dance. Classical ballet relies upon intervals of spectacle and dance that exceed the needs of the diegesis, carrying the ballet and the viewer into a space of movement as visual design, entertainment and energy. See Foster (1986), Scholl (1994) and Garafola (2007).
18. For a discussion of bodily training, specifically within the context of dance, and how it shapes the meaning of the body and its movement see Foster (1997).
19. See Foster (1998) for a theoretical discussion of how dance participates in the construction of social identity through the choreography of bodily movement/practices.
20. For an extended discussion of traditional partner roles, as well as a discussion of radical shifts in these roles and the actual dance technique, Contact Improvisation, that informs the partnering in this section of the film, see Novack (1990).
21. While our analysis of this number focuses on the applicability of Goodwin's theories of the musicology of the image, we want to note that this number's emphasis on the choreography of visual images also has historical precedence in the work of early twentieth-century experimental and avant-garde filmmakers – one example being Fernand Léger's *Ballet Mecanique* (1924).

22. Cultural Studies scholar Jeffrey Roessner argues that members of the New Left were critical of 'Revolution' when it was released (just a few months after the 1968 Paris student uprising). "Hoping for a more radical statement, the political left felt betrayed by Lennon's refusal to either condone the violence or to offer a solution" (2006: 149). Roessner argues that the *White Album*, of which 'Revolution' was a part, was more politically conscious than members of the left understood at the time, but that it offered "a postmodern politics" that "allowed the Beatles to contest the commodificaton of rock music even as they helped redefine the relationship between artistic style and political relevance" (*ibid.*: 147–48).

References

Altman, R. (1987), *The American Film Musical*, Bloomington and Indianapolis: Indiana University Press.

Arp, Robert (2006), 'All My Loving: Paul McCartney's Philosophy of Love', in M. Baur and S. Bauer (eds), *The Beatles and Philosophy: Nothing You Can Think that Can't Be Thunk*, Chicago: Carus Publishing, pp. 37–46.

Baur, M., and Baur, S. (eds) (2006), *The Beatles and Philosophy: Nothing You Can Think that Can't Be Thunk*, Chicago: Carus Publishing.

Baur, S. (2006), 'You Say You Want a Revolution: The Beatles and Marx', in M. Baur and S. Bauer (eds), *The Beatles and Philosophy: Nothing You Can Think that Can't Be Thunk*, Chicago: Carus Publishing, pp. 87–105.

Brannigan, E. (2011), *Dancefilm: Choreography and the Moving Image*, New York: Oxford University Press.

Calef, S. (2006), 'You Say that You've Got Everything You Want: The Beatles and the Critique of Consumer Culture', in M. Baur and S. Bauer (eds), *The Beatles and Philosophy: Nothing You Can Think that Can't Be Thunk*, Chicago: Carus Publishing, pp. 73–85.

Covach, J. (2006), 'From "Craft" to "Art": Formal Structure in the Music of the Beatles', in K. Womack and T. F. Davis (eds), *Reading the Beatles: Cultural Studies, Literary Criticism, and the Fab Four*, Albany: State University of New York Press, pp. 37–53.

Crooks, J. (2006), 'Take a Sad Song and Make it Better: The Beatles and Postmodern Thought', in M. Baur and S. Bauer (eds), *The Beatles and Philosophy: Nothing You Can Think that Can't Be Thunk*, Chicago: Carus Publishing, pp. 175–85.

Desmond, J. C. (1997), *Meaning in Motion: New Cultural Studies of Dance*, Durham: Duke University Press.

Dodds, S. (2004), *Dance on Screen: Genres and Media from Hollywood to Experimental Art*, New York: Palgrave Macmillan.

Dunagan, C., and Fenton, R. (2014), '*Dirty Dancing*: Dance, Class, and Race in the Pursuit of Womanhood', in M. Blanco Borelli (ed.), *The Oxford Handbook of Dance and the Popular Screen*, Oxford: Oxford University Press, pp. 135–54.

Dyer, R. (1992), *Only Entertainment*, London and New York: Routledge.

Feuer, J. (1993), *The Hollywood Musical*, 2nd edn, Bloomington: Indiana University Press.

Foster, S. L. (1986), *Reading Dancing: Bodies and Subjects in Contemporary American Dance*, Berkeley: University of California Press.

Foster, S. L. (1995), *Choreographing History*, Bloomington: Indiana University Press.

Foster, S. L. (1997), 'Dancing Bodies', in J. C. Desmond (ed.), *Meaning in Motion: New Cultural Studies of Dance*, Durham: Duke University Press, pp. 235–57.

Foster, S. L. (1998), 'Choreographies of Gender', *Signs: Journal of Women in Culture and Society*, 24(1), 1–3.

Garafola, L. (2007), 'Russian Ballet in the Age of Petipa', in M. Kant (ed.), *The Cambridge Companion to Ballet*, New York: Cambridge University Press, pp. 151–63.

Goodwin, A. (1992), *Dancing in the Distraction Factory: Music Television and Popular Culture*, Minneapolis: University of Minnesota Press.

Held, Jacob M. (2006), 'All You Need is Love: Hegel, Love, and Community', in M. Baur and S. Bauer (eds), *The Beatles and Philosophy: Nothing You Can Think that Can't Be Thunk*, Chicago: Carus Publishing, pp. 27–36.

Morris, G. (ed.) (1996), *Moving Words: Re-writing Dance*, New York: Routledge.

Novack, C. (1990), *Sharing the Dance: Contact Improvisation and American Culture*, Madison: University of Wisconsin Press.

Roessner, J. (2006), 'We All Want to Change the World: Postmodern Politics and the Beatles' *White Album*', in K. Womack and T. F. Davis (eds), *Reading the Beatles: Cultural Studies, Literary Criticism, and the Fab Four*, Albany: State University of New York Press, pp. 147–58.

Rubin, M. (1993), *Showstoppers: Busby Berkeley and the Tradition of Spectacle*, New York: Columbia University Press.

Scholl, T. (1994), *From Petipa to Balanchine: Classical Revival and the Modernization of Ballet*, New York: Routledge.

Womack, K., and Davis, T. F. (eds) (2006), *Reading the Beatles: Cultural Studies, Literary Criticism, and the Fab Four*, Albany: State University of New York Press.

Zigler, R. L. (2006), 'Realizing It's All Within Yourself: The Beatles as Surrogate Gurus of Eastern Philosophy', in M. Baur and S. Bauer (eds), *The Beatles and Philosophy: Nothing You Can Think that Can't Be Thunk*, Chicago: Carus Publishing, pp. 139–50.

Looking for the Past in Pastiche
Intertextuality in Bollywood Song-and-Dance Sequences

Usha Iyer[1]

Contemporary Bollywood cinema is marked by a proliferation of references to earlier Hindi films.[2] Pastiche, tribute and parody are familiar structuring principles; the very profusion of these intertextual devices points to a certain kind of 'memorialization' in this self-reflexive cinema. Analysing the political economy of the repeated cinematic sign in light of India's globalizing economy allows for an exploration of the nature of Bollywood cinema's investment in the past. Given the extensive quotation in its films, and the recent interest in remakes and tributes, the principal questions of this chapter are: what kind of narrative does Bollywood produce about itself through this intertextuality and what is its investment in producing this account? One of the most striking forms of intertextuality in Bollywood films are the song-and-dance sequences, composed of a collage of earlier styles of dance, music and choreography and *mise-en-scène* elements. In this chapter, I will analyse three such sequences – 'Woh Ladki Hai Kahan' from *Dil Chahta Hai* (Farhan Akhtar, 2001), 'Dhoom Tana' from *Om Shanti Om* (Farah Khan, 2007), and 'Phir Milenge Chalte Chalte' from *Rab Ne Bana Di Jodi* (Aditya Chopra, 2008) – each of which presents a veritable cinema of past attractions, with the protagonists enacting different eras of popular Hindi cinema. Song-and-dance intertextuality is thus used as a lens to focus on the presences and *presentations* of the past in the present.

In discussing the cultures of memory evoked and enlisted by the Bollywood film, this chapter will focus on the historicity of remembering and forgetting, that is, at what points certain films are remembered and others forgotten, and what that tells us about the current cultural moment; in this case specifically, to examine how "contemporary memory cultures in general can be read as reaction formations to economic globalization" (Huyssen, 2003: 16). Intertextuality as a visual proclivity often becomes evident in the context of cultural nostalgia. It functions to articulate issues and identities figured around the construction, representation and preservation of national memory. Part of this essay's interest in Bollywood intertextuality is motivated by an attempt to investigate how this cinema's investment in history is a recurrent cinematic style that signals, results from and participates in epochal social transfigurations. I will employ intertextuality as the macro category within which I particularly examine the devices of parody and pastiche. While intertextuality has been variously theorized as overt or unconscious, manifest or constitutive (Fairclough, 1992), my use of the term is mostly restricted to the overt relation between texts signalled by conscious and deliberate citations, as found in the song-and-dance sequences analysed here. Within this rubric, parody and pastiche are two devices that meet intertextuality's defining characteristic of referencing other texts, but adopt different tones and modes of address. Hoesterey defines pastiche as a quasi-homage to and assimilation of a great master (2001: 4). The element of homage is what sets pastiche apart from parody, and it is often this element that is employed in the discourse of Bollywood directors and producers as they choreograph their spectacular imitations of the past. Hutcheon (1985) theorizes parody as "rewriting" or "transposition", where the parodist confronts a canonical text of the past, dramatizing the difference between the two. Likewise, Hoesterey emphasizes that a parody dramatizes the difference between itself and the text it references, while pastiche simulates a relationship of similarity (2001: 13). While both pastiche and parody deform the style of the referent by selecting, accentuating, exaggerating and concentrating, "pastiche is more like its referent, less exaggerated, less discrepant" (Dyer, 2006: 56).

The potential tension in Bollywood's enlistment of the past may be analysed by examining the particular form of intertextuality these song-and-dance sequences adopt. There can exist a contrast between the language of tribute and homage employed by the directors – in interviews, for example – and the often parodic address of the song-and-dance text itself. Textual indicators such as the tone of the quotation (mocking/admiring), the relationship set up between the past and the present (disruptive/integrative), as well as paratextual information (for example, DVD features including interviews with directors) help determine whether a certain intertextual instance is a pastiche or a parody or an intricate combination of the two. The difference between parody and pastiche in the Bollywood context becomes important because of the link I seek to establish between cinematic and televisual mutations and cultural and technological transformations engendered by globalization.

Intertextual devices such as parody and pastiche perform the function of memorialization through their references to the past. Irrespective of the tone of the reference, what is significant is that the past is enlisted towards some project in the present. Where memorials are traditionally understood as monuments erected to preserve the memory of a group, within the discourse of memory studies they have been extended into various representational forms that are continuously produced in order to sustain a collective memory (Halbwachs, 1992; Anderson, 1991). The human body itself has been argued to act as a site for the propagation of memory (Connerton, 1989), which resonates with Bollywood's enlistment of the dancing star body as a memorial site within the range of intertextual means it employs to represent and *construct* a collective memory. Bollywood citations seek to establish an affective encounter with a cinematic past, which provokes the question of how films deploy spectacle in relation to history, ideology and national space.

In much of their memorializing of particular filmic styles and iconography, Bollywood song-and-dance sequences manufacture the past as an episodic narrative. This construction of the past through selective and strategic remembering in the present leads to the trope of the past as a succession of definable decades. In representing the past of Hindi cinema as consisting, for example, of the jazz-inspired 50s, the twist-obsessed 60s, the disco-dancing 80s, Bollywood fetishizes the star body, sets, props and costumes in a bric-a-brac collection of aestheticized fragments. In its selective and fetishized remembering, Bollywood intertextuality may display the "waning of historicity" that Jameson mourns (1995: 17), but more significantly, it points to a renewed *investment* in history. The obscuration of multiplicity atrophies the past into an entity that is continuous with the present, thereby legitimizing it. The selectivity of references from the past may be taken to indicate that a cinema of spectacle is recollected and resurrected to suggest a connection with Bollywood's own participation in and celebration of spectacle, as not an embarrassment anymore but a self-assured assertion of identity.[3] It is not surprising then that the cinema that these films remember is not the 'social' film of the 1940s and 50s,[4] the state-sponsored realist cinema of the 1970s and 80s, or even the anti-statist angry-young-man action movies that defined Hindi cinema of the 1970s, but rather the cinematic spectacle of cabaret shows, elaborate stage performances and dream/fantasy sequences. What is commemorated then is a cinema of dress, gesture, dance moves, sets and props: the very elements that take centre stage in the contemporary Bollywood aesthetic.[5] Even as it forges this link with the past to buttress its own status, Bollywood employs intertextual stagings of the past as conduits for the display of its perceived superiority over earlier popular cinema, often in terms of technical capability, special effects skills and its staging of larger-than-life spectacle. In being enlisted to mark Bollywood's difference from the cinema of the past, intertextuality thus fosters the economic and global aspirations of this new cinematic mode. The basic argument around which I shall organize my inquiries is that Bollywood is conflicted in its quotation of the past: it yokes itself to the past to lend itself legitimacy, but constantly strives to outdo it to assert its distance from the very cinema it quotes.

The first song sequence I examine is 'Woh Ladki Hai Kahan' from Farhan Akhtar's 2001 hit, *Dil Chahta Hai*. Viewed as a 'hip' self-reflexive film that interrogates the tropes of popular Hindi cinema, this song in particular was hailed as a clever parody of the typical song-and-dance moves from earlier eras of Hindi film.[6] The film follows the lives of three young men, Aakash, Sameer and Sid, and the ups and downs in their friendship and romantic relationships. The scene that leads into the song has Sameer (Saif Ali Khan) and Pooja (Sonali Kulkarni), a young couple, clearly marked as 'modern' by their speech, dress and class position, struggle with their embarrassment over their parents' attempt to set them up in an arranged marriage. They come to a movie theatre to watch a film that opens with the song, 'Woh Ladki Hai Kahan'. The sequence is constructed through a series of cuts between a two shot of Sameer and Pooja in the audience and their enactments on the screen. In the first segment, through this inter-cutting, they see themselves transposed into the Hindi cinema of the fifties. This first stanza is shot as a sepia-tinted 'fantasy' sequence in which a bricolage of cinematic tropes from the fifties is constituted through *mise-en-scène* elements such as smoke machine-induced vapours and ornate pillars with Art Nouveau-type curlicues that are found in song sequences such as 'Hum Aapki Aankhon Mein' from *Pyaasa* (Guru Dutt, 1957) and 'Ghar Aaya Mera Pardesi' from *Awaara* (Raj Kapoor, 1951). Sameer's moustache, white suit and bow tie echo that of Guru Dutt's character in *Pyaasa*, while Pooja's diaphanous gown, and her gesture of holding a veil over her face, mirrors that of the Mala Sinha character in the same film. Her curls-and-pearls coiffure is styled after Nargis's in the *Awaara* song sequence. Like in the *Pyaasa* song sequence, a big suspended painted moon dominates the background (see Figure 1).

Figure 1: Recreating the fifties, *Dil Chahta Hai* (Akhtar, 2001)

In the second stanza, the *mise-en-scène* shifts to a familiar 1970s song-and-dance routine: the hero and heroine out on a day-trip with a group of friends, all of them dancing in a whirl of bright 'kitschy' colours. The seventies are rendered recognizable by the back projection, bell bottom pants and Pooja's beehive hairstyle. This segment is meant to reference songs from the 1960s and 70s such as 'Mere Sapnon Ki Rani' from *Aradhana* (Shakti Samanta, 1969), or 'Yeh Sham Mastani' from *Kati Patang* (Samanta, 1970) among many others (see Figure 2).

Figure 2: The kitschy seventies, *Dil Chahta Hai* (Akhtar, 2001)

The third sequence spoofs typical 1980s and 90s dance routines that involved synchronized dance steps on mountain tops, heaving bosoms and chiffon saris (see Figure 3). The hero and heroine run towards each other in slow motion, the hero tugs at the heroine's sari, and the sequence ends in a long shot that emphasizes the scenery, with the point of focus being our gyrating protagonists. Unlike recent Bollywood films with their mandatory foreign location shoots, this sequence is shot in a clearly Indian location (the 'hill station' Lonavla, where many Hindi films of the 1980s shot their song sequences). This clearly parodic segment is meant to lampoon songs such as 'Keh Do Ke Tum Ho Meri' from *Tezaab* (N. Chandra, 1988) and 'Dhak Dhak Karne Laga' from *Beta* (Indra Kumar, 1992) featuring Madhuri Dixit and Anil Kapoor.

The song thus deploys a series of gestures, attitudes, costumes and locations to define and periodize popular Hindi cinema. The lyrics serve as markers of cinematic eras as well, with the first stanza including Urdu words such as "dildaar" (lover), "khwaab" (dream) and "Naazneen" (beautiful woman). By the third stanza, the Urdu, commonly perceived as the poetic and classical idiom, is replaced by more banal Hindi phrases such as "mere dil ko jaise dhadka diya,

Figure 3: Lampooning the eighties, *Dil Chahta Hai* (Akhtar, 2001)

mere tan badan ko pighla diya" (the way you've shaken my heart and melted my body), which in turn prompt the raunchy dance moves of the 1980s and 90s. As one of the first song-and-dance sequences to adopt an intertextual mode of referencing, 'Woh Ladki Hai Kahan' raises a number of questions: why use a historical survey of Hindi film song-and-dance sequences to cement the romantic relationship in the film? What particular moments of Hindi cinema constitute this episodic history? What function does this song-and-dance sequence play within the film? Attempting to answer these questions will help ascertain how this film relates to the past.

The function of this dance number is to resolve a set of complex tensions, given that Sameer has been unlucky in love so far, and has now fallen in love with Pooja, even though they both reject the idea of an arranged marriage. At the end of the third segment in the song, the camera pans left from the dancing couple of the 1980s and cuts to a shot/reverse shot sequence between Pooja and Sameer, the first in this entire song sequence. Where throughout we only see a two shot of them looking at the screen, here the editing finally consolidates the union of this couple as they affirm their love for each other. As the concluding chorus plays, Pooja and Sameer face each other while the audience around them performs the trademark movement for this song, suturing the divide between the screen and the spectator in a resounding celebration of the resolution of this couple's dilemmas. 'Woh Ladki Hai Kahan' thus enlists a specific history of spectacular romance to enable this fledgling romance. The romantic song-and-dance genre is vaunted as mitigating tensions between arranged marriage and 'falling in love', and, in the larger scheme of Bollywood's investments, between tradition and modernity. Sameer and Pooja emerge from the movie hall as an ecstatic couple, their romance structured by a remembering of the repertoire of popular Hindi film song-and-dance moves that have defined screen romance down the ages. Thus, Bollywood enlists the past to address the confounding questions that a global modernity imposes upon its subjects, and mobilizes visual culture to lay claim to more 'time-tested' 'traditional' affiliations and identifications.

On the surface, it would seem that, on account of the integrative role of the past in this song-and-dance sequence, its intertextual mode is more pastiche than parody. Where in parody, "characteristic features of the work are retained but are imitated with contrastive intention", in pastiche, this relationship is one of similarity (Hoesterey, 2001: 13). It may therefore be argued that even as it stereotypes three periods in Hindi film, 'Woh Ladki Hai Kahan' *extends* these very stereotypes through pastiche. Indeed, it creates a "relationship of similarity" by having the protagonists *embody* these historic cinematic types rather than distance themselves from them. Through pastiche, this couple continues the tradition of spectacular Indian film romance, to which, it would seem, song and dance is essential. The song and dance thus sets up an integrative relationship between past and present, where the conventions of the past resolve the predicaments of the present. That being said, there are various textual and paratextual indicators that complicate the song's address. Firstly, it is essential to note that *Dil Chahta Hai* was conceived of and received as a "refreshingly" anti-formula film.[7] Film trade analyst, Taran Adarsh, says in his review: "The storyline is diverse from the run-of-the-mill fares we've been subjected to since time immemorial",[8] while director Farhan Akhtar explains that he wrote the film's dialogue himself to create an "honest portrayal of Westernised urban youth in Mumbai: Most Hindi movies tend to dramatise events. They are very dialogue heavy. Characters don't speak like people normally do in real life."[9] The film was thus seen as aiming for a more 'realistic' narrative form than the typical Hindi film. One aspect that was designed to achieve this and to mark the film as 'different' was that most of the song sequences dropped the usual dance accompaniment which is seen as the quintessential mode of film song picturization in Bollywood. In fact, other than the opening song, 'Koi Kahe', performed in a discotheque, 'Woh Ladki Hai Kahan' is the only song sequence accompanied by overtly choreographed dance. It therefore becomes necessary to investigate the role of this song whose entire design is predicated upon dance moves within such an avowedly anti-formula film. Akhtar's depiction of Hindi film, especially of the 1960s–70s and the 1980s–90s, fits Hoesterey's definition of parody as imitation with satirical intention. In these two segments, the movements are exaggerated, the colours rendered too bright and 'kitschy', all of it pointing to a parodic take. However, the first segment of 'Woh Ladki Hai Kahan' aims for a more 'classic' tone, and its *relative* lack of deformation and discrepancy can be read as a homage to 1950s directors such as Guru Dutt and Raj Kapoor. Thus, within the same song, we can observe different degrees of homage and critique.

It is not insignificant in this context that within the diegesis, the romance between Sameer and Pooja is figured as simpler than the other two romantic relationships: between the painter, Sid (Akshaye Khanna) and a much older, divorced woman, Tara (Dimple Kapadia), and between the cynical-about-love Aakash (Aamir Khan) and the already-engaged Shalini (Preity Zinta). While Sameer and Pooja's romantic problems seem to be easily resolved by this song sequence, the more sceptical Aakash can only be 'converted' to the discourse of love by 'high art': a performance of *Troilus and Cressida* at the Sydney Opera House (exclusively commissioned for the film). A comparison of the two sequences reveals a deliberate contrasting of sombre operatic love with the frothy dance-based romance of Hindi cinema. Where in 'Woh Ladki Hai Kahan', Sameer and Pooja's fellow audience members, comprising of young urban Indians, perform a clearly comical dance move to join them in an exuberant and spontaneous affirmation of romance, here, the audience, composed of older white patrons, is shown crying in response to the tragic story of Troilus and Cressida. The address of the opera is shown to be much more complex than that of the Hindi song sequence. Already then, we see a complex negotiation between homage and parody in this inaugural intertextual Bollywood song-and-dance sequence. Further, the aesthetic hierarchy set up between Hindi film romance and *Troilus and Cressida* illuminates that the cultural nationalist discourse of contemporary Indian media narratives that bolster the status of the popular rests on rather shaky ground. Within a transnational realm of cultural production and reception, Bollywood hovers between self-conscious approbation of the local and discreet genuflection to the global/Western.

The second song-and-dance sequence to be considered here is 'Dhoom Tana' from the film, *Om Shanti Om* (Khan, 2007). This film is an intertextual extravaganza, riffing on the 1980 film, *Karz*, but also sampling a plethora of filmic references, styles and clichés. The first half of the film is set in the 1970s, while the second half takes place in contemporary times. The song sequence, 'Dhoom Tana', takes place in the first half when Om Makhija, played by Bollywood's biggest star, Shahrukh Khan, a poor 'extra' or junior artist in the Bombay film industry of the 1970s, slips into the premiere of the film, *Dreamy Girl* (an allusion to the 1977 Hindi film, *Dream Girl*). As he watches the object of his infatuation, Shanti Priya, on screen, he proceeds to displace the original stars of the films this song references who have been morphed into the sequence à la *Forrest Gump* (Robert Zemeckis, 1994). This re-embodiment functions as a literal substitution, inserting the bodies of contemporary stars – Sunil Dutt, Rajesh Khanna, and Jeetendra – into these films of the past: *Amrapali* (Lekh Tandon, 1966), *Saccha Jhutha* (Manmohan Desai, 1970), *Humjoli* (Ramanna, 1970) and *Jay-Vijay* (L. V. Prasad, 1977) (see Figures 4a-c).

Figures 4a-c: Dancing with the stars, *Om Shanti Om* (Khan, 2007)

Where 'Woh Ladki Hai Kahan' alludes to film texts of various eras, 'Dhoom Tana' directly quotes from a set of four texts from the 1960s and 70s. The suggestion is that the star-smitten Om constructs an elaborate fantasy of being on screen with Shanti Priya, who, as the leading star of the 1970s, acts in various genres, playing the courtesan, the cabaret dancer and the folk performer. Om's love for the star is enacted through a transposition into the space of popular Hindi cinema, where the expression of desire is carried out through song and dance. It is important here to consider how Om's class position – as urban poor – defines his relationship to the screen. He sneaks into the movie hall and sits in the lower 'stalls' section, from where he looks up to Shanti Priya on the screen as well as in her special box seat above. He embodies the participatory spectatorship ascribed to working-class audiences of popular Indian film, by whistling, dancing in the aisle, and in this case, fantasizing about being a star, dancing alongside his favourite heroine. However, the employment of intertextual fantasy here does not produce the same extra-filmic result as in 'Woh Ladki Hai Kahan'. Sameer and Pooja, the upper-class couple, can actualize their desires through intertextual intervention, suturing themselves into the narrative of the romantic Hindi film song. The audience joins them in celebrating this union, while in *Om Shanti Om*, the transposition remains a fantasy as class lines remain drawn and, by the end of the song, Om is led out for disrupting the film and runs away under the threat of being caught by the police. Thus, while the song-and-dance sequence allows for the eruption of subversive desires through fantasy, and the intertextual quotations provide approbation for these desires, the larger regime of the narrative reins in the cinema-induced fantasy.

By including original footage from the 1970s, 'Dhoom Tana' makes an explicit visual quotation. The performative tone of these quotations is determined by the film's figuration of Om Makhija as a clownish character, and casts the 1970s in general as tacky, exaggerated and embarrassing. Wilkinson-Weber, in an essay on costumes in recent Bollywood remakes, points out that the costume designers' brief for *Om Shanti Om* was not to aim for a naturalistic representation of seventies fashion but for a parodic masquerade, so that "the nostalgia that permeates *Om Shanti Om* is tinged with a sense that 1970s and 1980s Bollywood was, from the fashion standpoint, ridiculous" (2010: 140). She argues that remakes have to walk the line between mocking earlier fashion styles, so present-day Bollywood seems "naturally" superior, whilst retaining a sense of nostalgia for the past. This contrasts with the statements of homage espoused by directors and designers and used to promote remake films as "product[s] of their personal memories and longing for the names, styles, and culture of 1970s films" (2010: 140). This language of homage and longing does not prevent the film-makers from adopting a parodic attitude to this very past. The choice of the four films is also curious. These are hardly the most popular or canonized films of the 1960s and 1970s, but they provide the necessary ingredients of spectacle, via the elaborately staged courtesan dance of *Amrapali*, titillating pageantry, via the cabaret sequence from *Saccha Jhutha* and camp humour, via the badminton-dance sequence from *Humjoli* and the gypsy dance from *Jay-Vijay*. These elements – spectacle, titillating pageantry and camp humour – already serve as the signature style of popular Indian cinema within a global imaginary. Bollywood 'homage' reiterates the predominance of these elements through repeated quotation and a cultivated amnesia towards other attributes that a broader spectrum of popular cinema from the past would afford. Significantly, the intertextuality in 'Dhoom Tana' not only expresses a fond derision of the past, but also an assertion of pride in Bollywood's contemporary capabilities. Indeed, the publicity around 'Dhoom Tana' focused on the special effects used to match the contemporary action to the earlier film footage. In his book on the making of *Om Shanti Om*, the film's screenwriter, Mushtaq Sheikh, devotes an entire section titled 'FX the Past' to lauding the technical prowess of the *Om Shanti Om* team that "brought this technology to India for the first time" (2008: 87). There is an impetus thus to yoke intertextual quotations of the past to demonstrations of technical achievement in the present.

A comparison of 'Dhoom Tana' with yet another song from the film – 'Deewangi Deewangi' – further reveals the complexity of Bollywood's invocation of the past. In the second half of the film, Om Makhija is reborn as a famous film star, Om Kapoor. In this well-heeled, well-connected avatar, he is finally able to achieve his desire for cinematic fame. He receives the award that he had fantasized about as a poor junior artist and the song-and-dance sequence, 'Deewangi Deewangi', is a celebration of this award. Thirty-one star actors from the Hindi film industry, who have no other role in the film, make a 'special appearance' for this song-and-dance that simulates a Bollywood 'bash'. Each of these stars display their trademark dancing style, so that every-*body* comes to be a signpost for a certain phase in the history of this industry. Richard Dyer likens pastiche to synecdoche, "whereby the parts (the traits) are taken for the whole (the totality of the original oeuvre)" (2006: 57). By this estimation, 'Deewangi Deewangi' can also be conceived of as a 'pastiche' song where certain dance moves stand in for a star's whole career, and indeed for entire periods of popular Hindi cinema. Unlike in 'Dhoom Tana', these dance moves are not figured as comic, except, tellingly, those from the 1970s through the early 1990s: Dharmendra, Jeetendra, Mithun Chakraborty and Govinda. The more recent Bollywood stars, on the other hand, seem to receive more straightforward non-parodic treatment. A series of actresses such as Rani Mukherji, Kajol, Juhi Chawla and Karishma Kapoor join Shahrukh Khan in performing dance moves from the films they acted in together – *Kuch Kuch Hota Hai* (Karan Johar, 1998), *Phir Bhi Dil Hai Hindustani* (Aziz Mirza, 2000) and *Dil Toh Pagal Hai*

(Yash Chopra, 1997), respectively. Significantly, these very films are seminal instances of the Bollywood 'phenomenon', and, through their popularity, are regarded as major milestones in its cultural and economic ascendancy. Other actresses such as Urmila Matondkar, Shilpa Shetty and Priyanka Chopra re-enact their moves from *Rangeela* (Ram Gopal Varma, 1995), *Shool* (E. Nivas, 1999), and *Bluffmaster* (Rohan Sippy, 2005), highlighting in turn the increased importance of choreography in Bollywood films, which renders stars recognizable by their dance moves.[10] Thus, the choice of stars and of the trademark moves that define them marks 'Deewangi Deewangi' as a song celebrating contemporary stardom and the Bollywood industry that propagates it.

The third song sequence examined is 'Phir Milenge Chalte Chalte' from the 2008 film, *Rab Ne Bana Di Jodi*, directed by Aditya Chopra. It demonstrates how, as in the two previous sequences, the past is harnessed to yield larger-than-life spectacle. Circumstances force Taani (Anushka Sharma), a vivacious young woman, to marry Suri (Shah Rukh Khan), a boring middle-class middle-aged man. The only excitement in Taani's life comes from her dance class, where trainers from Mumbai bring the 'Dancing Jodi' competition to small-town Amritsar. Unbeknownst to Taani, her husband Suri assumes a new identity as Raj, a garrulous young man spouting clichés from Hindi films.[11] The song-and-dance sequence takes place after Raj backs out of the competition because he cannot dance well. Taani comes to a movie hall with Suri to watch a film, whose narrative is interrupted by her fantasy about Raj appearing on screen taking on the personas of various stars from different eras of popular Hindi cinema: Raj Kapoor from the 1950s, Dev Anand and Shammi Kapoor from the 1960s, Rajesh Khanna from the 1970s and Rishi Kapoor from the 1980s (see Figures 5a-d). In this fantasy world, Raj dances competently alongside actresses from contemporary Bollywood figured as heroines from earlier times.

Figures 5a-d: The spectacle of the past, *Rab Ne Bana Di Jodi* (Chopra, 2008)

Like 'Woh Ladki Hai Kahan', 'Phir Milenge Chalte Chalte' employs costume, sets, cinematographic idioms and trademark dance moves to make clear its allusions to the past. Additionally, the lyrics are composed of film and song titles associated with each of the star couples. These intertextual allusions are more specific and detailed than in the generalized referencing of 'Woh Ladki Hai Kahan' made seven years before. Further, unlike the two songs we looked at earlier, 'Phir Milenge Chalte Chalte' expands the canvas of each vintage vignette by creating more spectacular sets than found in the original and by introducing outside influences. The first vignette is thus a cross between quotations from Raj Kapoor–Nargis films and Busby Berkeley's design and choreography for films such as *Footlight Parade* (Lloyd Bacon, 1933). This hybrid approach to generating spectacle is probably what allows *Film Journal International* to describe 'Phir Milenge Chalte Chalte' as entirely influenced by Hollywood musicals:

> The song … gets a full-out treatment paying impeccable homage to Busby Berkeley, MGM's Arthur Freed Unit, Vincente Minnelli musicals, Andrew Lloyd Webber, and some candy-colored 1960s hippies-meet-Carnaby Street something. Topping it off, each change in sequence includes a famous Bollywood beauty: Bipasha Basu, Lara Dutta, Preity Zinta, Rani Mukerji and Kajol Devgan. (Lovece, 2008)

The vignettes also fetishize past images, for example, when a prop like Raj Kapoor's hat – which, in films such as *Awaara* and *Shree 420* (Kapoor, 1955), served as a symbol of his Chaplinesque rendering of the common man – transmogrifies into a giant hat lifted up by a clutch of dancing women. In the second vignette, instead of the real windows and homes referenced by the lyrics, we have a proliferation of repeated cut-out windows, while the fourth vignette features a toy train and fake trees. On the one hand, representation of the past through flat, decorative sets creates iconic signs of historical *mise-en-scène*, but, combined with the narrow selection of sources and the consistent investment in spectacularizing them, this flattening of the *mise-en-scène* leads to a flattened version of time, narrative and history.

Ordinarily, a quotation is used to point to a superior articulation, or to defer to the authority on a matter, which often helps affirm the status of one's own discourse. If Bollywood remakes were simple homage, as it is often claimed, then these would be the functions of the quotations we have seen thus far. Indeed, in re-naturalizing earlier tropes through their extension in the present cinematic aesthetic, Bollywood intertextuality can be argued to harness the energy and cultural mythology of older forms to lend credibility to its own accounts. Yet this apparent affirmation of the values and practices of earlier films is complicated when one considers that Bollywood pastiche rarely uses these quotations in their original form. Rather than a collage of original footage featuring the stars from the past, Bollywood always re-shoots these quotations, pointing, as mentioned earlier, to different investments in the present. In a *Rab Ne Bana Di Jodi* DVD extra discussing 'Phir Milenge Chalte Chalte', costume designer Aki Narula explains, "We had to bring in signature looks, yet modernize it". This 'modernizing' by adding the crucial ingredient of current notions of spectacle, whether through technical superiority or contemporary stardom, reveals a significant aspect of Bollywood's interest in the past. In infusing its allusions with this new spectacular charge, 'Phir Milenge Chalte Chalte' seeks to change the past to justify the investments of the present. These investments are articulated at the start of the song, when Raj flamboyantly announces: "Main love love ke baapon se seekhkar aaya hoon; romance te dance, Hindi film style" ("I've learned love from the fathers/gurus of love; romance and dance, Hindi film style"). The "fathers/gurus of love" refer to the various stars that the song pays homage to, as well as to Yash and Aditya Chopra, the producer and director of this film, who have, over the decades, produced the kind of spectacular, romance-driven films that Bollywood commemorates. The announcement also serves to cement the link between romance and dance, in that dance makes romance possible. Typically, the standard functions of the romantic duet in the Bollywood idiom are: to express love, to convey longing/heartbreak, as pre-romantic banter about the dangers of falling in love, or, as in these three sequences, as fantasy about being with the lover. Since the 1980s the romantic fantasy duet has frequently been shot in various settings, with changes in location and costume, contributing to the spectacle afforded by the song. In our three intertextual Bollywood songs, this spatial trope turns temporal, affording a certain type of 'cinematic tourism' where the fantasy is played out for all cinematic time, with setting and costume alterations signalling changes of entire cinematic periods. Sameer and Pooja, Om and Shanti Priya, and Raj and Taani whirl through baroque choreographic constructions that intra-textually are designed to address their sexual-romantic desires, and extra-textually, our spectatorial desire for spectacle.[12]

'Phir Milenge Chalte Chalte' adroitly coalesces these various desires through the intersection of fantasy and intertextuality we noted in the earlier two songs. At the personal level, Taani's fantasy of Raj's performance of this spectacular song-and-dance sequence effects a double addressing of her desire – for a competent dance partner *and* for a spontaneous and passionate romantic engagement that she finds lacking with her husband, Suri. Raj's supplanting of stars through the ages functions for her as an embodiment of multiple desirable dancing star bodies by her own object of desire, which, as played by Shahrukh Khan, produces a dual star reference – that of the referenced star, but always more importantly in the Bollywood film, of Shahrukh Khan's star body itself. This is where the song moves beyond the realm of personal fantasy, purporting to address a more collective spectatorial desire. The effect here is similar to what Neepa Majumdar describes as occurring in an intertextual film from the 1980s, *Naseeb* (Manmohan Desai, 1981), where "the subject of the sequence is star power itself" and the spectator "experiences the pleasures of recognition, desire, and identification with the star, all of which are basic to the experience of stardom" (2001: 164).

While on the workings of stardom in this song and dance, it is to be noted that a revealing choice is made in not having Taani (played by debutante, Anushka Sharma) play herself within this fantasy sequence, so that in addition to the spectatorial satisfaction of seeing Shahrukh Khan occupy various star bodies, we also have him dancing with a bevy of Bollywood's top heroines. This additional extra-diegetic star presence is generative of a *paisa vasool* or the 'getting your money's worth' discourse, in that you watch one film, but get to see all the stars in the Bollywood firmament. Specifically, the actresses in 'Phir Milenge Chalte Chalte' – Kajol, Bipasha Basu, Lara Dutta, Preity Zinta and Rani Mukherjee – are regulars in Yash Raj Films' productions, of which this film, *Rab Ne Bana Di Jodi*, is one. By having these actresses take on the personas of the major female stars of the past (Kajol as Nargis, for example), the song serves to buttress their own star status while promoting the prestige of the production company through this constructed 'tradition'.

The star cameos in these songs can be seen thus as acting as extra-textual markers of some kind of Bollywood star system. Significantly, in the three song-and-dance sequences, none of the contemporary stars actually bears a resemblance to stars of the past, for example Bipasha Basu as Nutan, Kajol as Nargis or Sonali Kulkarni as Madhuri Dixit, but through costume, make-up and dance, resemblance is constructed. The markers of stardom are thus inscribed not in physical appearance or in acting prowess but in exteriorized aspects that can be replicated by Bollywood. The intersection of fantasy and desire thus points to how Bollywood employs intertextuality with the past to showcase its own stars and pleasures.

In formulating a set of historical circumstances that favour the production of pastiche, Dyer cites periods when, under the pressure of geographical exploration, imperialism or migration, a multiplicity of traditions are brought together, creating the need to assert particular forms as indeed particular to certain cultures (2006: 131). Globalization can be argued to engender similar anxieties, to which Bollywood responds by relentlessly emphasizing its uniqueness and unprecedentedness within a global cinematic idiom, while simultaneously reiterating its ties with a specifically Indian film tradition. In an essay titled 'This Thing Called Bollywood', Madhava Prasad argues that Bollywood cinema signals the advent of a certain reflexivity, "becoming a cinema for itself as it were, recognizing its own unique position in the world, the contrastive pleasures and values that it represents vis-à-vis Hollywood" (2003). Through this study of intertextual song-and-dance sequences, I posit that spectacle, which is seen as a Bollywood signature, represents an otherness that is configured to command a certain desirable exchange value in the global market, which prompts a nexus with Bollywood's investment in producing a new canon as detailed above. This awareness of its difference enables the Bollywood film to "reproduce itself for a market that demands its perpetuation as a source of cultural identity" (*ibid.*), whether within India, for the Indian diaspora or for the growing ranks of global Bollywood fans.[13] "The desire for Bollywood is thus a desire for the reproduction of the difference that it represents on a world platform" (*ibid.*). Intertextual references to earlier popular cinema serve to retroactively mark this difference of the Indian cinematic idiom from that of Hollywood, so as to pronounce a grand tradition of an Indian cinematic vernacular.

The textual forms and textual effects of Bollywood cinema provide a lens to study the economic and cultural changes in the Indian subcontinent over the last two decades. As a transnational culture industry, Bollywood is engaged in ongoing strategies of incorporation by constantly referencing past cinematic forms. This genealogy of affiliations helps Bollywood to achieve credibility and legitimacy. The affiliations extend from and circulate between the cinema and newer media such as television, video and DVD technology and the internet, fostering an intertextual archive of memory. Within the economics of contemporary cultural production, where there is a proliferation of copies, versions, remakes and samples, intertextuality seems almost an inevitable response to this dynamics of sameness and repetition. Given that "[i]ntertextuality signals an *anxiety*, and an *indeterminacy* regarding authorial, readerly or textual identity, the relation of present culture to the past, or the function of writing within certain historical or political frameworks" (O'Donnell and Con Davis, 1989: xiii; emphasis mine), the study of Bollywood intertextuality becomes important for the examination of vectors of power and ideological formations in the Indian cultural economy.

In conclusion, an examination of Bollywood intertextuality reveals how a social memory is constructed by employing a past rendered through a set of emblematic gestures, manoeuvred through present sensibilities. In the three song-and-dance sequences discussed in this chapter, intertextuality is employed to manage desire and promote current configurations of interaction – between the romantic couple, the fan and the star, the spectator and the performer. In harnessing a cultural memory of certain periods in Hindi cinema, Bollywood's memorialization of the spectacular song-and-dance sequence acts as an assertion of pride in this cinema of the past, which was seen, in its time, as populist, retrograde and not deserving of a place in the Indian film canon. This new-found confidence that enables the commemoration of this cinema derives from Bollywood's participation in a global cinematic economy that valorizes and fetishizes the extravagance, lavishness and glamour of Bollywood cinema.[14] While the earlier statist discourse around cinema commended a realist aesthetic that would capture the 'authentic' idioms and rhythms of Indian life, Bollywood films suggest that spectacle *is* the authentic idiom of Indian cinema, and by extension, of Indian life. Bollywood intertextuality returns nostalgically to those elements of the popular cinematic past that it wants to enlist in the present – romance and spectacle. By connecting earlier eras to the present, Bollywood intertextuality aims to demonstrate that the object of nostalgia is not a lost or threatened ideal but one that continues to thrive in the present *through* Bollywood. In memorializing certain aspects of Hindi cinema, Bollywood films thus forge a reflexive reinforcement of their own mythologies.

Notes

1. Usha Iyer is Assistant Professor in Screen Studies at Clark University, Massachusetts. Her work focuses on dance and female stardom in popular Hindi cinema. She is the author of a forthcoming article on the Hindi film dancer-actress, Madhuri Dixit, in the journal, *Camera Obscura*, and her essay on Hindi horror cinema has appeared in the edited volume, *Figurations in Indian Film*.
2. My use of the term 'Bollywood' follows Madhava Prasad (2003) and Ashish Rajadhyaksha's (2003) description of Bollywood as a specific mode of popular Hindi cinema that developed from the 1990s, characterized, among other things, by family melodramas, NRI (non-resident Indian) or PIO (people of Indian origin) characters – characters who live outside of India, a conscious display of multinational brand names, and an unmistakable address to a diasporic audience.
3. Ashish Rajadhyaksha argues that Bollywood's 'culture of revival', its insistent reference to an earlier epoch (specifically, according to him, to the 1950s melodramas) serves to form a link with these earlier battles around cultural legitimacy, and celebrate its own triumph in that battle (2009). While Rajadhyaksha's cultural legitimacy argument underscores the continuing desire of the mainstream cinema to declare itself as the repository of national-cultural values, it is necessary to note that Bollywood cinema's intertextual references are not limited to Hindi films of the fifties, as he contends. Rather, Bollywood extensively appropriates cinematic tropes from the seventies, the eighties, and, in a cheeky act of self-affirmation, from Bollywood films of the nineties and the 2000s as well. This highlights the importance of more closely analysing the selectivity of Bollywood's narrative abductions, which would then allow us to investigate what this cinema itself proceeds to legitimate. Additionally, it is precisely the anti-statist action movies of the seventies, such as *Deewar* (1975) (which Rajadhyaksha refers to as an Ur-text for Bollywood) that Bollywood does *not* commemorate. Instead, a 'stylish' film like

Don (1978) is remade in 2006, the remake functioning as yet another element in Bollywood's reflexive reconstitution of itself, and as an affirmation of its investment in spectacle.
4. Even when the work of 1950s directors like Raj Kapoor and Guru Dutt is referenced, the quotations emphasize formal details such as *mise-en-scène* and costume (which are then further spectacularized), while the social critique in their films is entirely excised.
5. In addition to the most spectacle-driven segments from the past, these Bollywood song sequences also quote the most potentially 'camp' sequences (such as the badminton-dance sequence from *Humjoli* quoted in 'Dhoom Tana', or the gyrations-on-the-mountains sequence in 'Woh Ladki Hai Kahan'). This is true of most of the forms of intertextuality evidenced in the Indian mediascape, viz. Bollywood allusions, remix videos, television promos, and advertisements. Where an important post-economic deregulation question has been, 'what does it mean to be Indian in a global context?' the Indian mediascape has retorted by producing an intertextual mélange of caricature and exotica. This in turn leads to the Bollywood propensity for simultaneous parody and homage.
6. http://www.rediff.com/movies/2001/aug/10dil.htm (accessed 13 June 2010); Us Salam (2001).
7. The formula or 'masala' film refers to the Bombay cinema's omnibus aesthetic form consisting of family melodrama, action sequences, comic routines and song-and-dance numbers, each having a heterogeneous range of appeal within the film's loose narrative framework (Prasad, 1998: 7).
8. http://www.bollywoodhungama.com/movies/review/6738/index.html (accessed 13 July 2010).
9. http://specials.rediff.com/movies/2002/sep/23farh.htm (accessed 17 November 2009).
10. Two of the three song sequences I discuss – 'Woh Ladki Hai Kahan' and 'Dhoom Tana' – have been choreographed by the same person, Farah Khan, also the director of *Om Shanti Om*. It is important to note here the rise of the dance choreographer with Bollywood. This cinema has designated dance routines as all-important to its idiom, so that globally, Hindi cinema is increasingly associated with dance rather than with the song sequences that marked its difference earlier. Indeed, Bollywood has spawned a veritable industry around dance with international stage shows and numerous television reality shows.
11. In a double intertextual figuration, Suri's doppelganger, Raj, is named after the founding hero of Bollywood narratives, as played by Shahrukh Khan in *Dilwale Dulhaniya Le Jayenge* (also directed by Aditya Chopra), but also after Raj Kapoor (he mentions his full name once), the famous star and director from the 1950s who is commemorated in 'Phir Milenge Chalte Chalte'.
12. It is not incidental that the three films I discuss have been produced by major production companies in the Bombay film industry (Excel Entertainment Pvt Ltd, Red Chillies Entertainment, and Yash Raj Films) that can *afford* to stage this Bollywood 'spectacle of history' and thereby posit themselves as the worthy inheritors of

the Hindi film tradition. The seeming stylistic heterogeneity of these sequences reveals thus a discursive homogeneity that supports monologic power – of big production houses, and of geographical areas (North vs. South).
13. In her work on live performances of Bollywood dance by diasporic performers, Sangita Shresthova argues that the public display of Bollywood dancing constitutes a performance of cultural identity, highlighting the role of Hindi film dance as a form of cultural memory (2008: 261).
14. In an essay titled, 'Size Matters', Nitin Govil analyses Bollywood's fiscal-statistical portrait of itself, and how it is consumed by a "culture of enumeration" (2010: 107) that produces "big numbers" in terms of profit, projected growth etc.: "Hollywood once signified a certain form of bigness, with its star lifestyles, bloated economies of scale, world market share, and opulent *mise-en-scène*. As we near the end of the first hundred years of Hollywood, however, its Bombay counterpart now lays a legitimate claim to a new gigantism" (2010: 108). I tie this newly-found economic and cultural confidence to Bollywood's attempt to re-write the canon through intertextual means.

References

Anderson, Benedict (1991), *Imagined Communities: Reflections on the Origin and Spread of Nationalism*, London and New York: Verso.
Connerton, Paul (1989), *How Societies Remember*, Cambridge and New York: Cambridge University Press.
Dyer, R. (2006), *Pastiche: Knowing Imitation*, New York: Routledge.
Fairclough, Norman (1992), *Discourse and Social Change*, Cambridge, MA: Polity Press.
Govil, N. (2010), 'Size Matters', *BioScope: South Asian Screen Studies*, 1, 105–109.
Halbwachs, Maurice (1992), *On Collective Memory*, Chicago: University of Chicago Press.
Hoesterey, I. (2001), *Pastiche: Cultural Memory in Art, Film, Literature*, Bloomington: Indiana University Press.
Hutcheon, L. (1985), *A Theory of Parody: The Teachings of Twentieth-Century Art Forms*, New York: Methuen.
Huyssen, Andreas (2003), *Present Pasts: Urban Palimpsests and the Politics of Memory*, Stanford, CA: Stanford University Press.
Jameson, Fredric (1995), *Postmodernism or: The Cultural Logic of Late Capitalism*, Durham, NC: Duke University Press.
Lovece, F. (2008), 'Film Review: Rab Ne Bana Di Jodi', *Film Journal International*, 19 December, online at http://www.filmjournal.com/filmjournal/content_display/reviews/specialty-releases/e3iffab62725e964a29e971e890df03478f (accessed 15 July 2010).
Majumdar, N. (2001), 'The Embodied Voice: Stardom and Song Sequences in Popular Hindi Cinema', in A. Knight and P. Wojcik (eds), *Soundtrack Available: Essays on Film and Popular Music*, Durham: Duke University Press, pp. 161–84.
O'Donnell, P., and Con Davis, R. (eds) (1989), *Intertextuality and Contemporary American Fiction*, Baltimore: Johns Hopkins University Press.

Prasad, M. (1998), *Ideology of the Hindi Film: A Historical Construction*, New Delhi: Oxford University Press.

Prasad, M. (2003), 'This Thing Called Bollywood', *Seminar*, 525, online at http://www.india-seminar.com/2003/525/525%20madhava%20prasad.htm (accessed 30 November 2014).

Rajadhyaksha, A. (2003), 'The "Bollywoodization" of Indian Cinema: Cultural Nationalism in a Global Arena', *Inter-Asia Cultural Studies*, 4(1), 25–39.

Rajadhyaksha, A. (2009), *Indian Cinema in the Time of Celluloid: From Bollywood to the Emergency*, Bloomington: Indiana University Press.

Sheikh, M. (2008), *The Making of Om Shanti Om*, New Delhi: Om Books International.

Shresthova, Sangita (2008), 'Dancing to an Indian Beat: "Dola" goes my Diasporic Heart', in Sangita Gopal and Sujata Moorti (eds), *Global Bollywood: Travels of Hindi Song and Dance*, Minneapolis: University of Minnesota Press, pp. 243–63.

Us Salam, Z. (2001), 'Film Review: Dil Chahta Hai', *The Hindu*, 17 August.

Wilkinson-Weber, C. (2010), 'A Need for Redress: Costume in Some Recent Hindi Film Remakes', *BioScope: South Asian Screen Studies*, 1, 125–45.

The Call to *Rize*

Megan Anne Todd[1]

"Hit 'em with a little Ghetto Gospel"

The call[2] to *Rize* (David LaChappelle, 2005), heard, seen and felt, throughout the film is encapsulated in Tupac Shakur's posthumously re-engineered and slowed-down track 'Ghetto Gospel' (2004) produced by Eminem, that samples Elton John's song 'Indian Sunset' (1971). 'Ghetto Gospel' appears at the end of the film during credits and brings home the layered poly-vocal, multivalent and evocative calls re-iterated throughout the film. Tupac's cry to "Hit 'em with a little ghetto gospel" is answered in the last line of John's refrain, "Peace to this young warrior without the sound of guns", and echoes, among many things, elements of irony, tragedy and a constructed sense of hope. This fusion of voice, song, genre and content, cuts to the crossroads of the broader political paradox of USAmerican[3] culture that is at the heart of this film.

Shakur's legacy, for example, evokes a multiplicity of signifiers about USAmerica, hip hop, race and class. For many of Shakur's fans, he was the quintessential "young warrior" who, while calling "to end the war on the streets", died much too early with the sound of guns.[4] However, for Shakur's detractors, his legacy is framed not as a voice confronting social injustice, racism and poverty, but in the legal battles and bullets of his life. This polarization of perspective speaks beyond the multivalent legacy of Shakur to the broader political scope of commercial hip hop and institutional forms of racial and class discrimination which circumscribe and charge it. Tricia Rose writes at length about this in *The Hip Hop Wars: What We Talk about When We Talk about Hip Hop and Why it Matters* (2008). She asserts that:

> the public struggle over hip hop is waged over the images, stories, and market power associated with black and female bodies [and that] we need to arm young black men and women, and everyone else, with powerful critical tools so that they can expose and challenge the state of commercial hip hop, divest it from its pernicious brand of blackness, and make far more room for a wide range of alternatives. (Rose, 2008: xii)

In considering *Rize*, if we heed Rose's call, we must "arm ourselves" with critical tools with which to wade into the layered sonic and visual world of pastiche that is *Rize* to consider the "wide range of alternatives". This is the politicized charge and the inherent paradox, both implicit and explicit, in the call to *Rize*.

Situated squarely at a crossroads between fashion photography, documentary, MTV-like video and the genre of dance film, *Rize* maps the sonic and visual terrain of the dance styles of clowning, krumping and stripper dance, taking the viewer on a journey to the inner city of South Central Los Angeles through the lens of Hollywood. Fashion photographer, David LaChappelle, uses his compositional skills to situate these fresh hip hop dance styles in a way that creates visually striking scenography contrasting vivid colours against scenes of urban decay and sonic compositions that flow between the words of the dancers, beat-heavy tracks and appearances of some big voices from the music industry.

Invoking a call, as well as a response, *Rize* offers insight into the landscapes and soundscapes of the economic, psychic and cultural spaces where the dancers live and dance, albeit filtered through the lens and sound systems of those who engineer the images and sounds of 'cool' production.[5] Throughout the chapter I use the term 'call' to evoke the circular nature of call and response present in the dance forms the film highlights, but more importantly to politicize the film's performativity in an overt way. That is, I wish to call attention to how this film functions within a larger cultural framework. For example, as the dancers move they catalyse interaction of spirit, space, place, relationships, identities and power structures. Through mapping the overlapping, conflicting and complicit and cohesive circles of calls and response through the sonic and visual terrain, I consider how the film functions as a political 'agent provocateur', intervening at the intersections of mass media, spiritual practice, artistic practice and life. Although dance is framed clearly as a positive force within the lives of the dancers and the communities of South Central, *Rize* raises many vital critical questions but leaves them un-tethered to any type of critical engagement. In many instances, the film relies heavily on imagery montage to create vital critical commentary on many of the vexed issues which it highlights. This chapter hopes to create a critical framework for many of the political issues this film raises but does not address.

The Scenario of the American Dream/Freedom Dreams

The scenario of the 'American Dream' underpins *Rize* in a powerful way, evoking a raging political undercurrent that cuts to the heart of USAmerica's history and struggle for democracy, freedom and equality. The concept of scenario, set forth by Diana Taylor, asserts that "Instead of privileging *texts* and *narratives*, we could also look to scenarios as meaning-making paradigms that structure social environments, behaviours, and potential outcomes" (Taylor, 2003: 28; original emphasis).⁶ The scenario of the American dream, the concept that anyone can make it in the US through individual hard work, is repeated frequently in colloquial and political rhetoric, as well as dramatic structures of film and television. In *Rize*, too, this scenario is invoked not only by the film's title but also in its subject matter: young African-American people rising from the ashes of a burning city making their own way through the art of dance. The film's content and delivery act as a response to the American dream scenario by historicizing, confirming and/or challenging an audience's perceptions about that dream – in particular, who has been historically allowed to participate in the dream and how.

Rize's most successful call is the way that it draws firmly from the nostalgic bank account of the American Dream and evokes a multiplicity of responses that illuminate the inherent paradox of the dancing and the film as political acts. Throughout the film, the dancers, Dragon, Tight Eyez and Lil' C, testify to how the conditions of social inequities in the inner city are a catalyst for the need to cultivate and innovate. LaChappelle's framing of the dances certainly highlights this point as well. For example, Dragon talks about the lack of outlets beyond sports. Lil' C elucidates the same point, "In better neighbourhoods they have performing arts schools: you have ballet, you have modern, you have jazz, you have tap, all those prestigious academies you can go to. There's nothing like that available to you when you live where we live". These comments highlight the strong currents of alternative discourse to the American Dream.

In a book titled *Freedom Dreams: The Black Radical Imagination*, Robin D. G. Kelley chronicles artistic visions, works and dreams that 'imagined' a way beyond the structures of oppression in USAmerican society. Inspired by the vision of Dr Martin Luther King Jr, Kelley asserts that we need to "recover ideas" that reveal "a different way out of our constrictions ... tap the well of our own collective imaginations ... do what earlier generations have done: dream" (Kelley, 2002: xii). Although, as Kelley suggests, if we consider radical artistic movements through the criteria of success or failure, then we have to concede that most have failed, because they did not transform basic power relations in society. However, he asks, if we cannot produce a vision that allows us to see beyond and out of our current situation, then where can we go? (Kelley, 2002: x). The visions and dreams, which inspired these movements, in turn, still inspire people to struggle for change (Kelley, 2002: ix). Implicitly the work of *Freedom Dreams* attests to the fallibility of the American Dream and politicizes it.

Rize, on one hand, offers a glimpse of how some young people in South Central have tapped the well and found productive, creative alternatives to the trappings of poverty and limited options. However, on the other hand, it also illustrates, through its failures, that we must be ever vigilant of what Rose terms "hyper-behavioralism", an approach which she elucidates "over-emphasizes individual action and underestimates the impact of institutionalized forms of racial and class discrimination" (Rose, 2008: 8). In other words, Rose reminds us, as Foucault does, that people will always register distinct genealogical positionings in the webs of power in which they exist. As we lay bare these webs of power, we see that the scenario of the American Dream (crafted by regimes of power and historic white privilege) has always been inextricably woven with Freedom Dreams that include everyone regardless of race, gender, ethnicity, sex, class, and so on.

Los Angeles, California: Politics of Space and the Making of Place

We see the struggle between the American Dream and *Freedom Dreams* clearly delineated in cityscapes across the US, marked through demonstrations of power, wealth and privilege and through the city's re-use as well. The city of Los Angeles is possibly the ultimate example embodying the paradox of the American-Freedom-Dream. Regarding Los Angeles, we can ask is it "Disneyland's utopia or South Central's dystopia? ... The leader of the Pacific Rim or the leader of homelessness? A city reputed for its freedom of expression or police repression?" (Kelley, 2008: 1). Kelly affirms, Los Angeles,

> is all of these things, and the diverse communities who populate Los Angeles are the connective tissue linking these different worlds together. Although L.A is one of the most residentially segregated in United States capitalism, globalization, the criminal justice system, law, housing policy, popular culture, etc., bind varying groups of people together across lines of race, class and gender. (*Ibid.*)

This articulation of what segregates and disperses, as well as what binds and connects, is illustrative of de Certeau's theoretical estimation of "the city". De Certeau suggests that the city "serves as a totalizing and almost mythical landmark for socioeconomic and political strategies, urban life increasingly permits the re-emergence of the element that the urbanistic project excluded" (1984: 95). He proclaims that it is in the re-emergence of ways of use and the spatializing practices of the everyday that are resulting in the decay of what he terms "the concept-city". Furthermore, he wonders if "perhaps cities are deteriorating along with the procedures that organized them?" (de Certeau, 1984: 95). This is intriguing on several fronts. First, the USAmerica that elected the first African-American president is fraught with deep gauges of racialized injustice. Are the practices of clowning, krumping and stripper dance really going to change the deep structures of our society? Likely not. But as Kelley's work testifies, and Obama himself is so wont to repeat, it is in the recovery, inventing and investing in visions that gives us the imaginative capacity to move out of our present circumstance. For without the vision of the horizon towards which we want to move, "we don't know what to build, only what to knock down. We only end up confused, rudderless, and cynical, but we forget that making a revolution is not a series of clever manoeuvers and tactics but a process that can and must transform us" (Kelley, 2002: xii).

Call and Response

Taking off from Franz Fanon's statement,[7] "The circle of the dance is a permissive circle: it protects and permits ... there are no limits-inside the circle", we must consider what happens when this circle opens into an amplified space of hybridity (DeFrantz, 2004: 197). Paul Gilroy suggests that these hybrid spaces carry the vital charge of cultural re-formation. Fusing Fanon's circle within the frame of globalized hybrid practice, Thomas DeFrantz has suggested that:

> the aesthetic principles can be learned, and then the protective circle can form around a new, hybrid dance ... But this reformation often inspires failures in readings, as audiences, dancers, and choreographers don't necessarily understand their relationship to the circle. The circle protects and permits. When it is opened we are no longer protected, although we may be permitted. (DeFrantz, 2004: 199)

As the dance circle is opened and re-formed through the lens of LaChappelle and subsequently the intervening of mass media, we must ask can, and if so how, the sonic and visual fields continue to function as relational strategies for our common humanity? How do the dance circles formed in the streets and public spaces assert a psychic, corporeal and political presence that changes the space, place and power in their community? Then, how do these new dance circles re-create that presence in the psychic space of imagined community in USAmerica and the global community? Finally, can/does *Rize* somehow help to put South Central and the young people innovating new horizons of dance on 'the map'?

Geneologies of Talauega Brothers and LaChappelle

In 2002 Rich and Tone Talauega were working on Christina Aguilera's video *Dirty* (2002) with David LaChappelle, when they introduced him to communities of clowns, krumpers and stripper dancers in South Central Los Angeles

(Mitchell, 2004). This was the conceptual beginning of *Rize* when, as LaChappelle reported, he became convinced that he had to document what these kids were doing because they were so inspiring to him. He remarked, in an interview with the *NY Times*, "when you're shooting film and there's a Payless Caskets store right next to the Dance Academy – we pulled up the first night, and the headlights illuminated these little kids' coffins – you don't have to invent anything" (Mitchell, 2004). Maybe in that moment the dysfunctional marriage between his artistic vision and the genre of documentary was born.

The Talauega brothers are dancers, choreographers, musicians, producers and performers with an impressive array of A-list credits for their choreographic and consulting work. As well as connecting the clowning/krumping/stripper dance communities in South Central with the image industry of Hollywood and director David LaChappelle, these brothers co-wrote many of the songs that narrate the storyline of *Rize* in tracks such as 'Make You Dance', 'Clownin' Out', 'I Krump', 'Get Krumped' and 'Break It On Down (Battlezone)'.

While listening to the voices of the dancers narrating their experiences, *Rize* feels like a documentary, whereas at other moments we are struck with MTV-like glossy surreal images of black artists who remain within the glamorized ghetto-scapes in the film. This is problematic and buoyed by USAmerican histories that co-opt black art forms to feed mainstream popular culture. Instead of addressing this sort of historical alienation on any level, the visual image style of hyper-real fashion photography and the genre of documentary are instead hitched and combine to produce problematic and evocative relationships that continually straddle a crossroads of reality and music video.

Curator of the Tel Aviv Museum, Nili Goren, situates the visual style of LaChappelle's photography by calling on Jean Baudrillard's post-modern theory of simulacram. Goren observes the process of simulacram by which:

> The affinity between signs and their origins in reality weakens, and sometimes is even eliminated altogether; reality is replaced by a set of images and imitations, sometimes entirely devoid of origin.
>
> A flux of information rife with recurring images and ideas, that do not provide a clear notion regarding the state of affairs or events in the world; rather, they form a text, subject to interpretation, which serves as basis for the production of additional texts. The eye adapts itself to the dizzying whirl of the flickering images, as radical as they may be, and the mind becomes accustomed to their subversiveness.[8]

As Goren's apt observation highlights, LaChappelle's fashion photography work, as well as his video work, function through dizzying and captivating compositions that create a sense where the images convey no "clear notion regarding the state of affairs or events in the world". This strategy, while highly effective in fashion and music videos, is problematic for the genre of documentary, the most glaring examples of which I will discuss later.

If we consider *Rize* as the 'birth' of krumping into mainstream popular culture, then David LaChappelle would be the metaphoric midwife who assisted in the labour and delivery of krump and clowning from Los Angeles to its global sites of appropriation. LaChappelle was, until most recently, known primarily as a fashion photographer and was notably given his first job by Andy Warhol. He boasts an expansive and impressive resumé of photography exhibits and directing credits that range from music videos, advertisements and music shows, to films. *Rize* was LaChappelle's first full-length feature film, with two short versions, released earlier, one in 2003 titled *Clowns in the Hood*, and a second in 2004 titled *Krumped*. His visual works are vivid, surreal and exaggerated in their play with expression. Many involve nudity or partial nudity. LaChappelle's expertise in the music video style of presentation is most apparent in the last scene of *Rize* that I discuss below. LaChappelle's stylistic approach to documentation and imagery sequencing in *Rize* creates an evocative popular culture dance film, no doubt, but what are the stakes both for those who are 'documented' and those who consume the documentary as reality?

Speaking about his photography, LaChappelle emphasizes that he hopes that the narratives that emerge from his work allow people to engage and address issues that are challenging. He describes the charge of his art this way:

> I feel that we are living in a very precarious time, with environmental devastation, economic instability, religious wars waged, and excessive consumption amidst extreme poverty. I have always used photography as a means to try to understand the world and the paradox that is my life. There is the feeling that we are living at a precipice. My hope is that through the narratives told in my images, I will engage people and connect with them addressing the same ideas or questions that possibly challenge them.[9]

If indeed this was LaChappelle's goal as a producer of *Rize*, then he has been successful. The expressively evocative visual effects throughout *Rize* are classic LaChappelle imagery and effective at producing responses. This is evidence to the power of *Rize*, as well as the dance styles, which the film showcases. Conversely, it can also be argued that this ability to provoke might be evidence of sickness within USAmerican society. Responses illuminated vestiges of racism, notions of essentialism and voyeurism, while others document how art changes lives and creates social change. While acknowledging the limitations and failures of dance to evoke social change, there are also many instances in which the performative reach of dance succeeds in eliciting healing, hope, and the continued vision to struggle for change (Kelley, 2002).

Rize

The visual call that positions viewers in an active way begins with the title *RIZE*, which jumps out in red. In its appropriation and revision of the spelling of the word 'rise' there is a sense of something remade on its own terms. It speaks to the film's assertion of its own performativity. It is a proclamation of and to action. It at once tells us that the film is doing something and also commands us, the audience, to action, telling us to take our place. This repositioning and recasting of the audience is one of LaChappelle's first framing strategies that shape the film as a political act. It moves viewers from a purely voyeuristic positioning into one that is politicized, precarious and possibly responsible. The call can be construed as dangerous or threatening, precisely because it evokes responses, whether they be internal and self-reflective, or expressed and acted upon.

Rize begins with the words, "The footage in this film has not been sped up [sic] in any way". To someone unfamiliar with the dance style, this disclaimer may be apt, as it is impressive that dancers can move as these dancers do. Movements are strong and assertive in a way that is grounded in the spine and speaks out through quick and definite contractions, gestures and steps. There is an aggressive force in the movements, which are often executed rapidly, with strategic pause and style. The film weaves together footage of dancing, interviews and glimpses into lives of the dancers, as well as moments of historical footage. The second half of the film focuses on the Battle Zone, a competition where the krumpers and the clowns battle each other through dance.

After the opening disclaimer, we hear a historic newscaster's voice announcing, "six days of rioting in a negro section of Los Angeles … Civil rights leaders were quick to deplore the unbridled lawlessness. Dr Martin Luther King vowed to do all in his power to prevent a recurrence in Los Angeles or anywhere". We read "1965 Watts Riots Los Angeles, Ca" and then the film cuts to black and white footage of broken windows, looted storefronts and the city burning as our perspective moves through the city streets. As the images of devastation fill the screen, the sounds of the newscast gives way to a melodious female voice whose song counterpoints the visual devastation by sonically weaving a sense of hope, with the song 'Seek Ye The Lord'. This sort of paradox sets a tone that permeates the entire film. As the engulfing song fills our sonic experience, we read "1992 Rodney King Riots, Los Angeles, Ca". As the screen bursts into colour in the next frame, we see a panoptic view of the city, as if flying overhead. Then at street level we see buildings burning, cars burning and police watching looters. As a wall of fire approaches from across a street we see a man throwing small buckets of water on his roof. The camera angle sweeps wide again; as the city burns we watch from the air. Dropping back onto the street level, four African-American females engage in what appears to be an impromptu rhythmic street performance of the brutal beating of Rodney King by the Los Angeles police officer. The voice of Tight Eyez narrates, "This is our neighbourhood. This is where we all grew up. We were all kids back then when this happened. We managed to grow from these ashes. This is where we still live". We read "2002 Los Angeles, Ca" and observe the first krump session of the film, where Lil' C is getting amped up as other krump dancers including Tight Eyez and Dragon circle around him in an outside public space. The camera moves in close and listens as Dragon, a young African-American krump dancer with his face painted, asserts:

> If you're drowning and there is nothing around you but a board. You're going to reach out for that board. And this was our board. And from this board we floated abroad and we built us a big ship. And we are going to sail into the dance world, the art world. We're going to take it by storm because it's our belief. This is not a trend. Let me repeat this is not a trend.

Without commenting on the historic scenes of race-related violence and the present-day connections, the film then turns its focus to the hero of the tale: an African-American dancer named Tommy Johnson who originated the dance genre now called clowning. After being asked to perform as a circus clown for a little girl's birthday, Tommy created his trademark persona of 'Tommy the Hip Hop Clown'. Wearing a rainbow wig, whiteface makeup and clown attire, Tommy the Hip Hop Clown travels through Los Angeles neighbourhoods with loudspeakers in his car staging hip hop dance parties on lawns, in streets and public spaces. His loud music from the back of the car asserts place, defines space and calls people together. The assertion of a sonic presence makes way for a carnivalesque dance party that makes use of public neighbourhood streets and sidewalks. We see people of all ages, genders and body shapes clown dancing at Tommy the Hip Hop Clown's birthday parties. The re-purposing of space throughout the film calls us to consider Henri Lefebvre's (1974) theorization on the production of space,[10] de Certeau's (1984) theory of re-use[11] and ultimately how spatialized practices produce social spaces. The dance party footage is intercut with footage of dancers talking about clown dancing and what it has done for them in their lives. The track 'Make You Dance' narrates the scene as we see the clown dancers in action.

> Block party at the front porch on July fourth. Never bored because Tommy showed up in his Ford ... Come on come on come on skinny fat short or tall just get your back off the wall ... No violence. It ain't a fight. It's a dance craze. Like the old school ... It's not a fad – here to stay ...

After seeing the space Tommy creates in his persona of Tommy the Hip Hop Clown, we learn about his entrepreneurial beginnings and how he started the first clown dance group in 1992. In 2002 the dancers in the film report that there are now at least fifty clown groups in Los Angeles.

The focus of the documentary is on how clowning, krumping and stripper dance function as alternatives to gangs and violence, and cultivate new opportunities to 'rize' out of difficult situations. Throughout the documentary, we follow Tommy the Clown's journey as the founder of this contemporary dance movement. We meet the clowns, stripper dancers and the krumpers who, in their local dance practices, have created alternative options to gangs and to traditionally organized sports and other recreational activities. Although hip hop, krumping, clowning and stripper dance share many distinct cultural-aesthetic similarities with Africanist aesthetic dance practices, they also share commonalities with many other forms of embodied movement including boxing, punk mosh pits and capoeira (Zanfagna, 2009: 340). As Cristina Zanfanga (2009) points out, the many circles of dance often overlap and blur. Distinctions between the sacred and secular, between dancing and fighting, as well as style, can become difficult to distinguish in the hybrid spaces of contemporary USAmerica. *Rize* plays at/with the blurry edges of these hybridized spaces and amplifies many of the inherent paradoxes within.

While stripper dance is not a focus in *Rize*, LaChappelle includes a small segment on it. This section focuses mostly on three females and one young man and defines stripper dance specifically by a wide-leg second position stance with vigorous bouncing of the butt. However, they are quick to assert that stripper dance can and does incorporate anything into it. The young man says, "It's a flow. It's a vibe. It's like a connection. Everybody does it. Everybody sees it. We do everything … We'll put everything in it". These comments testify to the fluid and permeable nature of styles, as aesthetics and 'ways of doing' recycle through communities and times. Although some of the dancers in *Rize* insist that stripper dance is not sexual, Zanfanga points out the dance style references the "sexual and dynamic performance style of black strippers" (2009: 341). The track that drives this section, 'Fix up, Look Sharp', calls out the chorus, "I got the big beat, I hear the sound, I got the big beat, I get on down", as we see dynamic performances by a multiplicity of dancers.

In the next scene a group of young men are huddled together, as Lil'C and Tight Eyez assert, "you have stripper dance, or twerking, which we do not do". They articulate how their form and style of dance is totally different from clowning and/or stripper dance. The differences become obvious as we see the krump sessions. The song 'Get Krumped' tells us, "See this ain't a circus. We ain't clowns. Don't let the face paint fool ya". As we cut back and forth between the close-up documentary commentary, music and movement in the section devoted to krump, the sonic articulations in the customized for *Rize* tracks, 'Get Krumped', 'I Krump' and 'Beaztly', present these dance styles in a very specific way.

In the krump circle there is a masculinized energy and presence, with mostly men present, although there are female krumpers in the circle as well. The krumpers build the energy, at times pushing each other out of the way to take their place in the centre. Most notable of the female krumpers is Miss Prissy, who embraces the hard-hitting moves of krump aesthetics, albeit punctuating them at times in a distinctly feminized manner, such as with the swish of her hips and the flick of her skirt. Regardless of a dancer's gender, krump's aesthetic energy of asserting bodily presence and power, through the physical articulations of chest pops, arms swings, footwork and character embodiment, moves dancers in physical, emotional, social and sometimes spiritual ways, and carries a distinct masculinized charge.

We hear how these dancers, who started with Tommy's clown group, got together to develop their own style that could be more expressive of their aggression and intensity without the confining need to tone down the movement and interaction for the sake of entertainment. Again, the dancers emphasize that they created a style that could express and channel their fierce energy in a way that stripper dance or clowning did not allow. The critique of social inequity and struggle is implicit and explicit in its gestures of challenge and competition, which are negotiated generally in hip hop's, and specifically in krump's, bodily aesthetics. Hazzard-Donald observes how the negotiations of hip hop in popular culture change their charge when appropriated into the mainstream media.

> Hip hop dance permits and encourages a public (and private) male bonding that simultaneously protects the participants from and presents a challenge to the racist society that marginalized them. The dance is not necessarily observer friendly; its movements establish immediate external boundaries while enacting an aggressive self-definition. Hip hop's outwardly aggressive postures and gestures seem to contain and channel the dancer's rage. (Hazzard-Donald, 1996: 229)

These negotiations expand to reveal how krump is mobilized, by whom and towards what ends, and how it in turn is re-interpreted in these new sites. As Tricia Rose reminds us, it is imperative to engage dialogue around the current state of hip hop and the vital role of black culture in cross-racial exchanges in the mass-mediated world of today (2008: 7).

Problematizing Roots and Routes in the Sacred and Secular

How aesthetics of clowning, krumping and stripper dance are racialized, gendered, classed and sexualized changes with the contexts in which they are practised, for what purposes, and by whom, as well as with who is 'reading' the practice. As Foucault reminds us, "the body is molded by a great many distinct regimes" (Foucault, 1977: 153). This implies that everyone registers distinct genealogical positionings in the webs of power in which they exist. However, as de Certeau's theory of tactical navigations suggests, we have the power to remake our "register" within the webs of power – and in turn catalyse the remaking of the webs themselves (2004: 1248). And this is precisely why dance is such an interesting political practice. In this embrace, however, we must always keep the registers of power in full view so that they don't get lost in a celebration of ingenuity that forgets why the ingenuity is necessary in the first place. This is where *Rize* falls short. The audience is propelled into a liminal space of finding its way through an MTV-like hall of mirrors that moves through resonances/dissonances without paying particular attention to some of the scenarios that are being activated.

As these dance styles enter streams of commodification, they are set in contexts that play into and out of circulating realities of racism, sexism and classicism, though that is not addressed in *Rize*. The documentary is structured in ways that work both into and out of these scenarios it speaks to. The most disturbing example of this is in the middle of the film where footage of an unspecified African village, showing dancers in wrestling and face painting scenes, is interspersed with krumpers painting their faces and dancing. The scene is framed as transcendent, a collapsing, between different geographical locations, the present and the past, the sacred and the secular. It begins with Dragon stating "this is not something we had to learn because it was already implanted in us from birth" and culminates in a female krumper, Daisy, appearing to enter a trance state. As she does, Baby Tight Eyes exclaims, "She just struck. That's what we all been waiting on … Yup, that's what all of us been waitin' on". This scene is significant. It links the spiritual/religious intent present in krump to spiritual/religious dance practices of the African diaspora where dance and music are primary vehicles for manifesting spiritual religious connections. We see this in many diverse practices throughout the Americas and the continent of Africa. Reaching a spiritual realm through secular dance, the Africanist aesthetic of "sacred and the secular", as "deeply, often inseparably, connected" is expressed (Lawal, 2002: 42). Here in a crossroads of the sacred and the secular, krumping is framed as an embodied "recollection and interpretation of the past, memory", which facilitates "the transfer of cultural property from one geographical space to another" and acts as a "catalyst in the construction and negotiation of new identities" (*ibid.*: 43). This connection with Africanist aesthetics utilizes "the visual and performing arts" as a "means of embodying, affirming, revitalizing, and celebrating human existence itself" (*ibid.*: 42). This connection of revitalizing the community, the self, and that which is transcendent, through embodied movement, is what dancing and social justice are all about. However, the problematics of uncritically linking these two scenes, especially in light of Dragon's statement, as Hewitt states, risks "the interpretation that the movement is a product of racial memory rather than culture" which leads to a naïve and essentialist commentary for an undiscerning viewer (2005: 349).

The music playing throughout the background of this scene creates another collapse between diverse and non-specified pastiche of pan-African arts. According to a personal communication (21 November 2005), with a priest of Orisha Oko from a Cuban lineage of this Yoruba religion, the rhythm playing throughout this scene is one for the Orisha (deity) Shango, who is "associated with thunder/social justice" (Lawal, 2002: 53). The use of this rhythm adds another layer of political charge while at the same time, an etheric "ahhhhhhhh" sound, overlaid on the rhythm for Shango, cultivates a transcendent quality.

On a semiotic level, this scene creates a striking video montage that yokes the face painting of dancers in Los Angeles with masking in the unspecified African context. In *Rize* the first act of face painting we see is Tommy the Clown applying the white base paint for his whiteface clown makeup. From this, we see the practice re-shaped and reconfigured through the unique styles and expressions of the clowns' and krumpers' face paint. Masking certainly has a strong and varied tradition throughout the continent of Africa, where it is employed in many contexts and for varied purposes, sacred and/or secular. Even when masking in Africa occurs for "secular or entertainment purposes ... a mask is still considered sacred because of its social, political, or spiritual function" (Lawal, 2002: 41–42). In this way we can see the many varied designs and colours of creative face painting that both the clowns and the krumpers[12] wear through multiple levels. They can be seen as a way of identification with one group and not others (i.e., as a dancer and not a gang member); as an expression that is politicized in the heritage of multiple scenarios at work, in a way that allows the dancers (as Dragon and some of the other krumpers expressed) to conceal their own self-consciousness (worldly) self, while revealing and accessing a transcendent (spiritual) self. Furthermore, the face-painting depicted in this movie is a unique and empowering facet of this new African-American art form that shows unique styles and expressions which participate in Africanist traditions and speak back to white USAmericanist traditions as well.

This scene is both complex, overly naïve, beautiful and profoundly disturbing in some of the relationships it sets up. Africa is contextualized as primitive and as such plays into the USAmerican image of itself as progressive and first world. On another level the footage brings together traditions of the diaspora that show how Africans "transplanted to the Americas during the transatlantic slave trade ... held on firmly to their ancestral heritage, synthesizing it with

American (both European and Native American) elements" (Lawal, 2002: 42). This scene walks a dangerous line between promoting primitivist notions of African and African-American people and showing a continuum of heritage. It is a dangerous place, a crossing where, in the call to *Rize*, the audience has the opportunity to work itself as much into, as out of, historically constructed scenarios and racial stereotypes long embedded in the USAmerican imaginary. This call to *Rize* situates us, the audience, at the crossroads of our own perspectives where the dances and dancers turn, challenging us to come into relationship and understand, through our visual, auditory, cognitive and kinesthetic senses, our own unique resonances and dissonances to the political nature of embodied practices presented in the film, that are at once, among many things, a means of transferring knowledge and memory, contesting social norms, communicating hope and creating social change.

Battle Zone: Dancing and Fighting for Social Change

The second half of the film builds to the 'Battle Zone', where the krumpers and the clowns face off in a large auditorium. Tommy comments, "You know how battle-dancin' was back in the days. I just brought it back – with makeup". We see the pageantry, the preparation and the build-up towards the competition. Contestants are matched for age and gender. There is the lil' mama match, the big boy match, and others. Individual dancers innovate movement, continuously intensifying the energy in a one-upmanship that in this context is for battle, but can also be for fun, spiritual questing and community building, or a combination of these. Dancers use their best moves, taunting and prodding an opponent, getting as close to them as possible without touching them. Dancers at times include certain bodily manipulations that elicit visual effects, making it appear as if the dancer is doing more than they are actually doing. The effect could be seen as a sleight of hand and is referred to in krump as *illusion*. We see this same aesthetic articulated in the practice of *capoeira*, an Afro-Brazilian martial art/dance form. In *capoeira*, the notion of *malicia* involves an "awareness of what's going on under the surface of appearances of some form of social interaction between two people; then suddenly, at the propitious moment, the person with the subtlest *malicia* cunningly puts something over on the other person before he knows what's going on" (Merrell, 2005: 25). *Malicia* is the sense of doubling, of trickery, but good-natured and with a smile; it utilizes outward conformity and inward resistance that reveals itself only partially through cleverness, subtleness and appearances. It is said to be "an equalizer" in that it can make up for a lack of speed, ability or strength through deception (*ibid.*: 26). This aesthetic of *malicia* is at play in the practice of clowning and krump, in particular, where, within the circle, dancers try to outdo each other as much by how they do what they do as what they do.

Finally, the clowns win. If the film were to follow a more typical dramatic structure, it would seem that this would be the end of the movie; however, it is not. After the triumphant win at the Battle Zone, the story continues: we see Tommy the Clown's house trashed after someone has broken into it; we are shown the community's grief after 15-year-old Quinesha Dunford's death by random gunfire. Framed by scenes of violence past and present, the destructive home invasion and the crushing reality of senseless violence that ended a young life refute the representation of dance as a panacea for all social issues. So while *Rize* on many levels offers a portrait of South Central Angelinos that have created and continued to create positive change through dance, on another level it also engages a troubling re-inscription of the pernicious images of African-American communities rife with violence. We return again to the crucial paradox of the American-Freedom-Dream dancing at the crossroads of documentary and popular culture reverie. We must question how deep tragedy gets displaced in a succession of surreal images and be mindful of how history works on feeling and beyond facts.

Although dancing can be an alternative to gangs, may bring a community together and can be cathartic, we must acknowledge the harsh context from which this dancing emerges and address troubling essentialist notions that arise throughout some of the dancers' comments (i.e., that specific African-American kinesthetic talents are a product of racial versus cultural heritage, among others). It is also important to acknowledge what the dancing is doing as well. As represented in the documentary, dancing is effecting change on spiritual (for some), economic, artistic and social levels. In addition the film itself is effecting a re-evaluation of dance in society in general, and of African-American dance in particular. It is a testament to a community-prescribed pedagogy for social justice. It is an alternative to gang activity, a means for bonding a community, a place of spiritual expression and an art form in which to channel aggression about absent fathers and mothers and poverty productively. It now also provides a means by which some dancers can make a living and launch careers in the dance world and the music industry.

The role of Tommy the Clown in *Rize* functions both as hero and as a point of origin (or pre-origin) and differentiation for the genres of krumping and clowning primarily (and of stripper dance secondarily). Without Tommy's influence none of these forms would have manifested as they have, so the film does justice to documenting the genealogies of these dance forms. However, clowning (the genre that Tommy originated) becomes situated as the 'organized ball' or the mainstream genre, while krump, as Lil' C (one of contested originators of krump) articulates it, "is more of the black sheep, just the raw version, like you have organized ball and you have street ball. Krumping is the street ball." This positioning of krumping as the more edgy genre within *Rize* adds to its currency in mainstreamed and globalized hip hop and popular culture. So although this initial review of the film speaks much to Tommy's journey, it also provides the context within which to understand the emergence of krumping, as at least two of the three originators of krump were first clown dancers before they created krump.

Documentary and/or Music Video

The movie ends with a scene that flashes the names of dancers, interspersed with clips of dancing and footage of their lives, to the music of 'Oh, Happy Day'. The gospel song creates a sonic space of the black church, while the visual montage contrasts and problematizes the sonic narrative. Throughout, there is a strong sense of disembodiment in the visual and sonic pastiche of this scene. As Kim Hewitt asserts in her critical article on *Rize*, this last scene is the "most misplaced scene" in the entirety of the film (Hewitt, 2005: 350). It features the oiled and scantily clad krump dancers, sometimes in slow motion, in music video-like cinematography against the backdrop of urban decay and a bright blue sky. Hewitt states, "This scene pushes *Rize* from the arena of documenting popular culture to creating it, and from the task of documenting the black body to displaying it" (2005: 350). This is one of the many examples in the film that illustrates the contradictory juxtapositions between what the film does, what LaChappelle and the featured dancers state that the dances and the film do, and how both the dances and the film interact with the larger socio-political and historical realities at play. As the scene closes Dragon elucidates, "We have a belief that we can be somebody and that we're gonna be somebody. We're gonna, we're gonna rise no matter what", and Swoop, another dancer states, "the sky is there and there is no limit". The final video splices scenes of all the dancers as 'Rize Score Suite' plays "My people going to rise. Rise up".

Conclusion

Returning to Kelley's (2002) work, if we measure success and failure through whether or not certain movements or practices succeeded in changing the power structures, then most have been failures. If we look, however, at the interventions of dance in the lives of people such as Tommy the Clown who has turned the phrase, "In South Central where bustin' a cap is fundamental" to, "When you get to hatin' start shakin'", we begin to see how dance is effective towards social change. It is in the provocation of/through dance and films like *Rize* that we witness prismatic wounds of society revealing themselves more clearly through individual responses to the film. The performance of these dances, rooted in the African aesthetic of cultural transmissions, acts as a sort of ritual, a "reinvented" memory, or as Mark Pedelty writes in another context, "a living tradition born in the present" (Pedelty, 2004: 35).

Through its emergence onto the big screen *Rize* participates in illustrating, negotiating and remaking the scenario of the American Dream. This is a political act, a freedom dream. It diversifies the palette of hegemonic (read Europeanist) normalcy, where krumping and clowning are, as the krumper Dragon says, "just as valid as your ballet, as your waltz, as your tap dance". The film brings to centre stage Africanist aesthetics in these featured dance genres, which break the continuous kinesthetic line, mono-rhythmic orientation, detached performance personae and pseudo-apolitical assumptions many embodied Eurocentric art forms promote. It is in the exposure and the recognition and what the dance reveals that we have the opportunity to move towards a more radical humanism (Gilroy, 2000).

The dancing in this movie is political.[13] It is charged in the call to *RIZE*. It is buoyed in the scenario of the American Dream. Framed in the opening scenes of the movie, when we see the Watts and Rodney King riots and the footage of a burning city, the dancing, contextualized in chaos as a phoenix rising from the ashes, inspires. The film, in its successes and failures, moves us. And hopefully calls us, in the words of Dr Martin Luther King, Jr (2010 [1963]), to recognize "that social change will not come overnight", but work as though it is an "imminent possibility" (18). In this work, may we all become peaceful young warriors, wipe our eyes and see the light more clearly.

Notes

1. Megan Anne Todd received her PhD in Theatre/Performance of the Americas from Arizona State University. She has published in the *Journal of Pan African Studies*, *Theatre Journal*, and *Journal of Bodywork & Movement Therapies*. Dr Todd lectures, teaches and develops curriculum in the areas of performance studies, cultural studies, dance, somatics, pilates, yoga, kinesiology and injury prevention/post-rehabilitation. She is involved in ongoing performance-based research and artistic projects in the areas of social justice and wellness.
2. The call and response structure, or antiphony, is, according to Black Atlantic theorists such as Paul Gilroy (2000) and others, the foundational aesthetic structure of black artistic practices. It serves our thinking here about the dances in the film, and the film itself as a cultural text.
3. Gretchen Murphy in her work *Hemispheric Imaginings: The Monroe Doctrine and Narratives of the U.S. Empire* (2005) specifies various socio-cultural-political transcripts and processes spun from the Monroe Doctrine that positioned the US

so as to both dominate and express the concept "America". Murphy illustrates how this process also developed "the hemisphere" as "a meaningful cultural and geopolitical frame for American nationalism" (4). Therefore, when I utilize the term USAmerica(n) throughout the chapter, I do so to re-specify the geographic and cultural positionality of the US as a part, versus centrepoint, of the axes of power and control of the Americas.

4. Tupac Amaru Shakur (1971–1996).
5. The aesthetic of 'cool' has been appropriated and re-appropriated from Afro-diasporic cultures and drives much of USAmerican popular culture in distinct and specific ways. Dixon Gottschild (2003) reads Africanist aesthetics in ways of walking and talking, and in hairdos exhibited cross-culturally and cross-racially in the Americas. Coolness, in particular, is associated with youth in American culture. In this way we see the production and consumption of cool in its most marketable configurations.
6. Taylor details six ways of "using *scenario* as a paradigm for understanding social structures and behaviors" (2003: 28; original emphasis) that utilize both the archive (texts) and the repertoire (social actions, including performances).
7. Please note that I am utilizing DeFrantz's take on Fanon's statement, because I find it compelling to think through the 'opened circles' of dance in krump's diaspora. I am thus utilizing DeFrantz's contextualization and conceptualization of the dance circle, which is distinct from Fanon's.
8. http://www.lachapellestudio.com/about/ (accessed 10 January 2011).
9. http://www.lachapellestudio.com/about/ (accessed 10 January 2011).
10. Lefebvre (1974) asserts that spatial practices are the projection of political power, to which all elements are subjugated. He observes that although elements may be separated in the process, the overall control of the hegemony is never relinquished.
11. De Certeau (1984), as does Lefebvre (1974), describes the city as a product, a manifestation of hegemonic political and social power matrices. In this observation they are aligned with Foucault. However, in his essay 'Walking in the City', De Certeau goes to great lengths to speak about how space is produced in its use and re-use, as he develops his "theory of everyday practices, of lived space" that can be understood from the level of the haptic (1984: 96). Here is where clowning and krumping enter. In gathering they are remaking the space of the city (even as the police may attempt to halt it). The power paradigm is undeniable, unacceptable and must be addressed. It is, however, in the *"ways of use"* that one of many means to navigate and transform the power structure and remake the city on re-invested terms exists. The Euro-centrist hegemony, which instantiated itself in the cityscapes of USAmerica, is being remade by practices that re-interpret and re-utilize them.
12. In the early days of both clowning and krumping, dancers painted their faces in creative expressions. Now, as krumping has evolved into its own distinct style, face painting is no longer part of the practice.
13. In a 1966 article titled 'Dance and Culture: An Aesthetic of the Cool' Robert Farris Thompson described the aesthetic components of pan-African dance and music

as including "the dominance of a percussive concept of performance; multiple meter; apart playing and dancing; call-and-response; and finally the songs and dances of derision" (cited in DeFrantz, 2002: 14). For dance scholar DeFrantz, this last attribute – songs and dances of derision – most clearly signifies "the political dimension of 'black dance' performance. In this category, movement provokes meta-commentary and suggests narratives outside the physical frame of performance" (*ibid.*).

References

De Certeau, M. (1984), *The Practice of Everyday Life*, Los Angeles: University of California Press.
De Certeau, M. (2004), 'The Practice of Everyday Life', in J. Rivkin and M. Ryan (eds), *Literary Theory: An Anthology*, 2nd edn, Malden: Blackwell, pp. 1247–1257.
DeFrantz, T. F. (2002), *Dancing Many Drums: Excavations in African American Dance*, Madison: University of Wisconsin Press.
DeFrantz, T. F. (2004), *Dancing Revelations: Alvin Ailey's Embodiment of African American Culture*, New York: Oxford University Press.
Foucault, M. (1977), 'Nietzsche, Genealogy, History', in D. F. Bouchard (ed.), *Language, Counter-Memory, Practice: Selected Essays and Interviews*, Ithaca: Cornell University Press, pp. 139–64.
Gilroy, P. (2000), *Against Race: Imagining Political Culture beyond the Color Line*, Cambridge: Harvard University Press.
Gottschild, Dixon (2003), *The Black Dancing Body: A Geography from Coon to Cool*, New York: Palgrave.
Hazzard-Donald, K. (1996), 'Dance in Hip Hop Culture', in W. E. Perkins (ed.), *Droppin Science: Critical Essays on Rap Music and Hip Hop Culture*, Philadelphia: Temple University Press, pp. 220–35.
Hewitt, K. (2005), 'Review. Rize. Dir. David LaChappelle. Lionsgate Films, 2005', *Journal of Popular Music Studies*, 17(3), 345–52.
Kelley, Robin D. G. (2002), *Freedom Dreams: The Black Radical Imagination*, Boston: Beacon Press.
Kelley, Robin D. G. (2008). 'Syllabus: AMST 101gm: Race and Class in Los Angeles. Spring 2008.'
King Jr, Martin Luther (2010), *Strength to Love*, Cleveland: First Fortress Press [1963].
Lawal, Babatunde (2002), 'The African Heritage of African American Art and Performance', in P. C. Harrison, V. L. Walker II and G. Edwards (eds), *Black Theatre: Ritual Performance in the African Diaspora*, Philadelphia: Temple University Press, pp. 39–63.
Lefebvre, Henri (1974), *The Production of Space*, translated by Donald Nicholson-Smith. Malden: Blackwell.
Merrell, Floyd (2005), *Capoeira and Candomble: Conformity and Resistance through Afro-Brazilian Experience*, Madrid: Markus Wiener.
Mitchell, Elvis (2004), 'Critic's Notebook; on the Menu at Sundance: Quirky Chefs and Dancers', *New York Times: Arts Section*, 21 January, http://www.nytimes.

com/2004/01/21/movies/critic-s-notebook-on-the-menu-at-sundance-quirky-chef-and-dancers.html (accessed 23 October 2015).

Murphy, Gretchen (2005), *Hemispheric Imaginings: The Monroe Doctrine and Narratives of the U.S. Empire*, Durham: Duke University Press.

Pedelty, Mark (2004), *Musical Ritual in Mexico City*, Austin: University of Texas Press.

Rose, Tricia (2008), *Hip Hop Wars: What We Talk about When We Talk about Hip Hop-and Why it Matters*, New York: Basic Books.

Taylor, D. (2003), *The Archive and the Repertoire*, Durham: Duke University Press.

Zanfagna, C. (2009), 'The Multiringed Cosmos of Krumping/Hip-Hop at the Intersections of Battle, Media, and Spirit', in J. Malnig (ed.), *Ballroom, Boogie, Shimmy Sham Shake: A Social and Popular Dance Reader*, Chicago: University of Illinois Press, pp. 337–53.

Resounding Neurological Ecologies
Choreographing the Body's Lost Interactions with the World

Sarah-Mace Dennis[1]

> *The spirit, like the sea, is greater than any island or continent of sense-experience within its waters* - Madeline Gins (1994)

Introduction

Filmmaker, visual artist and transcendental meditator, David Lynch, says that ideas are like fishing. You have to have a hook and some bait. If you want to catch small fish, you don't necessarily have to go into deep water, but for the big fish, you have to be prepared to go much further out. Lynch believes that desire is the bait. In his analogy, desiring something is about focusing, and that is when attention becomes lively. This means that focusing on something is like putting bait on a hook: "if your consciousness, your awareness is expanded more and more, you are able to go deeper. And all things, anything that is a thing, everything comes from this field of unity" (Lynch, 2006).

What follows in this chapter is an interaction with a big fish caught, reeled in and examined through interdisciplinary lines of thinking.[2] The ideas that materialize here left their resonance inside my body in 2008. During a near-fatal car accident, I sustained severe brain trauma, which for some time left me physically and cognitively paralysed. In the weeks and months following the neurological fallout, I interacted with the environments that surrounded me through a succession of non-ordinary states of consciousness. *Mondo Ghillies* (Dennis, 2010)[3] - the short dance film that followed this - is a practical and experiential unfolding of the subjective and perceptual atmospheres that I came to see and hear as I moved through the world with a severely altered neurological architecture. Experiencing physiological and mental paralysis allowed me to develop a deep theoretical and corporeal understanding of what architects and philosophers Arakawa and Gins (2002) call the *thinking body*.

When speaking of an organism that 'persons' the world – as opposed to an organism that dogs, giraffes or cockroaches it – these theorists suggest that the ability to activate conscious reflection is sculpted by the organism-person that both feels and thinks its way through the environment as it subjectively unravels perceptual experience. Nerve tissue is interwoven throughout the body's organs, and the brain's synaptic pathways fire in constellations that communicate with this tissue, allowing the body to act in knowledgeable configurations as it moves through space (Arakawa and Gins, 2002: 3). Neurological patternings feed into and influence the body's incarnations of space. This idea is activated by Barbara Maria Stafford in her work *Echo Objects* when she notes that conscious experience is generated by our autonomic nervous system interacting with the world. This means that "the form of the resulting representation is more a construction of neural networks than it is a deliberate reflection about attending to aspects of that world" (Stafford, 2007: 194). The relationship between neurological function and the nervous system described in this statement can be amplified by aligning it with Arakawa and Gins's speculation that body might be understood as *sited*.

As a tactile, breathing materiality that initiates movement and that engages in a process of editing, determining and considering, the body can be conceived as constantly creating (Arakawa and Gins, 2002: 5). This is because each time a body moves, it propels dynamic corporeal possibilities that activate particular patterns of synaptic pathways. These pathways fire in configurations that allow the organism to realize its world through acute perceptual frameworks. In doing so, it creates and begins to understand its environmental surroundings. Often, as the body situates itself inside, and moves through, space it uses a process called *procedural learning*. This term refers to the skills, habits and modes of comprehension that become etched inside neurological memory and re-enacted on a regular basis through unconscious repetition (Koch, 2004: 193).

The potential for the repetitive re-enacting of thoughts and movements to modify neurological architecture can be explained by reading it against Norman Doidge's (2007) recent writings on neuroplasticity. In *The Brain that Changes Itself* he argues that the brain can change its structure and function in response to our actions, the way we sense and perceive the world, and the way we think and imagine it. The neurons – the most significant cells that make up the brain – wire together experiential and perceptual capabilities which are reactivated as the body repeats thoughts and movements that were previously familiar.

The body remembers. It remembers its physical interactions with the world, events that are neurologically triggered and fire every time we move. Neurons activated through the repetitive movement of the body in particular ways have the potential to become dominant, superseding other coalitions of neurons and influencing the ongoing ability to move our bodies in particular ways. This is because "the things that you do create coalitions of neurons that work well together and that are faster than the other coalitions of neurons" (Doidge, 2009).

The brain remembers. Generated through patterns of procedural learning, synaptic pathways fire in constellations that can become so deeply embedded, they often determine the re-enacting of familiar configurations of thoughts and movements in ways that go unnoticed. Sometimes the physiological moulding of these memories is so precisely etched that they can reform even after the brain has been wounded, shattered and partially destroyed. Predefined synaptic architectures affect the way that neurons fire together, with perceptual memory traces subtly influencing experiential encounters with the world.

Christof Koch, when speaking of conscious understanding, says that you are oblivious to much of what goes on around you. As organisms that 'person', we selectively attend to places and objects in our external worlds, using additional cognitive resources in order to focus. Everything else becomes diffused. As Koch notes, selective processing "comes at a price – a vast sea of never perceived events" (2004: 173). This means that "you and I are the prow into an ocean of ideas, or even shadows and ghost of ideas" (Strummer cited in Salewicz, 2007: 568).

Materializing through my instinct to communicate the sensations I had while sailing on those shadows and ghosts of ideas, the writing offered here is a textual exploration of the way my dance film *Mondo Ghillies* explores my body's sonic, visual and conceptual understanding of the brain wound that, for a time, erased my physical and intellectual understanding of the intersections between movement and space. After the accident, the damage to my brain resulted in a mental and physical paralysis that was neurologically induced. Believing that the plastic brain can change its structure even after damage, I began to dance again. *Mondo Ghillies* subtly evokes my encounter with the neuroplastic potential of dancing to articulate the way that the body's movement through space shapes and is shaped by perceptual experience. It is a film that explores the desire to sculpt and focus my attention in the conceptual reconfiguring and creative articulation of experience. If our bodies contain the memory traces of many sites, many hypotheses which unfold and are recast in the process of making a film, then in the context of my own interdisciplinary arts practice, filmmaking is one way that my body's memories become philosophically, visually and sonically activated.

If architecture looms as a great aid to critical thinking, as Arakawa and Gins (2002) suggest, then dance film, with its pondering of the philosophical and aesthetic implications of the body's movement through space, can surely contribute to the sort of critical theory that these thinkers propose.

In *Architectural Body*, the pair suggest that it is "architecture's task to mete out the world in such a way that it might be reflected on body-wide" (2002: 3). Extending this claim beyond the role of our built surrounds, I argue that dance film's exploration of the way that the body habituates, negotiates and moves through the environment makes it a practice that casts its atmosphere body-wide. As such, it uses the body's incarnations of space as its primary sculpting tool.

Perhaps Arakawa and Gins are right in suggesting that in our contemporary cultural climate, research should no longer be segregated to the spaces of school, library or laboratory. Instead, they propose that "where one lives needs to become a laboratory for researching, for mapping directly, the living body itself, oneself as a world forming inhabitant" (Arakawa and Gins, 2002: xxi). This may also be true about the spaces that one creates, be it the mental worlds that are evoked inside the space of narrative, or the physical worlds constructed at the site of the film set. I have come to consider all of these territories, including those cast by *Mondo Ghillies*, as laboratories for researching and mapping directly the living body, and the way that it creates itself as a world-forming inhabitant. The scenes cast inside this dance film are sites where the intersections between space, movement, the body and sound play out. The film uses these intersections to create a landscape that explores how the relationship between neurological memory and physical nerve tissue is activated at particular moments in time. It explores the way that the brain and body are neurologically mobilized through their interaction with an ecological surround in ways that are sometimes comprehensible, and sometimes belong to a place of no words. It also articulates how the fielding and perceptual imprint of our surroundings never ceases (Arakawa and Gins, 2002: 7), continuing even in meditation or sleep.

Following Arakawa and Gins, the textures of perception explored here are realized by a brain-body that has the potential to transcend the corporeal rhythm imposed on to it by the rigid architectural and social structures that compose the rational geometry of the Western world. Drawing on the sonic and visual experience of being neurologically paralysed, this work draws an analogy between water and the intensity of the human spirit: in this instance a spirit that is trapped inside a neurologically damaged shell. This is a story about a conscious encounter that is difficult to describe with language alone. It is a work that begins to articulate an experience of deep water, "as if water were the model for how we are or how we will become" (Gins, 1994: 172). "A mass of water with arms and legs", says Madeline Gins in *Helen Keller or Arakawa*. "And this as a more resilient and thorough version of ourselves?" (Gins, 1994: 172).

Paralysis

> 1. INTERIOR. DAY. RUN-DOWN ARCHITECTURAL SITE
>
> The film begins with a sequence of abstract lights, moving and flashing slowly. After a time, this footage is intercut with waves rolling from the shore back out into the ocean, and a woman lying still on the floor. We cut to a close-up of her shut eyes [see Figure 1], and then her left hand, which is posed for meditation. A sharp, diffused sound snakes in from outside the frame, marking its subtle presence. The sound gestures toward a world about to be unfolded.
>
> The still woman's eyes open, and we pan down on her body, lying rigid on the floor.[4]

Her body lies rigid, because when I woke up in hospital with severe brain trauma, I did not know if I knew that I was paralysed.

I would sense shadows around me drifting in a glared haze, their blurred outlines only occasionally beginning to materialize into conscious awareness.

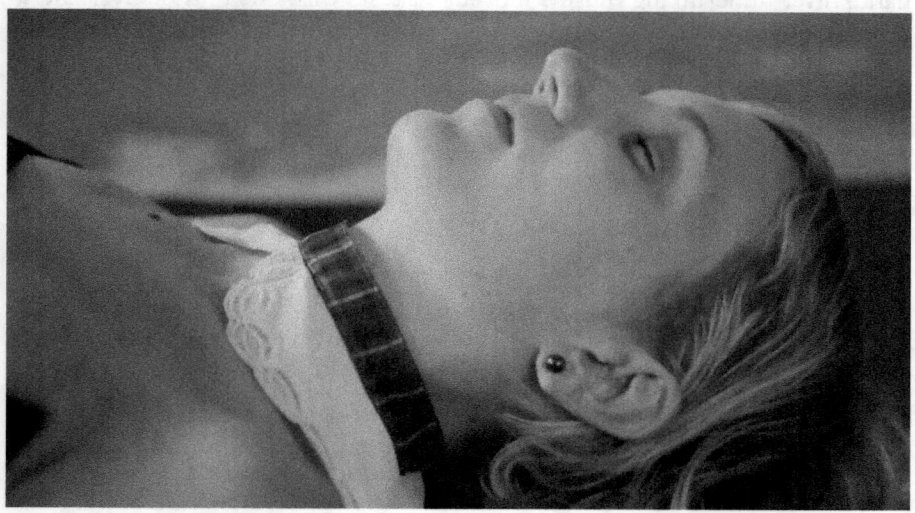

Figure 1: Production still (*Mondo Ghillies*, Sarah-Mace Dennis, 2010)

My awareness moved around the room like waves rolling in from the ocean. Occasionally, my mind would find enough momentum to give the objects that surrounded me perceptual content. More often, my attention would break in a frothy, uncontained mess across the stale hospital landscape that tried to unfold around me.

This is the perceptual texture that allowed the conceptualization of a dance film to begin. Although I had survived a car accident that I may never remember, I had sustained a very severe brain wound. After spending six days in intensive care in a coma-like state, there were three weeks in post-traumatic amnesia, where I was unable to form any new memories, or to remember past events.

The damage to my brain caused a paralysis that was neurologically induced. This meant that my experience of the world was mentally and physically *out* of time. After a small period of recovery, I regained control of the left side of my body, but only limited movement and feeling in the right. For the next two months I would immerse myself in an intensive rehabilitation process that involved learning to walk, write, eat and regain basic function of the right half of my body again. When I started walking around the hospital gymnasium, with almost no capacity to function symmetrically, I began to drag my right leg.

Three months after being discharged from hospital, my right-sided deficit was still noticeable when undertaking rigorous physical exercise, and I was unable to perform tasks requiring intricate coordination skills with my right hand. After undertaking routine movement tests with one of the physiotherapists at the hospital, she told me to accept that my recovery was probably complete. Reacting to this statement, I attended a Scottish dance class for the first time in 12 years.

Listening

2. INTERIOR. DAY. RUN-DOWN ARCHITECTURAL SITE

Lucinda enters, walking up to Luella and pulling her off the ground. They clutch each other's elbows, looking at each other for a moment. Lucinda leans in and whispers 'is it you' in Luella's ear. She pauses for a moment, then replies 'perhaps'.

They stare at each other and then begin to dance. In the beginning, Luella is softer than Lucinda but half way through the dynamic changes, with Luella gaining strength.

My cognitive function had returned. When I tried to dance again, I knew where, why and how I should be moving through space. But the mental representation that I had created of myself moving was *out* of time with my ability to physically manipulate and coordinate my limbs. I could not move myself into the right pieces of space at the right times, because the messages that my brain was sending were travelling too slowly.

As I moved through space, I turned my attention to a mental representation of myself dancing: imagining my whole body advancing through remembered patterns that I tried to manipulate in order to move properly. Perhaps this representational model was the problem. Perhaps the messages couldn't get through because the part of my brain that activated mobility in my right side was damaged to a point where it could no longer representationally or kinaesthetically comprehend or translate movement.

Watching me move, the physiotherapist told me to listen to the sound of my feet until the rhythm became even. If I focused on the sound, I would be able to hear when my weight was being unevenly distributed between the left and right sides of my body. Something happened. It was as if the experience of thinking through sound subtly reconfigured my neurological architecture, diverting the neurological pathways connected to movement to a new part of my brain. Was the topographical organization of my brain map changing? The idea that a brain map might be organized topographically means that the map is ordered as the body itself is ordered. This suggests that if your middle finger is positioned in between your index and ring finger, then the same is true of your brain map: the map for the middle finger is situated directly in between the map for your index and ring fingers. Doidge says that "topographical organization is different, because it means that parts of the brain that often work together are close together in the brain map, so signals don't have to travel far in the brain itself" (Doidge, 2007: 65).

In his investigation of the way that topographic order emerges in the brain, Doidge draws on Michael Merzenich's research, which suggests that topographic order emerges because activity in daily life involves repeating sequences in a fixed order. This means that the way that we procedurally learn to interact with the spaces that surround us cognitively shapes the structure of our brains. Doidge states:

> When we pick up an object the size of an apple or baseball, we usually grip it first with our thumb and index finger, then wrap the rest of our fingers around it one by one. Since the thumb and the index finger often touch at almost the same time, sending their signals to the brain almost simultaneously, the thumb and the index finger map tend to form close together in the brain (neurons that fire together wire together). (Doidge, 2007: 66)

Extended experimentation by Merzenich demonstrated that if parts of the body were affected so they weren't used (demonstrated by blindfolding different animals or severing their median nerve) then other parts of the body would invade the unused map space and use it to process their input. This demonstrates that "when it came to allocating brain-processing power, brain maps were governed by competition for precious resources and the principle of *use it or lose it*" (Doidge, 2007: 59).

Although I had learnt to *think* again, my damaged brain map was still restricting the ability to move my right side. This changed when I began to listen to the sound of my feet on the floor. When movement was manipulated and controlled by listening to my body, did the part of my brain map that listens become larger, compensating for the damaged area that limited mobility on my right side? If the neurological infrastructure that translated the mental representation of my body into a physical procedure for moving through space was damaged, it is possible that diverting the way pathways fired and wired together by listening altered the structure of my brain map.

In *Listening*, philosopher Jean-Luc Nancy (2007) draws attention to the physical properties of our aural senses, discussing the relationship between sound and the body. Of the body, he reminds us that we define ourselves through feeling: by the way we hear ourselves, see ourselves, touch ourselves and taste ourselves. As feeling subjects we think of ourselves and represent ourselves, approaching ourselves and straying from ourselves, always "feeling a 'self' that escapes [*s'echappe*] or hides [*seretrance*] as long as it resounds elsewhere as it does in itself, in a world and in the other" (Nancy, 2007: 9). For Nancy, listening contributes to our ability to sense, for sense as a possibility is aligned closely with resonance, or with sonority itself:

> Sense is first of all the rebound of sound, a rebound that is coextensive with the whole folding/unfolding [*pli/depli*] of presence and of the present that makes or opens the perceptible as such, and that opens in it the sonorous exponent: the vibrant spacing-out of a sense in whatever sense one understands or hears it. (Nancy, 2007: 30)

When I began dancing, I would create a mental representation that was mimetic. Not only was there a delay in my brain function, there were also multiple processes of translation occurring: the movement of my body represented by my brain which then attempted to fire together constellations of neurons in ways that would create particular physical actions. With limited neurological function, and a complex process of translation, it follows that the imitative trace of my body as it tried to keep up with this mental representation could only ever be slightly out of time with the sequence of events unfolding around me in space. Listening allowed me to be in time in a different way: by sensing and modifying my body's movements in the moment. This is because, as Nancy suggests, "in the case of the eye, there is a manifestation and display, a making *evident*", whereas in the case of the ear, there is "withdrawal and turning inward, a making *resonant*" (Nancy, 2007: 3; original emphasis).

Sound's potential to generate a sonorous present that resonates through the body and the room is noted by Nancy:

> In this open and above all opening presence, in acoustic spreading and expansion, listening takes place at the same time as the sonorous event, an arrangement that is clearly distinct from that of vision (for which, incidentally, there is no visual or luminous 'event' either, in an entirely identical meaning of the word: visual presence is already there, available before I see it, whereas sonorous presence arrives – it entails an attack, as musicians and acousticians say). (Nancy, 2007: 14)

The sound that was being made by my body was simultaneously resonating through my nerve tissue, allowing me to sync both heard and felt sensations as they moved through my organs (see Figure 2). I listened as the sound resonated, manipulating my body's rhythms according to aural cues as they unfolded around and through me. I learnt to dance again.

Figure 2: Production still (*Mondo Ghillies*, Sarah-Mace Dennis, 2010)

Mondo Ghillies

3. INTERIOR. DAY. RUN-DOWN ARCHITECTURAL SITE

In the beginning, Luella's dancing is weaker than Lucinda's but half way through the dynamic changes. Now Lucinda becomes softer, before she begins to lean backward and eventually falls down. Luella stands still for a moment, looking at Lucinda who says 'where are you going'. After thinking for a moment Luella says, 'I'm going back'. She leaves the room, picking up the mirror near the doorway on her way out.

> Lucinda remains still as Luella walks outside to the river. As she walks we hear Lucinda repeat 'I saw her spirit and it was the sea'. When Luella arrives at the river she stands there for a moment, before holding the mirror up to the waves, the water reflected in the glass. This image is intercut with a shot of Luella lying on the floor of the empty building. Eventually the picture fades into MRI scans projected over a close-up of the water.

When I was not willing my brain to clutch onto ideas and temporalities from the ordered world, I would drift to another place: an ambience of no logical comprehension and no words. In finding ways to visually, sonically and textually communicate this terrain, I have had to tap into what I call the invisible spaces of perception. I use this term to describe those ways of comprehending our external worlds that exist outside of pre-defined habits embedded inside the body by procedural learning. They are ways of moving through, seeing, hearing and understanding the spaces around us that are not pre-conditioned or even logical. Rather, these intuitive rhythms of comprehension are experienced and sensed by the body, but not always able to be articulated with scientific, rational explanation. Are these invisible functions, these different ways of being in, hearing and perceiving our external surroundings, things that linger somewhere inside everybody's consciousness? What if these functions are always there, somehow unrecognizable because the corporeal languages that our bodies have learnt to interact with space on a daily basis have overwritten them?

Although these other ways of perceiving might be part of a conscious experience, their affect is difficult to articulate with language alone. This is why dance film, with its potential to cast and unfold a dynamic sonic and visual world, provided an important pallet of movements, tones, textures and temporalities with which to describe this embodied state. Here the dancing or 'choreographed' body was drawn on because of the possibilities it offered for moving through, resisting and reconfiguring the rational, ordered dimensions of perspectival space.

By casting its attention towards a landscape that is visually and aurally located at the periphery of rational comprehension, *Mondo Ghillies* evokes the tone of a world that is habituated by a body learning to move after a period of physical and mental stillness. The neurologically paralysed body that habituates the perceptual ecologies that echo here, initially comes to know its external world through constellations of sense experience that are activated outside of the patterns of thinking and learning etched into synapses and cells through a lifetime of procedural learning. This means that, at times, the film becomes a practical and experiential thinking through of those invisible spaces of perception that I was able to access when many of my synaptic pathways were shattered. Gesturing towards this ambient terrain, the work intersects a fragmented narrative with residual imprints of those ethereal rhythms that each character senses, but cannot articulate with rational, logical explanation.

It is inside this environment that 'mondo' leaves its conceptual trace. In *Zen and the Brain: Toward an Understanding of Meditation and Consciousness*, neurologist James Austin uses the term 'mondo' to describe the many bizarre answers and behaviours that are carried by old zen masters. In this illustration he says:

> We encounter the story about the earnest young monk who asks old Joshu about the real meaning of Buddhism, and promptly hears this no sequitur: 'The Cyprus tree in the courtyard'. What is one to make of these old, incomprehensible replies? Such questions, and answers, are termed mondo. If we permit them to, they can help us interpret where the masters of old and the roshi of today are coming from. (Austin, 1998: 110–11)

When one comes to grips with the essence of mondo, they are able to realize the limitations of logical concepts. This means that form, rather than content, is key. There is little use in trying to make literal meaning out of the scenarios cast by mondo. Insisting on uncovering these sort of logical answers will lead to bafflement and disappointment, possibly leaving one intellectually offended (Austin, 1998: 110).

Set in a surreal world at the edges of logical comprehension, *Mondo Ghillies* suggests that we give volume to our external surroundings by the way we frame them with our conscious awareness. Exploring the way that both external and internal worlds are framed by the embodied intersections between movement, ecology, subjectivity and desire, the work suggests that the perceptual spaces we unravel aren't always completely logical, understood through notions of time that are constructed through linear comprehension. Rather, they often belong to another state of consciousness: an atmosphere closely aligned with Buddhism's mondo. In this space, logical comprehension is somewhat limited because consciously embodying every moment of the encounter is key. This is the description of a sensorial terrain that is similar to the world I caught glimpses of in the weeks and months following neurological damage. Only able to summon enough cognitive momentum to understand my surroundings as they perceptually unfolded around me, it was as if my spirit were the sea, as if water were a metaphor for who we are and what we will become.

The two characters in *Mondo Ghillies*, Luella (played by myself) and Lucinda (Megan Williams), are different variations of the same person: both women are me. As such, they symbolize the different subjective atmospheres, deterritorializations, levels, thresholds and distributions of intensity that I experienced after the injury (see Figure 3). Acknowledging that subjectivity is never fixed suggests that our identities are capable of metamorphosis, because the neuroplastic conditions that enable one to gather the world through intensities of feeling are in a constant process of structural change. The decodings and over-codings, de-constructions and reconstructions, double articulations and contradictions that begin to form the mental traces configured by these women, are all traces of my own subjectivity as an "inescapable work-in-progress: subject there will be" (Doel, 1995: 232).

Figure 3: Production still (*Mondo Ghillies*, Sarah-Mace Dennis, 2010)

The film opens with Luella lying static on the floor. Lucinda enters and picks her up, and they begin to dance, before Lucinda is lowered to the floor, and Luella leaves and walks towards the river. At the beginning of the film, choreographed movement intercut with images of water builds to a sequence of the two women dancing. The first part of the film pieces together my memories of what it felt like to learn to dance again after enduring severe brain trauma. Even after a substantial period of recovery, my limited neurological function meant that my body was *out* of time with the events that unfolded in real time around me. Eventually my neurological architecture began to reconfigure, and I was able to move again, but my right side was still weak and partially paralysed. Believing that the plastic brain can change its structure even after damage, I began to dance again. By listening to the sound of my feet, I believe I reconfigured damaged neural pathways, and in doing so, gradually regained use of my entire body.

In the early stages of recovery, my attention was *out* of time. Mostly it would drift around the room, and I was only able to give the objects that surrounded me perceptual content when I could summon enough cognitive strength to focus long enough to clutch on to an idea or event taking place inside my external world. The experience of only being able to consciously adhere to the things that surrounded me for brief moments in time is explored in the shooting technique that I began developing with Director of Photography, Richard C. Bell, in the making of this work. Informed by what Australian cinematographer Christopher Doyle refers to as "the dance between the camera and the actor" (Doyle, 2006) for *Mondo Ghillies* I asked Bell to begin to explore an approach to filming that meant frequently taking the camera off the tripod and intuitively beginning to move with the performers as they travelled through the space of the set.

Working with Bell to explore the experiential potential of the dancing camera was part of my desire to evoke the sensorial complexity of the dancing body. The decision to extend my interdisciplinary arts practice to the discipline of dance film was motivated by a conceptual interest in discovering a way to articulate the complexity of full-bodied movement. I wanted to explore strategies for communicating the way that the act of dancing activates and is activated by an intricate network of perceiving senses that are tactile, visual and auditory. Having been a dancer myself, I knew that dancing inspires the senses in ways that materialize an embodied affect that would be difficult to articulate with the static framing inherent to traditional cinematic language.

My interest in experimenting with a dancing camera emerged through my ongoing engagement with Doyle's work and his use of this technique in films such as *Chungking Express* (Kar-Wai, 1995) and *Paranoid Park* (Sant, 2008). When talking about this approach to filming he says:

> What happens with camera movement is what I call the dance between the camera and the actor. And I think the dance is what really engages people. And how well we dance is really what camera movement is all about. (Doyle, 2006)

In the opening scenes of *Paranoid Park* and *Chungking Express*, Doyle's camera moves around his characters, transiently sculpting their habituations of space with his flowing, almost otherworldly, shooting style. Intimately moving with each character to reveal glances of hands, shoulders, faces and bodies as they move through their surrounds, Doyle's camera intimately follows and breathes against the bodies that are the subject of its gaze. In much of the imagery depicted in the opening scenes of these films the camera trails rather than frames. Moving with and around the action, rather than depicting it with the limitations of a detached frame, Doyle reveals the lines of presence imprinted into the landscape by sited bodies. This is a cinematic dance that sculpts the movements of the identities it frames, creating a perceptual echoing that reveals the plastic intersections that unravel between the film's subjects and the external worlds that their bodies activate. In doing so, he unmasks the lines of presence etched into the landscape by subjects who inhabit the spaces that they move through body-wide.

In the initial explorations of our own dancing camera technique, Bell's camera moves to reveal the intimate details of two bodies that are tactile, breathing material forms. These are bodies that are sited in their interactions with the things that surround them. The camera hovers over Luella's hand in meditation pose, before hesitantly dancing over the look on her quiet face. Moving across her body it lingers as Lucinda reaches down and pulls her up by the elbows. The camera dances against lips, necks, ears and eyes, revealing the details of sited bodies that are activated by the way they interact with and move through the spaces that unfold around them.

At other times in the film, the camera intimately dances across the details of an ecological surround that is perceptually fragile. This outside world is only in focus when the camera's attention moves towards it with concentrated desire. During these moments, the environment is organized by the subtle movements of Bell's camera, with its angles and vantage points that visually carve into matter, giving it meaning and shape.

All scenes in the film were cast through the intersection of a range of sited bodies. These are the sited bodies of the actors becoming characters inside the film set and my own sited body as director, imagining, recollecting, rehearsing and performing the story to give it shape. Other aspects of the film were activated by the sited bodies of the production and post-production crew, who, after listening to my story and hearing the contours of my vision, engaged in their own process of sculpting, editing, framing and perceiving. As we began to create the world that is *Mondo Ghillies*, our own memory traces were activated every time we moved, recalled a step, a line of dialogue, or a direction or idea about how the characters and the camera should proceed.

The film's sonic environment was created by composers Michelle Xen and John Teh and layered by sound designer Clare Andreallo. The sound is an aural exploration of my sited body, as it unfolds and undergoes metamorphosis by the characters of Lucinda and Luella. Sonically, the work describes the way that I (Lucinda/Luella) rhythmically unfold into the spaces around me, and the way that these spaces embed their sonic resonance inside my synaptic architecture, activating new patterns of movement and thought. If, drawing on mondo, form rather than content is key to creating a meditative space that exists outside of the limitations of logical concepts, then the sonic world cast by the composition and sound design in the film is a way of enhancing this contemplative atmosphere. The soundtrack opens the narrative spaces depicted in the film to the presence of something other than the events that are occurring inside them. Here sound gestures towards an elsewhere that resonates outside of language, logical comprehension and words. It folds and unfolds the presence of this elsewhere into the bodies of the two women dancing and moving across the screens. As such, sound reverberates and rebounds the complex memory traces that compose these sited bodies, allowing one to sense the resonance of their experiential worlds.

The potential for the sonorous to contribute to and enhance the possibilities set into motion by vision is echoed Nancy (2007) who describes the way that the sound enhances visual form. He notes:

> It does not dissolve it, but rather enlarges it; gives it an amplitude, a density, and a vibration or an undulation whose outline never does anything but approach. The visual persists until its disappearance; the sonorous appears and fades away into its permanence. (Nancy, 2007: 2)

The sound of drums, bongos and the subtle howl of bagpipes are interwoven into the film's visual sequences to materialize a whispering of hidden events. As Luella's still body is being pulled from the floor, the sound of running water is subtly interwoven with the resonance of breath to gesture towards the fluidity of a spirit not yet fully contained by the cognitive function of a rational brain-body. At repetitive intervals, drum beats punctuate the body with rhythm to signal its emergence from that still place of mental and physical paralysis.

This beating first resounds when Luella, lying still on the floor, opens her eyes for the first time. The rhythm repeats and builds as Lucinda pulls Luella up and they start to dance, the pulsating drums giving tempo and energy to a neurologically damaged body that, as it dances in time with the sound, is regenerated and remade. Towards the end of the fling sequence, these compositional passages are overlaid with the subtle aural trace of dancing feet, a sound that continues to strengthen Luella's body and bring it alive. As sound and image touch each other, a fuller and more embodied network of senses is activated, both in the bodies of the women moving and dancing on screen, as well as in the bodies of those engaging with the cinematic spaces that the work unfolds.

Coda

Jean-Luc Nancy argues that communication is not transmission but "a sharing that becomes subject: sharing as subject of all 'subjects'. An unfolding, a dance, a resonance" (Nancy, 2007: 41). The role that communication might play as an unfolding and sharing of subject is expanded by aligning Nancy's thinking with the thoughts of Gins who says "that a network of possible alignments might come about from the writing of this" (Gins, 1994: 9). Considering this statement, I wonder if perhaps we not only need to tell stories about our lives to make sense of them, to know how we exist, but also to materialize tangible events that can be aligned with the thoughts of others, a continued casting and reconfiguring of ideas that allows new thinking to materialize. Writing on the potential of observable events, Gins says, "observable events are potentially reproducible ones; eventually, from these sequences, a whole new perceiver of a new other might be generated" (Gins, 1994: 10).

The dance film *Mondo Ghillies* recasts my own experience of severe brain trauma to unfold a conversation about the brain, the body and perception. It uses the dynamic possibilities of the moving image to gesture towards those textures of feeling that exist beyond the logical operations of the brain, with its learned sensory behaviours and ways of being in the world that many of us re-enact in our everyday lives. By experimenting with new rhythms for constellating ambient perceptual atmospheres with images of the body in motion, it configures a cinematic space that is more textually rich and has a greater sensorial impact than the lines of thinking able to be cast with language alone. Drawing on the sonic and visual possibilities offered by dance film, *Mondo Ghillies* becomes a filmic trace of the experience of being *out* of time with the world, physically and mentally. This trace evokes and resonates with Gins's affirmation that "the spirit, like the sea, is greater than any island of sense experience within its waters" (Gins, 1994: 84).

Figure 4: Production still (*Mondo Ghillies*, Sarah-Mace Dennis, 2010)

Notes

1. Sarah-Mace Dennis is a filmmaker, video artist and independent scholar based in London. Her work, although interdisciplinary, primarily focuses on the intersections between critical and creative writing, video and performance. In 2008, after a serious car accident, she sustained a very severe brain injury, which left her mentally and physically paralysed. She attributes some of her recovery to the hours she spent dancing to songs written by seventies punk band The Clash.
2. The writing offered here is part of a larger research investigation that I describe as becoming-narrative and the edges of a poetic-criticality. It is a strategy for producing cinematic, literary and theoretical texts from an anomalous position at the border zone of poetry and philosophy, theory and fiction, historical concepts and imaginative ideas. The spatial and temporal residues set into motion by *Mondo Ghillies* have opened a space for new types of writing and critical thinking to occur. What follows is perhaps best read as a companion piece to, rather than a discursive explanation of, the scenes that unfold the film. It is a strategy that seeks to know the ways that it might be possible to allow the sensation experienced in the process of practice to influence the structuring, framing, writing and unravelling of a critical text. This means that theory might explore new and experimental territory that is sensitive and responsive to the trajectory that practice engenders.
3. The film is available at https://vimeo.com/37572264 (among other places), and readers are encouraged to view the film in conjunction with this text.
4. This, and all subsequent references, are taken from the script of *Mondo Ghillies* (2010).

References

Arakawa, S. and Gins, M. (2002), *Architectural Body*, Tuscaloosa: University of Alabama Press.
Austin, J. H. (1998), *Zen and the Brain: Toward an Understanding of Meditation and Consciousness*, Massachusetts: Massachusetts Institute of Technology.
Doel, M. (1995), 'Bodies without Organs: Schizoanalysis and Deconstruction', in S. Pile and N. Thrift (eds), *Mapping the Subject: Geographies of Cultural Transformation*, London: Routledge, pp. 226–40.
Doidge, N. (2007), *The Brain that Changes Itself*, Melbourne: Scribe.
Doidge, N. (2009), 'Your Brain: How it can Change, Develop and Improve', *Melbourne Conversations*, https://www.youtube.com/watch?v=ibpbkV7xc24 (accessed 21 October 2015).
Doyle, C. (2006), *BBC Culture Show w/ Christopher Doyle*, http://www.youtube.com/watch?v=iuWZI0yUUHU (accessed 6 August 2009).
Gins, M. (1994), *Helen Keller or Arakawa*, New York: Burning Books with East-West Cultural Studies.
Kar-Wai, W. (1995), *Chungking Express*, C. Yi-kan (producer). Hong Kong: Mirimax Films, Rolling Thunder Pictures, The Criterion Collection, Artificial Eye, Ocean Shores Video.

Koch, C. (2004), *The Quest for Consciousness: A Neurobiological Approach*, Englewood, CO: Roberts and Company.

Lynch, D. (2006), *David Lynch Ideas*, http://www.youtube.com/watch?v=ZPc1N7kf_AQ (accessed 10 December 2010).

Nancy, J.-L. (2007), *Listening*, translated by C. Mandell, New York: Fordham University Press.

Salewicz, C. (2007), *Redemption Song: The Definitive Biography of Joe Strummer*, London: HarperCollins.

Sant, G. V. (2008), *Paranoid Park*, Charles Gilbert and N. Kopp (producers). United States: IFC Films.

Stafford, B. M. (2007), *Echo Objects: The Cognitive Work of Images*, London: University of Chicago Press.

Index

42nd Street 4

added value 82–83
Advance 35
Aggiss, Liz 20, 34
Akhtar, Farhan 213
Altman, Rick 134
Anarchic Variations 34
Anderson, David 20
Anderson, Peter 33
Aragon, M. 171–72
Arakawa, S. 248–50
Arledge, Sara K. 17
Austin, James 257

b-boy 58
b-girl 58
Bacon, Lloyd 4
Badham, John 2
Bándy, Miklós 18
Baur, Steven 200
Bel Geddes, Norman 19–20
Berkeley, Busby 4
Beyoncé 4
BKLYN 34, 35
black cultural dysfunction
    see cultural dysfunction
Blitzstein, Marc 18
Borelli, Melissa Blanco 2, 47
boy 32, 33
Boyz n the Hood 63
Brannigan, Erin 1, 3
Breakaway 29–30
Browder, Stony Junior 168
Buckland, Theresa 1
Burrow, Jonathan 32

Cannon, Terry 17–18

Carroll, Noël 2, 21
Carswell, Leon 'Vietnam' 54
Chang, J. 124
Chion, Michael 51, 82, 87
classical musical
    see musical (genre)
clowning (dance genre) 235, 239, 241
colourblind meritocracy 79–80, 93, 102
'Come Together' 194
Conner, Bruce 29–30
Cordova, Sarah Davis 151–53, 160
Cornered 34
Cowie, Billy 20
Coyle, R. 6
Crazy Legs 97
Croce, Arlene 22
Crooks, James 187
cultural dysfunction 83–84, 86, 93, 95, 100, 104–106

Dance of the Hands
    see *Tilly Losch in Her Dance of the Hands*
Darkchild
    see Jerkins, Rodney
Davy Jones Locker 16
de Certeau, M. 230
de Jong, Bettie 28
Decouflé, Philippe 31–32
'Deewangi Deewangi' 217–18
deFrantz, Thomas 231
Deren, Maya 2–3, 14, 20
'Dhoom Tana' 214–17
Dil Chahta Hai 210, 211–12
Dodds, Sherril 3, 22, 26
Doidge, Norman 248–49, 253
Doyle, Christopher 259
Dr Buzzard's Original Savannah Band 168

Dyer, Richard 64

experimental screendance 25–26

Feuer, Jane 61
Fitzgerald, J. 6
Flashdance 2, 131–32
Fosse, Bob 4
Foster, Susan 154
Fuller, Loïe 3

Gale, Robert 179
'Gangnam Style' 7
Garafola, Lynn 163
Geritz, Kathy 17
Gibson, LaurieAnn 115
Gins, M. 248–50
Goodwin, A. 2, 184, 188–90
Gordon, Suzanne 151, 153, 160–61
Goren, Nili 232
Greenfield, Amy 25, 30
Grossberg, L. 2

Hale, Catherine 33
Hände: Das Leben und die Liebe eines Zärtlichen Geschlechts 18
Hands 32
Hands: The Life and Loves of the Gentler Sex
   see *Hände: Das Leben und die Liebe eines Zärtlichen Geschlechts*
Harris, Hilary 27–28
Hawks, Howard 4
Hazzard-Donald, K. 237
Hinton, David 32
Hoberman, J. 131
Honey 67–68
Horak, Jan-Christopher 19
Houstoun, Wendy 32
'Hungry Eyes' 140
hyper-behaviouralism 82–83, 88–90, 92–93
hyperchoreography 35–36
hyperdance 36

'I Want You (She's So Heavy)' 194–97

'In the Mood' 174
Introspection 17
Ipapo, Ami 35
'I've Just Seen a Face' 190–93

James, David 17
Jerkins, Rodney 112–13

Kelley, Robin D. G. 229–31
Kenney, Marie 178
Koch, Christof 249
Krims, Adam 65
krumping 233, 237–38, 241–42

LaChappelle, David 231–33
Le P'tit bal 31–32
Lee, Rosemary 33
Little Ease (outside the box) 34, 35
Lockyer, Bob 30–31
Lovece, F. 219
Lumière Brothers 3
Lynch, David 247
Lyne, Adrian 2

malicia 240–41
Man Act 32
'Maniac' 139
Marks, Victoria 31
McPherson, Katrina 22
McRobbie, Angela 47
meritocracy 90, 92
Midgelow, Vida L. 154, 161
Miller, Glenn 174
mondo 257
Mondo Ghillies 247–64
Moore, Annabelle Whitford 15–16
Morton, C. 170
Mothers & Daughters 31
Motion Control 20
MTV 131
Music Man, The 133
musical (genre) 132–34
Musser, C. 3

Nancy, Jean-Luc 254–55, 261

Nathan, David 168
Neptune's Daughters 16
'Never' 139–40
Nine Variations on a Dance Theme 28–29
Nymph of the Waves, A 16

Om Shanti Om 214, *215*
'Ooh Wee' 115
Outside In 31

pachuco 170–71
Parfitt-Brown, Clare 4
parody 208, 213
Pearlman, Karen 23
Peterson, Sidney 17
'Phir Milenge Chalte Chalte' 218–21
Physical TV Company 22–23
Platt, Marc 112
Porter, Jenelle 21–22
Posner, Bruce 16
Powell, Michael 4
practice montage 72–73
Prasad, Madhava 221–22
Pressburger, Emeric 4
Prince, Kate 51
Procter, Tyrone 4
Psy 7

Rab Ne Bana Di Jodi 218
Rainer, Yvonne 2–3
Red Shoes, The 4
'Revolution' 200–201
Reynolds, D. 5–6
Roberts, Adam 32
Rock Steady Crew 95–97
Rose, Mitchell 35
Rose, Tricia 68, 71–72, 81–82, 112, 227
Rosenberg, Douglas 23–25

Sandy, Kenrick 51
Saturday Night Fever 2, 6
Save the Last Dance 64, 66–67, 70
screendance 185
Serpentine Dance 15
Sherwood, Diana 20

Simon, Stella 18
Sitney, P. Adams 14
Smith, Jeff 6
Soul Train 4
Step Up 68–70, 73–74
Step Up 2: The Streets 43, 53, 71–73
Step Up 3D 47–51, 54–56
Step Up trilogy 64
Straight Outta Brooklyn 63
'Strawberry Fields Forever' 198–200
Street Dance 3D 51–52
stripper dance 236
Stubbs, Mike 32
Study in Choreography for the Camera, A 14

Tarr, Matt 35
Tilly Losch in Her Dance of the Hands 19
Touched 32
Transport 30
Troika Ranch 35
Truth: The Truth, The 36
Tuckett, Will 51

Unseen Cinema 16

Valdez, Luis 170
van Eijck, Koen 162–63
Vimeo 27
Vize, L. 7

waacking 4
Warner, T. 112
whiteness 81–83, 87, 90, 93, 104
Williams, John 167, 180
Williams, Margaret 31
'Wipe Out' 140
'Woh Ladki Hai Kahan' 210–13
Woodruff, Billie 110
Wulff, Helena 161

You Got Served 52–53

Zigler, Ronald Lee 202
zoot suits 170

www.ingramcontent.com/pod-product-compliance
Lightning Source LLC
Chambersburg PA
CBHW050213240426
43671CB00013B/2319